you both.
Pat Gould

ABRAHAM'S JOURNAL

The Life & Times
of
Abraham Blish
1616 - 1683

Patricia B Gould

Patricia Louise Blish Gould

PBG Press   Congress, Arizona

Though based in part on historical records, this is a work of fiction. Some names, characters, places, and incidents may be the product of the author's imagination and/or used fictitiously.

This special edition was prepared for printing by
Ghost River Images
5350 East Fourth Street
Tucson, Arizona 85711
www.ghostriverimages.com

Cover photo by: Patricia Louise Blish Gould

ISBN: 0-9727171-0-2

Library of Congress Control Number: 2002116169

Printed in the United States of America

Third Printing: May, 2003

10 9 8 7 6 5 4 3 2

Contents

DEDICATED TO

MY MOTHER
ALICE HELEN WHEELER BLISH - 1921-2002
WHO BELIEVED IN ME
I THANK THE LORD FOR ALLOWING HER
TO HEAR BITS AND PIECES OF SOME OF THE
CHAPTERS OF MY BOOK,
I AM SORRY THAT SHE IS NOT HERE
WITH ME NOW TO HEAR ITS COMPLETION.
My mother was blind and loved to hear me read to her.

MY FATHER
FREDDIE EMERY BLISH - 1912-1977
WHO WAS MY INSPIRATION FOR THE
MAIN CHARACTER OF MY BOOK

MY HUSBAND AND SOULMATE
ROBERT L. GOULD
OF FORTY-FIVE YEARS
WHO SAT FOR MANY HOURS ALONE
WAITING FOR ME TO FINISH A CHAPTER
SO HE COULD READ IT

**MY CHILDREN, GRANDCHILDREN
AND GREAT-GRANDCHILDREN**
WHO UNKNOWINGLY BECAME A PART OF MY BOOK

MANY THANKS TO

The wonderful people at the Sturgis Library
    3090 Main Street
    Barnstable, Massachusetts 02630

The wonderful people at the Trayser Museum, Cobb's Hill
    Old King's Highway
    P 0 Box 1174
    Barnstable, Massachusetts 02630

Mary Ann Paulic, Director of the Congress Library
    P 0 Box 380
    Congress, Arizona 85332

Robert and Lorraine Puzey of North Somerset, England

FORWARD

"Abraham's Journal" is the life story of Abraham Blish, a Puritan who came to New England in 1637. I am the 10th generation from Abraham and I have written this novel in his honor as well as for all of the people depicted in this book that came to this great country of ours to find freedom.

I do not know if he kept a real journal but I like to think that he may have. Most of the names and dates and events in this book are factual except for those characters with criminal intent.

I mean no disrespect when the word Indian appears in the text, it seemed out of place for the time that this book takes place to use the words Native American.

Abraham Blish was born in 1616 and raised in Devonshire, England until he was 21 years old. In 1637 he moved to Duxbury, Massachusetts graduating from Cambridge University in England.

He moved to Barnstable, Massachusetts in 1640 after he married Anne Pratt on September 7, 1640. They had two children, Sarah born in 1644 and Joseph born in 1648. When Anne died he married Hannah Williams Barker in January 1654. They had one son, Abraham, Jr. born in 1654. When Hannah died he married Allice Derby in 1659.

He was a Freeman five times during his lifetime in 1641, 1651,1652,1658 and 1670. He took the Oath of Fidelity in 1643 and again in 1657. He gained the right to bear arms in 1643 and held that distinction all his life. He was a Grand Juror in 1642,1643,1658 and 1663. He was a Surveyor of highways in 1645, 1650 and 1652. He was elected Grand Enquest in 1658 and 1663. He was Constable from 1656 to 1660 and again from 1667 to 1671. He was Hayward in 1668 and 1673.

He was known as a great farmer and landowner, owning 200 acres of land in Barnstable at one time. He led a Christian life as a Puritan and was highly regarded and respected as a friend to all those who knew him. He was a very loving husband, father, stepfather and father-in-law and was grandfather to 30 children when he died on September 7, 1683.

I sincerely hope that you enjoy reading this book as much as I have enjoyed writing it.

Patricia Louise Blish Gould

CHAPTER ONE
FEBRUARY 1637

It was February 22, 1637 and Richard More had just posted his letter to Abraham Blish with the captain of the '*Friendship*', which was docked in the Boston harbor. He had no doubt that Abraham would be on the return trip from England, and he chuckled as he said out loud to himself, "I sure can write a convincing letter." He would have many stories to tell his friend when he arrived. He was certain Abraham would take him up on his offer. Abraham was ambitious and enthusiastic and was the kind of man that was needed to help establish the new colonies further. How could an adventurous man like him refuse? He hoped the voyage would be good for him.

As he left the dock the wind blew little stinging ice crystals into his face and he pulled his hat down and hurried on toward the inn. 'Another winter storm,' he thought, and he shivered. The cold reminded him of that first day in 1620 when the '*Mayflower*' landed in Plymouth. The suffering they had all endured that first winter was heartbreaking. He shivered again not sure if it was from the cold or the bad memories.

He remembered the meeting of all the men while they were still on board the '*Mayflower*'. The leaders, William Bradford, William Brewster, Edward Winslow, Isaac Allerton, Myles Standish and all of the passengers combined together into what Mr. Bradford called a Civil Body Politic. They represented the Crown in exercising local sovereignty over the new land and its native inhabitants and formed the "Mayflower Compact." This contract was the security that declared that all of the 102 people that had left England for the New World would arrive there as a civil community. No one had been made to feel that his or her part in this great adventure would be too small, they were all just as important as William Bradford or William Brewster.

Yes, he thought to himself, there were many hardships that first winter. He opened the door to the Anchor Inn and the smell of good food brought him back to reality and made him realize how hungry he was as he entered the warm room.

"Another storm is brewing out there," he said to the Innkeeper. He took his hat off, brushed the icy rain from its brim and hung it on a hook near the door, and then he removed his coat, shook it and hung it up beside his hat.

"I heard the wind start up a while ago, I was hoping you'd get here soon," the Innkeeper said, "my wife has a good meal prepared for you," as he motioned to a table near the fireplace.

"That's wonderful, I'm hungry and something hot will surely warm me up," Richard replied. 'How thankful I am,' he thought as he pulled the chair away from the table and sat down. He was glad he was not back in Plymouth in the common house with the dirt floors and leaking roof, the dampness that never seemed to go away and the sickening smell of mildew and sweat. That was an odor that he never wanted to encounter again.

The Inn keeper's wife was at his table in no time with a steaming bowl of stew, a loaf of fresh corn bread smothered with butter and a large mug of beer. He thanked her politely and ate his meal quietly. Several other men entered the inn while he was eating, all complaining about the weather. Richard smiled thinking; 'they don't know what cold is.'

After he finished eating Richard retired to his room and sat down at the table and lit the lamp. Mary had been encouraging him to write some of his stories and had given him a book of plain paper bound in soft leather for his birthday. He opened his pack; found his quill, ink and new journal, adjusted the lamp for the best light, and started writing. He had a good memory for dates and times and he found that if he picked a date, he could remember the things that happened very clearly on that date, he always started his stories that way when telling them, so he wrote:

November 5, 1620

We were ill prepared for the horrible cold and snow and had no idea how hungry we would be during that first winter. Of the 102 passengers that left England, four had died before they saw land, and almost half had died before the next summer.

Many of my new friends died of starvation and disease within the first year of their arrival in the new land. Many of them were gone within the first three month during the depth of the winter, and by summer a total of 46 men, women and children had succumbed to the horrible scurvy and other diseases which the long voyage and poor conditions aboard the ship had brought upon them. Most of the women died of exposure trying to protect their children from cold and hunger while still on board the 'Mayflower' anchored in the harbor. Since there was not enough shelter ashore for everyone the men felt that the women would be safer on board, but the dirty conditions and cold salty air was worse than the crowded shelter the men had built on shore.

The Captain of the 'Mayflower,' Mr. Christopher Jones, wanted to put ashore all those aboard that were sick and return to England at this time, but he feared that God would cause more mishaps upon them if they left the passengers alone to the elements and without supplies. Many of his men were also sick and weak and he did not dare to put to sea until he saw that they were going to recover and the heart of winter was over.

Only 12 heads of families were left, many fathers had to care for their small children alone.

I was one of the 4 unattached young men that was still alive and at age eight I took on the responsibility of caring for some of the younger children, helping the few women that were still alive. We tended to the cook fires that were built for warmth as well as cooking. We washed the children's filthy clothes and then dressed them and shared our food with them. We worked long and hard to fetch wood, hunted for meat and cleaned it. We even helped cook what little food was found.

These hardships helped me develop a strong sense of concern for my fellow man. I try to make my public and private interests indistinguishable and hope that I have grown to become a strong, caring and passionate man. I believe that a colony can not succeed without people whose selflessness is not tempered by virtue, courage, hard work and piety. But enough about me, I have many more interesting stories to write.

It was on January 8, 1621 when one of the sailors of the 'Mayflower', Master Jones, a younger cousin of the Captain, and some of the men with the energy to fight the cold, went fishing and brought back three seal and a codfish, enough to last for several days. They were all cooked and served, much of it going to those that were sick and weak.

The next day, January 9, 1621 a 20-foot square common house built for storage was finished except for the roof and several house lots were laid out surrounding it. The men had been working to construct this shelter since they had come ashore, living in lean-tos covered with pine and fir branches for shelter. About twenty women and children were allowed to come ashore during this time.

A few days later John Billington and Samuel Fuller were sent out for grass to thatch the roof for the common house. It was the 12th of January, and they didn't get back until the next day, after being lost and spending a terrifying night in the woods listening to wolves thinking they were lions. John's spaniel, mastiff bitch, had flushed a deer and the men gave chase and they got themselves lost. The men were unhurt but still shaking with freight when they returned, however, they did manage to bring back enough thatch to cover the roof.

Two days later the newly thatched roof of the common house caught fire and was consumed. Most everything was saved because of the quick thinking of several men who threw snow and mud onto the flames as the fire fell on to the floor. Thankfully no one was injured, though Mr. Bradford had been lying sick in the common house when the fire broke out, Mr. Winslow had brought him to safety. John and Samuel were again asked to fetch more reeds to recover the house roof. This time they knew where to find them, but they were extremely careful taking several men with them and being sure to leave a trail so they would not have to spend another night alone in the dark woods. They returned with enough thatch to finish the roof before it snowed again.

After the fire, some of the women and children were taken back to the ship for shelter, but then the sickness started to befall them again so they were moved back to the common house and other surrounding lean-tos. The weather grew colder, and the sickness subsided.

On January the 19th John Goodman, a hunter, beat off two wolves that had chased his spaniel, Beauty. All he could think of was that his dog was his only true friend and no mangy wolf was going to harm her. John was a solitary man, but a hard worker and had cared for his dog on the long voyage across the Atlantic when she grew sick and refused to eat. Everyone thought he was a little crazy, when he would hold her tight against the swaying of the ship and spoon water into her mouth trying to keep her lips wet. After a couple of weeks when she found her sea legs, she got over her seasickness, and was everyone's pet, always laying with the little children on cold nights, keeping them warm with her body.

Another fortunate incident happened on February 9th. Master Jones shot five wild geese and found a deer that had been killed by the Indians, which was being consumed by wolves. He shot the wolves and brought them back along with the remainder of the deer and the five geese. The hides of the wolves and deer were tanned and used to help keep the sick warm. The geese were roasted on a spit and the grease that dripped from them was saved and used to soothe the throats of the people that had the coughing sickness. The deer was saved for the next day's meal.

When we awoke on the morning of March 3rd the wind had turned south bringing warmer weather and the singing of the birds in the woods was most pleasant to hear. There were more smiles and laughter from the children that day.

By March 25th, the beginning of spring, it pleased God to cease the sickness among us and bring new life into everyone. Shortly after that, on April 5, 1621, to be exact, the 'Mayflower' and her ragged crew left to go back to England for supplies. God rewarded Captain Jones by giving them an easy voyage and they arrived safely back in England on May 6th, just one month and one day after she left the new colony.

The Wampanoag Indians had been watching us struggle throughout the winter, not sure just how much they should help, we were strange and smelly people. They were reluctant to become friendly with us because of our sickness. They still remembered the horrible losses their people had endured in 1615 when Captain John Smith brought the epidemic of small pox to their shores. The fever sickness had killed more than half of the coastal Indian population. When spring came and there were fewer of us left alive, the Indians approached our makeshift settlement cautiously, holding their noses with their fingers and thumbs or covering their faces with their robes. They had decided during the winter to befriend the settlers if any were still alive when spring came, so, instead of maintaining a hostile distance they made their approach.

On March 26, 1621 a dark skinned man dressed in fur and feathers boldly walked into our settlement, his name was Samoset, an English speaking Abenaki from Pemaquid whose people had been trading with Sir Francis Popham for ten years. He had another young Indian with him who had once been a captive of the French he was called Squanto, who spoke French, Dutch, English and several Native dialects.

Within a few days, Chief Massasoit of the Wampanoag Indians, his brother Quadequina and about 60 of their men were our guests and on the April 1, 1621, the first historic treaty that reflected the good intentions of both parties was formed between the Wampanoag Indians and the Plymouth Colony. They each agreed to aid the other in the event of an attack by a third party, and to disarm during their meetings with each other.

Although I was young at the time I knew there had to be a reason why these Indians were so friendly. Unbeknown to us, the Narragansett had been a constant thorn in the side of the Wampanoag Indians for more than 5 years, and our friendliness toward them and our firearms would be a great advantage in keeping the Narragansett Indians at bay. They were frequently at war with each other. The Wampanoag believed that the Narragansett would not attack the Pilgrims, because they were fearful of the weapon of fire, so this treaty was beneficial to them as well as to us. We are still to this day at peace with the Wampanoag Indians.

I am sorry to have to write that another small Pox epidemic broke out in the summer of 1633, it destroyed even more of the Indian population. Even some of our people were stricken, I remember hearing that about ten English children died of the dreaded disease that year.

• • •

When the light from the oil lamp flickered a few times Richard decided that he had written enough for one night. His fingers were stiff and cold and he shivered a little as he put his pen down and covered the little bottle of ink with the cork stopper. He stood up and stretched his legs and then laid down on the small feather bed and pulled the warm quilt over him. He went to sleep thinking about Mary and his new baby, little William.

• • •

Before Abraham Blish stepped out of the barn he heard the jingle of the bells that young Master Dudley had attached to his horse's reins. Billy Dudley was trotting up the lane on his old horse High Stepper waving a letter. Billy had been delivering letters in Devonshire County England for a shilling or two from each party, the sender and the receiver, for about five years. Everyone knew he charged both ways, but he was a likable boy and the money helped him support his mother and younger sister.

"Hello Billy, you're out early this afternoon," Abraham called, "What have you got for my Pa today?" It was April 1, 1637.

"It's not for your Pa, Abraham, it's for you," Billy said. "From Richard More of the Plymouth Colonies," he continued, handing

Abraham the letter. "The *'Friendship'* docked last night and I'm delivering letters for the Captain." Billy turned his hand so that his palm was up and held it there waiting for his shilling.

"For me? From Richard?" Abraham said with surprise. "I haven't heard from Richard for over a year, I'd almost given up ever hearing from him again," he continued. "I thought that something had happened to him and no one had taken the time to write me about it," Abraham said as he dug into his pocket and found a shilling and two pence and put them into Billy's still outstretched hand.

"Thank you Billy, I hope there's only good news in here," Abraham said and patted 'High Stepper' on the nose.

"I'm sure there is, Mr. Blish, the Captain didn't tell me any bad news from the Colonies," Billy said happily, he put his money into his pouch and turned his horse toward the lane waving to Abraham as he trotted back down the road toward town.

Abraham and Richard had written to each other as often as possible during the last ten years. They had been friends as children. Their two families were neighbors for many years. Their fathers, James Blish and Thomas More had political influence in their town government and were considered to be fair and decent men. Sarah Blish and Elizabeth More were like sisters always helping each other as neighbors did in those days.

Seventeen years before, although just a young child, Abraham wanted to go with Richard when he left on the *'Mayflower'* with Mr. Brewster. He had secretly wanted his parents to join the group of men that called themselves Puritans as Richards father had done. When he was five he remembered asking his father if he could go to the same church that Richard went to, but his father wouldn't hear of it. He could still hear his exact words, "We are not changing our religion and we are not moving anywhere Abraham, you are going to finish your schooling here and that's all I will say to you about it." Abraham didn't understand what his father meant at the time, he hadn't asked him to move anywhere, but he knew better than to ever bring the subject up again.

Abraham waved back at Billy and hurried into the house. "Mother, I have a letter from Richard," he shouted excitedly and then started to sit down at the table to open it.

"What is it Abraham?" his mother called from the parlor where she was busy cleaning?"

"I've just received a letter from Richard," he repeated as Sarah came into the kitchen.

"Oh, you must read it to all of us," she said excitedly, "why don't you go and get your father and brother while I make us some tea."

"All right," he said a little reluctantly turning toward the door. He could hardly contain his excitement as he ran down the hill to the Mill where his Pa and brother John were grinding wheat.

"Pa, I have a letter from Richard More," he shouted breathlessly as he stepped into the Mill, "Mother has tea ready, come and I'll read it aloud."

Seeing the excitement on his son's face James said, "I guess this is as good a time as any to stop for afternoon tea." He finished filling a bag with flour and tied it, he was always happy to hear how Richard was doing.

John put his arm around his brother's shoulder in an affectionate hug and laughingly said, "It's about time you heard from him, I was beginning to think the Indians had captured him." Abraham laughed too, and they all headed toward the house for tea and to hear what news Richard's letter held.

Sarah poured tea when they were all seated. Abraham carefully opened the seal on his letter and began reading.

February 21, 1637
My dear friend Abraham,
May this letter find you and your family in the best of health and prosperity.

As you know it has been a while since I have had the opportunity to sit down with pen and paper to answer your letters. I hope I have not brought worry to you and I wish to apologize to you now if I have.

This last year has been a very busy year for me and quite eventful. So I shall try to begin at the beginning.

Mr. Bradford purchased a large quantity of land from the Mattakeeset Indians last year and I was granted about a hundred acres. We have named our newly settled town Duxbury and I have laid out my land in sections for planting, orchards, and my dwelling lot. I have just completed my new house and barn and I am pleased at the way I have arranged everything. I have another plot of land, about 20 acres with a small dwelling on it for sale. We lived there while I was building our new house. There are about ten other families now living here.

The weather here was gentle with us during this past year and has provided us with plenty of crops to harvest and hay for our cattle. Trading with the Indians last fall was successful in bringing us many useful items that they provide us and I am sure it was satisfactory for them as well.

I understand that the weather last year shortened your growing season and has caused you much concern, for this I grieve for you all. The weather one wonders how, must also be the cause of the trade problems that we are having between our two countries. The great drought that you had last Spring, with no rain for many weeks must have destroyed your hay crops, I understand that you are now paying an unbelievable 5 pounds a load. We have had to accept very low prices for our beaver skins and other trade goods.

We have sent numerous letters to the Merchant Adventurers Council in England, but they will not agree to consider our accounts with them settled. We have shipped many more skins than we have received credit or trade goods for, and it seems that the more beaver and other commodities that we send to England, the more our debt grows.

So, last month we resolved to send no more beaver and otter skins until the previous balance owed to us has been paid in full. Believe it or not, the balance due us here in New Plymouth was well over 3,000 pounds. This is almost the same amount that our sponsors loaned us sixteen years ago. As of this day, this controversy has still not been settled, and it may be years before it will be, if ever. But enough of this, it is nothing that you must concern yourself with at the moment.

The rest of my news shall be about the good fortune that God has bestowed upon me. The most important being that I was married on March 3, 1636, to Mary Sprague of New Plymouth and we are expecting our first child within the month. Mary has been improving our new house every day with her fancy way of sewing and quilting. She is handing me one tool or another whenever she sees that I might have a minute or two, and asks that I build her a shelf here or there. I have never been happier in my life.

So, at this point in my letter to you Abraham, I will reveal to you the reason for writing you this especially long letter. I am inviting you with urgency to come to Duxbury and help us establish it into a new colony. We are in need of honorable men of high character who will be influential in building our new country. I have known you and your family for a long time and can assure you that I am offering you an opportunity of a lifetime. I know, as sure as I know the Lord Jesus, that some day this New World will become a nation bigger than the King's England.

It will be in your own best interest and beneficial to all of us here if you could bring as many carpenter tools that you will need for building, as well as any farming tools that you may have available. Clothing, bedding, dishes and crockery packed in reusable casks and kegs of all sizes are in great demand now and will be very helpful to you when starting your own home.

Cattle are available for sale here, but at this moment are quite expensive, as are sheep. Other livestock such as chickens, goats and hogs are available at reasonable prices.

A good horse can be purchased from Mr. Edward Rogers of Yarmouth. Several years ago he was successful in developing a new breed of work horse by breeding a young chestnut colored mare called a Narragansett pacer with a large stallion that he traded for several yards of cloth from an Indian. The Indian did not know when the horse came to be in the Colonies, probably in 1624 when we received some of the first animals from England, but he insisted that he was the true owner. Edward believes that it may have been an offspring of several horses that were given to the Indians by the French many years ago. His herd is of some size now and he has been selling several each year. I have made a choice of one for you, though I have not purchased it yet, Edward has promised me that he would not sell it until I have heard from you.

This is a wonderful new land and a great opportunity for you and I do hope that you will consider this letter as my invitation to you to join Mary and I here in Duxbury for as long as it takes to get you settled into your own home.

If your decision is to accept my invitation, I shall be in Boston on business during the first week of May and shall await the arrival of the 'Friendship' hoping to greet you then. We shall then journey to Duxbury by boat, about 25 miles south of Boston, it will be faster than trying to go by land, as most of the road way is no wider than a deer trail. I realize that this does not give you much time to make arrangements or settle your accounts, but I do hope you will accept my invitation. If it is not possible to join me here at that time, please do send an answer as to whether or not you will be able to accept my invitation at a later date.

So, now I will close with best regards to your parents and brother, and no matter what your decision regarding this great endeavor,

I will always remain your very loving friend in our Lord Jesus,

Richard More

CHAPTER TWO
APRIL 1637

Abraham was standing on the dock preparing to board the 'Friendship' in Plymouth England on April 8, 1637, just a little over a week after he had received Richard's letter. He shivered slightly pulling his coat a little higher onto the back of his neck. Though it was quite a nice day with just a slight breeze blowing from the south and a few high clouds to the north he felt a chill. 'The excitement of what is to come,' he thought and shrugged off the foreboding feeling of sadness that he may never see his family again that was already creeping into his mind.

When he hugged his mother goodbye he knew she was still crying, she hadn't really stopped since he had made his decision to leave his home in Devonshire County England where he was born.

"I love you, mother," he said, holding her tight in his arms.

She hugged him even harder than he was hugging her, "I know my son, and I love you, too, please write to us every chance you get."

"I will, mother," he promised, "and you do the same." She said she would as she slipped out of his arms so that his brother could embrace him.

"Have a great adventure brother," John said as he gave him a huge bear hug.

Abraham hugged him back and said, "Take care brother, and be sure to give Molly a hug for me."

"I shall only give Molly hugs from me, you scoundrel," John said and punched him playfully on his arm.

"Then I shall give her one myself the next time I see her," Abraham said laughing.

Abraham gave his father a long affectionate hug and held his hand in a firm handshake for a minute or so.

James had tears in his eyes as he handed his son a pouch and said, "Invest it wisely, son."

Thanking him, Abraham took the pouch and slipped it into the inside pocket of his heavy coat vaguely thinking that it would probably help him buy the horse Richard had mentioned in his letter.

When the ship's First Mate rang the bell for all to board Abraham picked up his satchel and ran up the gangplank onto the deck of the 'Friendship'. He waved to his family as the ship's anchor was hauled out of the water and he watched them until they became tiny specks on the shore. He wiped the tears from his eyes and shook his head to rid himself of the lonesome feeling that filled his being; even his excitement couldn't take away the homesickness he was already feeling.

Abraham found his berth in the first class section of the ship and settled himself into the small tidy quarters. The 'Friendship' was an old fishing boat that had been turned into a quite comfortable passenger ship, for ten first class passengers. However, the decks below were not as comfortable as there were about twenty-five middle class families and fifteen young men that were hoping to be hired as apprentices or servants sharing that small space. They all wanted to find a better way of life. Abraham had hired and paid passage for three of these men to go with him as indentured servants, and they were among those second class passengers.

Now, at last he was on his way to the Colonies and a whole new life. Abraham had been waiting for this day since he was a small boy when he watched Richard go aboard the 'Mayflower'. What an adventure his friend was going to have he remembered thinking, and he wanted to go with him.

Now that he was older he understood many of the reasons why the Puritans left England in 1620. They wanted a greater reformation of the Church of England and separated themselves from it and formed their own religion. Some people even called them Separatist though he himself preferred the word Puritan and had become a member while in college in London. The Puritans did away with many of the elaborate ceremonies, thereby purifying the church. They felt that they could serve their Lord Jesus better by setting examples of themselves, by practicing better moral habits and by preaching a closer form of religion they felt the bible expressed.

Abraham also remembered sadly why Richard and his brothers and sister were part of that adventure. A tragic fire had ended the life of Richard's parents on January 20, 1619. They both died while saving their four children from their burning home. It was a sad day for everyone in the small village of Barnstaple, England. Abraham could still remember his mother running toward the More home screaming Elizabeth's name over and over.

Thomas More was at a town council meeting that morning and was on his way home when he saw the dreaded black smoke of a house fire. Almost immediately he realized it was coming from the direction of his own home, "Oh my Heavenly Father," he cried aloud and gave his horse a kick. He saw Sarah Blish hurrying the children back to her house demanding that they stay there and telling Richard not to let them out of his sight. He rode as near as he could to the burning house and when his skittish horse would go no closer he dismounted and started running as fast as he could. He watched horrified when he saw Elizabeth run back into the house. He screamed her name as he heard the explosion of burning thatch fall into his home.

She had pushed little Jasper out of the door and into the arms of his older brother Richard. Then as Elizabeth turned back into her house to gather as much of their clothing as she could the roof collapsed upon her covering her with burning thatch. He could hear her screams over the roar of the fire and without any thought of his own well being he ran into the inferno to try and save his beautiful Elizabeth.

Thomas's body was found covering hers as if to shield her from the horrible death by fire. Elizabeth was just barely alive when the fire had finally burned itself out. She lived two days, suffering from severe burns over most of her body. She never gained consciousness and did not know that her husband had perished in the fire trying to save her. They left their four children orphans for the village to raise.

Several members of the newly reformed Puritan church that Thomas More was a member of took charge of the More children, as families often did when tragedy struck and there were no relatives to take them. Richard, age 8, and his younger brother Thomas, age 6, were in the charge of William Brewster and his wife, Mary. Ellen age 4, was a charge of Edward and Elizabeth Winslow, and his youngest brother Jasper, age 2, was a charge of John and Katherine Carver.

A few months later William Brewster, leader of the Puritans secured a patent from the Virginia Company for a tract of land in the Plymouth Colony. He believed there would be more freedom of religion in the new Colony so he and many of his followers, including the Winslows and the Carvers, all boarded the Mayflower and fled from the Church of England taking the More children with them.

Nine years later in 1629 many others sailed to this new freedom of religion with John Endicott who had been granted a charter from the king to form the Massachusetts Bay Colony. Abraham had wanted to go then, too, thinking that at age 13 he was old enough to be an apprentice, but his father told him again that he had to wait until he finished his education.

Now at last the time had come for him to leave, he was 21 years old, had finished with his studies and had collected his inheritance. He was ready for a great adventure. 'No one can tell me "No," now,' he thought. His brother John had also finished his education and, not as adventurous as he was, had opted to stay in England and take over the duties of the family farm, run the gristmill and help care for his parents. Besides he was in love with Molly James and was planning to get married later this year.

Abraham's thoughts as he stood on deck of the '*Friendship*' looking out at the ocean were both happy and sad. He hated leaving his family but Richard's letter had given him the encouragement he needed to begin this new adventure. He was on his way to the Colonies and there was no turning back. He had enough money to purchase land there and start a small farm. Then as a young man's thoughts often do he envisioned a beautiful girl, marriage and a family. He could picture his life in front of him as if in a wonderful daydream and he prayed for the courage and guidance to succeed.

CHAPTER THREE
MAY 1637

It was sunny but still cold with a slight breeze blowing in from the south on May 10, 1637 when a sailor in the crow's nest high atop the mast called out, "Land Ho." Everyone on board the *'Friendship'* went forward to the bow for a better view, grateful that this trip would soon be over.

As the Captain steered the *'Friendship'* into Boston harbor the view that Abraham saw did not quite meet the image of New England that he pictured in his mind. There were hills with small houses setting precariously on them, the landscape was covered with trees and here and there he could see huge rocks covering the shoreline. There was a sandy beach in a small cove south of the town and on the north side huge rocks jutted out of the water as if they were waiting for ships to find them. There were rowboats, schooners, pinnacles and long narrow boats with a point on each end, canoes he thought, they must be canoes, the Indian boat that Captain Smith talked about. There were ships of all sizes anchored in the harbor or tied to the wharf.

Abraham remembered the vivid descriptions that John Smith had planted in the minds of his friends when he told them about this new land. The land that he called New England. It was 22 years ago that Captain John Smith proclaimed to all those he met that he was the discoverer of a new land. Abraham remembered meeting him at a church meeting many years before, he couldn't have been more than three or four years old, but the stories that the great Captain told left vivid pictures of wilderness and Indians in his imagination. Friendly and hostile Indians wearing animal skins and feathers in their hair. Eating strange plants, as well as squirrels, deer and fish. Captain Smith told stories about these frightening people living in mud houses and playing games with a fur ball and fighting with other tribes of Indians. He told of the boats that could go forward or backward without turning around, he called them canoes. According to the many tales he remembered about him, Abraham knew that much had happened to Captain Smith since then. One in particular was about a beautiful Indian Princess named Pocahontas. 'I'll have to ask Richard if any of these tales are true,' he thought.

He searched the shore again for the funny looking boat and spotted one with two Indians in it paddling down the coast toward a cove with a sandy beach. He watched it until it disappeared.

The harbor was full of people with the anticipation of meeting loved ones or receiving word from them. He didn't realize how many people had actually found their way to the Colonies. Sailors and servants and gentlemen and women of all races and in all forms of dress were wondering about as if in a frenzy. There was shouting and grunting and groaning from men carrying heavy loads from one ship to another. The wharf was covered with wooden crates and kegs and barrels of all shapes and sizes. It looked like chaos from where he was standing. Several men ran to the sides of the ship grabbing the ropes that the sailors on board threw out to them and then together they pulled the 'Friendship' to the pilings on the pier and tied her up. When the gangplank was secured to the wharf the Captain called the order for all passengers to disembark.

A man of large stature dressed in a fine suit of tan color and a dark green cloth coat with silver buttons caught Abraham's attention when he waved his broad brimmed hat. Richard was waiting for Abraham as he had promised.

Abraham waved and smiled as he stepped off the gangplank and grasped Richard's hand.

Richard pulled him into a great bear hug that almost took the air from his lungs. "I knew it had to be you," Richard said, his voice gruff with emotion.

"And I would know you anywhere," Abraham replied with the same amount of emotion, if not more.

"I pray you must have had an uneventful voyage in order to have arrived so soon," Richard said.

"Yes," Abraham replied, "thanks be to the Lord that the wind was brisk, and rather warm, there was only one storm of any size and that only lasted an hour or so." As they stood on the dock chatting about the size of the harbor and the weather Abraham's men found him and stood nearby waiting for their orders.

"Well, come then we still have a lot to do before dark," Richard smiled patting him on the back, "Our pinnace is ready to load."

Abraham returned Richard's smile and grabbed a large leather bag with both hands and hauled it onto his shoulder. He motioned his men to follow them.

Together, with the help of the other three men that Richard had hired they loaded his cargo onto the thirty-five foot boat that would take them to Duxbury. There were several leather bags and many large trunks, casks and kegs of all sizes. Abraham had spent about 300 pounds of his inheritance on supplies that he knew he would need as well as those that he thought others would need. It took them most of the day to move his belongings from one ship to the other.

In one of his trunks he had four pairs of shoes and four pairs of boots in his own size, and five pair of each in various sizes. There were four dozen pairs of stockings of fine Irish linen. Several trunks were filled with bolts of Kersey cloth, linen cloth, canvas and rudge, which was a coarse thick woolen cloth used in making rugs. He also had several bolts of grogram material and soft leather in one trunk, some very fine Holland linen and other coarser types that were excellent for making cloth coats and trousers. He had kegs of pitch and tar, ropes and twine, knives and scissors. There were hatchets, hoes, axes, scythes, reaphooks, shovels, spades, saws, files, nails, iron pots and other items too numerous to mention.

From a Dutch trade ship that had landed in England before his departure Abraham had purchased four barrels of raw sugar and three barrels of molasses. He also purchased spices such as cinnamon, ginger and nutmeg that were packed in small wooden boxes and then covered with wax and then packed in wooden crates.

When he purchased his tickets for New England he paid a goodly sum of money to the Captain and the first mate to insure that all of his possessions would be stored in the driest part of the '*Friendship*'. He inspected his supplies as the men loaded them onto the pinnace and found that all was in order.

As the last of his belongings were put aboard Richard's boat the Captain of the *'Friendship'* approached him and asked, "Is all well with the cargo, Mr. Blish."

Abraham assured him, "Everything is in order," he said as he shook the Captain's hand.

The Captain saluted him by tipping his hat and said, "Well, I'm off to find a pub, I'll see you again, Sir."

"Thank you for my safe passage, Captain," Abraham called after him.

Richard was already aboard the pinnace and reached down toward Abraham to give him a hand aboard. "I'm so glad that you're here, Abraham."

"So am I, Richard," he answered, "I've wanted to come here since I can remember."

"Well we shall see in a few weeks if you still feel the same way," Richard chuckled and then said, "Remember the old saying, 'be careful what you wish for, you might get it.'"

Abraham smiled and said, "I hope I do."

When they were about ten miles from Richard's home, the wind started to pick up and it looked like an early spring storm was coming. The wind was blowing quite hard and it was almost dark by the time the pinnace reached the small sheltered cove near the Duxbury wharf. Richard suggested that it would not be wise to try and unload all of Abraham's cargo in this weather, it would be better to leave it in the boat during the night where it would stay dry. There was still another two miles inland to go by oxen and wagon before they'd reach Richard's house.

The little town of Duxbury consisted of only about a dozen houses, but they were all built to last and stand against the weather. They were built of sturdy timbers, rough cut lumber, then thinner boards cut at angles to form clapboards were attached to the outside and they had shake roofs made of cedar. Windows were glassed in and the doors were of heavy oak. Abraham could see that some of the first temporary houses were still standing, they were more crudely built of roughly cut lumber or logs and still had thatched roofs and made good housing for the indentured servants.

Four days before Richard had left his wagon and oxen in John Pratt's barn and taken a pinnace to Boston to meet Abraham. He knew that if Abraham was coming they'd need a way to haul his belongs back to his house.

Behind a small grove of trees that protected them from the wind and sea the Pratt's had a cozy cottage. It over looked the cove and was located just a short distance up a small hill from the shore.

As they approached the small house they saw an older man carrying a milk pail toward his barn. The barn looked larger than the house and it was. Richard whistled to get Mr. Pratt's attention and waved to him.

In a strong voice Mr. Pratt said loudly, "Who's there."

"It's me, Richard More, and Abraham Blish is with me," Richard replied in a friendly tone.

"Well, Richard, we didn't expect to see you so soon, is everything all right with you?" John Pratt called back as they approached him.

"Well, the *"Friendship"* docked quite early this morning and we made good time coming down the coast, but now it looks like it might rain and the wind has started to pick up," Richard said. Then he gave John a friendly smile and continued, "So I decided that we might ask if we could impose on you and spend the night."

John shook Abraham's hand after shaking Richard's and said, "You would not be imposing Richard and your timing is perfect. I'm about to do my evening chores and milk the cows."

"Maybe we can help you," Abraham suggested.

"Well, I never refuse help," John smiled and led the way to the barn. In the north end there was a pigsty and along the west wall there were stanchions for several cows. There was a horse stall on the south side of the barn and there were about 15 chickens nesting in their coops on the eastern side. The loft was full of hay and a big old cat sat on top of a grain barrel. Several sheep and a goat were in a pen near the chickens.

John got the milking stool down from the peg on the wall and Abraham took the shovel and started cleaning the horse stall. Richard found the pitchfork and gave the horses some hay, then moving the cat he opened the grain barrel and gave the hogs a couple of scoops of feed corn, throwing some to the chickens as he passed by them.

Richard then went to check on his oxen and gave them a few forks full of hay. They were great beasts; he had raised them from the day they were born. "I hope the beasts were not too much bother for you John," Richard said.

"Not at all," John replied. "They're a great pair, you can be proud of the way you trained them to haul as one, it's not always easy to get these animals to work together," he continued.

"It took me over a year to make them obey my commands," Richard replied pleased with the compliment, and then he continued, "I do thank you for keeping them, and if you ever need to use them, feel free to do so."

"I certainly shall," John replied with a chuckle.

After he finished the milking John hung the milking stool back up on its peg near the barn door and picking up the steaming pails of warm milk he said, "Now that you good fellows have finished my chores for me I'll let Sarah know you're here." Then he said, "Come with me and we'll wash our hands," and he led them to the back door of the house. There was a small bench near the steps with a bucket of warm water on it and a linen cloth hung on a peg nearby. John sat the milk pails down on the top step and dipped his cold hands into the warm water. He smiled and said, "By the time you finish washing your hands, Sarah will have a good hot meal ready for us," and he went inside with the buckets of milk.

"That's very neighborly of you, John," Richard said putting his hands into the water. "This feels so good Abraham, remember to do this whenever your hands are cold and you'll never get swollen knuckles."

"My mother used to tell us the same thing," Abraham replied as he put his hands into the bucket.

"A good wife will always know when to put warm water out for you," Richard chuckled.

"Mary does this, too, I'm sure," Abraham said laughingly taking the damp linen towel from Richard.

"She sure does," Richard laughed back.

Sarah Pratt opened the door at the same time Richard did and closed it quickly after the two men entered the warm cozy house. Sarah and Anne had prepared the table so the five of them could all eat together. Sarah Pratt smiled at Richard and Abraham and she gave them each an affectionate greeting.

"Come in and warm yourselves, I'm so glad you're here," Sarah said to the young men.

Richard gave her another hug and then said, "Sarah, this is Abraham Blish."

"I have met Abraham, in fact I think he was about 13 years old when we left Barnstaple," she said as she took Abraham's hand and patted it. "It's so good to have you here safely, Abraham," she smiled.

'She still looks the same,' Abraham thought, 'she hasn't changed at all in the last eight years,' and he smiled at her and hugged her, too. "It's so good to be here, Mrs. Pratt," he said politely and laid his hand on top of hers. "Thank you for your hospitality, I hope we are not intruding," he said.

"Not at all, Abraham," she replied.

John laughed and said, "My Sarah is always ready to feed everyone and anyone at any time. And how about your men, where are they?" John questioned.

"They're down at the shore building a lean-to shelter," Abraham answered. "They had a fire started before we had even left the wharf," he added.

Richard said with a chuckle, "My men were telling tales of the great hurricane and eclipse of the moon to Abraham's men."

Abraham added, "They're going to stay there for the night to watch the supplies."

"They have enough food for three or four days and I'm sure they'll be warm enough," Richard said. Then he laughed and said, "After all, most of the men have probably slept in worst places."

Abraham laughed too, and said, "I'm sure my men won't mind where they sleep as long as it's not on a boat, they are most happy to be on dry land for a change."

John said, "I know I would be, I would rather my feet be planted on dry land." He shook his head as if to forget the unpleasant journey and said, "I couldn't wait to get here, I was sick all the while we were at sea."

"Our meal is almost ready," Sarah said changing the subject. She still remembered her husband's painful journey to New England.

"I told you that we would be back with you in time to enjoy your evening meal when I left yesterday," Richard said as he walked toward the warm fireplace. He had been delighted to accept John's invitation, the mention of food reminded him of his hunger, and a nice hot meal would certainly make this day complete. He knew what a good cook Sarah was; he had been invited to eat with them several times.

"You have made good speed on this trip Richard," Sarah said helping him take his coat off. Then taking Abraham's coat she said, "And you Abraham, you haven't changed at all since last I saw you, you look just like your mother, and how is the dear lady?" Sarah missed her friends back in England and wished she could see them again, but that was not to be she thought as she brushed her eyes with the back of her hand.

"She's feeling quite well Mrs. Pratt and sends her greetings to all her friends," Abraham replied, "and I have a letter for you in one of my trunks from her," he continued as he gave her another hug. Sarah Blish and Sarah Pratt had known each other growing up. They not only shared the same name they also had the same kind of twinkling of the eyes and happy dispositions. Abraham missed his mother already. Sarah Blish had sat down and written several long letters to five of her friends in New England and had them ready for Abraham to bring with him a week before he was ready to leave.

Then as if to change her thoughts to happier ones Sarah smiled brightly and turned to Richard and said, "Richard, I must ask about Mary and your baby son, William, how are they doing?"

"They are both just fine, her sister Remember is staying with us for a while," he replied, happy to just hear Mary's and William's names. "Thank you for asking, you are so thoughtful, Sarah," he continued.

"Well, you certainly are welcome and I am so happy to see that you made it back safely," she said. Then she turned and handed her lovely daughter the heavy coats and said, "Anne, please hang these dear, while I finish our table." Sarah had a small tear in her eye as she busied herself with their evening meal.

Anne Pratt was just 16, her birthday was two days before, May 8th, but she knew she was going to marry the man with the most beautiful blue eyes she had ever seen. Her lips were slightly curved, with just a hint of a smile as she looked at Abraham shyly.

Abraham had never seen anyone with hair the color of hers. It was a golden red, pulled back into a loose pile on top of her head, little natural curls framed her pretty face and fell down the back of her neck onto her light blue high collared dress. She was just a little girl the last time he saw her before the Pratt's moved to New England eight years before. She sure did grow up to be pretty he thought as he smiled back at her.

Then blushing slightly, she turned to the coat rack and hung the coats up knowing that Abraham had not taken his eyes off her since he had entered the door. When she turned around the two men followed her into the large eating room. "You can sit here, Richard," Anne said giving his arm a quick shy hug. "Mr. Blish, you may sit beside Richard here," Anne said as she pulled a chair away from the table motioning him to sit.

John Pratt pulled his chair away from his side of the table and they all sat down. "Shall we pray?" he said. As the women bowed their heads, John proceeded to thank the Lord for the safe trip that Abraham had had and the wonderful food they were about to eat.

Abraham bowed his head too, but he didn't close his eyes. He couldn't take them off Anne. While they were passing the food, Abraham tried to listen to the conversation, but his concentration was focused on Anne, the lovely girl across the table from him. 'I'm so happy, I think I'm in love,' he thought.

"I am so pleased that you are here to help settle our new little town Abraham," Sarah said as she handed him a plate of corn bread.

"Thank you, Mrs. Pratt," Abraham said tearing his eyes from Anne and looking at Sarah, "I am so happy that Richard has invited me to stay with him and Mary until I can settle myself into my own home."

Abraham spooned some of the corn and beans that were closest to him onto his plate, handed the bowl to Richard and took another dish filled with an orange colored squash from Sarah's hands. He helped himself to a big spoon full and then passed it to Richard. This passing of dishes continued for several more servings of delicious smelling food. A large platter of ham and a bowl of hasty pudding were also served. Abraham didn't know he was so hungry until he started eating. They all ate in silence for a few minutes, but Abraham continued to look at Anne as often as he dared, all the while thinking how lovely she was. 'I have never seen anyone so beautiful, I wonder if she's spoken for,' he thought.

The next morning the hired men had the wagon loaded with everything that they could get into it by the time Richard got there with the oxen, they hitched the team securely to it and were ready to go shortly after sun up.

"We'll have to come back tomorrow for the rest Mr. Blish," one of the men said.

"Will it be all right to leave it here, Richard?" Abraham asked.

"I'm sure it will be," he answered, "but leave everything in the pinnace, where it will stay dry in case it rains again tonight."

"It will be easier to keep an eye on, too," one of the other men said.

"Please stay and guard everything for Mr. Blish, Jonas," Richard said, "Bernard can stay with you." The two men shook their heads agreeing and then one of them put the last of the wood on the fire while the other said he would gather some more.

Richard and Abraham walked on ahead of the men and wagon. Richard was anxious to see his Mary he had hated to leave her so soon after their baby son was born, but her sister was with her and their hired hands were nearby if she needed help.

The trip from the Pratt's to Richard's home was uneventful. Richard pointed out some more of the devastation that the great hurricane had caused which was most unbelievable to Abraham. Hugh piles of trees that had been caught on a ledge looked exactly like a huge beaver dam as Richard had described to him on the way down the coast. Where the trees once stood there was now nothing but barren land covered with sand and grass.

"It must have been frightening," Abraham said.

"It was the most horrible sound I have ever heard," Richard replied, and then added, "the people laid down on the floor of their homes covered their ears and prayed that it would end."

When they were almost to Richard's home, they encountered a small troop of militiamen from Plymouth headed south to Long Island. They learned that the Pequot Indians were causing problems again with some of the settlers there and they had orders from Governor Bradford to see if peace could be made.

Abraham questioned Richard about the militia and whether or not he still believed that peace with all Indians could be obtained someday. Richard told him that several peace treaties had been signed, but there were still some Indians that did not trust the white man to live near them.

"Do you think that I could be of help by joining the militia?" Abraham asked Richard as they continued walking toward home.

"Well," Richard replied, "I believe that you could be of more help by settling in as a farmer."

"How can that help?" Abraham asked a little perplexed.

Richard had a little smile on his face but his tone was serious as he said, "Because we need more food and goods to trade with, you see, the Indians are willing to sell the land, but they don't want us to take it from them."

Abraham thought about this answer for a minute, then said, "I don't believe that we are any different from them in that matter, no one wants to have things stolen from them do they."

"No they don't," Richard agreed, "most of them are willing to help us by exchanging the knowledge they have for growing things, for our tools and iron pots. Or any other items they find fascinating that they think they have use for," he said smiling.

Then Abraham changed the subject to the land Richard had told him about, "How much land is in the plot that you have for sale?" he questioned.

Richard said, "I have paced it off to be 20 acres, almost square and it has a small house on it near the southeast corner, in fact we lived there until my new house was finished."

"Have you decided on a price yet," Abraham asked, trying to decide what a fair price would be without having seen the property yet.

"I do believe that 21 pounds would be an honest figure," Richard said after seeming to do a little figuring in his head. "There's also plenty of good land for a pasture, and for growing hay, barley, corn, vegetables and there's a small orchard in one corner and a wooded area where there is good hunting for small game and deer."

"That would be about one pound per acre, is that in line with the value of land here?" Abraham questioned

"Abraham, I know you have learned much since I last saw you," Richard said as he stopped on the trail and turned toward him, "I have read your letters many times over, and I have not once thought about over charging you for this land." Then he continued with a smile, "You and I have always been and will continue to be, the best of friends, even though we do business together."

Abraham also stopped walking when Richard did, and after listening to the sincerity in Richards voice returned his smile and extending his hand said, "I am sorry if I sounded as if I thought you would take advantage of my wealth, and I do apologize." They shook each other's hand and headed toward home with the men and wagon full of supplies following along slowly.

Mary had seen them coming up the road before Richard noticed her and was hurrying toward them. When he heard her call his name he started running toward her. He caught her in his arms taking her off her feet and swung her around in a circle. Then he stopped and kissed her full on the mouth in front of everyone. Abraham blushed a little, as did Mary when Richard introduced them. Abraham lifted her hand and brought it to his lips and kissed it in a friendly manner and said, "Hello Mary, it is such a pleasure to meet you."

Mary made a small curtsy and smiled up at Abraham, while still holding tight to Richard's arm, "I'm so glad you were able to come to this wonderful new land Abraham. It will be a joy to hear all about your journey," she added.

"I'm grateful to you for inviting me here," Abraham replied.

Richard then took baby William from Mary's sister Remember's arms and holding him gently introduced him to Abraham.

Abraham peeked into the little bundle of blankets at the tiny face and touched William's smooth cheek with his fingertip, "How beautiful," he said.

Mary looked at Remember and smiling she said, "Abraham, this is my little sister Remember, she's been helping me for a while."

Abraham shook her hand and giving her a friendly smile he said, "Hello, Remember, how are you."

Remember gave him a little curtsy and shyly said, "Hello, Mr. Blish."

Although Remember was quite attractive, he couldn't get Anne Pratt's loveliness out of his thoughts.

Abraham and his men moved his belongings into Richards shed that afternoon, May 11, 1637 and then his men went back to the wharf to get the next load. They would return the following day.

That evening he found his writing pen and paper and wrote a short letter to his mother, father and brother John telling them briefly that he had arrived safely and all was fine with him.

May 11, 1637
Dear Mother, Father and Brother John,
I am writing to let you know that I have arrived in good health and with all of my belongings intact. You can address your letters to me in care of Richard More, Duxbury Colony.
Sarah Pratt sends her love and thanks you for your letter. She will be writing to you very soon.
Richard and Mary had a baby boy they named William and all is fine with them, too.

I will be attending church with Richard and Mary and, of course, John, Sarah and Anne Pratt will also be there. Anne Pratt has certainly grown up to be a lovely young lady.

I have to get this finished so that the men that Richard hired to help us get my cargo here can post it for me. They will be leaving tomorrow to go back to Boston. I will write more at another time. Please write soon.

In God's hands I leave you. I will always be your loving son,

Abraham

• • •

For the next few months he settled into his life as a gentleman farmer helping Richard with the farming chores and meeting the other men in town. He joined the church and was accepted as a man of good standing in the small town of Duxbury. Every Sunday at church Abraham made it a point to talk with John Pratt about farming or cattle, just so he could see Anne's beautiful smile. He knew he was in love and felt that Anne had the same feelings for him but he was cautious about announcing his intentions to her father until he was established in his new home and community, after all he had only known her for a short while.

Patricia Louise Blish Gould

CHAPTER FOUR
AUGUST 1637

It was during this time that Richard told him stories about the many hardships that the pilgrims had endured during those first years. He would start his stories by remembering a date and then he would say to Abraham, "You know, Abraham, it was 16 years ago today that a young lad was lost in Plymouth. Would you like to hear about him?"

Abraham always answered, "Yes, of course," and then stopped what he was doing and gave his undivided attention to the story he was about to hear.

Richard had a way of telling a story that would give you a clear picture in your mind of everything he was saying and he would always have you laughing or crying before it was over.

"The date was June 11, 1627, a young boy named John Crackson left the village settlement of Plymouth and became lost. He was after small game and eggs and birds for his mother. When he had not returned to eat his evening meal, which he never missed, his mother became worried and went to Governor Bradford's home and reported that her son was not home yet. After forming a group of men as a search party they searched the woods around the village, ringing the small bell that had helped many men return home, but they still were unable to find him.

The next day Governor Bradford sent word to Yanno, Chief of the Cummaquid Indians, that John was lost. Yanno was about 26 years of age, and very personable, gentle, courteous and fair conditioned, and except for his clothes he did not look like a savage. The young Chief agreed

29

to help them find young Crackson and sent a party of about a dozen young men, himself included, in search of the boy through the woods along the shore.

About eight of us, including two Indian guides set forth in a shallop toward Nauset. The weather was being very fair when we left Plymouth, but after being at sea just a short time a storm arose of wind and rain and much lightening and thunder and a waterspout arose very near the boat. We were both fearful and thankful that when night fell we were near a harbor at a place called Cummaquid where we thought we might find shelter from the storm. But the Indians that were with us, Tisquantum our interpreter, and Tokamahamon, a good friend of mine, thought that we would be safer at sea in the middle of the bay and so we stayed there through the night.

In the morning we awoke with the sun and found several young Indian lads on the shore seeking lobsters, so we sent Tisquantum and Tokamahamon to tell them that we were looking for a lost boy and we would not harm them. They told us that the boy was well and that he was in the village of Nauset which was a few miles further down the shore. The boys invited us to eat with them and then they took us to Chief Yanno, who was camped just off the shore in a small clearing where he and his men had spent the night.

Yanno was cheerful that he had helped us discover where young John was and that he was safe. While we ate he entertained us with stories about the time when he was lost at a very young age and was found by his father asleep in a tree. He was scolded for not telling anyone where he was going, and then praised for climbing the tree where he was safe from bears.

There was however, one thing that was very sad about this event. It seems there was an old woman in Yanno's village, whom we judged to be no less than 100 years old, who came close to us to see us because she had never seen an English man before. When she looked at us she broke forth into a great passion, weeping and crying excessively. We were quite taken back with her carrying on like this and demanded to know the reason of it and then they told us her sad tale.

It seemed that in the year 1614, she had three sons who, along with twenty-four other young Indian men and boys, were lured into going with Captain Thomas Hunt aboard his ship to trade with him. A short while after dark the ship left the harbor along with all three of her sons and the other young men. Captain Hunt had kidnapped them and he carried them as captives to Spain and sold them into slavery.

This action caused her to be deprived of the comfort of her children in her old age and she had only what people discarded and what she could *grow and gather for herself. There were two other old women that lived with her whose husbands and sons had been killed in Indian wars or other ways. To have no man to support you in your old age was very sad in the ways of the Indians and many women would just go off into the woods alone and die.*

We told her we were sorry that any Englishman should give her that offense and that Captain Hunt was a bad man and that all the English condemned him for his terrible deeds. We assured her that we would not offer her any such injury even if we gained all the skins in the country. We gave the old woman some small trifles and a cloth coat, which she took with pleasure and then she wandered off, muttering as old Indian women do.

Later that afternoon, after the stories were told and we had eaten our noontime meal we took our shollop down the coast to Nauset. Yanno and our two Indian friends went with us to show us were the Nauset village was. When we arrived it was almost dark and the tide was almost out which made it difficult to go ashore in our shollop, but Yanno and Tisquantum went in with their small canoe, while we spent the night in the boat.

The next morning Chief Aspinet of the Nauset Village came to the shore with about a hundred of his men and brought the boy with him. John's feet were wrapped in soft deerskin and he was clothed in fur. Though the days were warm there were still patches of snow and ice in the woods and John had walked through a cold swamp for hours. His feet had been almost frozen when he was found, and were still bright red and he was unable to walk on them, otherwise he seemed fine and was smiling from ear to ear. One of the Indian men carried him through the water to us with about 50 of the Indians following him unarmed. The others stood on shore with their bows and arrows ready watching to see if anyone would cause them harm. When the boy was handed aboard the shollop to us the Indian bowed his head and made peace with us. We gave the man carrying the boy a knife and also gave one to Chief Aspinet.

Chief Yanno had left Aspinet's village shortly after he arrived there and was already back in his village when we returned to Cummaquid later that afternoon. He brought us water and food and the women and children joined hand in hand singing and dancing before us. The Indian men also showed all the kindness they could. We gave young John a small knife, three silver buttons and a waistcoat to give to Chief Yanno in payment for saving his life and Yanno took a necklace from his neck and gave it to young John. We left by moonlight and arrived safely home around midnight."

"These are not the Indians that are causing problems to the south of us are they?" Abraham asked when Richard ended his story.

"No," Richard answered smiling; "Yanno is still a friend of the English and has helped many. You will meet him soon," he said still smiling.

"When?" Abraham asked a little shaken.

"I don't know," Richard answered, "he will just appear in front of you someday and scare you so much your knees will shake."

"What do you mean?" Abraham asked looking around.

"You sure have a lot of questions," Richard said looking at him with laughing eyes. "I mean, that Yanno loves to frighten new settlers, he means no harm, I think he just likes to test the courage of people."

"Oh," Abraham said, "I guess I'll have to keep my guard up and my eyes open."

Richard just smiled and went back to work.

Abraham stood still looking toward the forest wondering if they were being watched.

• • •

Word came to Richard and Abraham on August 5, 1637 that English troops had been ordered to surround and burn a Pequot village about 250 miles down the coast from Duxbury, near the Long Island. All inhabitants were to be killed, take no prisoners was the order.

The Pequot were arrogant and called themselves Moor-hawks, meaning a clean and beautiful people and they considered themselves better than the white man. They believed that the white man's God was just a fly, an annoyance to deal with. The English were also nothing, just filthy hairy people.

There were also many other reasons why the Pequot hated the white men. Many years before a white man by the name of John Smith brought a disease to them called small pox and over 30,000 Indians died from this dreaded sickness. They also believed that the white man violated the land by growing crops of tobacco and other unknown vegetation that was not considered edible by them. They believed that the white men wanted their women and children to become their slaves or servants and tried to bribe them with small amounts of clothing and 'magic' tools to change their native ways of living and to believe in the white man's God as they did.

Some of the men in the Plymouth militia newly arrived from England were more than willing to carry out such unthinkable deeds, they believed that the Indians were sinful people and followers of Satan. It was not uncommon to hear that these men harassed the Indians, took their land without payment and then told them that they had no right to hunt on it. Both Richard and Abraham were totally against this treatment of the Indians. They thought that retaliation for such horrible treatment to the Pequot village would be inevitable.

With this news, however, Abraham and Richard, along with most of the able bodied landowners, their servants and hired hands had no choice but to side with the English so they signed up with the militia. They wanted to be ready for anything that the Pequot may decide to do. Although this village was miles away and the Indians rarely invaded another tribe's territory without warning, they all thought it best to be prepared for the worst. Governor Bradford gave the order that all towns should build a fortification house for protection. The town of Duxbury built theirs on the western side of town and it took them most of the summer to complete it.

The burning and killing that took place that fateful day in August in the Pequot village on the Long Island, caused many problems between the Indians and some of the early settlers that had tried to befriend them for many years. However, because of the destruction of their village the Pequot had no choice if they wanted to survive, they had to submit to the English or be killed. Though the order to take no prisoners was given, many of the militia could not bring themselves to kill innocent women and children and defenseless old men and they were taken as prisoners.

This horrendous deed, the building of the fortification houses and expanding the militia did, however, cause the local Narragansett Indians to become friendlier toward the settlers of Duxbury making it easier for the settlers there and in the surrounding towns to bargain with them.

After this burning things quieted down between the Indians and English with very few skirmishes between them. However, everyone was always on the lookout for any suspicious looking Indians. The other Indian tribes settled their differences with the white man and each other peacefully without any further war or retaliation.

Harvesting and the preparation for winter took up the rest of that summer and fall. Wood cutting and stacking for everyone was beginning and Abraham sold several of the axes and saws that he had brought with him.

On September 5, 1637, in a friendly gesture the Indian women from Yanno's village came to town with baskets of corn, beans, squash, pumpkins, cucumbers, artichokes, berries and soft rabbit and squirrel furs and other items to trade and sell to the settlers.

Sarah, Anne, Mary and Remember were among the many white women that traded, pots, pans, candles, cloth, quilts and needles, for warm furs to be made into hats, mittens and hoods for winter cloaks. They also bought warm fur lined moccasins from them and traded many items useful to both white and Indian women alike. Many of the small towns throughout the colonies traded with the Indians every fall and this tradition grew each year.

Abraham traded several barrels of the tools and supplies that he had brought with him to the Indians and sold some of his other supplies to his neighbors for money. He had well over 30 pounds sterling and felt that he could well afford the land Richard wanted to sell him.

Richard More signed the deed over to Abraham for the 20 acres of his land that included a dwelling house and a large barn, on November 1, 1637. This parcel was the same piece of land they had talked about when Abraham first arrived in Duxbury. They both had walked around the property and surveyed it during the summer. There were fields where Richard had planted wheat, barley and oats the previous years and there was a small apple orchard that covered about an acre of land. Wild Concord grape vines covered a small grove of beach trees and there was a small cranberry bog in the lowest corner of the land. Richard pointed out where Mary had planted her vegetable garden not too far from the house.

The small sturdy house was almost on the southeast corner of his land at the top of a hill and he like its location. There was a majestic view from the front door overlooking the entire town, the harbor and the ocean beyond. 'This must be what the eagle can see when he's soaring over the trees,' he thought. So he named his new home "Eagles Nest."

It was a small house in comparison with his parents home in England, but he liked the way it was made with the back of it tight against the side of the hill and the front facing east. The roof was newly thatched and the front room window was made with small diamond shaped panes of glass and set in lead cames. They were closed by a hinged casement that helped to keep out the cold. The window casement was made of wood; however, the casement for the door was made from iron that Richard had forged himself

Richard had built this house in the summer of 1632. It was a small four-room frame house covered with weatherboarding and then clapboards. The walls inside were sheathed up with boards molded at the edges in an ornamental manner and the intervening space was filled with clary and chopped straw and imperfect bricks. This was done for warmth and was known as nogging. Good bricks were purchased from the Salem brickyard that had been in operation since 1629. Clay was easily found along the coast and was used to make bricks for chimneys. These brick were laid upon huge stone foundations in puddles of clay up to the ridge line and then lime was used at the chimney top because it held up to the weather better.

Richard built an oven with an iron door into the side of the fireplace and forged the heavy strap hinges of wrought iron to keep it closed. This same wrought iron was used to secure the front and back doors, as well as for the butterfly hinges that he used on the cupboards and windows. He forged the thumb latches and fitted them into the hard maple handles that he carved for the inside and outside of the door. It was the first house that he built, but not the last. He always enjoyed the satisfaction he received after all the hard work of building a house was done.

During the following week Abraham moved all of his belongings that he had stored in Richard's woodshed into his new home. His men stayed in the house with him for a few days while they cleaned and winterized one corner of the barn but they all continued to cook and eat their meals in the house. Like many new settlers before him, Abraham came to the new land prepared. He brought with him enough food to last a year, eight bushels of meal; two bushels of dried peas, two bushels of oatmeal, a gallon of brandy, a gallon of oil, two gallons of vinegar and a large variety of spices. He had also made many good trades for corn and beans with the Indian women.

When he unpacked his casks and kegs he took great care to build shelves and pegs to store and hang his possessions. As he was taking his winter clothes from his trunks he noticed that the strings of a pouch were hanging out of the inside pocket of his great coat. He pulled the pouch out and realized that it was the one that his father had given him when he left England. He opened it and found 200 pounds sterling in it. "Invest it wisely," his father had said to him.

"How could I have forgotten that," he asked himself out loud. Tears came to his eyes as he realized that he had never thanked his father for this generous gift. He immediately got his pen and paper out of the special wooden box that he kept them in and wrote his father a letter.

November 8, 1637
Dear Father and Mother and Brother John,
 This letter will be longer than the last one and Good news is all I have to tell you. I am a landowner now as I have recently purchased a home from Richard that I named 'Eagle's Nest' because there is a beautiful view of the Duxbury Harbor and of the ocean beyond from my front door.
 I have twenty acres of land and a nice house and barn that Richard built about five years ago. I have been moving in for about a week now and have everything about settled. I have been very busy with buying pigs, sheep and chickens and getting ready for winter. I also bought the horse that Richard mentioned in my letter.
 Richard and I have joined the militia and all of the able bodied men in town helped in the building of a fortification house to guard against the Pequot Indians. The other Indian tribes have been friendly enough, but the Pequot are rascals. Have no fear though; no one in town has seen any of them this year. So please don't worry about us, we are all quite safe here.
 Richard and I went to Boston last month and I found some of the furniture that I needed and we brought it back by schooner. The roads here are very scarce; most of them are only deer trails or Indian trails. Horses are able to get through single file, but it is most difficult for oxen and wagons. The roads in the small towns are better, but traveling is much easier between towns if we travel by water.
 I did not tell you in my last letter about Anne Pratt, only that she had grown up to be pretty. Well, anyway, she is the most beautiful girl I have ever seen. She has beautiful reddish blonde hair that curls around her face and is always escaping from her bonnet. Her skin is so white with just a

smattering of freckles across her nose and cheeks. Her eyes are as blue as the ocean and they sparkle when she smiles, and she smiles at me every time I see her.

I wanted to tell you about her because my intentions are to ask her father if I can court her. I know she is young, but I believe that I will never find anyone else that pleases my eye as much as Anne does. I am sure that my next letter to you will have more news about her.

Well, father my main reason for writing this letter is to thank you for the money that you gave me as I boarded the 'Friendship'. I just tonight found it in my great coat pocket. It has been there since I put my winter clothes away in my trunk. In fact I did not remember that it was there until I saw the pouch strings hanging out of the pocket when I was unpacking my trunk this evening. This will give me more than enough money to buy the cattle that I will need to start my herd.

Bless you father and mother for all you have done for me. I hope this letter finds its way to you soon. I miss you and hope you will write soon. Have John and Molly set a date to marry yet?

In God's hands I leave you. I will always be your loving son

Patricia Louise Blish Gould

CHAPTER FIVE
1638

The winter was harsh with cold but there was not very much snow to hinder traveling. In some instances it was easier because the ground was frozen. On February 6, 1638, Abraham and fellow townsmen powwowed with a group of Narragansett Indians and offered them a wide range of goods such as axes, hoes, hatchets, knives, crowbars, plows, wagons, cloth, spinning wheels, and more, in exchange for a chance to tell them about the white mans God. The Indians were also interested in the technology that the white man had and so learning the language and moral philosophy appealed to them.

After listening and trading for a few days, the Indians left town and went about their own way of living, but whenever they wanted or needed the white man's goods they would listen again about God and then go about their own business again. The settlers knew this would happen but had decided that a little religion was much better than no religion at all. So whenever the Indians wanted to trade, they had to learn a lesson about God and spend a day or so listening to the preacher.

Later that spring, on April 27, 1638, the Indian women of a nearby Narragansett settlement were called upon by some of the farmers in Duxbury for help in planting their fields. Abraham along with Thomas Dimmock and his friend Edward Fitzrandall traded rakes and hoes and other tools for their secrets of how they reaped enough food to sustain their people throughout the long winters. The men had seen the large quantities of vegetables the Indian women's gardens produced last fall when they brought them to town to trade.

The women gladly told them about plating beans and corn in the same hill along with a small fish and they showed them how to plant squash, pumpkins, cucumbers and artichokes in mounds or "hills" which allowed the roots to intertwine and strengthen the plants against the winds. This method also prevented the birds from finding the seeds. When the fish decayed it provided fertilizer and other nutrients and the crops were larger. This was no secret, they said, it was a gift from mother earth and she had given the old ones a dream about the way of planting many years before. They showed the farmers that by keeping the fields clear of all weeds they were able to grow better crops and found that they could have, by mid summer each year, fresh beans and cucumbers.

Many of the Indian women and children were paid well by the farmers to help them in the gardens during planting and harvest time. They were very instrumental in keeping peace between the men of their village and the white settlers, persuading them that trading was good. Hunters and fishermen were always bringing a deer or turkey or huge codfish to the white men to trade for iron pots or coats or cloth for themselves and their women.

The Indians showed the settlers how to fire small sections of the forest. In late winter and early spring they set fire to the undergrowth letting it spread only near the ground and just so far up the trees. None of the trees were damaged because lower limbs were cut away or burned off when the tree was young. Doing this every year or so made hunting easier as well as traveling and it also prevented forest fires that were caused by lightening from burning too many acres of their land.

Indian women showed the white women where to pick wild strawberries, blueberries, raspberries and blackberries. These were welcomed treats when made into cakes and cobblers and tarts.

There were still, however, other Indian villages that did not find it so easy to be friendly, always finding little ways to irritate the new settlers. One such occurrence happened on January 3, 1638 when one of the Pequot tribes decided to go on a retaliating raiding party.

This was one of the first stories that Abraham wrote about in his journal it was about the first man in the new colony that was ever tried for treason. Abraham titled his stories by a person's name, where as Richard always started his with a date. The title of this story was '*William Baker*.'

"*A small raiding party of about six young Pequot Indian men found and captured William Baker, an unmarried man living alone in a small shanty near their woods. He was chopping wood on that day and did not hear the Indians until one of them grabbed him from behind. He was beaten severely and then bound by his wrists and dragged until he regained his senses enough to get up and walk. It was then that he realized there were two young girls with them that had been captured earlier that day from a nearby farm. Their hands were tied too, but evidently they had not been beaten, as he could see no bruises or blood on them.*

Judith and Jennifer Walker were out gathering brush for kindling when the young warriors captured them. The girls were about nine and eleven and were so scared that they couldn't talk. William could see that their coats and dresses were dirty and their stockings and shoes were wet, he guessed they had probably wet their pantaloons a few times since they were captured. "What is your name," he said to the oldest one.

"Judith Walker and this is my little sister Jenny," the scared child whispered.

When William realized that they were his new neighbors living about a mile south of him, he whispered back with swollen lips, "It will be all right as soon as we reach their village little ladies."

Both girls looked at him as if he was crazy, then Judith, asked sobbing, "How can you say it will be all right when we will probably all die."

"Hush, now, don't cry, be brave so they don't hurt you," William said quietly.

One of the young warriors said quite plainly in English, "No talk!"

About a half-hour later they arrived at the Indian village, the girls were white with fear and cold and shook so badly that they were unable to make their legs move anymore. They sat down on the cold ground as soon as the warriors let go of the their tethered hands. William was pushed to the ground and kicked several times by each of the warriors but as soon as they stopped he stood up and tried to look brave and he tried his best to stop his legs from shaking from fear and the cold. His shirt and frock had been torn and his trousers were nothing but rags hanging from his waist.

Many of the women and children swarmed around the captives touching them and staring at them until one Indian woman shooed them away. She took them to her hut and untied their hands then motioned for them to sit near her fire pit. She put fur robes around them and after a few minutes they stopped shaking. She talked softly to them in her native language and smiled at the three dirty captives as she ladled out a dish of stew for each of them.

It took a few minutes before Williams eyes adjusted to the darkness of the hut and he noticed two little children huddled on a bed of furs on one side of the room. They were both holding a bowl of food and were eating quietly, staring at the dirty white people.

The woman busied herself in some packs that were hung on the wall beside her sleeping mat while the captives ate and then she left the hut with a large jug.

William saw a gourd hanging on the wall by the door and a bucket of what he thought might be drinking water sat directly under it. He was so thirsty and knew that the girls must be, too, so he got up carefully, so as not to scare the little Indian children, went over to the bucket and dipped the gourd into the pail. He smelled the clear liquid and then tasted it, clean water he whispered to himself. He filled the gourd and took it over to the girls and offered them a drink. They drank the clear water from the funny looking dipper and handed it back to William. He took it back to the bucket and dipped it in again and then drank his fill of the cold water, then held the cold gourd to his swollen lip for a minute before he hung it back on the peg.

The Indian woman came back into her hut with the big jug full of water just as William was sitting back down. She stopped short and looked at William with a slight frown. He looked up at her and then motioned to the water bucket and then to the little girls. She smiled and nodded her head up and down understanding him, and sat the heavy jug near the hearth then sat down between the girls and William and warmed her hands over the fire.

In the little English that she knew she told them that her name was Santumtanya. The white men, on the Long Island far away had killed her husband, leaving her with two children to take care of by herself; she pointed to the bed of fur. Her people had lost many men, women and children; there had been enough death she said.

"I not let you be hurt," she said pointing to each one of them. "No more people die here, room for all to live," Santumtanya said to William.

William nodded his head in agreement. "There has been enough killing between the English and your people. I wish to harm no one," he said looking at the pretty Indian woman now standing with her hands on her hips.

"I will speak for you when the sun rises," she said as she put her fingers into the jug of water. It was still cold so she pushed it nearer to the *fire pit and then busied herself again with some of the bundles near her bed.*

Judy said quietly to William, "Can I have some more food, I'm still hungry," and she held her dish out to him.

William winked at the scared little girl and said, "Excuse me Santantantan," he knew he wasn't pronouncing her name right, so he cleared his throat and held Judy's dish out toward her, "more food for girls?" he said and gave her a slightly embarrassed smile.

Santumtanya stopped what she was doing and shook her head yes and took the dish and refilled it, then filled Jenny's and William's empty dishes. She offered them some corn cakes that were in a flat plate like dish with a rounded cover over it. They each took one and used it to clean the bottom of their bowls.

After the little girls had finished their meal they became sleepy and started yawning. Santumtanya put her hand in the water jug again and decided it was warm enough, she dipped a gourd full out and poured it into a large round bowl and put a piece of soft deer hide into it. She looked at William and said, "Turn back to fire, no look," and then she sat down beside Jenny and gently removed the fur robe, pulled her dirty coat and dress over her head and washed her face, hands, arms and legs and even her bottom side. She rinsed the soft hide in the water several times before she was satisfied that the little girl was clean enough to put on a clean deerskin shirt, it was so long that it became a dress on little Jenny. She put a pair of soft moccasins on her little feet and then she took the little girl's hand and led her to the bed and covered her with a big fur blanket.

Judy's eyes were big when Santumtanya came back to her with a clean dish of water. She pulled away a little when the water first touched her skin but Santumtanya smiled at her and crooned soft sing-song words to her as she cleaned the very sleepy girl's dirty body. The dress that she gave Judy was also a little too long so Santumtanya found one of her belts and tied it around the thin little body smiling approvingly as she put a new pair of soft moccasins on her feet. Then she led Judy to the soft warm bed that her sister was now fast asleep in, she covered her and then patted her hair back from her forehead in a motherly gesture of love. Tears of sadness for them filled Santumtanya's eyes and she quickly turned her head so Judy wouldn't see them and went back to the fire.

Now it was William's turn. She smiled as she took the dirty dish of water, lifted the door flap and poured it just outside the door. She closed the heavy hide securely, went to the large pot by the fire and poured a big gourd full into the dish. She took another soft deer hide and put it into the warm water and handed William the bowl. He looked at her a little bewil-

dered and then she motioned for him to wash himself by making circular motions with her hand on her face. He smiled and turned his back and took his shirt off and started washing himself with the warm water. He couldn't remember the last time he had bathed, it must have been late last fall he decided. I must look a sight he thought to himself, and felt his beard.

When he had washed down to his waist, Santumtanya tapped him on his shoulder and motioned to a clean pile of clothes lying near the mat that the girls had been sitting on.

"I go to see stars in sky, be back soon time," she said smiling and then pointed to his crotch and made another circular motion with her hand. Then she turned and went out of the door pulling the heavy hide securely over the opening again.

William smiled to himself and muttered, "I guess she wants everything clean," as he turned his back to the sleeping little girls, untied his trousers letting them fall to his feet and finished washing. The Indian children watched him and giggled at his bare backside, it was as white as the snow. He turned his head and looked at them and they quickly hid their faces, 'they look like little fur balls,' he thought. He smiled as he finished his bath and put on the clean clothes she had laid out for him. He laid down facing the fire and pulled the fur over his back and must have fallen asleep soon after because he didn't hear Santumtanya come back or anything else until daylight.

The next morning after she fed her children and guests Santumtanya went to meet with the elders. She was prepared to defend her guests and knew she would be met with some opposition. The young warriors wanted to torture William and send the little girls to live with the Cummaquid Indians to the South but Santumtanya said glaring at them sternly, "No, there has been enough killing." She pleaded with her brother-in-law Yapanto for their lives, "I have no husband to hunt for me now so I will take the white man for my new husband, he will hunt for me and my children," she said looking at Yapanto.

Santumtanya's first husband, Sotawan was Chief Yapanto's brother. "He will care for me and my children, please do not kill him, give him to me, I like the looks of the white man's face," she said a little shyly, "it is a kind face."

Yapanto looked at his sister-in-law trying to decide if she was right about too much killing, he was still bitter over some of the things that the white man had done to his people. He knew she wasn't done pleading her case yet so he motioned for her to continue. "I will care for the white girls, too, they will learn the Indian ways, they will make pretty wives for your young warriors," she said looking back at the painted faces of the young Indian men.

Now Yapanto held up his hand, a sign for Santumtanya to stop talking, he had heard enough, he had already decided to keep the white girls alive to replace some of the Indian children that had died from the white man's attack on his village. Yapanto was a Medicine Man as well as the new Chief of his village and he knew that it would be his duty to take care of his dead brother's wife if she could not find anyone to marry her soon, he already had three wives and four children. There were not very many unmarried men left since the attack. Those that were with him now had escaped the burning of their village on the Long Island because of a vision of fire that he had described to them the week before. The rest had followed him here after escaping when the fighting first began. Santumtanya was one of them but she was alone now and needed someone to look after her and her children.

Yapanto could see nothing in the dirty man's face but he told her she could keep him if he could prove that he was worthy of being an Indian because if his life were to be spared he would have to marry her and stay with her in their village.

Santumtanya was smiling when she lifted the flap on the door of her hut. She held two little dolls in her hands and told the girls to stay quiet as she handed the toys to them. She turned to William and said, "You be safe if you no afraid. I tell Yopanto come, you answer Chief with truth, you be safe."

William shook his head and said, "I'm not afraid."

"You be talking to Chief Yapanto soon," she said repeating herself, wanting to be sure that William understood her English words, "you be true with tongue when he comes to see you," she continued quietly. "Santumtanya," she said pointing to herself, "like William to stay here. No be dead," she said shaking her head no as she used her finger as a knife and pulled it across her throat.

William nodded that he understood and then made a motion as if to shave. His face itched and he could feel the dirt that had become imbedded in the hair of his beard while he was being dragged. He usually shaved only in the summer months, in the winter he left his beard on for warmth. He put his hand to his face and felt his swollen cheek; it had been cut on the inside from his teeth when he was kicked.

Santumtanya looked at him for a few seconds and then went to her pack near the wall, pulled a sharp knife out of a leather holder and filled a pan with hot water. She handed them both to him and said smiling, "No cut," and used the same gesture of cutting her throat again.

45

He smiled back, "No cut," he repeated and dipped the knife into the water and carefully shaved his hairy face.

While she waited for him to finish shaving she gathered some small pouches that were filled with herbs and bear grease. She carefully mixed several different herbs and a small amount of the grease in the palm of her hand and then sat quietly for the white man to finish his tedious chore.

When he was clean-shaven she applied the salve to the bruises on William's cheek and forehead. She wet another piece of soft hide and carefully applied it to William's scalp holding it there for a few minutes to loosen the dried blood. She could feel the hard bump and William winced when her fingers pressed the contusion. He said, "Ow," and pulled away.

She said, "Be still, I try to feel if head open under bump." She held the bump with two fingers and her thumb and moved it back and forth a little. "Be brave," she said and rubbed some salve on the bump. "You be good, strong head, no broke," and she smiled at William again. Then she got up and went to her basket hanging on the wall over her bed and took a funny looking piece of shell from it then sat down again in back of William.

He turned a little to see what she had in her hand and said, "Now what?"

"Be still, no hurt you," she said quietly. "First comb your hair, you no cry, so little ones no cry when Santumtanya comb little girls hair. They cry maybe, girls hair bad."

William looked over at the girls still playing with the dolls that Santumtanya had given them. She turned his head back with her hands and pulled the comb through the tangles of his dark brown hair that just recently started to have white hairs scattered through it. Then he sat still and didn't say anything while she gently pulled and tugged on the long tangled mess. She tied it back with a piece of rawhide string and then patted him gently on the top of his head smiling.

He smiled back at her thinking, 'It might not be a bad idea to look presentable when I meet the Chief.'

"Come girls," she said as she motioned her arm for them to come to her. The girls had been watching her comb William's hair out of the corner of their eyes, waiting for him to object to having his hair pulled, while they played quietly with the strange looking little dolls made from ears of corn and rabbit fur. Jenny got up first and walked slowly across the small room to the pretty smiling Indian lady.

"I comb hair, no cry," she said as she pulled the comb through her own beautiful black hair. Jenny sat down on Santumtanya's lap and didn't cry as her light blonde hair was carefully smoothed and then twisted into *a long braid that hung halfway down her back. By the time Santumtanya was done Judith was standing by her side waiting for her turn. She didn't cry either.*

'Both girls look lovely,' William thought and smiled at them and patted himself on the head. They smiled back at him and went back to the bed and picked up their dolls.

Santumtanya went to the other bed and talked quietly to her children for a few minutes, then her daughter took Jenny's hand and they left the hut for just a minute or so, then she came back and took Judy outside.

William realized that she had shown them where they could relieve themselves. When they were back she tucked them into the bed of fur and sang a song to them before she kissed them on their heads. He had to go too, but thought he would wait until she had the children settled before he asked her where he should relieve himself.

Then she motioned for William to follow her and she opened the flap of the door and pointed to a nearby tree several feet away from the hut. "No run," she said.

"No run," he said smiling and walked slowly toward the tree and peed against it keeping his back to her. He had no intention of running, his ribs still hurt and the bruise on his leg felt like a knot.

When he was through he turned and walked back to Santumtanya, he was blushing because he was a little embarrassed he couldn't remember ever peeing where a woman could hear him before.

Santumtanya smiled at him as she opened the door of her hut and motioned for him to enter first. It was so quiet that he could hardly believe that there were four little children in the room.

Santumtanya had just finished putting her little hut in order when Yapanto knocked on the roof of her shelter. She said enter in her own language and the tall Indian Chief lifted the heavy flap and bending down he entered Santumtanya's home.

William was standing with his head bent in a slight bow as she had told him to. His hands were at his side, relaxed, he wanted to appear brave and not to look threatening, at the same time.

His stance must have pleased Yapanto because he told him to sit and they both sat facing each other across the fire pit. Both men eyed each other in silence, William had been told not to speak until Yapanto did.

Santumtanya busied herself preparing their morning meal over the fire and after she served both men their hot food she prepared five more dishes, one for each of the children and one for herself. She quietly passed a dish of corn bread to everyone and sat down on her bed with the two captive girls. She put her finger to her lips and shook her head no, they both understood that they should not talk at all. They ate quietly.

Yapanto questioned William for several hours; it was well into the afternoon before they were finished. Yapanto learned that William had a gun hidden at his shanty and that he knew how to make gunpowder.

William agreed to show the Chief how it was done and where he could get the sulfur, saltpeter and charcoal that was needed to make the explosive, on one condition. He wanted the Chief to let the little girls go home, unharmed. William bravely held his ground as he bargained with the Chief of the Pequot Indians until Yapanto finally agreed to his terms.

The Chief also insisted that William live with his people in their village and he was to marry Santumtanya. At first William was against getting married, but the Chief told him that he would not agree to release the girls if he did not marry his sister-in-law.

William finally agreed after Yapanto convinced him why he should marry her; she had seen to his well being since he had entered the village, and he had been washed, shaved, clothed and well fed by the beautiful Indian woman and she had pleaded for his life. Yapanto convinced William that it would please her and give her comfort after loosing her husband, and it would be an honor for him to marry her. Her first husband was his brother and the white man would be taking his dead brother's place in this small village.

This agreement spared his life, as well as the little girls, he would not be tortured, Yapanto had agreed to that, and Judith and Jennifer Walker would be taken home. He smiled inwardly when Yapanto left.

It did not bother William that he would be helping the Indians make ammunition; he reasoned that they needed to protect themselves as much as the white man did. He also reasoned that the Indians did not own very many guns and if they did they considered them only a possession because they were afraid to use them. The noise frightened them.

Santumtanya was all smiles as soon as her brother-in-law left her home. She got up from the bed and went to the fire pit and sat down in front of William in the same place that her Chief had been sitting. She smiled openly at William and was not the least bit shy.

He smiled back, 'She sure was pretty,' he thought.

After a lengthy discussion and arguing among themselves the Pequot agreed to the decisions that Yapanto had made. The next day they took the young girls, cleaned and in new clothes and unharmed, back to the edge of the woods and pointed them in the right direction toward their home.

The story they told was only believed because of the new clothes they had on and the Indian dolls that Santumtanya had given them. Their *mother was happy to have them back unharmed and allowed them to keep the dolls, but she made them change into their own clothes.*

William had not been allowed to go with the young warriors, but Chief Yapanto went, not only to protect the girls, but also to collect William's belongings. William had told the Chief where his gun was hidden and requested that the rest of his belongings, meager as they were, be brought to him. The Chief agreed.

William was treated well and given plenty of food by his new wife. He was grateful that he didn't have to forage for it as he had always done in the past. He made small amounts of gunpowder for the Chief, but he also showed him how to sharpen the hoes and axes and other tools that they had. He also learned their ways and some of their language. Within a month everyone in the Pequot village had learned to trust him and liked him.

Santumtanya was about the same age as William. Her son's name was Nanatimo, who William nicknamed Timmy, her daughter's name was Yapatinotum, a name he didn't even try to pronounce, he called her Jenny after the youngest of the little captive girls. Timmy was about the age of five and Jenny was about four.

Santumtanya insisted that he wear the clean buckskins that she made him, and cooked his meals and cleaned his dwelling for him. He found that his new life with a wife and family in the Indian village was much easier and better than it had been living alone in the white mans settlement. Even though he was made to bathe almost daily by his new wife, whom he called Sandy, and shave the hair from his face much more often than he thought it necessary, his life was happier.

Sandy's children learned that they did not have to fear him and they loved to hear his stories even though they didn't understand all of the words. He was at peace with himself and the village.

Santumtanya's father was a white man who came to her village with Captain John Smith. Her mother was the daughter of a chief and was given to the white man as a gift. When the white man left to go back to England with his Captain on the big ship, Santumtanya's mother was not allowed to go. It was said that her mother died from shame and heartache shortly after Sandy was born and she was left in her grandmother's care.

Soon after the Walker girls were returned to their home the militia was told to be on the look out for a white man that may be living with the Pequot. William was to be arrested for treason if he was found. The girls told their story about how William had talked for a long time with the Chief and had smiled a lot at the Indian woman. They heard him agree to live with the Indians and had stayed behind when they were taken home. They had no idea that he had saved their lives by making this agreement.

About eight weeks after William was captured the militia saw him with a Pequot hunting party. The militia surprised the Indians and had their guns aimed at them ready to fire as they ventured into a small clearing where they were following deer tracks. William was immediately arrested for treason and went peacefully with the militia to protect his new friends. He did, however, manage to tell Yapanto that he did not want to go back to Duxbury to live and would try to escape as soon as he could.

When he arrived back in town the people were shocked by they way he looked, one could hardly tell William from the Indians. He was taken to the Constable and the next day at a special court hearing he was put on trial. William told the jury how well he had been treated and that he did not want to stay in town, that he was married now and wanted to be with his new wife in the Indian village.

Richard More questioned William for about an hour and after he confessed to showing the Indians how to make gunpowder he was considered guilty of treason by a unanimous vote of the jury. The court sentenced him to be tied to the whipping post that very afternoon and he had to stand there all night. His punishment for becoming a traitor was thirty lashes to be carried out the next day at sunrise, if he was still alive and not frozen to death. As fate would have it he was still alive at dawn and his punishment was carried out. He fainted after the first eight lashes but received all thirty of them from the Constable. After he was whipped he was put into a shed that was located near the stockade and used as a jail.

That night he was in such pain from the lashes and the frostbite that he could hardly move without moaning. He thought he saw his wife and then he thought he could hear Yapanto whispering. The stars were out but there was no moon. 'Where's the moon?' he wondered, 'I must be dreaming.' These thoughts flickered through his mind for several hours and he shivered uncontrollably. He opened his eyes at last and realized he was in his own hut with Sandy.

Santumtanya, Yapanto and several other Indian friends had managed to help him escape during the night from the makeshift prison and carried him home to his village on a stretcher made from two poles and a piece of bear hide. With Sandy's herbs and constant care William recovered from his ordeal, but he was very careful for many years never to be seen near Duxbury again.

William Baker, by joining the Pequot Indian culture, became one of the earliest white men to conform to the Indian way of life and he was always thereafter, thought of as the first traitor in the colonies.

William and Sandy had a son a year later. William named him Elisha. Sandy named him Nauhaught. His full name was Elisha Baker Nauhaught."

• • •

There was a great and fearful earthquake that summer; in fact the date was recorded forever in many peoples minds, June 1, 1638. The epicenter was in Weymouth about forty miles south of Boston but it was felt in Duxbury and all of the surrounding towns.

Abraham could hear a low and reverberating rumble long before he felt the earth move under his feet. The noise came from northward and passed southward and it came with a low murmur, like low thunder far off in the distance and close to the ground. As the noise grew louder and louder the earth began to shake with such violence that platters and dishes and such things that were on the shelves and tables fell to the floor.

Abraham ran from the house only to find that the trees were swaying all around him. He was suddenly thrown to the ground and thinking that he might be safer crawled back into the doorway of the house, he stayed there, he couldn't get up anyway. He thought that if the house started to fall he would be able to run to the meadow nearby.

He thought that the shaking would never stop. He had heard stories of the earth moving but had never experienced it, an earthquake he said aloud. The barn shook knocking saddles and harnesses and tools off their hooks, the animals were frightened and bellowing and stamping their feet. When the ground stopped shaking Abraham ran to the barn to check the animals, then to his servants quarters to see if his hired hands were all right. He found them wallowing in the muck in the barnyard, they were so afraid that the roof would fall upon them, as he had been, they ran from the barn and were knocked to the ground, they were covered in mud and dung, Abraham could not help laughing at them.

"Mr. Blish, what was that?" one of them asked.

"Why are you laughing?" another one said.

"It was an earthquake," he said holding his side, "and I'm laughing at the sight of you, you look worse than the pigs." He couldn't help it, all he could see on some of their faces were their eyes, big and round, the only white thing left on their bodies was the white part of their eyes.

The men looked at each other and then realized what their master was laughing at, and then they started laughing, too.

After several minutes when they had all gained their composure Abraham explained that it was a phenomenon that occurred in all parts of the world once in a while and he admitted that he did not know why. "Maybe God is trying to help us remember that He's the one in charge," he said trying to look serious.

Then he burst out laughing again and held his side as he said, "You all had better go down to the brook and get cleaned up," he turned toward the barn and said, "I'll tend to the animals."

Though it had been only about a minute or so that the ground actually trembled, for many it seemed like a long time before the earth was still again. When the tremors did stop, everything grew strangely quiet, even the sobbing and crying stopped and the people were almost as afraid of the quiet as they were of the horrible noise, they thought that the world was coming to an end.

Many of them admitted that they were not able to stand and were thrown to the ground or to the floor as Abraham had been. Some of them were still holding onto the doors or posts when the trembling stopped and were so afraid that they could not let go for many minutes. Some of the men told that they had been thrown around as if they were made of straw and they feared that God was showing them that He was still almighty and powerful. Many of them vowed to mend their evil ways from this day forward and they were on their knees praying out loud to God for their salvation. Children were screaming and crying and the women were trying to comfort them as they themselves sobbed and prayed.

The shaking was not only felt on the land, but also on the sea. The men on the ships that were in the harbor could see the trees shaking and hear the noise. The quake caused great waves in the ocean and tossed the ships in the harbor about like baskets in a rushing brook after a long rain. Many of the captains and sailors were in fear of their lives, praying that the ships would hold their moorings and they would not be thrown onto the reefs or shores. There were no clouds in the sky and many sailors knowing nothing about earthquakes, could not understand why the ocean was tossing them about when there was no wind or rain. Prayers were shouted and most of the frightened people, both on land and sea, were on their knees still in prayer when a few minutes later there was another quaking of the earth. This aftershock and was not as strong as the earthquake and it was quickly over.

They all agreed that the Hand of the Lord was so powerful, that just by raising it He could make both the land and the sea shake and the mountains to tremble before Him whenever He pleased. Many men became Christians after this frightening day and some of them moved their family inland in fear of another great shaking of the earth not knowing that an earthquake could happen to them wherever they were. People talked of nothing else for weeks; each one had their own tale to tell.

Abraham later found that more Indians than usual were questioning him and his friends about their God. Asking if He was the cause of the earth moving and the sea churning without wind or rain. He tried to explain to them that this shaking of the earth had happened before in other parts of the world, but he did not know why. Abraham didn't think that God had anything to do with it, though, and tried to reassure the Indians and others that God was the protector of man, and would not do them any harm.

Richard and Mary were in their garden planting when they heard the rumbling and felt the ground shaking. Remember was holding little William and they were all thrown to the ground. They crawled toward each other and prayed. "Earthquake," Richard said remembering the stories he heard as a boy. Governor Bradford told him that it was not unusual for the ground to open up and swallow people during one of these events. He prayed that this would not happen to him and his family or anyone else. The trees still swayed after the ground stood still and Richard held his family for several minutes before he let them loose. They all prayed together. When it was all over he explained to his hired hands and their families what had happened and assured them that the world was not coming to an end.

• • •

Later that month after a special meeting of the Town Council, Ann Hutchinson, known as a 'disbeliever' was asked to leave Duxbury. Ann had gone about after the earthquake accusing God of causing the problems that the people were having. She irritated many women in the community with her whining and cursing in front of the children and anyone she happened to meet. At church she would whisper during the sermon and contradict the words of the Reverend. Her actions caused the women to complain to their husbands so much that they finally placed a formal complaint against her and asked the Town Council to do something to keep her from being such a nuisance.

Ann's life had not been easy during the last several years. Her husband of nine years had died about three years before, shortly after they moved to Duxbury from Liverpool, England. They had purchased two acres of land in the new settlement from William Bradford as soon as they arrived, it was mostly wooded and on the side of a hill but it was all they could afford. Everett Hutchinson was a strong man and between him and Ann, and with the help of their older children they managed to clear enough land to build a crude shelter and plant and harvest a suitable vegetable garden before the first winter cold sat in. They were well known for their fortitude and their children were healthy and had good manners. Ann was a large woman well over five feet six inches tall and weighed at least two hundred pounds, she was about the same size and weight as Everett, and was respected for being a hard worker and a good mother to her five children.

Everett was accidentally killed shortly after they built their house when a tree fell on him while he was helping a neighbor clear some land that adjoined his property. They were planning to plant a wheat field and share the profits from it.

Ann became very distressed and depressed with all of the responsibility of running a farm and the raising of five children falling onto her shoulders with no one to help her. She believed that God had struck her husband down and that He was cruel and evil. She said that God was responsible for the great earth shaking and the many accidents that had happened to several of her friends and all of the Indian wars that were happening all around them.

She became outspoken at church and was forever contradicting the ministers and deacons. She would become so adamant about her beliefs that she would use bawdy language in front of the whole congregation caring little that the children were listening. She tried to convince the ministers to agree with her and when they would not she would stomp out of the church screaming that evil would prevail on everyone that did not believer her. Her children would follow her with their heads bowed and cheeks all pink with embarrassment.

She was critical of everything from the governing of New Plymouth to the way the stockade was built. Ann was very outspoken and she had her one view of religion and politics and no one could change her mind once it was made up.

Ann became so troublesome that during a secret town council meeting held in Plymouth on June 24, 1638 at Governor Bradford's home, they voted to excommunicate her and her children as well as any of her followers, from the church. The court charged her with blasphemy (swearing), heresy (rejection of church beliefs) and traducing the ministers (trying to change their beliefs).

After her excommunication Ann did managed to convince several families that her ideas about God were true and on July 1, 1638 they all left Duxbury for the new settlement of Rhode Island. A few years later it was learned that Ann was remarried and had settled into married life with her new husband and had several more children.

• • •

On July 3, 1638 Governor Bradford held a Town Council meeting to select a grand jury for the trial of four white men accused of robbery and murder by Chief Quintanta of the Narragansett Indians.

This story was written in Abraham's journal under the name of *"Posanto"* which was the name of the murdered Indian boy.

About the middle of June in the year 1638 four men of little means decided to leave the small town of Duxbury for an easier way of life. Arthur Peach persuaded Thomas Jackson, Richard Stinnings and Daniel Crose to go with him and help him rob Randall Shave, a prominent landowner in town.

Thomas Jackson was an indentured servant to Randall Shave and one evening during a drinking spree he told his friends that he knew where his master kept his money. He had seen Mr. Shave put come coins in a pewter pitcher on the mantle over the fireplace earlier that week. One of Thomas' chores was to fill the wood box every afternoon. "I heard Mr. Shave drop his money into the pitcher," Thomas said, "then he put it up on the mantle. He didn't know I saw him," he said giggling. Thomas giggled most of the time, especially when he was scared.

Upon hearing Thomas' story Arthur got the bright idea that if they all joined up together they could escape to the Dutch Colony that was about 250 miles away, buy land there from the Indians, real cheap and start their own farm. "I think I've got an idea how we can get our hands on some money," he said looking at Richard and grinning.

Arthur Peach had been a good soldier in the Pequot war, fearless and always first in line to attack an enemy, and he obeyed his commander's orders without any hesitation. However, he was not very well thought of by the other soldiers, though he was strong in body he was considered weak in his head. He was extremely lazy when it came to work, and would pick a fight in an instant and for no reason when he was drinking rum. He was a most despicable man when it came to women; he was forever trying to seduce all of the maidservants in town. They were afraid of him and tried to stay away from him.

Daniel Crose was also a very cruel man and was known to torture animals. Arthur was his only friend, probably because they were so much alike, especially when it came to drinking, fighting and women. The one difference was that Daniel was sadistic. It was said that when he went hunting he would wound a deer and instead of killing it when it was down, he would cut out its eyes and tongue while it was still alive. The Indians knew about this man and they hated him.

Richard Stinnings was also a servant of Randall Shave. He worked with Thomas Jackson and picked on him unmercifully. Thomas being the smaller of the two was easy prey and his constant giggling irritated Richard so much that he was always hitting or kicking him. Richard wasn't educated, but he had been a sailor on several crossings of the ocean from England to Boston and he thought he knew everything. He was also very filthy, no one had ever seen him take a bath, once in a while he did cut his beard with his knife when it became too flea invested. Richard and Thomas were probably friends because they were opposites of each other. Thomas hated to be dirty and washed himself and his clothes as often as possible, he also knew how to write his name and he could count having gone to school for two years before his parents died.

That same evening after another jug of rum, Arthur laid out a plan to steal Randall Shave's money and run away. About midnight the four men met quietly behind the Shave home. Thomas Jackson, being the smallest of the lot, therefore less likely to make any noise, let himself in the front door and crept across the floor to the fireplace. He stood up carefully when he reached the mantel and quickly grabbed the pitcher, careful not to jiggle the money in it. Without a sound he made it back to the door closing is carefully behind him. They all ran as fast as they could down the trail out of town. Arthur planned to steal a boat at daybreak and be gone swiftly with out a trace.

After running for about two miles without stopping they came upon a small farm where Daniel stole two chickens and some eggs. He grabbed them by their heads and gave their necks a twist so fast that they didn't have time to squawk.

The men were tired but Arthur urged them on, but at a somewhat slower pace, for about another half-hour or so until they came to a little gully. Actually Thomas fell into it and he refused to get up even when Daniel kicked him in the ribs. Thomas yelled and Arthur said, "Shut up," looking around cautiously, then said, "This is as good a place as any I guess to stop and rest a while."

They were about three miles out of town by this time and had run most of the way. He knew they were somewhere between the Bay of Massachusetts and the Narragansett Indian country and felt that it should be safe enough to build a fire and rest for a while. Arthur got the fire started with his flint stone and some dry leaves while Daniel gathered some dead tree branches. They divided the eggs and ate them raw while the chickens were cooking. Arthur had thrown them into the fire as soon as it was blazing, feathers, innards and all.

They were all laughing and sipping a bottle of rum while they were waiting for the chickens to cook when suddenly they heard a noise.

Two young Narragansett Indian boys had smelled the smoke for several minutes before they saw the light of the fire. Curiosity took over their good sense and they crept closer, wondering who would build such a smoky blaze. It had to be a white man; Indian fires were almost smokeless and hardly noticeable. When they could see the men they made the signal to each other for 'white man' and smiled. 'Stupid men' they signed.

They watched them from the trees for a few minutes and then quietly crept closer, maybe they knew who these white men were. A twig broke under Santinomo's moccasin; they stopped hoping they hadn't been heard.

Arthur pulled his knife out of his boot and called out, "Who goes there?"

The loud voice startled them and they jumped a little, then gaining his composure Posanto, the older of the two stood up and said calmly, trying not to sound frightened, "I am called Posanto, I am from the village of Chief Quintanta."

Arthur thought he could see the outline of another person kneeling on the ground near Posanto's feet and said, "Who's that with you?"

Posanto looked at this brother and made a motion for him to stand up and said, "This is my brother Santinomo."

The four men could see the young boys and were afraid that there might be others with them. Arthur deepened his voice to make himself sound fierce and said loudly, "Show yourselves."

Posanto and Santinomo could see the four men in the firelight and knew that they should act very friendly and appear to be unafraid. Most white men were friendly toward the Indians, but they had been taught to be cautious because there were still men from some of the ships that would try to steal young Indian lads and take them away to a land unknown. 'We were not careful enough; we never should have stopped here,' Posanto thought. Then taking a deep breath to gather his courage he took a few steps toward the fire and said, "We are alone, we saw your fire and thought that we might warm ourselves, we are still a few miles from our village."

Arthur laughed when he realized that Posanto was just a young Indian about the age of 14, his brother had to be even younger, maybe 11 or so. He changed his voice to sound friendly and said, "Well, come and join us we have nice fresh chicken cooking." He kicked at the fire and than sat down and said, "You can have some when it's done."

Daniel said selfishly, "Well, they can't have any of my share, by gawd, I killed these birds and half of one is mine."

Arthur said, "Shut up, Daniel, don't worry, you'll get your share, there's enough for everyone."

"We have our own food," Posanto said quickly. He had no intentions of sharing the putrid smelling meat.

"Well, make yourself at home," Arthur said and motioned for the boys to sit down.

Richard said sarcastically, "What are you doing out this time of night, you should be home in your hut with your mama. Snot nosed Indian kids," he said and picked his nose and wiped it on his pants.

Thomas giggled, and Daniel hit him in the arm. Thomas groaned and moved away a little.

Posanto was not offended; he wasn't sure what the smelly man meant and he really didn't care. "We've been trading all day at the Wampanoag village," then added quietly, almost as if he was reprimanding himself, "we should not have stayed so long." Posanto sat down on the ground where he had been standing and Santinomo took a step back and sat down on a flat rock.

"Dumb Indians," Richard said under his breath.

"Dumb Indians," Thomas repeated him and then giggled.

Arthur grinned and said, "Let's see if the chickens ready," and he reached his dirty hand toward the fire and tried to touch the burned meat.

A spark hit his hand and he pulled it back quickly and then picked up a stick and poked at the chicken trying to lift it out of the fire.

Daniel laughed at his stupidity and cursed, "Damned fool".

"Damned fool," Thomas repeated. Daniel hated it when Thomas mimicked him, but this time he only laughed.

When Arthur finally had one of the chickens out of the fire he took out his skinning knife and cut its head off. The feathers were gone and the bird had been charred to a black lump but the feet were still attached so he cut them off and tossed them back into the fire. As he cut the bird in half, the guts spilled out onto the hot coals and sizzled, and he handed half of the chicken to Daniel and the other to Richard. He did the same thing to the other chicken giving the smallest half to Thomas, keeping the biggest piece for himself, cleaned his knife on his breeches and put it back in his boot.

The men had no manners whatsoever, they ate with smacking noises and the juices dripped down their chins and onto their clothing. It didn't seem to bother them at all. They sucked the marrow out of the bones and then tossed them into the fire.

Posanto reached into his pack and took out his Bannock, or as the white man called them, corn cakes, that were neatly wrapped in cornhusk and took a bite, Santinomo did the same. The smell of the chicken feathers and guts cooking was horrible and both Indian boys held their breath as long as they could then covered their noses with the sleeves of their shirts.

Santinomo turned his eyes toward the food he was eating and tried not to listen to the slobbering sounds.

Posanto could not watch them either he had never seen anyone eat that way.

Posanto thought about leaving, but he wasn't sure if they would follow him, he thought that they would probably not harm him and his brother if they didn't feel threatened. He decided that they would be safer where they were, they could watch them better, besides their fire was warm, though it wasn't really cold; it was just damp and chilly, and he was tired.

After they had all eaten Arthur brought out his tobacco and rum. He offered some of the rum to Posanto but the young boy refused. Arthur took a long swallow and then handed the jug to Daniel. Daniel drank a couple of swallows and then said as he handed the jug to Richard, "The boy looks like a man, but he doesn't act like one."

Richard took a big swig and then handed the jug back to Daniel. Daniel got up and went over to where Posanto was setting and handed him the jug and said, "Go ahead, be a man, it won't hurt ya, it's only watered down rum."

Thomas was on his knees and said in a whining voice, "Don't give that rotten Indian any, I haven't had mine yet."

Arthur kicked him on his thigh and said, "Shut up, you'll get your share."

Thomas fell over onto his side and whimpered, "I want some."

Posanto decided he'd better take a sip before any more violence erupted, so he put the jug to his lips, after he wiped the top with his sleeve, and let just a little of the burning liquid touch his tongue.

Thomas grabbed it out of his hand as soon as he took the jug from his mouth and shouted, "Save some for me you rotten Indian."

After that every time the jug was passed to him he took only little sips and then was sure to hand it to Thomas. Posanto was glad that Santinomo had laid down beside him and pretended to be asleep after he ate his corn cake, the men didn't try to make him drink any of the putrid rum.

Then a strong smelling pipe was passed around. Posanto sucked on it a couple of times when it came his way but was sickened by the taste of the tobacco and spittle that was in the stem. They didn't seem to mind him refusing after the second time the pipe was offered to him.

Posanto didn't realize that these men were evil thieves and as they were smoking the pipe and sipping the rum he answered their questions about his day of trading.

"What ya got in your packs?" Arthur asked Posanto. Daniel snickered and poked Richard in the side with his foot. He knew what Arthur was thinking.

"I still have five feet of wampum left," he answered Arthur innocently as he opened his pack, "and I have three coats of cloth, a new pair of moccasins and two buckskin shirts." He took the shirts out of the pack and unfolded them on his lap.

Richard said, "Ya did good, huh." He was almost drooling over Posanto's belongings.

Santinomo sat up and joined the conversation when he saw Posanto take the shirts out of his pack. "I have three necklaces and four pair of earbobs, too," he said proudly holding them up toward the light of the fire.

"Can I see them?" Thomas asked Santinomo, holding out his hand.

Santinomo looked at him cautiously and then handed him one of the necklaces.

Thomas held them closer to the fire for a better look and then handed them back and said with a leering smile, "Pretty."

Santinomo smiled back and said, *"I have some arrowheads and skin-ning knives left that I will use the next time I go trading."* The boys were very proud of their trading skills but too naïve to realize that these men were not to be trusted. When the four white men were finished looking and handling the necklaces and earbobs, Santinomo put away his new possessions and Posanto folded his shirts and repacked all of his things.

After a little more small talk about how far away the young Narragansett Indian boy's village was and where the Wampanooag village was, Richard and Daniel began to yawn. Arthur Peach said, *"Well, men it's getting late and we have a long way to go tomorrow, we'd better all get some sleep."* The fire was dying down and it was becoming hard to see each other, there was only a crescent moon and it was dark beyond the shadows of the fire.

Thomas was snoring already.

Posanto used his pack for a pillow and tried to close his eyes but his head was spinning a little from the rum so he turned over onto his stom-ach and fixed his eyes on a burning ember in the fire until the dizziness stopped, he was soon fast asleep.

Santinomo took a cloth coat from his pack, put it on and then found a big tree a little way from the fire and curled up under it and went to sleep.

Richard got up and turned his back to relieve himself and laughed when his pee splashed on Thomas' foot.

Thomas woke up and cursed him and hit him in the leg with his fist, Richard in turn cuffed him on the head and called him an idiot.

Arthur told them to stop. There'd be time enough for fighting tomor-row.

Thomas rolled over with his back to the fire.

Richard took a couple of steps away from the puddle he had just made and laid down and went to sleep.

When Arthur could hear the young lads snoring softly he drew his knife and quietly crawled over to Posanto, hit him on the back of his head with his fist and then stabbed him twice in the back. He pulled his pack out from under him and kicked Thomas awake. *"Hurry up and get your stuff, we're leaving,"* he whispered. Richard and Daniel didn't need to be kicked or shouted at, they knew what was happening when they heard the sickening sound of Arthur's fist hitting Posanto's head.

When Santinomo heard the commotion he instinctively got up and ran into the forest, tripped over a big log and crawled under it and cov-ered himself with leaves. He heard the cussing and arguing between Arthur and Daniel about looking for him, but he stayed still. He knew the men *were drunk and stupid but he never dreamed they would attack him and his brother.*

After Richard found Santinomo's pack under the tree where the young boy had been sleeping, Arthur decided that it was too dark to chase wild Indians around in the woods. They quickly gathered up their own meager possessions and with their newly stolen wealth in the Indian boy's packs they headed south on the trail leaving Posanto for dead.

Santinomo stayed in his hiding place for about a half-hour and then decided it was safe to come out. It was just becoming light enough to see the outlines of the trees against the sky. He found Posanto just as he was regaining consciousness. He cradled his brother's head in his arms for a few minutes until Posanto asked for some water. He found his gourd and gave him a sip. He knew he had to get help for Posanto soon or his brother would be visiting his grandfather in the afterworld.

Posanto's head throbbed and his back was burning as if it were on fire. He could hardly breath and as Santinomo helped him slowly sit up, he coughed up blood. By sheer willpower and strength he didn't know he had, he managed with the help of Santinomo, to stagger and crawl the three miles to his village, making it home by early afternoon.

Posanto's family was furious when they managed to understand what had happened to him. His father, Tiamino, a great Narragansett warrior, and about ten men of the village, started after the four thieves who had about a twelve hour head start on them. But, being much more familiar with the country then the four fugitives, the Narragansett's caught up with them by the next morning. Later that evening Tiamino and his warriors had them back in the village so that Posanto and Santinomo could identify them.

When the four men saw that they had not killed Posanto they tried to lie their way out of the situation by swearing on their mother's graves that they had never laid eyes on the young Indian boys before. Posanto's father was so angry that Chief Quintanta and some of the Indian men had to hold him to keep him from killing them where they stood.

Chief Quintanta decided that he should take them to the English fathers on Aquidneck Island just north of Plymouth to stand trial in the white mans court. If they had taken the matter into their own hands the chief knew it would start another outbreak and many people, both Indian and white would suffer as Posanto's family was suffering now.

Governor Bradford sent word to the members of the grand jury, Abraham Blish, Richard More, John Willis, John Williams and Myles Standish to meet them at Aquidneck Island immediately shortly after Chief Quintanta had arrived there with the criminals. Richard Shave was also notified that he should be there, too. He also sent a message to Dr. Fuller requesting him to go to Chief Quintanta's village a see if he could be of help to the injured boy and also requested his presence at the trial.

The four men were put into the stocks for three days and given only bread and water until the grand jury convened. On the fourth day they were brought before the court and accused of robbery and assault, with the attempt to commit murder.

The jurors examined the evidence, that being the packs and the wampum belonging to Posanto and Santinomo found in the accused men's possession and heard the testimony of Santinomo. Chief Quintanta, the Medicine Man, Mopotamina and Tiamino also testified that Thomas had told them when they were on their way to Aquidneck Island, that Arthur had been the one to hit Posanto on the head and stab him in the back.

Dr. Samuel Fuller testified that when he examined Posanto he found that the poor boy had indeed been hit on the head with such a force that it had dented his scull. He also testified that one of the stab wounds had pierced his lung causing him great pain and to cough up blood. The Doctor also reported that these wounds were fatal and upon oath before the jury in open court testified that young Posanto would not live and that his stab wounds were caused by a knife about the size of the one found on Arthur.

In court Thomas whimpered uncontrollably and muttered that he was innocent. Daniel cursed and kicked him whenever he was close enough to him.

Richard sat slouched over and seemed to be praying all during the trial.

Arthur sat still with his head held high and moved only his eyes glaring at Santinomo as if he was trying to scare him.

The courthouse was full; many townspeople had to stand against the walls. All of Posanto's family and friends were at the trial which lasted two days and before it was over all four men freely confessed to all they had been accused of. The jury found them all guilty of attempted murder and they were condemned to death, they were all sentenced by the jury to hang by the neck until dead.

Posanto died that afternoon after hearing the outcome of the trial; it was as if he had been waiting to hear the judgment of his attackers before he left this earth.

The murderers were taken to New Plymouth that afternoon where they were to be executed the next day.

That night Daniel Crose escaped presumably with the help of a 'friend', though no one would admit to it, or with the help of a few vengeful Indian 'friends,' no one knew for sure.

However, about a week later a rumor circulated that he had been found. He had been hung by his ankles in a tree about five miles from Plymouth and his body looked like it had been tortured for several days before he died. There were gaping holes in his face where his eyes should have been and his tongue was not in his mouth. It is presumed that the Narragansett Indians had found justice in their own way without causing a war with the English.

The other three men were hung from a newly constructed gallows in front of the New Plymouth courthouse and left there for three days for all to see.

It was a matter of great sadness to all colonists to think that there were such people living among them who would commit such a crime. Posanto's murder was the second one committed in New Plymouth since the Pilgrims landed in 1620.

• • •

"You know, Abraham, the first person executed for murder in New Plymouth was John Billington, Sr.," Richard said when they were on their way home from the hanging. "He was hung on September 10, 1630. Would you like to hear about him?" he asked.

"Yes, of course," Abraham answered smiling to himself, he had no choice, he was a captive audience, but he like Richard's stories and usually wrote them in his journal afterward.

"It's not very long because I don't know many of the details, but it is a true story as I know it," Richard said.

"John Billington, Sr. was born in London and was a member of one of the most profane families among the Pilgrims. Many of his family members had been punished for their misconduct and unfavorable behavior before this incident. However, his wife was known to be a kind and loving mother to her young son Johnny and would protect him by hiding him in the woods when his father came home drunk. It is believed that it was on one of these occasions when young John wandered off and was lost.

"But that's another story," Richard said interrupting himself.

"John Billington, Sr., shot a young man named John Newcomin after quarreling with him over beaver pelts that Newcomin had purchased from Billington several months before at a fair market price. Billington way-laid the young man as he was coming into town one evening, and after starting the quarrel by accusing young Newcomin of still owing him money, he cold bloodily aimed his gun at Newcomin's head and fired. John Newcomin died shortly after a passerby found him in the muddy road.

This incident was of great sadness to everyone in the colony and the court took all possible means to carry out a fair trial and consulted all of the leading men of Massachusetts Bay as to the punishment that should be bestowed upon Billington.

After several hours of discussion it was agreed that Billington was to be put in the stockade with his feet, hands and head in the stanchions all during his trial. He was given only water to drink twice a day and a slice of bread each the evening. This position was truly painful and on the fifth day of the trial he confessed. All members of the jury concurred and he was found guilty of this great misconduct and they sentenced John Billington to be hanged by the neck until dead. The following day his sentence was carried out.

There was much sadness, I remember, for weeks people talked of nothing else. Mrs. Billington and little Johnny were taken in of by a man named Anthony Dix and a month later Governor Bradford suggested that they be married. Mrs. Billington was grateful to Anthony and gladly accepted his proposal; she hated the name of Billington and asked the good governor if he would change Johnny's last name to Dix in all of the public records. Governor Bradford agreed that from this day hence her son's name would be listed as Johnny Dix.

"And so it was," Richard said, "I don't believe I have heard the name 'Billington' since then."

"This certainly has been a sorrowful week," Abraham said and Richard agreed as they continued their journey home.

• • •

On September 2, 1638 Abraham paid John Cole of Duxbury, 30 shillings for a young heifer that had just been bred. When the heifer freshened he would have the start of his own herd of cattle. He had made arrangements to pay John another 30 shillings when he was sure she was pregnant, and indeed two months later on November 3, 1638, Abraham paid John another 30 shillings for the heifer. She would have her calf in the spring.

On September 29, 1638 Abraham sold the easterly half of his twenty-acre homestead to John Willis for 8 pounds sterling, 10 shillings, keeping the 10 acres of land that his "Eagles Nest" house was on.

Two months later on November 27, 1638 John Willis divided this same lot in half again and sold the easterly side to William Paybody of Duxbury for the sum of eight pounds.

Abraham's farm, though smaller now, was beginning to pay him for the hard work that he had put into it, and by selling the wooded easterly half to John Willis, he was able to purchase another cow and two hogs.

During the winter Abraham learned from Richard More and several other members of the Duxbury Church about a new settlement that was being planned in a place called Mattakeese about forty miles south. He listened carefully to the men and discussed the possibility of joining the association with several of them. He was very interested in taking part in this great adventure and that evening he and Richard talked for several hours about it. Abraham took Richard's advice very seriously, after all Richard was there when Plymouth, the very first settlement was started, and he was one of the first settlers of Duxbury, he was well aware of the hard work that would be involved.

Richard also suggested to Abraham one evening while they were smoking their pipes after their meal that it might be a good idea if he were married before he moved, for several reasons. The first being that he would be granted more land, second he would need the help of a wife to keep his house and help with the many chores there would be, and third he wouldn't have to hire as many hands. Of course, Richard chuckled over the last reason.

"Your reasoning is very sound," Abraham said smiling.

"So, how long is it going to be before you find the courage to ask Anne Pratt's father if you can court her?" Richard asked Abraham during their conversation.

"Um, well I've known her for about a year and a half now, I guess it would be proper to talk to her father," he said. He blushed as he said almost in a whisper, "I knew from the very first day I arrived here that I wanted to marry her."

"Everyone knows how you feel about her," Richard said smiling and paused, letting Abraham think about this statement too.

"I don't know if she thinks of me the same way, do you?" he asked anxiously.

"I think everyone except you might know the answer to that question, Abraham!" Richard laughed.

"I will talk to Mr. Pratt as soon as I can," he said more or less to himself.

Richard stood up and walked to the fireplace to get a firebrand to light his pipe, Abraham hardly noticed.

Abraham would have to ask Mr. Pratt's permission to court Anne very soon if he wanted to move to Mattakeese when everyone else did. He was anxious to become a part of the new settlement and he didn't want to leave Anne in Duxbury; he wanted to take her with him.

He realized she was young, but he couldn't wait any longer, she would be 18 in a few months, her birthday was May 8th. They had greeted each other in church every Sunday since Abraham had arrived in Duxbury and they often made eye contact and smiled at each other discretely. He was careful to keep his distance from her, he was always sure to be proper and polite to her when they were together and he had never allowed himself to be alone in the same room with her. He was deeply in love with Anne and he didn't want to spoil her reputation by any improper flirtations that could be interpreted in a bad way. He also wanted to stay on the good side of her father.

It was about two weeks later, just before Christmas, when the townspeople were gathered for an evening church service, that Abraham finally gathered the courage to ask John Pratt for permission to court Anne. "Good evening Mr. Pratt," Abraham said politely.

"Good evening Mr. Blish," John returned the greeting.

They talked about the weather for a few minutes and then taking a deep breath Abraham said, "Mr. Pratt I would like to ask your permission to court Anne." He could feel his face turning red but before he lost his courage he continued quickly, "I have a Christmas present that I'd like to give her, but I would like your permission first." His heart was pounding and he was short of breath, or maybe he had been holding his breath, he wasn't sure.

John smiled and put his hand on Abraham's shoulder and said, "I thought you'd never ask." His eyes twinkled and he continued,

"Anne has been begging us to let her see you on Christmas day, I do believe she has a gift for you, too."

Abraham grinned from ear to ear and could hardly contain himself. He was so happy that he wanted to jump up and down with joy and shout to high heaven, but instead he shook John's hand so hard that John finally had to pull it away before it was crushed. "Oh, thank you, thank you Mr. Pratt," Abraham said as he turned and walked across the room toward Anne.

Anne could see the joy on Abraham's face as he crossed the room toward her. She instantly took several steps in his direction, with her mother following close by. When they met, Anne held out her hand to him and he took it, gently squeezed it, then put it to his lips and kissed it.

He really wanted to kiss her lovely mouth right there in front of everyone, but he knew he couldn't, so he smiled and said, "Your father has given me his permission to call on you, Anne. Of course," he continued quickly, "I will need your permission, too." He glanced at Sarah who was smiling and it gave him the courage to add, "Could I come by your home tomorrow evening to see you?"

She glanced at her mother and Sarah nodded her head yes and Anne very politely said, "I would love to see you then, about 7 o'clock?" she asked looking at him and then at her mother.

Sarah nodded again and said still smiling, "I think that you should come for our Christmas dinner at 5 o'clock Mr. Blish."

Anne had begged her mother for months to allow her to talk to Abraham and once in a while Sarah Pratt would have Richard and his family over for their Sunday evening meal and she always included Abraham on these occasions.

Abraham said excitedly, "Yes, of course, I would love to join you then. Can I bring anything?" He asked quickly remembering his manners.

"No, thank you Abraham," Sarah answered. "We'll be looking forward to seeing you then," she said and she patted his arm gently and the ladies turned and walked toward John who was waiting for them at the door.

Anne was delighted; her feet barely touched the floor.

Abraham could not have been happier and all he could do was stand there and stare at their backs with a silly grin on his face. 'I've never been so happy. I'm in love!' he thought.

That evening was the beginning of a wonderful relationship.

On Christmas day Abraham gave Anne a beautiful China Teapot with two matching cups and saucers, they were decorated with little blue flowers. "Oh, Abraham they are beautiful, I shall cherish them forever," she said with tears in her eyes.

"Where ever did you get this," Sarah asked as she carefully touched one of the shiny porcelain cups.

"It comes from the Orient," Abraham answered, "and the flowers were painted on before it was glazed," he said trying to sound knowledgeable about such things. He was actually only repeating what the Chinese man had told him when he bought them from him the last time he went to Boston.

"It is absolutely lovely," Sarah said, "I don't know if I would ever use it, I'd be afraid I'd break it."

"Oh, Mother, I'm sure you would drink a cup of tea with me if I served it to you in this beautiful cup," Anne said smiling brightly holding one of the cups gently.

"I'm sure I would," Sarah agreed, "I'd feel like a queen." She pretended to hold a cup in her finger and thumb and held her little finger out in a sophisticated manner. Everyone laughed.

"I have something for you too, Abraham, but I'm sure it is no way near as costly," Anne said handing him a small wooden box.

"Well, now," Abraham said, "I am not accustomed to receiving gifts, I'm not sure what to say." He opened the box and found a beautifully carved wooden pipe. It had an oval shaped bowl and a curved stem and it was almost white in color. "It's perfect," he said smiling as he turned it over in his hand and put the stem to his lips. It tasted clean and it fit his mouth and teeth just right.

"It was made in Holland," Anne said.

"It's wonderful, Anne," he said quietly. He wanted to get up and kiss her full on the mouth. He looked at her hoping she could read his thoughts. His eyes said 'I love you' as he smiled at her.

She smiled back and then lowered her eyes, 'he really did like it,' she thought.

Sarah could feel the awkwardness between them and quickly handed Anne another gift.

Abraham was delighted that she loved the china. 'I am so happy, I know I'm in love,' he thought to himself. He really wanted to shout it from the tallest tree.

Patricia Louise Blish Gould

CHAPTER SIX
1639

On February 20, 1639 Deborah Barker was born to John Barker and his wife Hannah Williams Barker. Deborah was their first child. John and Hannah were neighbors of the Pratt's. Sarah and Anne Pratt and Mary More were with Hannah when Deborah was born and though Hannah was very weak afterward, she was able to set up and was nursing her new baby girl before John arrived home that evening.

John Barker stopped by the Pratt's house on his way to his fishing boat early that cold morning and asked Sarah if she would look in on Hannah after a while. "I think she's going into labor, she has a bad back ache," he told Sarah.

"Yes, John I'll be glad to go and stay with her today," she smiled patting his arm, "I'm sure she'll be just fine," she continued.

"Thank you very much, I'll try not to be late tonight," he said as he opened the door and headed down the path toward the wharf.

"I'll tell her you said that, and I'll hold you to your word," Sarah called after him chuckling. She had never known John Barker to be on time for anything; the man was always late.

After John left Sarah sent Anne to Mary More's house to see if she was feeling well enough to help her with Deborah's delivery. Sarah knew that Anne was capable of helping her, but she did not have enough experience yet. Anne had only helped her once and that was when Mary delivered little William. Anne did just as she was told that day but if Mary was available to help it would be better for Anne just to watch and learn.

Anne hitched her horse Penny to the small buggy and did as her mother asked. She was glad that the sun was shining though it didn't seem to be warming the day up very quickly. She shivered under the heavy fur robe that was always kept in the buggy.

Anne drove her buggy as close to Mary's house as she could and then hitched Penny's reins to the hitching post and ran to the door.

Mary answered almost immediately, "Hello Anne," Mary said, "what brings you out so early on a cold day like this."

"Good morning, Mary," Anne said a little excited, "Mother would like to know if you feel well enough to help her, Hannah may have her baby today."

Mary was not surprised when Anne knocked on her door that morning. She knew that Hannah would be having her baby soon. "I certainly can, and I'm feeling just fine," she said, "Please come in for a minute while I get ready," she added quickly closing the door behind Anne. Mary asked her sister Remember to tell Richard where she was going and kissed little William good bye and said, "I'll try to be back before dark."

Anne helped Mary into the buggy when she came out and they went directly to the Barker's house.

Mary was pregnant again and her baby was due within the next three or four weeks. She checked in on Hannah at least two or three times a week lately and she also made sure that she visited Sarah and Anne once a week or so. They all lived about a mile apart from each other with Sarah's house being between Hannah's and Mary's. If Mary started at her house and walked to Sarah's house and then on to Hannah's and then back to hers it was about a three-mile walk. The four women were very good friends. Sarah was like a mother to Hannah and Mary and they loved Anne like a little sister.

Mary and Anne bustled about making sure all of Hannah's chores were done for her while Sarah made sure Deborah's birthing pad was in order and then she made a pot of 'new mother's' tea. They tried to keep Hannah's mind off the pains with idle chitchat. They talked of church and the new people that were arriving in town daily and of course they talked about the whale that John Barker had caught. Hannah also mentioned that John was interested in moving to the new settlement in Mattakeese.

John owned fifty acres of farmland in Duxbury but his main occupation was fishing; he had three men working for him, one on the farm and two on his boat. He owned enough land to grow the crops his family needed and hired a young man and his wife to help in the fields. But his first love was fishing, leaving the farming up to Hannah and the hired hand.

Hannah knew that she was his second love but she understood him. She loved to pick on him about being out all hours of the night with '*Tilly*', the name of his boat, but she wasn't jealous of an old smelly fishing boat, she was proud of his ambition.

John's fishing boat was thirty feet long and he supplied many of the small towns up and down the coast with fresh fish every day. Most of the fish that he caught were Cod and Sea Bass but once in a while he would tow a fish as large as his boat into the harbor, he called it a brown shark. He would harpoon these giants with a sharp iron hook attached to a long pole with a rope that was looped to one end and then follow them, or let the huge fish tow him, until they weakened or died from loss of blood; then he would tow them home.

Once he towed a whale about fifty-foot long into the Duxbury harbor. He found the monster fish floating about a mile off shore. He poked at it with an oar and found it to be almost lifeless. It didn't struggle at all when two of the John's men harpooned it. It only expelled its last breath from the top of its head and started to sink. They quickly tied the whale's jaws shut to keep the great beast from filling with water and sinking, then they secured it to the boat and towed it to shore. It took them until well after sunset to get home, but when they arrived at the dock people gathered around with torches and lanterns and helped for several hours to pull the monster onto the beach.

The children and women were seen touching the whale knowing that a creature like this one most surely could have swallowed Jonah. Many children stayed awake most of the night too excited to sleep, and were still excited when they awoke early the next morning. They couldn't wait to see the whale in the daylight.

The townspeople talked of John's catch for many months. The oil from the blubber that was rendered from that whale was used to light lamps for many people for many months. The bones were whittled into useful items such as eating utensils, dishes and combs.

John loved his work, he was good at it and though he was gone from sun up to sun down Hannah didn't mind. He was a very resourceful man providing a good home for her, and he was a good husband and well liked throughout the community.

Little Deborah was born about 2 o'clock in the afternoon. Sarah, Anne and Mary made sure a nice meal was prepared and Hannah and the baby were resting comfortably when they left her house. It was getting late and they wanted to be home before it got too dark.

John was coming up the lane from the dock just as the ladies were getting into the buggy. "Is Hannah all right?" he asked.

"She's doing very well, John, and I'm happy to see that you kept your promise for once," Sarah kidded him, "It isn't quite dark."

John laughed and said, "Thank you for helping, Sarah." Then he tipped his hat to Anne and Mary and quickly opened the door to his cozy warm house.

Hannah was sitting on the settee in front of the fireplace with their baby in her arms. "So what do we have here?" he asked with a smile on his face from ear to ear. He leaned down and kissed Hannah on the forehead.

"Our new baby girl, John," Hannah said softly. "I'd like to name her Deborah, after my mother," she added.

"I love the name Deborah," John said and reached for his baby. Deborah opened her eyes and looked directly at her father. John smiled and a lump caught in his throat as he said, "She's beautiful, just like you are Hannah." He kissed his baby daughter's soft cheek and held her tight.

"I'm sorry she isn't a boy, John, I know you wanted a son," Hannah said tears filling her eyes.

John handed Deborah back to Hannah and then got on his knees in front of her chair and hugged both his beautiful wife and new baby girl close to him. "I only want healthy children Hannah, I don't care if they are sons or daughters, just as long as they are strong and healthy. I love you Hannah, I want you to be healthy, too," he said and he kissed her on her mouth and then her eyes, kissing the tears away.

Hannah sniffed and said, "I love you, too, John." She put her arm across his shoulder and then stroked his cheek, "I'm fine John, I'm just tired tonight." She was tired she thought and scolded herself a little, she knew it was really she herself that wanted to give John a son, "Tomorrow I'll feel better and I'll be back on my feet in no time," she said trying to smile.

He kissed her lips lightly again and said, "Is anything in the stew pot?"

Hannah smiled and said, "Yes dear, Mary and Anne made some this afternoon, it should be just right, there's some corn bread in the cupboard, too."

John helped himself to a big bowl of stew and scooped out a smaller dish for Hannah and then buttered them each a piece of corn bread. He sat Hannah's bowl on the small table by her chair then poured each of them a mug of milk.

John had never waited on Hannah before and it touched her deeply. She really did have a wonderful husband; she thanked God with a silent prayer. 'He'll be a wonderful father, too,' she thought smiling softly.

It wasn't long after Hannah had her baby that Mary More had hers. It was March 22, 1639 when Edward More was born. Another son Richard marveled when he held his new baby during his baptism. He was surely blessed.

Mary had given birth to him with Sarah and Anne's help, her labor had been easy and the baby was healthy.

• • •

On May 26, 1639 Richard asked Abraham to join his family for their evening meal of roasted pork, apples and hasty pudding. Abraham accepted the invitation without hesitation he loved Mary's cooking. After they ate the men sat before the fireplace smoking their pipes.

"As you know Abraham," Richard said, "I have been in Plymouth for several days."

"Yes, Mary told me you had business there," Abraham replied, "was your meeting successful?"

"Yes it was, thank you for asking," Richard said, "but I also have some information about that section of Colonial land called Mattakeese. A little over two years ago, on March 5, 1637 just before you arrived here, William Bradford granted the Mattakeese lands to Richard Collicut and a few of his associates?"

"Yes, I remember when we talked about it last year. I was interested in moving there at that time. Some of the men were planning to form an association, but I haven't heard anything about the grant since then," Abraham said. "Is Mr. Collicut planning to move there soon?" he asked before Richard had a chance to tell him anything.

"No, I don't believe so," Richard said. "No one has moved there yet," and then continued, "You see Richard Collicut was unable to secure the land and his grant has been forfeited. I visited the Mattakeeset Indian lands several years ago, about the time Yarmouth was being settled it was 1636. Mattakeese is located between Sandwich on the east and Yarmouth on the west."

"Yes, Yarmouth is one of the oldest colonies, right?" Abraham questioned, and then without hesitation he asked, "How far is it to Mattakeese?"

"It's about forty miles from here by land, and about twenty miles by boat," Richard answered.

"Only about sixty miles from Plymouth, then," Abraham calculated.

"That's right," Richard said.

"Is the land good for farming?" Abraham asked.

"Yes," Richard said and in his story telling voice he described Mattakeese, "it has been long cultivated by the Indians and is well known to many. If one closed his eyes he could still see a young Indian sitting alone and silent on a hill there, his spirit appealing to the Great Spirit for guidance. And young Indian girls loping down the trail south of the hill on their way to see how the corn and beans and pumpkins were growing. The great hay fields and crooked channels twist seaward, with low, easy shorelines on both sides. The lands cleared for the planting of corn are just part of the rare beauty of the land. It stretches through woods, beautiful and commodious, from the ponds to the hill and then down to the beach. It also has a large stretch of salt marsh that could offer hay for many cattle, horses and sheep."

Abraham was mesmerized and had his own vision of cattle and sheep grazing on the tall hay. "The demand for cattle and sheep is growing steadily and large fields of pasturage could offer the opportunity to make handsome profits from healthy livestock," he said.

"You're right," Richard said, "A new grant will be made out later this month and if you're interested, I will take you to a meeting next week at William Bradford's home."

"Yes, I do believe that I am very interested," Abraham said enthusiastically.

"Then we shall plan on going," Richard said smiling.

"Why did Richard Collicut forfeit the grant to settle such good land?" Abraham asked.

"Well, in all fairness to Mr. Collicut, he was probably so busy that his duties prevented him from going to Mattakeese as he had intended when he received the grant." Richard said.

"I know that he is a selectman and deputy to the General Court in Dorchester," Abraham said.

"Yes, and at the same time he was suppose to settle Mattakeese he was appointed Commissary by the Plymouth Court and he was in charge of making provisions for the troops during the expedition against the Pequot Indians," Richard said. Then he added, "He was also asked to rectify the bounds between Dedham and Dorchester during that time."

"No one can be in two places at the same time," Abraham said.

"Mr. Collicut is a very valuable man in the Massachusetts Colony General Court and Governor Bradford did not hold him accountable for forfeiting his grant," Richard said trying to cover a yawn.

"I guess it's time for me to leave," Abraham chuckled as he stood up, "I shall have to hurry if I want to be home before dark."

"I'm sorry," Richard apologized for yawning, "it's been a long day for me." Then smiling he said, "you are a wise man Abraham to take advantage of an opportunity to help settle a new colony."

"I am very excited about it," Abraham said as he went to the door, "I probably won't sleep a wink tonight," he added as he closed the door behind him. He whistled most of the way home.

The following week on June 14, 1639 a meeting of the General Court in Plymouth was held in Governor Bradford's home. Abraham was introduced to the other men who were also interested in forming an association to establish a new colony. The grant stated that the land called Mattakeese was to be inhabited within the next two months by no less than forty-two residents. The court also expected that the individual parcels of land were to be surveyed and portioned off into home lots and common fields by that time. Thomas Dimmock reported that the Reverend Lothrop of Scituate along with the majority of his church was in the process of removing their church to the new town and should be established there before winter. Governor Bradford accepted this information as the truth and assigned a grant to them that very evening.

Most of these men were from Scituate, and Boston, but like Abraham there were one or two each from Duxbury, Weymouth and Yarmouth. The association consisted of a mixture of prominent and well-educated men from all walks of life with many different talents. Abraham wrote their names down so that he could remember them. Reverend Joseph Hull, Thomas Dimmock, Henry Coggin, James Hamblen, Thomas Allyn, Nathaniel Bacon, Austin Bearse, John Bursley, Thomas Huckins, Roger Goodspeed, Laurence Litchfield, John Mayo, Samuel Mayo, John Scudder, Thomas Shaw, John Smith, and of course Abraham Blish.

The next week at the first official meeting of the association the new town was incorporated. Reverend Joseph Hull was voted to be their Chairman and Abraham was elected to keep the records of each meeting. Governor Bradford was also in attendance that day and gave him a new journal and he wrote his first entry as follows.

The Reverend Hull made a motion to rename the new settlement Barnstable, Thomas Dimmock seconded it and the motion carried unanimously.

Joseph Hull suggested naming the new settlement after the town of Barnstaple in Devonshire, England, because nearly all those in the association were from the counties Devon and Somerset in the west of England. Many of the men sailed with Joseph Hull to New England from Barnstaple Harbor in England, which was the most convenient port to their homes, in the fall of 1635 on the 'Griffin'. The shorefronts of the two places at low tide were very similar to each other. There were miles of sand flats in both the long narrow harbors, and both harbors reminded everyone of the old English town of Barnstaple.

No one disapproved of the re-naming and Barnstable became the official name of the new settlement. They did however, change the spelling of the two towns. The English town was spelled Barnstaple with a 'p' and the New England town was spelled Barnstable with a 'b'. Abraham noted this change in his journal.

William Carsely was elected the first Constable and was sworn in although he stated that he would not be able to move until later that year.

Abraham also inscribed the following information that was given him by the men of the newest town in the Colony. He wrote the total number of people in each family at the end of each person's paragraph.

The good Reverend Joseph Hull was a minister in Weymouth and preached his last sermon there on May 5, 1639 and joined the association. He was also a farmer and a businessman and arrived in New England in 1635. He was known to have taken care of cattle sent from England and shared the profits gained here with the wealthy English owners. This new area of land appealed to him because of the pasturage for stock raising. Its cleared fields invited settlement and its stretch of salt marsh offered hay, which of course was necessary in raising cattle, horses and sheep. He was a surveyor, naturally interested in land, and was active in public affairs and was well known by Plymouth officials. Governor Bradford also ordered him to train the inhabitants of the new town of Barnstable at arms as soon as possible in case of an Indian attack. He was married to Patience Adams of Weymouth and they had a daughter named Julia. 3

Thomas Dimmock was an Elder of Rev. Lothrop's church in Scituate. He was married to Ann Marie Hammond on December 5, 1638 in Scituate. He stated the reasons for his coming to New England were not to amass wealth, or acquire honor; all he wanted was the freedom to worship his God according to the dictates of his own conscience and to enjoy the blessings of civil and religious liberty. He stated that his duties to his God, to his country and to his neighbors would never knowingly be violated. He would not judge his friends by their religion because he believed that to be a prerogative of only the Lord and no man had a right to interfere with another mans beliefs. He read a message from Reverend Lothrop stating that although he was not yet a member of the association he was intending to move to Barnstable later in the fall. Thomas intended to build his own home and had promised Reverend Lothrop that he would secure a refuge for his family as well. Thomas' wife Ann Marie, who insisted that everyone call her Marie, was a woman known for healing wounds and sickness, using herbs. She was taught by her mother in England and was now enlisting the Indian women as teachers and gatherers for her. She had learned many of their ways and uses of the unfamiliar herbs here in this new land. They had no children. 2

Henry Coggin was a sea captain and admitted that he would be at sea most of the time but wanted to establish a new home for his family. He married Abigail Bishop in England on April 2, 1635 and they had two children, a daughter named Abigail, after her mother, age three and Thomas born March 2, 1639. He agreed to enlist the services of as many hired hands as it would take to keep his farm and home in order while he was at sea. He was a man of good standing and was considered wealthy. 4

James Hamblen came from London to Boston in 1635 and bought a schooner and a pinnace and started a transport service between Boston and Plymouth and all ports in between. He had several indentured servants working for him. As a member of the association he had agreed to move to the new settlement and bring his service to Barnstable as well. He married Agnes Hall of Boston on December 3, 1638 and had no children at this time. 2

Thomas Allyn was a farmer from Scituate and was interested in bring-ing his surveying knowledge to the new town. Thomas was also a bee-keeper and had been successful in transporting live hives from one farm to another in Scituate. The association welcomed him upon the recom-mendation of William Bradford. He was not married. 1

Nathaniel Bacon was a tanner and currier of leather. He was deputy to the colony court in Plymouth and an assistant to the governor. He was married to Hannah Mayo, daughter of the Reverend John Mayo. He was well received into the association because of the skills in his trade and because of his knowledge of the court. They had no children. 2

Austin Bearse arrived in Boston on April 24, 1638 on the ship 'Con-fidence' from London having been born in Southampton, England, and moved directly to Scituate. He was a young man, only 21, and he was married to Mary Baker on May 1, 1639, they wanted to settle in the new town and were ready to move without further notice. Austin was recom-mended highly by the Reverend Lothrop to the association. In England Austin's father was a well-known vegetable farmer and Austin had learned from him the knowledge needed to produce much of the food that would be needed by the new settlement. He stated that he had brought many pro-duce seeds with him and he needed to plant them as soon as possible. They had no children. 2

John Bursley was married to a woman named Mary and was of middle age, he was well educated and had been a surveyor for many years in England. His skills in that field were very valuable. He was also a man of means and had two hired hands that were able carpenters who had agreed to move with him. They had no children. 2

Thomas Huckins was a young man who was not married, but he was well mannered and a hard worker, skilled as a mason and carpenter. His services were much needed and he was highly recommended by Reverend Lothrop. 1

Roger Goodspeed was well educated and though he was not a member of Reverend Lothrop's congregation the Reverend recommended him highly. He was a farmer and lived a quiet and inoffensive life. He was also well to do having been left a large inheritance from his father. He was not married. 1

Laurence Litchfield was a friend of Reverend Lothrop and because he was unmarried he was asked to go to the new settlement immediately to lay out the land. His father was a farmer in England and Laurence had studied agriculture in college before he came to the colonies. 1

John Mayo was a teaching elder of Reverend Lothrop's church and because he was a widower he was chosen to move to the new settlement as soon as possible. He was well educated and considered a fair and decent man. He would also be available to preach a Sunday service if the Reverend had to be away on a matter of business. 1

Samuel Mayo owned a boat and was called Captain Mayo by many of his friends. He considered himself a fair and honest businessman and was well learned in boat building. Captain Mayo and Robert Shelly were planning to go into the boat building business together. He was brother to John Mayo. He was not married. 1

John Scudder was a stone mason, a valuable trade for anyone wishing to move to a new settlement. He came from England at the age of 15 in 1632 as an indentured servant to Michael Metcalf of Dedham. John worked for Mr. Metcalf for two years as a hog yard cleaner and never complained about any of the work that he was asked to do. During this time he also built durable and beautiful stone walls all around Mr. Metcalf's land. When he was 22 he married Margaret Linnett, who had also been in servitude to Michael Metcalf as a dairymaid. They did not have an education but Mr. Metcalf gave them a letter of recommendation stating that John was a hard worker and also clever in the laying of stone walls and Margaret was a quiet girl and a good mother to their son Matthew, age one. The letter from Mr. Metcalf was accepted and John was admitted into the association. 3

Thomas Shaw, only 21 was said to be a hard worker. He first arrived in Plymouth in 1636 with enough money to purchase a small apple orchard in Hingham and had a good business making cider. He had his land for sale and as soon as it was sold he would move to the new settlement. He planned to bring his knowledge of apple trees and fifty saplings from his orchard with him. The making of cider was a good industry to have in a new town and the association readily admitted him. He was not married. 1

John Smith and Susanna Hinckley, daughter of Samuel Hinckley were recently married and were excited about moving to a new colony. Susanna's father, Samuel Hinckley had been opposed to this marriage because he considered John to be too liberal; however, Susanna insisted that she would never love anyone else and finally convinced her father to allow her to marry him. John was very influential in the government of the colony and was gladly admitted to the association because of his expertise in government policy. Susanna was also the sister of Thomas Hinckley and Hannah Hinckley Lewis, both of whom were planning to move to the new colony. They had no children. 2

A total of 29 people would be ready to move to Barnstable within two weeks. Keeping the Journal of Barnstable up to date kept

Abraham very busy, often writing for several hours in the evening, entering the new residents names and pertinent information that was requested by the Governor.

On July 6, 1639 the Reverend John Lothrop and his congregation held a day of humiliation in Scituate, praying for the presence of God in mercy to go with them to Mattakeese. He gave Abraham a copy of his prayer and Abraham copied it into his journal word for word.

"Today is a day to be thankful for the grace of Our God, and we pray that he will guide us and grant us his blessing, and settle us there in the new colony of Mattakeese as a new Church, and to unite us together in holy walking and to make us faithful in keeping our covenant with God and one another. Amen."

Four months later, on early October 11, 1639 the following men, all from Scituate, became residents of Barnstable and were granted their land from the association when they arrived. Some of the men who owned cattle and other animals came on foot driving their livestock over land. Abraham entered the new arrivals in his journal each evening.

John Crocker was illiterate and had a bad temper when drinking. He was married to Joan Lawton in Scituate in 1637. They came with Reverend Lothrop though he was never a member of the church. He was a good farmer and was recommended by the Reverend as a hard worker so the association granted him 40 acres of salt marsh and thirty acres of upland. They had no children. 2

Henry Ewell was a member of the Reverend's church and was not married. He was a carpenter and for the past five years he had helped build several houses in Scituate. His services would be very useful in Barnstable. 1

William Crocker, brother of John, was a member of the Reverend's church and married to Alice and they had two children born in Scituate, John was born May 1, 1637 and Elizabeth born on September 22, 1639, was only 20 days old. He was a Deacon and a great help to Reverend Lothrop. Being industrious, economical and a good manager had made him wealthy; but he was also generous, well respected and honest. 4

William Betts was a young man and had recently received his inheritance. He was a gardener and anxious to start planting as soon as possible. His specialty was vegetables and he had talked at length with many

Indian women learning as much as possible about growing corn, beans and the large orange squash they called pumpkins; as well as the other strange edibles this new land provided. He was not married. 1

Robert Shelly was skilled in boat building and would be welcomed in this new community and was recommended and held in high regard by Reverend Lothrop. He was a friend of Samuel Mayo and they planned to go into the boat building business together. He was not married. 1

John Cooper was a deacon of Reverend Lothrop's church in Scituate. He was married to Priscilla Wright. He was a very well educated man and also a good carpenter having built several houses in Scituate. They had no children. 2

Henry Bourne was a member of Reverend Lothrop's church and was recently married to Sarah. He sold his house in Scituate and moved to Barnstable with the Reverend. He was well educated and a skilled surveyor. His services were welcomed in Barnstable. They had no children. 2

Thomas Hinckley was a young man, just 21 but he took a leading role representing Barnstable at Plymouth Court and was appointed by Governor Bradford to act as magistrate in local disputes, or any negotiation that was needed for the purchase of Indian lands. He was also capable of guiding the town's course through any troubled periods. He had worked as an assistant to the Governor for two years and was well respected, but not always popular, some people considered him a haughty person. One man had the audacity to call him a stiff-necked pompous ass, that being Captain Matthew Fuller, although he did acknowledge his fault when Thomas sued him. Reverend Lothrop recommended Thomas having known him since he was born. The Reverend had baptized him in 1619 in Edgerton, County Kent, England when Thomas was just a few days old. Thomas came to Plymouth on the "Hercules" in 1634 with his parents Samuel and Sarah Hinckley and his 3 siblings when he was 16 years old. Thomas was not able to move immediately to the new settlement but the association agreed to include him and granted him a portion of land if he promised to build a home there within a year. He was not married. Susannah Smith and Hannah Lewis were his sisters. 1

Samuel Jackson and his wife Henrietta were indentured servants of Thomas Hinckley and they were sent to Barnstable to oversee Mr. Hinckley's property and build him a home. Their servitude would expire in three years and Thomas promised Samuel that he would give him a house and five acres of land if he would move to the new colony now and help him build a house there. The association approved this agreement and accepted Samuel as a member under Thomas' recommendation.

Henrietta was required to help in the Hinckley house whenever called upon. Samuel and Henrietta had a son age one. 3

Isaac Robinson started a small dairy herd in Scituate in 1638 and agreed to move some of his cattle to Barnstable knowing that the meadows there were known to be the best in the colony producing the best hay. He had two hired hands that were to move there immediately and take his place until he arrived, they were to start building his house. They were not married. 2

John Carsely was indentured to Isaac Wells and the association accepted him on Mr. Wells' recommendation. John was not a man of good character, he was brash and bold in his speech, but he was knowledgeable in growing flax and hemp and was granted permission to watch over Mr. Wells' fields. Hemp was used to produce twine and rope as well as sailcloth and flax was used to make linen cloth. Isaac Wells' rope making business was located in Boston but he owned land in several other colonies and the association welcomed his business. He was not married. 1

William Carsely was sworn in as Constable several months before and was now ready to move to the new settlement and was quite excited to belong to the association. He was to be married to Martha Matthews of Yarmouth the following month, on November 28, 1639 and was anxious to begin building his new home. 2

Robert Linnet owned several young cows and a prize bull that he brought with him to Barnstable. He was a friend of Isaac Robinson and together they had increased their herds of cattle twice over in the last three years. He was not married. 1

Thomas Lothrop was a nephew of the Reverend Lothrop and was an apprentice to Robert Shelly the boat builder. He was not married. 1

Thomas Lumbert and his wife Judith had anticipated a large family when they married in 1633 but as yet there were no children born to them. They decided to move to Barnstable with the intention of building a home with extra rooms, large enough for two beds in each one and open their home up to the many travelers that would soon be coming to the new settlement. Judith was a good cook and they felt they could prosper in this business knowing that in a few years traveling would probably be easier as the roads opened and the wharf in the harbor was completed. The location of their property was situated so as to be the first place that travelers came upon when entering the new town. The association agreed to their idea and welcomed them to the community. 2

Henry Rowley owned twelve of the best sheep in Scituate and did not have enough pasture land to increase his herd so was pleased to join the association and move them to Barnstable. His wife was one of the best spinners of wool in the surrounding towns and was called on often to teach the young girls. She was worried, however, that her spinning wheel might be damaged on the journey to the new town. Henry assured her that every precaution would be taken to keep it safe, they would go by boat and would crate it securely. They had no children. 2

George Lewis was married to Hannah Hinckley and considered a very knowledgeable cattleman. He also owned a prize bull hat would insure a healthy herd of cattle for the new town. They had no children. 2

Edward Fitzrandolph was a young widower anxious to move to a new community, he wanted to leave the memory of his loving wife and baby in Scituate both having died soon after his baby was born. He was a planter specializing in fruit trees and grapes and cranberries. 1

Bernard Lumbert was a young man with no particular skills but known as a hard worker and willing to do any job he was asked to do. Reverend Lothrop recommended him as he was a younger brother of Thomas and lived with him and Judith. 1

Henry Cobb was an Elder in Reverend Lothrop's church and was asked to come to the new settlement and help with the layout of the land. He was married to Patience Hurst of Plymouth in 1631 and they had two sons born there, John born January 7, 1631 and James born January 14, 1634. After he moved to Scituate they had two daughters, Mary born March 24, 1637 and Hannah born October 5, 1639 was only a week old. Patience was not a strong woman so Henry hired a maidservant to help her after her baby was born and she came with them. Henry was also skilled in raising cattle and agreed to bring them with him. 7

Richard Foxwell was considered another one of the best carpenters in the new colony. He had a hired hand named Nathaniel Morton that worked with him and they were both welcomed in Barnstable. They were both unmarried. 2

Reverend John Lothrop was from Lowthorpe in York County, England and held two degrees from Cambridge, a bachelor's degree that he received in 1605 and his masters in 1609. He married Hannah Howse, a clergyman's daughter, in 1610 and in 1611 he became curate of the parish church at Egerton, Kent County, England. He parted from the Church of England in 1624 and became a member of the Separatist Church.

When Henry Jacob, the founder of the Separatist died, John became the clergyman for a congregation of about 60 people. They met quietly in private homes every Sunday. He and Hannah had nine children during the next 21 years. On April 29, 1632, their meeting was raided and John was arrested and imprisoned for two years.

His wife Hannah died in 1633 while he was in prison leaving his children to be cared for by the church members until he was released a year later.

On September 18, 1634, he and his nine children arrived in Boston aboard the Griffin and settled in Scituate living there for about 4 years. He met his second wife, Elizabeth shortly after arriving in Scituate and they were married on June 5, 1638 and their first son James was born there on August 5, 1639. They packed all of their belongings and their 10 children and headed for the new little settlement.

The good Reverend John Lothrop and his family arrived in the new colony by water along with some of his congregation. A few of the other men and their families that were also in his congregation did not move to Mattakeese immediately but they came as soon as their individual circumstances rendered it convenient.

The Reverend John Lothrop was the first minister to hold a church service in Barnstable. John Lothrop's family of 12 and his congregation of 6 families, about 40 people in all, made the long trip from Scituate to Barnstable, arriving by water on October 11, 1639. They left early in the morning and arrived in late afternoon.

The people of Barnstable had no way of paying a preacher, but the town council agreed to build a parish house for the Reverend and those that could find the time helped him build it. It was completed just before the first snow and it was considered quite a large home; it had to be in order to house his family of 10 children comfortably. He designed the roof to be raised higher than most homes in order to form a great loft for sleeping. He hewed great boards from the fallen trees that were toppled by the great hurricane that still laid askew on part of his property. Some of these boards were twelve to sixteen inches wide and were use to make some of his furniture, including a long dining table with benches on either side. It was long enough to seat all of the members of his family at the same time, as well as anyone in his congregation that needed his council.

The common room was about 30 feet square and large enough to hold 50 people. On cold Sundays everyone would gather in the Lothrop home, sitting on benches placed against the walls, the fireplace would blaze and John would preach for at least two hours. The children were made to sit quietly in the loft; sometimes the younger ones would nap on pallets while the older ones fidgeted soundlessly. The people of Barnstable gave him a food supply and allowed him to keep any moneys exchanged between man and man. He managed to handle his finances quite well, he had always been an ambitious man and able to care for his family while also helping his fellow man whenever they needed him.

He was usually desirous of peace, but nevertheless, he was precise, insistent and uncompromising in adherence to what he personally thought right. He was considered a holy reverent and heavenly-minded man. He was a preacher endowed with a competent measure of humility; he was meek but not submissive. John Lothrop believed in baptism by a sprinkling of water on the head and the church was the center of all life, religious, political and social.

He was assertive in manner, but humane and liberal in his thinking. He and his family and followers were well received by the new community. These traits had driven him from a comfortable living in the Church of England to prison, to Scituate and now to Barnstable. Many believed that he had become a better man after facing these hardships. John Lothrop and his growing family were welcomed and well respected in Barnstable. 12

Antony Annable was a member of Reverend Lothrop's church and was very influential in government affairs in Plymouth and Scituate. He and his wife Jane came to Plymouth in 1623 on the 'Anne' with their daughter Sarah. They were granted four acres of land there and in 1634 he sold his property and they moved to Scituate. His knowledge of governmental policies would be most useful in the new settlement and he was highly recommended by Governor Bradford. Jane's skill as a healer and close friend of Marie Dimmock's would be of great value to the new colony. They had two more daughters while they lived in Plymouth, Hannah was born in 1625 and Susannah was born in 1630. Another daughter was born in Scituate in 1635 but she lived only a short time. Their fifth child, another daughter they named Deborah was also born in Scituate in 1637. Anthony told the association that we did not feel that he should move his large family until he had a home for them and the association agreed to grant him land if he would start building on it within the month. He agreed and the association welcomed him and his family.6

There were now 53 new residents in the town of Barnstable making a total of 82, including men women and children. Abraham did not include himself or Anthony Annable in this count, as they had not officially moved into their new homes.

On December 21, 1639, John Lothrop held a special day of thanksgiving at his new partially build home for God's exceeding mercy in bringing them safely to Barnstable. Many of their homes were just temporarily built of poles and sticks and mud, but their new homes were under construction. The winter months were hard, but they all managed to survive them. The Reverend would tell the story of his trials and tribulations whenever he was asked and Abraham remembered them and wrote them in his journal often repeating them to his family.

CHAPTER SEVEN
1640

One Sunday afternoon while the men waited for their evening meal Richard told Abraham the reason why Governor Bradford insisted that more than one person keep records for each town.

"Just before you arrived here," Richard said, "there was a fire in the home of Myles Standish. Nothing was saved not even any of his furniture. He had to start all over again. Of course many people helped him by donating many useful items that he needed to keep a house."

"I remember the fire that left you homeless, Richard," Abraham said sadly.

"Yes, fire is a terrible thing," Richard replied pausing a minute to reflect. He cleared his throat and then continued.

"The fire was March 10, 1637," Richard said positive of the exact date of the event. "It destroyed much information that was considered very important. Many of the records of all the settlers in Duxbury were lost. And of course, when it was rewritten many important dates and items of interest were never remembered. There was one thing that Myles was grateful for though. It seems that earlier that day his assistant, Daniel Smith had taken three books home with him to record information into from notes he had received that morning. Thus they were not in Myles' home at the time of the fire," Richard said pausing again as he recalled the horrible event.

"During the following months Myles and Daniel made a huge effort to reconstruct the records and with the help of everyone else in town they were able to gather much of the information that was lost. After the fire it was decided by the town council that the Reverend should also keep records of everything that went on in the church, such as marriages, baptisms and funerals," Richard stated.

"My journals that I have been writing over the years were also used to help reconstruct the lost records," Richard said smiling.

"Your journals are very valuable, Richard," Abraham said, and then added, "maybe mine will be useful someday, too."

"I'm sure they will be," Richard said and then continued. "When Myles built his new home he had a huge stone hollowed out and placed above the foundation so that the hole opened into his commonroom. An iron door was made special for it and all of his records have been kept in it from that day to this."

"Now I fully understand my duty to keep complete records for the Governor," Abraham said, " I thank you for this information, Richard."

"Myles Standish has been our magistrate here in Duxbury for 4 years now and is also the colony's treasurer and has been on its governing council for 19 years. He visits all of the area towns in his jurisdiction at least once a year. He was married to Rose Morgan when he arrived in Plymouth on the Mayflower, but she died during the first year we were here in Plymouth. He has a son Josiah about the age of 15," Richard said.

Mary called the men to eat and Abraham made a promise to himself that he would keep as many journals as it took to insure that the records for the new town of Barnstable would be forever kept.

Abraham traveled from Duxbury to Barnstable for each town meeting from that time on and diligently completed his records as soon after each meeting as he could taking pride in the accuracy of his journal.

Abraham spent most of the winter in Duxbury drawing plans for his new home, making the doors and some new furniture. He also made sure that he had nails and other hardware that he would need. He started building his new home in the Great Marshes that overlooked Sandy Neck Cove on the western side of Barnstable, Massachusetts on April 5, 1640. He built his new house in the same fashion as Richard More built his. The outside of the house was covered with weatherboarding and then clapboards. The inside walls were sheathed up with boards molded at the edges in an ornamental manner and the space between them was filled with clary, chopped straw and imperfect bricks making a form of insulation to keep the cold out and the heat in.

He covered the roof with shingles that he split from the log by means of a frow, which was a hatchet like tool and then he hand shaved them into thin tapered pieces. Some of the men with lesser means would thatch their roofs as their fathers taught them in old England.

He made the window openings small and he closed them with hinged casements. The casements were made of wood and inset with diamond shaped glass set in lead cames. Abraham had brought the glass, safely packed in a barrel of flour, with him from England. In the windows of the barn and in the hired hand's house he used oiled paper that supplied a surprisingly large amount of light.

He built a huge chimney with a fireplace that was large enough for a grown man to walk into. It had a hanger fitted into the brick to hold a large cook pot and the flat surface of the floor was large enough for two sets of trammels, which were used to set iron pans and kettles on for baking and cooking. It also had an oven built into one side for baking bread. The completed fireplace covered almost the entire west wall leaving only a small area that he used as a cooking area on one side. He built cupboards at the north end of the fireplace and he made a large shelf under them that he used to hold a water pail and a large basin. An eating area with a large table was on the south side of the fireplace and the rest of the area, known as the common room, in front of the fireplace was where everyone gathered most of the time. He added another room onto the north side of the house that was used as the master bedroom. At the back of the house toward the west he built a shed and a barn with a covered walkway that connected all three buildings.

Upstairs there were three bedrooms with floors of hard wood that were polished with whale oil to preserve them and hand woven rugs were scattered beside the beds and in the hallway. Abraham purchased cornhusk mattresses from Boston and had them delivered by ship along with the rugs.

The China dishes that he bought for Anne were placed in the cupboard on special shelves that he made for them. There were small grooves in the back of each shelf and small pegs placed in the cupboards in front of the grove to hold the plates securely. He placed all of the dishes that matched Anne's tea set in the cupboard and latched the hinged doors with small pieces of wood. He did not tell her about these dishes and did not plan to until they were married and moved into their new home.

Another gift that he did not mention to her was the Tall Clock that he bought from Thomas Harland a clock maker of Boston. He paid 25 pounds sterling for the clock and it never left his sight from the time he left Boston until he arrived in Barnstable. At the time he believed that he was the only one in the new settlement to own a clock. He knew she would love it.

Richard often went to Barnstable to help Abraham work on his new home and with his help and the help of his two hired hands his new house would be finished by late fall or early winter. One evening when the chimney was almost finished and the men were settling down with their pipes after they had eaten their evening meal, Richard tapped his pipe on the edge of the stone hearth of the fireplace, the sparks from it reminded him of a story.

"Would you like to hear another one of my stories?" he asked. Of course, the answer was yes, and as usual it started with a date.

"I was about 11 years old in 1623. The men, women and children in New Plymouth had been working very hard for the past two summers. They had managed to build over a dozen great houses in pleasant situations in the new colony, but some of the poor people still lived in tents and wigwams. The wigwams were made of small poles pricked into the ground and bent to fasten at the tops and on the side, then matted with boughs and covered with sedge and old mats. They were copied from the Indians and the mats were purchased from the Indians by trade. They also used old pieces of sailcloth to keep out the elements those first few years. The roofs always leaked and when it rained for a long time the rains penetrated through the thatch and disturbed their sleep. The people prayed, and sang psalms daily asking God to provide them with warm homes and good food. During the winter a fireplace built of stones would be constructed at one end and a door with a hewed frame and wooden hinges was installed on the opposite end of the one room shelter. The floors were covered with rushes or straw. Every dwelling was different. Each man had his own idea of what would keep the wild animals, cold and rain from coming into his home.

The following summer proved fruitful for everyone. The Indians in the nearby villages were friendlier, the gardens and wheat fields produced great crops and the people were beginning to feel better. In the fall they harvested and prepared their food for storage, along with many deer, tur-

key and pheasant. *There were also many other birds and fish which had been salted, and put away in the storeroom for winter.*

Four or five more homes were built as well as a great storeroom of sturdy logs and they covered it over on the outside with boards and a heavy thatch roof. They attached a shed to one end and it was wattled up with boughs and daubed with clay. It was used to store hoes, rakes, axes and other tools that were of great value for survival.

Well now, a very large man by the name of George Sowle had a habit of smoking his pipe all day, not just in the evenings as most of the men did. He was always tapping out the dead ashes on trees and door cases and anywhere else he needed to. In the late afternoon of November 20, 1623, about two days before Thanksgiving, he put his hatchet away in the shed and of course, he tapped his pipe out on the door case as he left the small building.

At midnight John Howland's wife Elizabeth awoke when their smallest child cried out after having a bad dream. She settled the child down and then went out to the necessary. When she came back, she thought she smelled smoke. The moon being almost full gave her the light, and the courage to take a few steps toward the storehouse. She ran back to her house and shouted to John that there was smoke coming from the storehouse. Then she woke the older children telling them to watch the younger ones, grabbed her warm coat and ran to William Bradford's home and banged on his door as hard as she could. When he opened the door she pointed to the storehouse and shouted fire, fire! Then she ran from house to house shouting the alarm as loud as she could.

John, by this time, was almost to the storehouse, and the flames were shooting up through the roof of the shed where the tools were. He had nothing to fight the flames with except an old shovel that had been left by the door. He opened the front door and the heat was on him with such force that he was nearly knocked to the ground. He could see only smoke, but he went into the storehouse anyway knowing that he had to save as much food as possible. He knew that the grain was on the left and the vegetables were on the right and not really knowing why, to headed toward the vegetable bins and grabbed as many baskets as he could and turned and ran for the door.

Several other men had arrived by this time, including William Bradford, Edward Winslow and Isaac Allerton, as well as some women and a few of us children. We saw John coming out with his arms full of food and in the excitement we all started to follow his lead, but Mr. Bradford shouted that we should form a human chain with only two or three of the men going into the storehouse at one time. The rest of us waited at the door to take the food from them and we carried it about 50 feet from the fire. The women wet rags and put them over the faces of the men.

After four of five minutes the three men inside came out and three others went in. They took turns until it became too smoky and too hot. We all had to stand back near the trees as the fire took over the whole building. There was nothing we could do then but watch the shed and storehouse and the rest of our winter supplies become a blazing inferno.

The next day some of the men that had been inside the burning building were sick with terrible coughing and choking. They did recover after a few days and during that time we all helped to clean up the mess. By spring a new storehouse was completed.

Needless to say we had a pretty skimpy winter that year, but we didn't starve, there were plenty of deer and fish to eat. Our Indian friends helped us by supplying us with squash, corn and beans. And as I have said many times, without their help we would have starved to death during those first years. I remember them well.

Mr. Sowle, however, lost a lot of weight that winter, he vowed he would not eat any of the rescued provisions and he never smoked his pipe again during the day.

Mr. Bradford did not allow any men to punish Mr. Sowle, as the punishment he put upon himself was harsh enough.

After Richard's story the men all found their sleeping pallets and bedded down for the night, happy that they were fortunate enough to have a warm bed by a nice warm fireplace.

• • •

Governor Bradford called a special town council meeting for the new town of Barnstable on April 16, 1640. He attended this meeting and signed a Charter, or an official document, declaring the town as established as the newest Colony in New England. Everyone in town attended this meeting and a celebration was held afterward.

Abraham also noted that the new town of Barnstable had many distinctions. It had a town meeting form of government and it was influential in the affairs of Plymouth colony, the Province of Massachusetts Bay and the Commonwealth of Massachusetts. Most of the people were well educated; they were well to do farmers, seafaring men, wealthy landowners and businessmen. Barnstable was the 9th colony established by the Plymouth Plantation and it covered an area of eight square miles.

The first Full Town Council meeting in Barnstable was held on June 2, 1640. They voted that no one could sell his house, or land, without giving the town the first opportunity to buy it. The council would have to provide a purchaser or approve of the buyer. William Carsely was officially sworn in as Constable and Thomas Allyn and Henry Bourne were appointed Surveyors and Abraham Blish and Henry Cobb were appointed Haywards. Jurors were also appointed.

They also gave Thomas Lumbert and his wife Martha permission to open an Inn as soon as it was completed. Thomas and Martha built their home overlooking the ocean between the harbor and the main road leading into Barnstable.

After the meeting Abraham and his hired men worked on his house for almost two weeks until he was needed back in Duxbury. He also missed Anne. He left instructions for his men to finish the roof and when they were finished they were to start mowing the hay that was in the field next to his home. He told them he would be back in a couple of weeks. This routine continued until the end of August, his wedding date was coming up in early September and he told his men he would send word to them whether or not he would be moving in before winter or wait until next spring. He also told them if they ran out of supplies they should go to Duxbury and he would supply them with whatever they needed.

• • •

Timothy Dimmock, son of Thomas and Ann Marie Dimmock was born on June 15, 1640 he lived just a few minutes. He was buried in the lower side of the Calves Pasture on June 17, 1640. Timothy was the first baby to die in Barnstable and many women grieved for Marie. He was born prematurely; Marie was pregnant only about seven and a half months when she went into labor. The poor baby took a few breaths, wiggled a little and then he died. He was so tiny only weighing about three or four pounds. Marie took the herbs that she knew would stop her premature labor, but it was too late, her baby wanted to be born and that was that.

The women all consoled Marie and as the warm months passed her sadness passed, there was no time to dwell on such things Marie chided herself, she had way too much to do to get ready for the next season.

• • •

John Mayo was invested as teaching elder of the Barnstable church on August 5, 1640 and he was elected to teach the 12 children old enough to attend school how to read and do their numbers. History lessons were also taught as well as the scriptures. Elders substituted for ministers, and their duties were to teach the doctrine the same as the pastor. David Linnell age 9, and Hannah Shelly age 8, were two of the oldest children of the church and often helped teach the smaller ones. After the age of 15 or 16 children of the colonies had a choice, go to Boston or back to England to finish their education or stay at home to help their parents carry on with the farming, cattle raising or the family business.

Although most everyone attended church not everyone was a member. The Barnstable church now had about 43 members in all, 24 men and 19 women. There were 20 young men that were not yet the legal age of 24 and were not eligible to become members and young children were not considered members of the church until they reached legal age.

• • •

Abraham Blish and Anne Pratt were married on Wednesday, September 7, 1640 at 11 o'clock in the morning at the Duxbury Church. The ceremony was quite lengthy, as weddings were for the Puritans, with many prayers and blessings given by the Reverend Ralph Partridge. There being three prayers lasting about 5 minutes each, the first prayer was for Abraham, requesting that God help him to be faithful to his wife, be a good provider to his family and a father who would give good advice and strong discipline to his children. The second prayer was for Anne, praying to the Lord Jesus to help her become an obeying wife to her husband and a loving mother to her children. After taking their vows and becoming man and wife, there was a third prayer beseeching God to bless this couple and make them strong and fruitful in their union.

After the wedding wonderful dishes of food, prepared by Sarah Pratt, Mary More and her sister Remember and several other neighbor ladies, were served to all that attended and best wishes were extended to both Abraham and Anne. Everyone admired Abraham for his thoughtfulness, good humor and good looks and complimented Anne for her beauty and the lovely white dress that her mother had made for her. Sarah had embroidered tiny white flowers at the neckline, wrists and around the hem of the dress and on the brim of her bonnet that was made of the same lightweight cotton material as the dress. Anne carried a bouquet of lovely dried wild flowers tied with a blue ribbon.

Just before sunset when all the food had been eaten and all congratulations had been repeated several times over, Abraham and Anne walked slowly home, holding hands. They didn't say much to each other; they each had their own thoughts.

Abraham was planning to move to Barnstable within the next few weeks and wondered if Ann could be ready by then. They had not discussed a date to move yet but he was anxious to go as soon as he could. He had purchased much of the furniture for his house during his trips to Boston and had it sent directly to Barnstable. He told her about all of the things he had bought and made, but of course, he couldn't tell her of special little things he had found just for her, what surprises lay ahead for her, especially her set of China and the Tall Clock.

Anne was wondering whether or not Abraham would be upset when he found out she wanted to take her horse, Penny, with her when they moved to Barnstable. It would mean that they would have to travel overland if she did, she was sure Penny would not fair very well going by boat. Anne had not seen their new house; it was not proper to go anywhere with a man without a chaperone, even if he was going to be your husband. But she was very excited about moving there and could hardly wait to see their new home. It was almost finished and Anne had started making quilts and pillows and featherbeds to furnish it since the day after Abraham had asked her father for her hand. Anne couldn't wait to see it all.

When they reached their house she squealed in surprise as he picked her up just outside the door and carried her over the threshold. Then he sat her down gently and said, "Anne, you are so beautiful," as he bent his head toward her and gently kissed her on her lips, their first kiss.

Her heart was beating so fast she could hear it in her ears and her face redden and her hands shook. She wanted to kiss him back but she was sure he would think badly of her. 'Women were not suppose to have these feelings, were they?' she wondered. She just smiled up at him she couldn't say anything.

He took off his hat and coat and seeing that she was still standing there, not quite knowing what to do, he gently removed her shawl and bonnet and laid them on a chair near the door.

Then he turned back toward her, took her hand, lifted it to his mouth turned it over and kissed her palm, then folded her fingers onto the kiss he had placed there. He smiled and said, "If I'm ever out of your sight for more than two minutes and you get lonesome for me, just open your hand and think of that kiss."

She smiled up at him again and blinked back a tear. She was so full of so many mixed emotions all at once that she thought she might faint. She quickly sat down on the chair where her shawl and bonnet were and slowly opened her hand looking at her palm as if she could see his kiss; she could certainly still feel it. She closed her hand again.

Abraham went into the kitchen and took two small mugs out of the cupboard and filled them with sweet cider that had just started to turn fizzy, and went back into the common room where Anne was sitting. He handed her one of them and asked, "Are you all right Mrs. Blish?"

"Oh, yes, thank you Abraham," she said quickly liking the sound of her new name. "I'm just kind of emotional, and a little afraid," she added shyly.

"You mustn't be afraid my dear Anne," he said softly and then added, "I'll never hurt you," and he took her hand and pulled her to her feet gently and slowly led her to the settee in front of the fireplace. He sat down beside her and said, "We must talk about moving to our new home in Barnstable," trying to keep the emotions he was feeling in check. "I think we should go as soon as possible, before any bad weather comes, it will be getting colder soon."

"Have you hired a boat, yet?" Anne asked, thinking that he could not be consulting her in such a matter, it would be up to him to decide when they should leave he did not need any help from her in making this decision did he?

"No I haven't," he said slowly, "I wanted to know how much time you thought you would need to get ready, how many trunks you will have, then we would know what size boat we would have to hire and when we would be ready to leave."

Anne looked a little startled because no one had ever asked her to make a decision like this and she wasn't sure what she should say. So, not wanting to sound to excited she said slowly, "Oh Abraham, I do need time to pack the things we have here that you might want to take." And then she added, "I have my quilts and pillows, and will need to take my clothes and dishes, and I have sewing things and, oh dear, my spinning wheel and the furniture and everything." Her voice was beginning to rise as she began to realize how much work needed to be done. She looked up at Abraham and he was smiling, she tried to relax a little and sipped her cider, enjoying the tingle it left on her tongue.

Abraham took her hand and said, "You don't have to think about anything except your own personal belongings, my love, everything in here has already been taken care of."

"Well, I do have most of my clothes and such already packed, I could just leave them in the trunks. I do have a few things still at home, I mean at my parents house, but I, we, could probably be ready by, well," she stammered, "Ah, maybe Monday or Tuesday?" She looked at him shyly to see what his reaction was.

He had a big grin on his face and said, "I knew you could make a decision." He squeezed her hand and said, "So, from now on we will make all decisions together, and even if I don't ask your opinion about anything, I will expect you to give me one anyway, if you have one," he chuckled. "Are we in agreement on this?" he added.

Anne looked at him full in the face this time and said quietly, "Yes, we are in agreement." She knew that she would never fear him again, she would be his equal, his partner she would be his wife in every way. Then quickly before she lost her voice altogether, she whispered, "I want to take Penny with me if I can, but I know she doesn't like water, she'll have to go by land."

"Of course you can," he said, "she can go overland with the other animals," he was a little concerned that she might think he wouldn't let her. He knew how much the beautiful little Narragansett pacer meant to her. She had had her since she was born; Penny was as gentle as a kitten and Anne had trained her to pull a small buggy and also to a little saddle and she rode her every where.

"I would never separate the two of you," he said sighing a little. "Besides she'll be a good mare someday and we could breed her with my horse, Sam, and start our own herd of plow horses," he said, grinning at his own joke. His horse was an excellent workhorse, as well as a good riding horse, harness or saddle, Abraham could coax him to do whatever needed to be done.

"I love you so much," Anne said with a little sob of relief. Then her face turned a bright red from his talk of breeding their horses together and she said, "Plow horses?"

Abraham laughed at her blushing face, stood up and taking both of her hands he pulled her to her feet. "I love you, too, Anne," he said, his voice was husky and this time he led her toward the bedroom.

As Anne followed she knew that Abraham would never be gruff or loud like her father was, and he would never be inconsiderate about his manners and cleanliness. In fact, Abraham had never smelled bad to her, his clothes were always clean and neatly pressed, she had always wondered, but never dared to ask, who he hired to keep his clothes so nice. She'd have to remember to do that, but right now there were other things she should be thinking about.

Abraham lit the candle on the nightstand, pulled the curtain across the window and was now pulling the quilt down from the pillows. She was unsure if she should be getting undressed now or not, so she took a deep breath, let it out silently and sat down on a chair to take off her shoes. Before she knew it, Abraham was in front of her on his knees with her foot in his hands undoing the buckle on her shoe.

"Oh, Abraham, I can do this, myself," she said a little embarrassed.

"But I want to do it for you," he smiled, "in fact, I want to do everything for you tonight, I don't want you to do anything, all right?" He was looking at her with such a sincere and loving look on his face that she couldn't have refused him if her life had depended on it.

"Oh, Abraham, you are so loving, you make me feel like a princess," she said softly and sat back and let him pull her shoes from her tired feet. No words had to be said after that, by either one of them.

Abraham lifted her off the chair by putting his hands around her waist then turned her around so that he was standing in back of her. He undid the buttons at the top of her dress slowly and carefully, little shivers ran down her back as his fingers touched her bare skin tenderly and then he kissed the back of her neck as he slid her dress off her shoulders. He turned her around toward him and pushed her dress down over her hips to the floor. He untied both her petticoats, one at a time, and let them fall to the floor on top of her dress.

She thought she should stop him and pick them up and hang them on the hooks on the wall, but then she changed her mind as his hand slid back up to her shoulders and his fingers slid under the straps of her camisole. An audible sigh escaped her lips as he moved his hands down her arms and pulled her to him gently stroking her bare back and bottom as he kissed her soft shoulder.

Abraham could hardly contain himself as he caressed her body, he wanted to take her right then, but instead he moaned and carefully pushed her back toward the bed. He gently lifted her up, laid her on the bed and pulled the covers over her after he took a long lingering look at her nakedness in the candlelight.

Anne was so self conscious of her body, not knowing whether he would approve of the curve of her round breasts, small waist and flaring hips so she closed her eyes tight. She was glad when he covered her up realizing that she had been cold for the last few minutes, but the featherbed was soft and it snuggled up around her back.

She lay there very still wondering if she should look at Abraham while he removed his own clothes knowing she would be forever embarrassed if he caught her. But she couldn't resist the temptation and she slowly opened her eyes and turned her head toward him, his back was to her, and he was naked to his waist, how beautiful the muscles moved. His shoulders were broad and tanned and she thought absently that he must work without his shirt, as he lowered his trousers and bent slightly to pull them over his knees. Then he sat on the edge of the bed and lifted the covers and slid his body in beside hers. She was startled when she felt his manhood on her leg and stiffened slightly, but he was kissing her cheek and then her mouth and she had to kiss him back, she didn't care if it was right or wrong. As he caressed her body slowly she let her emotions carry her wherever they wanted to go, it was so wonderful to love her husband like this.

Abraham was quite surprised at Anne's permissiveness, but he didn't want her to be any different. He knew she wasn't going to resist him, but he wasn't sure that he could hold himself back long enough to keep from hurting her. So slowly he raised himself up over her body and she spread herself under him so that their bodies would become one. A little hurting moan escaped Anne's lips, but she didn't push him away. He stopped moving and just held her kissing her mouth tenderly. Anne relaxed and after a few minutes, their passion found a life of its own.

After their lovemaking they held each other close, Anne went to sleep thinking 'I am the happiest woman ever to be on God's great earth.'

Abraham went to sleep thinking, 'I am so happy. I am in love!'

September 8, 1640
Dear Mother, Father, John & Molly,

While Anne is preparing our morning meal I thought that I would write you a short letter of good news. Anne Pratt and I were married on September 7, 1640 at 11 o'clock in the morning at the Duxbury Church. I am now the happiest man in the world.

Anne looked absolutely beautiful in her lovely white dress. Her mother made it for her and it was trimmed with little white flowers embroidered around the neck and cuffs and all around the bottom. She carried a small bouquet of lovely dried wild flowers tied with a blue ribbon that matched her eyes. I am telling you this Mother because I know that you and Molly would want to know about these things. And yes, because I also enjoy remembering how she looked.

We are not going to give each other a wedding gift until we move to our new home in Barnstable. Everyone in town attended our celebration and there was so much good food prepared by the ladies of the church that everyone stayed until almost dark offering congratulations and of course, their advice.

The weather has been wet with much rain of late; however, the sun was out all day yesterday and it was warm. It was a perfect day.

Anne has our breakfast ready so I will end this letter now and I shall write to you again very soon.

I leave you in God's hands. I will always be your loving son,

Abraham

• • •

Abraham and Anne decided not to hire a boat the week after they were married because it rained for three days in a row, a downpour. Then it took several more days before the roads were dry enough to travel. Several town council meetings also took place that Abraham was obliged to attend during the next few weeks and before they knew it winter had set in. They resigned themselves to the fact that they had to wait until spring.

Abraham sent word to his men in Barnstable that they would not be moving into their new house until spring, he would let them know the exact date as soon as he could.

The winter was cold and snowy and Abraham and Anne spent many nights curled up in each other's arms in front of the hearth, making love and discussing their move to West Barnstable.

• • •

Anthony and Jane Annable and their four daughters moved into their new home on November 1, 1640. Anthony had worked all summer and was in hopes to have his house finished before harvest season, but one of his hired hands died of pneumonia and he could not find anyone to take his place. However, the weather cooperated toward the end of October and he was able to move all of their belongings to Barnstable by schooner before it snowed.

CHAPTER EIGHT
1641

Two of Abraham's hired men returned in March to report that the house was completed and everything was in order for them to move in. One of his men stayed to keep a fire going and make sure everything was clean and neat when they arrived. He was also cutting wood and putting the finishing touches on the barn.

It was late winter before Abraham and Anne decided that they would be ready to move by the first week of April. They spent much of February and March packing and getting ready to take as many of their belongings as they could on the first trip. They left everything else packed and stored in the commonroom so that the men would know what to bring in the second load. They planned to take a boat to Barnstable with their personal things as soon as the weather would allow. They could move their trunks, casks, kegs, chests, beds, tables and chairs by ship without too many problems, leaving the livestock, chickens and geese to be taken overland by wagon.

The trail was not very wide in some places, winding along the shore, over stretches of sand, behind creeks, through woods, up and down and around hills, and around swamps. They would have to go slow and it would be hard traveling, probably taking them eight or nine days. Abraham thought that his men and the animals, the two oxen, six sheep, and the two horses would be able to get through if they took their time and were careful. The ten chickens, four geese and eight small hogs could be put into cages and go by boat. He decided to sell the two large hogs that he had planned to butcher in the fall, they were too big to keep track of during the journey.

As each day passed and the weather grew warmer Anne put their winter clothes and quilts and the new pillow cases and sheets that she had made during the winter into a trunk or cask, things she was sure she wouldn't be using until the following fall or winter. Lately she was beginning to think that sitting around with Abraham was making her gain weight, she was happy to be able to get out side into the sunshine now, as the days were growing longer and warmer. She loved to take Penny out to exercise and she had not been able to for several weeks because of the snow.

Then one morning toward the middle of March as she got out of bed, she was overwhelmed with nausea, thank God Abraham was already up and out doing the morning chores. She sagged to the floor and pulled the commode door open and lifted out the night pot just in time. She knew as soon as her head cleared that she must be with child. She stood up slowly and poured cool water from the pitcher into the wash bowl added a little bayberry soap ball and washed her face.

After a few minutes she got dressed and slowly went about emptying the night pots, making the bed and doing her morning chores. If she was with child she didn't want Abraham to know yet. She prayed that the sickness would go away soon because Abraham would be in expecting his morning meal and she had put off cooking as long as she could. Then she remembered hearing her mother tell about an old remedy for morning sickness, soda biscuits and ginger tea. So while she was getting her pans heated and the table set, she nibbled on a cold soda biscuit and sipped a glass of cold ginger tea. Her stomach settled down and she felt much better by the time Abraham came in for breakfast. She was even a little hungry her self when she sat down to eat with him.

She knew that he would be excited about her good news, but she decided she'd wait a couple of days to be sure she didn't have the flu or the grip. Besides, they were planning to leave for Barnstable the following week, and she was sure he'd change his mind if he knew she was sick and she didn't want to ruin their plans. So she said nothing about the baby, she just continued packing and getting ready to move. How excited she was though, a new town, a new house and a new baby, all in the same year!

It was April 6 about mid afternoon when Abraham and Anne left the Duxbury harbor for their new home and it was getting dark by the time they reached Barnstable Harbor. The Captain anchored about a half mile off shore and told them he would dock at first light. The weather was a little cold, but it was clear and calm and though the moon was in its last quarter there were lots of stars giving them enough light to see each other. Abraham and Anne found a trunk full of their bedding with two feather pillows and a big lovely colorful handmade quilt in it. They found a nice comfortable spot on the port side of the ship spread out their bedding and tried to get some rest. But they were both so excited they couldn't sleep so they chatted about their new home and laughed about nothing and everything; finally toward morning they dosed off for a little while until the sunlight woke them up. The Captain had just given the order to raise the jib and the ship was moving slowly toward shore. They would be home before noon.

That evening after all of their belongings were brought into the house and a nice fire was glowing, they ate the last of the bread and cheese and cold roast beef Anne had packed for their trip. They were sitting in front of the warm fireplace holding each other almost asleep. "I have a surprise for you, Anne," Abraham whispered as he kissed her cheek.

"Oh, Abraham, another one?" she said breathlessly. "What is it?" she asked excitedly.

The beautiful clock standing tall against the wall by the window was more than she could ever have hoped for, it was such a wonderful surprise when she walked into her new home. She had given him a big kiss for it and then asked him to teach her to tell the correct time, he promised her he would and told her it was exactly 10:32 o'clock in the morning. She told herself she would remember that time for the rest of her life.

"Go over to that top cupboard and open it," Abraham said.

"You are spoiling me," Anne said kissing him lightly on his mouth and then she went quickly to the cupboard, but could not quite reach the little wooden latch that locked it. Abraham got up and turned the latch and opened the door for her.

"Oh, my," Anne said, covering her mouth, "Oh, my, oh Abraham, what a wonderful surprise." She couldn't say anything else she was speechless. "My teapot matches these dishes, oh what a wonderful gift," she said and threw her arms around his neck and kissed him passionately.

'This is the perfect time to tell Abraham about our baby,' she thought, and whispered, "I have a surprise for you too."

"Oh?" he said with a look of wonder on his face. 'What kind of a surprise could she have for me,' he thought, he hadn't seen her bring anything in to the house that they hadn't packed together.

"I hope you're not going to be upset with me but I just couldn't tell you about it until we were here safely in our new home," Anne said softly.

"Now you know I won't be upset with you, but maybe you should tell me so I won't stay awake all night wondering about it," he said smiling.

"Well," Anne said with a tear of happiness in her eye, "I'm going to have a baby sometime in early October."

Abraham was stunned for a second, but then he was overjoyed and he pulled her to him and kissed her gently and held her for a full minute before he said anything. "I'm so happy I don't know what to say," he whispered, "you couldn't have given me a nicer surprise," and he kissed her soft lips. Then he said, worried about how hard she had been working getting ready to move, "Are you all right after our long trip and all the lifting and carrying you've been doing?" he asked holding her tighter.

"Of course I am," she replied smiling, "but I didn't tell you sooner because I was afraid you'd put off moving until next year, and I wanted our baby to be born here, and besides, we were almost all packed before I realized I was pregnant."

Abraham kissed her again and holding her close against him said, "You're probably right, but please don't keep anymore secrets from me again, all right?"

Anne whispered, "All right," and smiled inwardly knowing that everything would be wonderful from now on.

Abraham was writing at the table the next morning when Anne woke up so she quietly washed and dressed and started breakfast.

April 9, 1641
Dear Mother, Father, John & Molly,
We moved into our new home here in Barnstable yesterday. We have not unpacked any of Anne's trunks and we have not placed any of the furniture that we brought with us. We have our work cut out for us today, and for several days hence I believe.

I gave her the China dishes that I wrote you about last Christmas, they match the tea set that I gave her. I made a cupboard special to hold them and put them all away in it. When she opened the door last evening she was completely overjoyed. She also gave me a gift that I will cherish forever; she told me that we would be having a baby in early October. I am so happy and I know that she is, too.

Anne has our breakfast ready so I will close this letter now and hope that it finds you well and prosperous.

I leave you in God's hands and will always be your loving son,

Abraham

But it wasn't all right, because several weeks later, on May 1, 1641 Anne began vomiting shortly after Abraham left to go surveying with Thomas and John Lothrop. By that afternoon she had developed a high fever and could hardly stand and almost fainted, she had to lie down.

When Abraham came home about 6 o'clock that evening, there was no sign of Anne who was usually bustling around the fireplace getting his evening meal ready. He called loudly to her while he was taking his boots off but she did not answer. He looked in the shed thinking she might be getting wood for the fireplace, when he didn't see her there he went to the bedroom.

She was lying on the bed, he could tell something was very wrong the minute he opened the door, it smelled like a sick room, of vomit and fever. He ran to the bedside, lit the candle and held it close to Anne's face. She looked flushed and when he put his hand to her forehead he could tell that she had a high fever. He could hardly believe that someone could feel so hot. He put his face to her mouth to see if he could feel her breath on his cheek and then touched her neck, he could feel her pulse. He sat the candle down and ran to the water bucket, found a cloth, wet it and ran back to Anne. When he put the cool cloth to her forehead she turned her head a little and opened her eyes.

Abraham whispered a thankful prayer to God. He knew he had to get help or she would lose the baby, maybe he would lose them both. He told her that he would be right back, he was going to get Jane and Marie. He shoved his feet into his boots, grabbed his coat and ran to the barn.

He practically threw the saddle onto his horse and was headed toward Marie Dimmock's house before he remembered that he had left the candle lit. He decided he had no choice he would have to take a chance and hope that Anne would not knock it over.

Marie Dimmock and Jane Annable were neighbors. Both Marie and Jane were skillful physicians and dispensers of many safe, good, and useful herbal medicines. One of their famous recipes was called new mother's tea made with Red Raspberry Leaf, Dandelion Root, Nettle, Oats, and Yellow Dock all boiled together and made into a tea. They gave this to new mothers who were apt to be anemic or had their children close together. Yellow Dock and Alfalfa Oil made into a salve was used to help heal the wounds of childbirth and both Jane and Marie had the skills to administer them. They were welcomed by every new mother-to-be in Barnstable.

When Marie heard the loud knocking at her door she could tell that someone was in trouble.

Abraham hardly gave her time to say hello when she opened the door. "Please, you must come quickly," Abraham said in a loud breathless voice."

"What is it Abraham," Marie replied in shock. She had never seen him in such a state of mind.

"Anne has a high fever and I'm afraid she'll lose the baby if she hasn't already." He said anxiously.

"Yes, yes, Abraham," Marie said as she pulled her coat from the hook by the door. She knew that something was drastically wrong because Abraham was usually a quiet man, and did not get excited over trivial happenings like some men did.

"I'll get your buggy hitched," he said as he ran toward the barn.

"Thomas, I'll be at Abraham's house, Anne is very sick, I'll be home as soon as I'm through helping her," Marie said to her husband.

He was sitting by the fireplace reading his bible when Abraham knocked on the door and he had heard his neighbor's frightened voice and their conversation. "Yes, dear, be sure to send for me if I can be of any help," he said.

"I will," she said as she ran to the back door and called to the young son of their hired hand, "James, come quickly." When James was almost to the door she said in a loud voice, "Hurry James, Anne Blish needs my help and I want you to go and tell Jane Annable that I will meet her at Mrs. Blish's home as soon as she can get there."

"Yes, ma'am," he said running toward the stable to get his horse.

She turned and went quickly to her room and grabbed her medicine bag and then rushed out of her house toward the barn.

Abraham had the buggy almost hitched to the Dimmock's horse by the time Marie ran into the barn. "You ride on ahead, I'll be right behind you," Marie called. Abraham handed her the reins and then mounted his horse as she climbed into the buggy.

When James arrived at the Annable's home Jane was coming from the shed at the back of the house with an armful of wood. She dropped the wood near the door before James had finished relaying his mistress' message and said, "Oh, James, I'll get my medicine bag, go to the barn and saddle my horse for me please, I'll meet you there in just a minute."

"Yes, Ma'am," he said turning his horse toward the back of the house.

"Sarah, please watch your sisters while I go and help Mrs. Blish, Jane said to her oldest daughter, "tell your father I'll be home as soon as I can."

"Yes, mother," Sarah said, she was used to watching her sisters, her mother was often called upon to help the sick.

It was only about a mile from the Dimmock's to Abraham's house, but it seemed like a hundred by the time they arrived. Marie was out of the buggy and into the house almost as fast as Abraham was. She asked Abraham to open the bedroom window and then get her a pan of cold water and a clean cloth. She took several small packets of herbs from her bag and went to the fireplace and found that the water kettle was full and still hot. She put the herbs in a small kettle and poured some hot water over them then hurried back into the bedroom.

"Abraham, please put some wood on the fire," she said breathlessly, "we'll need boiling water in case we lose the baby." She hadn't intended to scare him by saying such a thing, but it was her way of warning him of what might happen.

He did as he was told trying not to think the worst. "What do you want me to do now?" Abraham said when he came back into the bedroom.

Marie tried not to sound as worried as she really was so she said in a calmer voice, "Maybe you should tend the horses now, Anne will be all right, don't you worry." She patted his arm. She knew it would be better for him if he had something to do. Marie was still washing Anne's face and body with cold water when Jane entered the bedroom.

"Is she going to lose the baby," Jane asked as she put her hand on Anne's forehead.

"I'm not sure, I'll leave that up to the good Lord," she replied sadly. "I have the herbal tea brewing, it should be ready."

"I'll get it," Jane said. She was back in a few minutes with a steaming cup and sat it down on the cammode near the bed.

"We must take her nightgown off," Jane said as she held Anne's feverish head so Marie could spoon little sips of medicine into her mouth. "She needs to be cooled down or her blood will heat so much that it will cause her to miscarry."

Then Jane lifted the covers, she gasped and looked up at Marie and whispered, "Oh, no, we're too late for the little babe, Marie." The bed sheet and Anne's nightgown were covered with blood.

"Well, we're not going to be too late for dear Anne," Marie said determined to bring Anne back to the living.

Jane changed the bedding and was sponging her with cold water by the time Abraham came back in from settling the horses. Marie was holding Anne's head up so she could sip more of the tea. Anne was awake now; the cloth was so nice and cool against her skin. The cold cloth and the taste of the bitter medicine had raised her back into consciousness.

Anne knew she was losing the baby just before Abraham came home from the Lathrop's, but she could do nothing about it. She was so weak she couldn't get out of bed. When the first pain came she fainted and could hardly remember Abraham telling her he was going to get help, it was as if she were dreaming. She looked at Abraham with feverish eyes and started to cry. He knelt beside the bed and took her hand.

"I've lost the baby," she sobbed.

"Yes, but you will be all right, love" he whispered.

"Yes, I know I will, I feel much better now, but I'm so weak and tired and our baby's gone," she said still crying.

"Oh my dearest Anne, please don't worry about our little baby, God needed another angel," he whispered softly. Tears were running down Abraham face and he kissed her hand and then her cheek. "We can have another baby dear Anne, but I just don't know what I'd do if I lost you." He held her tight as she sobbed and their tears mingled together.

Softhearted Jane picked up the soiled bed linen and left the room with tears running down her face.

Marie went out to the well for more cold water, the tears were running down her cheeks, too. When she came back in both she and Jane began washing Anne's still hot body again with more cold water. She wasn't quite as feverish now; the medicine was beginning to work. But they were both still worried because Anne's fever had not broken yet. The cold water and the cold air from the window were helping, but it would probably be morning before she would be able to tell whether Anne would recover completely. Sometimes this kind of a fever left a person with a weakness that they never recovered from.

It was about 1 o'clock in the morning when Jane woke from dozing in the chair by the bed. Anne had been talking in her sleep. "No, God, please don't take my baby," she had shouted.

Marie and Abraham were drinking tea trying to stay awake in the commonroom when they heard Anne's voice. They ran to the bedroom to find Anne thrashing about the bed, the sheets were wrapped about her legs and were wet with perspiration; the quilt was on the floor. Jane was trying to calm her down, but Anne could not hear her. Anne was having hallucinations that it was raining inside the house and everything was wet and ruined.

Abraham took Anne's arms and held them tightly and said loudly, "I'm right here, Anne, I'm right here, I'm helping you Anne, see? Look at me Anne, open your eyes, Anne."

After a minute or so, Anne calmed down and opened her eyes and blinked a few times, then she grabbed Abraham around the neck and cried and cried, hugging him as hard as her weakened body would allow. When she loosened her hold on him he gently laid her back down on the bed and Marie gave her more medicine tea while Jane changed and straightened the bed sheets and quilts.

"She'll be all right now, Abraham," Marie said, "her fever was breaking, that's what caused her to cry out and thrash around."

"But you won't be leaving yet, will you?" Abraham asked worriedly.

"Oh, no, we'll wait till morning," Jane assured him.

Marie said, "I can stay with her all day tomorrow."

Abraham gave her a little smile and took her hand and held it to his chest in a gesture of thanks.

"You'd better get some sleep now," she said softly, "you've had a very trying time of this."

"I'll see about getting our baby properly laid to rest first thing in the morning," he said as he turned toward the commonroom. He hadn't realized just how tired he really was as he lay down on the pallet near the fireplace.

Marie sat down on the chair beside the bed and put her head down on a pillow near Anne's feet, Jane laid down at the foot of the bed. They both were asleep a few minutes later.

Marie knew that tomorrow would be a sad day for Anne, but she was a strong willed lady, with faith in God, believing He would let nothing happen to her that she and He couldn't handle together.

Abraham woke up a little before dawn and could not go back to sleep. He got up quietly and went to the fireplace and put another log on the fire, found the lamp and lit it with a fire stick from the fireplace. He looked in on Anne and she was sleeping peacefully. Both Marie and Jane were still asleep, too. Then he gathered his writing pen and paper and sat down at the table. He had to write to his mother and father. It always made him feel better when he wrote his thoughts on paper.

May 1, 1641

Dear Mother, Father, John and Molly,

We are about settled in our new home and have made many new friends here. Everyone is busy planting and building. Barnstable is growing every day and I hardly have time to keep up with my journal. I am going to try to catch up on it a bit when I finish this letter to you.

I am sorry that this letter has sad news for you. Anne was about four months pregnant and she had a miscarriage, we lost our baby last night. I believe that God needed another angel to watch over us.

Anne is going to be well and Marie Dimmock has assured us that Anne will have other babies, maybe even next year she said.

I hope that all is well with you and hope you receive my letter in good health.

I leave you in God's hands and will always be your loving son,

Abraham

The next morning Abraham laid their tiny infant to rest in the shade of a large maple on the eastern side of their house. Anne watched from their bedroom window with tears flowing down her face. When he finished he came back inside and sat with her on the bed, holding her against him for a long while. They said prayers for their baby and then sent its spirit to heaven to be with God as his littlest angel.

Anne recuperated nicely with the help of her new friends Marie Dimmock and Jane Annable.

Abraham was kept very busy writing in his journal as more and more people were arriving in Barnstable. He recorded marriages and births and tried to add important details to each new arrival's entry.

• • •

On April 3, 1641 William and Elizabeth Lewis Bills had a baby girl they named Sarah. Marie and Jane were with her and both new mother and baby were in good health.

On May 14, 1641 Thomas and Mary Hinckley arrived in Barnstable and moved into their new home. Thomas Hinckley and Mary Richards had just recently married and were from Weymouth, Thomas was 23 and Mary was 18, they were anxious to be a part of the new settlement.

Joseph Hull took it upon himself to break communion with the Barnstable church on May 11, 1641 by joining the Yarmouth church as their Pastor. Members of the Barnstable church were saddened when Joseph asked that both he and his wife be excused from the church. They had been members in good standing for two years, but he was needed as an elder in Yarmouth now. So, at a special town meeting, it was agreed by all council members that they be dismissed from the church immediately and Joseph was excused from any and all official duties in Barnstable.

• • •

Anne cried when she received the good news that she had been expecting from Mary More. On June 4, 1641 Richard and Mary More's third child was born, a little girl, they named her Ellen after Richard's little sister. Anne was delighted to hear that Mary was in good health and wanted to go to Duxbury to see the new baby as soon as possible. Abraham promised her he would take her as soon as she was well enough to travel.

• • •

Matthew Graves was a Tinker going about the settlements patching and mending pewter pots and pans. Most of the time he did a good job and was considered an honorable person. However, in July of 1641 he mended a large pot for Mrs. Lothrop melting one of her good spoons, which she agreed to let him do, but then he had the audacity to charge her for fixing the pot, as if the spoon had belonged to him. She was so angry that she had him arrested but when he explained to Constable Carsely that it was a mistake and promised to give Mrs. Lothrop a new and larger spoon as compensation he was released.

The following week when he was about finished with all the repairs of the village he was heard calling Mrs. Lothrop bad names. When Reverend Lothrop heard about it he sent for Constable Carsely again and when they confronted Tinker Graves he confessed not only to the name-calling but also to kissing Reverend Lothrop's daughter Agatha. He said he was in love with her and would gladly take her for his wife. However, the Reverend would have no tinker for a son-in-law and because Agatha was only 15 years old he refused to allow his daughter to become involved with him. Matthew Graves was sentenced to the whipping post and stocks. He was given 10 lashes after sitting for two days in the stocks. Four days later when he recovered enough to walk, he left Barnstable and it was a long time before he was seen in town again.

• • •

William and Elizabeth Bills' baby Sarah died in her sleep on May 7, she was just a little over a month old. Jane and Marie called her death an unfortunate accident. She had somehow pulled a small blanket over her little face and suffocated. Elizabeth was horrified and heartbroken, they buried her the next day and everyone felt very sorry for Elizabeth and helped her all they could.

• • •

The first criminal case in Barnstable was a matter of public drinking. It concerned two of Henry Bourne's hired men, John Bryant and Daniel Pryor. Henry Bourne had met them drinking on the highway leading to Yarmouth when he was on his way back home after visiting Joseph Hull in a matter of business. Public drunkenness and disorderly conduct were causes for severe punishment and always dealt with immediately. He ordered them back to his house and then summoned Constable Carsely who took them to the stockade.

Constable William Carsely brought them before a special session of the court held on June 2, 1641. Henry testified that the men were falling down and acted very undignified by exposing themselves openly and urinating in the middle of the road.

He reported that he had been able to hear the two men for about two miles before he come upon them. They were shouting and telling bawdy stories and had a gallon jug of rum they were passing back and forth as they staggered toward him. They told him that they were on their way to Yarmouth to get another jug of rum and some tobacco, as no one in town would sell them any.

The two men had no defense at the hearing as they could not remember very much of that day. They also knew that Henry Bourne was a fair man, had always treated them well and would be believed sooner than they would. They smelled of rum and tobacco and they were very dirty which did not help their case at all. It only took a few minutes for them to be found guilty by the jury. They were sentenced to the stockade for six days and to the church woodshed at night. They were given only bread and water three times a day for the first three days and full meals the last three days.

After these six very uncomfortable days and nights they were assigned to the common hay fields to help with the cutting and stacking of hay until haying season was over. Then Constable Carsely escorted them out of town, Daniel Pryor went to Duxbury and John Bryant went to Scituate. Men of such conduct were not welcomed in Barnstable.

• • •

On June 4, 1641, Abraham became a freeman, along with William Betts. A freeman was a gentleman that owned property worth at least two hundred pounds, a member in good standing of the church and was able to afford to wear nice clothes. He also had full civil and political rights as a citizen of Barnstable.

• • •

On June 17, 1641 at the first court at Yarmouth the original purchase of lands in the northeast section of Barnstable was purchased from Chief Nepoyetum and Chief Twacommacus, with Myles

Standish, and Josiah Winslow representing Plymouth Colony. The Barnstable town council promised in consideration that they would build the Indian Chiefs a dwelling house with a chamber, wooden floorboards and a chimney with an oven in it. Land ownership, as white men knew it meant little to the Indians, they believed that all lands except for lands that they were living upon at the moment belonged to Mother Earth. If they could retain the right to hunt and fish and hold small plots to grow their corn and other vegetables, their wants were supplied.

• • •

On August 3, 1641 Samuel and Henrietta Jackson's son was born, they named him Herbert. Their home on Thomas Hinckley's property was completed and they had just recently moved in. Marie and Jane were with her and both new mother and baby were in good health.

• • •

James Cudworth was a fisherman and on September 2, 1641 he hired two Algonquian Indian friends to show him their fishing habits, what baits to use and when the fishing seasons were best in the rivers and bays and at sea. After a long morning of sailing in James' bark they came upon a great Leviathan whale about a half-mile down the beach from Barnstable harbor.

The whale had beached itself on the sandy shore and was still breathing long shallow gasps of air, but it wasn't long before no life was left in the poor beast. The Indians thought that the great creature from the ocean was only there to make their lives miserable for the next few months because the smell would become overwhelming in the very near future and continue for most of the winter. However, being the fisherman that he was, James Cudworth knew that this wondrous creature called a whale would provide at least a hundred barrels of oil for the people of Barnstable and its bones would be made into useful utensils.

James immediately sent one of the Indians into town to find as many people as they could to help cut the blubber of the great beast into easy to handle slabs. He told them to ask the women for the loan of as many boiling pots as they could spare. He then set about finding stones to make crude hearths to set the pots on and enough driftwood to keep the fires going for the next few days.

Many people took turns keeping the fires hot and the pots full of blubber. Huge amounts of oil for lamps were derived from this wonderful find on the beach and it was divided among the people of Barnstable each providing their own kegs and barrels. Though the work was hard, it was well worth it. The white man looked upon the great whale as a Godsend, the Indians looked upon it as something evil. Many people talked about it for months remembering John Barker's whale in Duxbury.

• • •

The harvest season went by without much of anything happening except for the courting of Alice Layton by Roger Goodspeed. Roger was a quiet man but everyone knew that he was in love with Alice and had been since earlier in the spring when he met her.

Alice was almost as shy; however, she made it known to all that she and Roger were to be married before the end of the year. She convinced her father to talk to Roger and shortly afterward Roger proposed to her. She took it upon herself to make arrangements with the Reverend for their wedding. Roger Goodspeed married Alice Layton on December 1, 1641 in the Barnstable Church. Everyone in town attended the wedding.

Patricia Louise Blish Gould

CHAPTER NINE
1642

On January 23, 1642 Anne's horse Penny had her colt, a little mare she named Star. Star had a five pointed white mark on her brow and the rest of her was completely copper colored. She was beautiful.

"I'll train her just like I did Penny," Anne told Abraham.

"She's a beautiful little horse," he said. Then he laughed and put his arms around his pretty wife, "I told you my old plow horse would make beautiful babies."

Anne blushed and said, "Yes you did," she looked at him and blushed even more.

Abraham kissed his embarrassed wife and then they watched as Penny nudged her baby into a standing position and waited until little Star found her mother's teat and took her first mouth full of warm milk.

Abraham piled stacks of hay all around the stall to keep Penny and Star warm and then they went into the house.

He was proud of his farm it was growing fast. The cow he purchased in Duxbury and brought to Barnstable had two calves now and she was going to be pastured with the other cows and Mr. Linnett's prize bull in the spring. Now they had a new colt, his farm was prospering. Cows were selling for 5 pounds each, goats 8 to 10 shillings and hogs were 5 or 6 shillings each.

• • •

A good farmer planned his chores by the season. In March the tapping of the Maple tree produced sap for the boiling of Maple syrup. In April Abraham, along with the other farmers in town had the worse job known to them; they had to get the winters accumulation of manure spread onto their fields. These were not happy weeks for Anne or any of the other women in town. When their hungry, ill-smelling men came in for their meals their odor lingered throughout the house for the rest of the day.

After the second day, Anne decided she would meet Abraham outside with his lunch and made sure that he left his smelly clothes in the shed when he came home in the evening. She also had clean warm water in the outside wash tub ready for him to bathe in before she allowed him to enter her house. He complained that it was too cold to be practically naked out of doors, but she promised him she would see that he was warmed up properly as soon as he came in smelling nicely.

Sheep washing came the first of May at the Indian ponds that were perfect for the job; the ponds had a little cove with a sandy beach and a long stretch of shallow water. On the pasture hills above the cove children gathered with their dinner pails for this favorite holiday. After the washing, came days of shearing. Expert Edmund Meigs of South Sandwich was in high demand for his shearing skills and made his rounds teaching and helping those that needed his expertise.

Then followed several days of cold, dreary rain, "the sheep storm" it was called, because inevitably after the poor sheep were shorn of their warm fleece it would rain and they would have to stand dripping wet and shivering in the barnyards and meadows.

The women liked the coming of summer though it meant that everyone had to get up very early. The men had to go into the marsh to cut their hay and wheat and the women had to fix their breakfast and then pack their dinner pails by 4 o'clock in the morning. The good farmer had his English hay in the barn by the 4th of August, and if he had the luck of good weather, the cornfields would be in tassel by the 10th of August. The women made jugs of switchel, a nourishing drink of water, cider vinegar, ginger and a little sugar, for their husbands and they kept this nourishing drink cool by setting the jugs in a nearby brook. The women did not mind rising early because it meant long blissful hours when the men were out of their way. However, for the men it was another story, they never looked forward to this tedious job because they and their poor beasts suffered with the bites of black flies that also crawled into every crevice of their bodies.

Before it was time to shuck the corn there were days when the barn floors had to be cleared for the threshing of the wheat, rye, oats and flax. Some of the seed was saved for next year's sowing and the rest was bagged and taken to the mill for grinding. The flaxseed was bagged and taken to a press where the oil was extracted and the broken straw was swingled and hatcheled and the fibers were spun into thread to make linen cloth.

Corn was dried and ground into corn meal. Wheat was ground into flour. Barley was thrashed and put into cloth bags and stored high and dry also. The women used this grain to make pancakes, and to thicken and flavor soups. Honey was also produced by a few of the farmers and used to sweeten cakes and pies when sugar was not available.

After the harvest season the women worked hard to preserve their produce for winter. Most of the vegetables were dried and stored in high, dry places such as the attics of the houses.

In fall and winter Cod and Sea bass were caught daily and cleaned and hung in each fisherman's fish house. The Indians provided wild ducks, geese, swans, turkeys and deer to the townspeople in trade for breads and corn cakes or other goods. Sometimes the townspeople even paid them to hunt for them.

In the orderly planning of the year the winter days were spent in the woods cutting firewood for the next year or laying up stone walls. In late winter lambing had to be carefully watched. And then a good farmer's routine would start all over again and he would set his buckets and taps to the Maple trees.

• • •

On February 8, 1642 John Coggin was born to Henry and Abigail Coggin. He was baptized on February 12 at the Barnstable Church. Henry was not at home when Abigail's time came; he was in England on business. Before he left Barnstable he employed his widowed sister Mary Gaunt to live with them and help Abigail with the new baby. Abigail liked Mary but she wanted Henry with her or at least nearby when her baby came.

"It seems like he is gone most of the time," she pouted to Mary every time he left.

"Stop complaining, look at all the money he brings home for you to spend and all the presents he brings you," Mary said. Mary was not an affectionate person and was very jealous of Abigail. Abigail looked like a porcelain doll she looked like a cornhusk doll.

• • •

Abraham was elected by the Barnstable Town Council on March 7, 1642 to hold the office of Grand Juror from the town of Barnstable for the colony of New Plymouth for the ensuing year. He knew he would have much to write in his journal this year.

Much drunkenness and uncleanness among the newcomers of the colonies was beginning to be seen. Even knowing the punishment for these actions the men continued to find a reason in their own minds for swilling the jugs of rum that were easily found at any of the harbors where the ships were docked. Beside the drunkenness laws that were broken there seemed to be more robberies, fighting adultery and even murder. The law read that if a man did smite or wound another with a full purpose or desire to kill him, yet he did not die, the magistrate could not take away the would be murderers life. In the case of adultery, if it is admitted that the body was not actually defiled, then death could not be inflicted. In the case of sodomy and bestiality, if there was no penetration, then a death sentence could not be served.

• • •

Joseph Hull and his wife were restored to fellowship on March8, 1642 when they moved back to Barnstable from Yarmouth and acknowledged their sins and renewed their covenant with the Barnstable church. At this meeting it was agreed that they could return as full members of the Barnstable Church if they pledged their allegiance in front of all the members of the congregation. They had asked for forgiveness at the council meeting for their sins against the church with heads bowed. They were granted their request after they promised never to leave the church again.

• • •

Thomas and Marie Dimmock's second baby Mehitabel was born on April 18, 1642. She was baptized the following Sunday, April 22, 1642. Things went well with Marie's pregnancy this time and her baby was healthy. Jane Annable was with her when her time came.

• • •

On May 21, 1642 John Carsely, and his wife Alice, were presented before the court for public fornication. This was not tolerated by the Church, or by the townspeople.

The day before Reverend John Lothrop saw them cavorting and kissing in the orchard that bordered his land. The Reverend knew they were married but could not understand their behavior, he watched them for a few minutes thinking that surely they were on their way home. However, when he looked toward the orchard again about a half-hour later he saw them both lying on the ground beneath an apple tree. He was appalled and immediately took his coat from the rack by the door and headed toward the orchard.

When he was within hearing distance to called loudly, "John Carsely."

There was much giggling and a scrambling of clothes and patting their hair. He called again, "John Carsely, just what are you doing!" The Reverend's voice did not intone a question; it was indeed an exclamation of disgust.

"We were not doing anything Reverend," John said in a husky voice. Alice was still giggling.

"I know that you are married but you have no right to act this way in broad daylight where you can be seen by the public," the Reverend said loudly. "I have no choice but to take you both to court and will do so this very day," he continued.

Alice stopped her twiddling and gasped. "We haven't done anything wrong, Reverend, honestly," she said trying to sound innocent.

"I happen to know that you did young lady," the Reverend replied, "and I will see to it that you both are punished. This sort of thing may be tolerated in the old country, but not here," he was still angry that anyone he knew would be bold enough to be fornicating in the open like animals. 'It is cold, too,' he thought to himself, 'they could catch their death.' He told them to go on home and he turned on his heel and headed toward Abraham Blish's house. "What is this world coming to," he muttered as he stomped away.

The two were taken to court the following day and after the Reverend finished his detailed description of the scene he had witnessed John Carsely was sentenced to be given 10 lashes, Alice's punishment was to sit in the stocks while the punishment was inflected upon her husband. The punishment was duly performed on May 22, 1642. John was also fined 3 shillings and 5 pence for breach of public peace and within a week or so they moved to Yarmouth.

• • •

William and Alice Crocker's son Samuel was born on June 3, 1642 and baptized on June 3, 1642. Jane Annable and Marie Dimmock helped Alice and her delivery was easy, her baby was small but he seemed healthy and nursed well.

• • •

On June 10, 1642 John Humfry was called back to England to help his wife Judith settle her mothers estate. When Judith's mother, Mrs. Monroe became ill during the fall of 1641, she decided she should go back to help care for her mother, she had missed her mother dearly and didn't want her to die alone. After eight long months of a terrible suffering Mrs. Monroe finally passed away leaving Judith to sell everything. Judith, knowing nothing of these matters, sent for her husband. John had no choice but to leave his daughters, Mercy 8, and Caroline 9, in the care of his hired help, Nathan and Catherine Johnson.

Nathan Johnson was a boisterous man and was very demanding especially when he drank too much beer. Catherine was a big stout woman always complaining that her head ached or her feet hurt or her legs were swollen. Especially when there was work to do, but everyone suspected it was just her way of getting attention from Nathan. Jane and Marie gave her herbs for a tea that should have helped her, but they didn't think she took them.

Before John Humfrey left for England he promised to pay them extra wages when he returned. He was sure they had the means to care for his girls as he was paying them monthly wages now. He had paid for their passage to New Plymouth and in return they worked for him for five years and had obtained their freedom from indentured servitude just last year. They had gained their status as good citizens of the community and were both members in good standing of the Barnstable church. When their servitude ended they had saved enough money to purchase two acres of land and start a small farm and were successful in making a living growing cucumbers, squash and pumpkins.

John thought that the girls would be more comfortable with them than anyone else because they knew Catherine so well, having grown up seeing her everyday since they were babies.

Catherine hired a servant girl named Hessie who was about 16 years old, shortly after they purchased their land the summer before. Hessie loved the two little girls. They reminded her of her little sisters she had left behind in England.

Hessie lived in the shed attached to the back of the Johnson's house that she had furnished with other peoples thrown away junk.

Nathan hired Jonas Williams, a young man about the age of 18, the same time Hessie was hired by Catherine. Jonas was new in Barnstable, having just arrived from New Plymouth and needed work. There were many young men roaming from town to town looking to be hired during the summer months. He was allowed to sleep in a corner of the barn that had been partitioned off from the cows with pieces of slab wood. He had an old mattress and an old chair that he had found and he made a table from a couple of old boards. It was the best home he ever had.

From the minute Jonas laid eyes on Hessie he started leering at her. He was always trying to kiss her and would touch her breasts or bottom every time he came near her. She tried to avoid him as much as possible, but there were times when their duties coincided with each other's and she couldn't escape his hands.

He would catch her feeding the chickens and pretend to help her by reaching into the pail of feed she held in her arms and 'accidently' touch her breast. When she was milking the cow he would sneak around in front of her and try to look up her dress. Hessie was a little afraid of him, but she thought that he was harmless enough if she didn't make him mad at her. She didn't smile at him very much and she always told him to leave her alone, he would just laugh and give her a leering grin.

127

About six weeks after he moved in to the Johnson's barn, Jonas had his way with Hessie. One evening he caught her on the pathway between the barn and her shed. He put his hand over her mouth and dragged her back into the barn. He held her down and tore her clothes off from her saying in a harsh whisper, "If you scream I'll beat you real bad." He took his hand from her mouth and pulled her tight against him while he loosened his belt and let his pants fall down around his feet.

She struggled and cried and pleaded with him and begged him not to hurt her. "Please don't hurt me," Hessie sobbed, "I'm not going to scream." She gasped when she saw his erection. "Oh God please help me," she sobbed.

"God can't help you now Hessie," he said laughing at her, "I've got you right where I want you."

Hessie struggled and moaned when he entered her, but he didn't care how much pain she was in, he wanted only satisfaction for himself.

He was smothering her with his large body and she could hardly breathe, she fainted. When she came to, he was pulling up his pants. She turned her head and tried to set up, but he pushed her back down onto the straw with his dirty shoe as he pulled a harness strap from the beam over his head. "I'm going to make sure you won't tell anyone about this," he said as he raised the strap over his head and turned her over with his foot.

"No, no," she pleaded, "I won't tell anyone, honest."

But he beat her anyway; on her naked back and buttocks, "One, two, three," she heard him say, and she fainted again.

She could hardly move when she woke up, but somehow she managed to crawl back to her shed. She washed herself in her water bucket, slumped down on her bed and cried herself to sleep. She thought he enjoyed beating her as much as he did raping her.

Several days after Jonas had dragged her into the barn he told her that Nathan knew what she had let him do and that if she didn't let them both do it Nathan was going to send her away.

She couldn't believe this was happening to her. 'God, what have I done, please help me,' she prayed silently. Jonas never beat her again, but he still threatened her every time he raped her. She didn't move or plead or anything, she just lay there waiting until it was over for Jonas and then Nathan would take his turn. She always cried herself to sleep on those nights

Finally, after several months of this treatment the inevitable happened, she was pregnant. She was almost grateful because when she was about six or seven months along, they didn't bother her as much and left her alone except for calling her bad names and laughing at her.

Now, eight months pregnant, she was big and fat in the belly carrying a baby she resented. She felt so alone and frightened all the time.

Catherine had assumed that she had been willing to be with Jonas and said as much when Hessie tried to tell her what both men were doing to her. She cried and tried to convince her that she was not that kind of girl. But the more she asked Catherine for help the more Catherine laughed at her. She knew she would have to do something soon, knowing that Catherine would give her no help when the time came to have her baby. She wasn't sure if she loved it or hated it. She could feel it kicking more and more and her back hurt every night. She was so tired.

It was about ten days after John Humfrey left for England that Mercy and Caroline Humfrey ran away from the Johnson's house to the Rev. Lothrop's rectory. They knocked loudly on the door and shouted his name. The Reverend was appalled at the sight of them when he opened the door. They were crying and sobbing and very upset.

"What has happened to you," he asked as he put his hands out toward them to guide them into his home. Their hair was messy, with straw sticking out of it, and their clothes were dirty and torn. They began to cry even harder and were shaking all over.

"What is it dear?" Elizabeth Lothrop asked entering into the room to see what the fuss was all about.

She couldn't believe her eyes when she saw the two little girls. She immediately took charge taking both girls into her arms and comforting them. After a minute she led them across the room to the fireplace. She told one of her girls to fetch them a drink of water, plucked some of the hay from their hair and sat them down on the bench near the warm hearth still holding their hands.

Mercy, after sipping the cold water, and still shaking, whispered, "Mr. Johnson hurt my underneath and Jonas Williams hurt Caroline in the same place."

Elizabeth gasped and looked up at the Reverend who was standing there speechless, and said, "John you must do something about this, these children have been severely damaged."

129

John gathered himself up and said, "I certainly will," and turned, took his coat from the wall rack and stormed out of the door.

Elizabeth gently urged the girls into her daughter's room and settled them down on the bed. She found clean nightclothes and helped them wash themselves and get dressed. She persuaded them to allow her to examine them with her eyes only and found there to be blood on them as well as their under clothes. She then sent her oldest daughter to the Dimmock's home to fetch Marie.

Elizabeth was so angry that two grown men would do such a thing to small children, especially in this new land where everyone felt safe from crime and criminals. It seemed that everyday, something bad was happening. Fighting, arguing, thievery and now this. 'What could happen next,' she wondered?

The first place John Lothrop headed was to Abraham Blish's house his closest neighbor. He knew that Constable Carsely would be away for a few more days, he had taken a drunken man to Plymouth the day before.

When John and Abraham arrived at the Johnson's home Mrs. Johnson came to the door and as usual was still in her nightgown with a shawl thrown over her shoulders. She was evidently eating her lunch, though it was only about 11 o'clock in the morning, because when she greeted the men with a mouth full of corn bread she sprayed little bits of food all over them. "Hello, Reverend, Mr. Blish, how do you do," she said.

The men at her door did not return her greeting. They were both extremely upset. Reverend Lothrop, with a scowl on his face asked in a gruff voice, "Where is Nathan?"

With a startled look she said "He must be doing chores, or in the garden, I haven't seen him since he left at sunrise." They turned without thanking her and headed toward the barn.

Nathan and Jonas were headed toward the house and were surprised to see the Reverend and Abraham coming toward them.

"Good day," called Nathan, what brings you here, would you like to help us with our cucumber harvest," Nathan said grinning as they approached each other.

"Not today," Abraham said with a frown.

John Lothrop was in no mood to joke, as he said in a low growling voice, "I have the Humfrey girls at my house and I want you to tell me exactly what happened to them, and I want the truth, now!"

Nathan could tell by the tone of the Reverend's voice that he was very angry, he had never seen him like this before. A frightened look came over his face, but he managed to keep his voice from shaking as he asked, "Now, Reverend, what do you mean, the truth about what?"

It seemed to the Reverend that Nathan grew a little shorter and he started to shake. Jonas was shaking too, his knees grew weak and he reached out to the fence for support.

Abraham reached a hand out toward the front of Nathan's coat, but the Reverend put his hand on Abraham's arm and said with his teeth clenched, "Nathan Johnson, you will tell me now, exactly what you did to the little Humfry girls this morning."

By this time Nathan could not help himself, he turned white and then stammered, "It wasn't our fault, it wasn't my fault, it was his fault," he whimpered as he looked at Jonas, "the girls were to blame, they were showing themselves to us. You know Catherine," he whined, "with her being sick all the time I wasn't able to keep myself under control. A man is a man, you know," he was so scared he was blubbering.

By this time, Abraham had had enough of this sniveling fool's stuttering. "Tell us right now what happened this morning or you shall be put in the stockade immediately without a trial."

Nathan could tell that Abraham meant every word of the threat and in a shaking voice he said, "The girls were in the barn feeding the chickens and gathering the eggs with Hessie." He took a big gulp of air and continued, "Hessie ain't any good anymore, being big and pregnant, what is a man to do when he has the urge to relieve himself."

Jonas Williams had nothing to say. In fact he was so frightened that he wet himself right in front of Reverend Lothrop and Abraham. This was a sign of guilt as far as they were concerned, and both men were taken to the stockade that very morning where it was agreed upon that they would spend the night and would be tried the next day.

Hessie testified in tears at the trial that she was present when Nathan and Jonas raped Mercy and Caroline Humfry. Her story was heart rending and by the time she was through with her testimony everyone was horrified at the way she had been treated during the past year.

She told the jurors that she and the two little girls were in the barn feeding the chickens when Jonas and Nathan came in.

"I knew by the look on their faces what they were about to do," she said in a shaky voice. "They had been drinking rum again, I could smell it on them. So I told the girls to go and get another pail of chicken feed from the grain bin. I thought I might be able to persuade them to let the girls go in the house and help Catherine. I didn't want them to see what was about to happen to me. But Nathan said 'No' in a very frightening voice, they were to stay there."

Her lips quivered as she continued, "I tried to protect the little girls by getting in front of them and I told the men to leave them alone and take me. But I guess they had other things on their minds because they only laughed at me."

Hessie had tears running down her checks as she remembered the horrible scene. "Then they grabbed some ropes, tied the little girls hands behind their backs and then tied the other end of the ropes to their own wrists. I was still trying to make them let the girls go and I pulled on the ropes trying to get them loose. Then Jonas yelled at me to shut my mouth and he hit me in the face with the back of his hand, and I fell to the floor, I knew it was no use talking to them any more."

Hessie put her head down and covered her face with her hand-kerchief for a minute quietly sobbing. Abraham asked, "Are you all right, Hessie?"

She shook her head yes, blew her nose and lifted her face up toward the ceiling and closed her eyes for a minute praying for strength and then continued, "Then they made me take my dress off and they both took turns trying to have relations with me. I kept telling the girls to keep their eyes shut, don't cry think of the birds singing. 'Please, don't cry', I kept saying to them. But the men were hurting me, and my belly is so big, they couldn't satisfy themselves and they were so rough that I was afraid that I was going to faint. I begged them to please stop, I thought I was going to have birthing pains and my baby was kicking so hard that I thought I would have my baby right then, it hurt me so much," she was sobbing again.

Hessie blew her nose again and took a deep breath and said in an angry voice, "That was when they untied the girls and tore their dresses and forced them down into the hay. The girls cried and screamed and kicked as their bodies were being invaded and I was pleading with those horrible men to leave them alone and I was crying, too."

The courtroom grew silent waiting for Hessie to continue, she sniffed and said, "When the men finally rolled off of them I screamed at the girls to run. 'Run,' I said, 'Go to Reverend Lothrop's house,' and I was sobbing. 'Run as fast as you can and don't stop until you get there,' I screamed after them."

"The men were both laughing and pulling their breeches up as I carefully stood up, they didn't pay any attention to me as I walked slowly back to my shed, I had to vomit and I had to lay down. I prayed that the men would not follow the girls, I guess they probably didn't dare," she concluded lowering her eyes to the floor.

After a few seconds of silence, Abraham asked her if she could remember anything else.

Hessie lifted her head and looked at the two rapists and said between clenched teeth, "I have never hated anyone as much as I do Jonas Williams. That monster is the father of my baby and he has been forcing himself of me for months." Hessie wiped her eyes and lifted her chin and continued, "Nathan Johnson has also been having relations with me against my will and I hate him, too. I tried to tell Catherine, but she called me bad names and told me it was all my fault and she could do nothing about it."

The jury had listened to Hessie's testimony carefully, but despite the opinions of the Reverend and Abraham the jury found the men not guilty of a capital offense of Massachusetts's law, which was punishable by death. Nathan Johnson and Jonas Williams were however, each given 10 lashes with a 'cat-o-nine-tails' and both were fined 20 pounds each. They each survived their whipping and Nathan paid his fine but Jonas was unable to pay his so he was taken to Plymouth and sent back to England.

The children were not at the trial. They were taken to live with an aunt in Yarmouth until their father and mother came home. Marie Dimmock talked to them and explained to them what had happened and assured them that they would be all right. She also told them that their mother would explain further when they were older.

Hessie was taken in to live with the Lothrop's until after her baby girl was born. She then moved to Boston where she found a job as a nanny. The new family allowed her to tend her own child while caring for theirs and she eventually married a nice young man and lived peacefully as a well respected lady for many years.

• • •

The laws governing the New Plymouth colony were somewhat perplexing. The punishment did not always fit the crime. But being that the church was involved with the government some matters became very complex.

For instance, on August 5, 1642 Thomas Granger, a young man of 16 years, who happened to be a friend of Jonas Williams, was seen committing buggery with a mare in Laurence Litchfield's pasture. Thomas was accused and then confessed to having sex with the mare at several different times.

Laurence Litchfield feeling sorry for the homely young lad had hired him about six months before to clean the barn, pigpen, and chicken coop.

Thomas was quite an ugly little fellow, very thin and short in stature. His hair was like straw and stuck up all over his head. Of course, he was quite unclean and ill mannered as no one had ever taught him anything. Thomas was orphaned since he was about 6 years old and was brought to New Plymouth to live with a man that used him as an animal. He was given an old blanket and he had to sleep in the barn. Once in awhile he was given an old shirt or pair of breeches, he never had any shoes. In winter someone might throw him a pair of old boots and a coat which he kept hidden in an old bucket that he found. He was not allowed to eat with the other members of the household and was punished if anyone else did something wrong. He was called 'scapegoat' by the other servants, or sometimes just 'goat'.

On the day Thomas was seen in the pasture in an obscene act with a mare he was taken directly to the stocks. At his trial he confessed that he had used this mare as well as a cow, two goats, five sheep, two calves and a turkey for this purpose over the past few months.

Thomas confessed that when he was a young boy back in England, a man that he knew had used such actions and he had watched this man many times and did not know it was wrong. The man had told him once when he had seen Thomas watching him that it was human nature and nothing to be ashamed of. As Thomas grew older and the forces of nature turned his body into that of a young man it was only natural for him to act out what he had seen.

Thomas was indicted in court on August 10, 1642 and sentenced to death by hanging. But before he was to be hanged, and as part of his punishment, he had to dig a large pit and watch all of the animals that he had buggered be killed.

It took about a month to find the animals that Thomas had used and bring them back to Barnstable. Their owners were more than willing to turn them over to the Constable when they were told what had been done to them. Thomas cried as the animals were bludgeoned before him.

Everyone thought that he was ashamed for what he had done, but he was crying because he hated to see an animal being beaten. He was use to cruelty being done to him, but it hurt to see animals suffer. He had always tried to soothe a horse after its owner had whipped it. He would rub ointment on the welts and talk to it until it stopped shaking. Whenever he buggered the animals he was careful not to hurt them, except for the turkey which he was never able to catch afterward.

When the animals were all dead they were buried together in the large pit that Thomas had dug. No use was made of any part of them.

Thomas was executed by hanging on September 8, 1642. His death was a lesson to those who were not careful about the people they invited into their life, as one wicked person may infest another. Some people believed that Thomas Granger's death was much less cruel than his life had been.

• • •

Two days later on September 10, 1642 Joseph Hull and his wife left Barnstable for good. They went to Dover, New Hampshire to minister at the church there. Reverend Hull had studied theology and was a minister in his own right, but his preaching wasn't needed in Barnstable. It had been only six months since he and his wife returned to Barnstable for the second time and he tried to find his place among the men again but it seemed that he could still not see eye to eye with some of them.

As a juror at both trials Joseph Hull wanted Jonas Williams and Nathan Johnson to be hanged and he wanted Thomas Granger to be sent back to England. The rest of the jurors opposed him and it was then that he decided that he would never be able to enjoy living in Barnstable. This time many townspeople conceded that

Joseph was not happy in their town and they wished him well in his new home in Dover.

Ralph Partridge had many of the same feelings. He was also a minister and decided about this same time and for many of the same reasons to move. He packed his family up a week after his friend Joseph Hull left and moved to Duxbury to serve there as a minister and magistrate.

• • •

Roger Goodspeed and his wife Alice had a baby boy they named Nathaniel on October 6, 1642. Many tongues stopped wagging then; Alice and Roger had been married for 10 months and 5 days. Alice looked very pregnant early in the spring so everyone assumed that she and Roger had not been able to wait to consummate their marriage on their wedding night.

• • •

On December 4, 1642 Nathaniel and Hannah Bacon moved into their new house that had taken Nathaniel nearly a year to build. It was two stories high and built in the common style. He used oak timbers that were cut from the surrounding forest and hewed by hand. He had no hired hands so he had only himself to rely on unless a good neighbor found the time to help him. In those early years many men worked together cutting down and sawing into boards the huge oak trees found in the nearby forest. This was also necessary to clear fields for their cattle and farmland.

Many homes were built during this time with the idea that they needed protection from the Indians. Not unlike most of the newly built homes in the colonies Nathaniel's home was about 22 feet in front and 26 feet in the rear. The lower story was divided into three rooms. The front room was 16 feet square, with low walls and a large beam across the ceiling. The bedroom floor was elevated two feet above the other floors to give more height to the cellar underneath it. The second story also had low walls and was divided into three rooms corresponding with those in the lower story.

Some of the ovens were built on the outside of the house with the mouth opening into one corner on the backside. The cooking area was very small with the fireplace taking up most of the space on the north wall especially when the oven opened into the room instead of outside. Hannah was pleased that the fireplace in her new house opened into the cooking area though it was small it was much easier to bake bread. In the winter she didn't have to go outside through the snow every time she baked and the oven also stayed hot longer and the food cooked better. Hannah had requested that Nathan build her oven the same way after she visited Anne Blish's new house. Abraham had built her oven to open into the cooking area and though it made her house quite warm in the summer she told Hannah it was much easier for baking to have the oven door open inside the house.

The chimney was of stone and the fireplace in the front room was eight feet wide, four feet deep and with a mantle so high that a tall person could walk under it by stooping just a little. When a fire was built in the center of the fireplace on a cold winter evening a seat in the chimney corner was a luxury. There was a fireplace in the front bedchamber as well. The windows were small and covered with oiled paper that was used instead of glass.

The newlyweds were very happy in their new home and Nathaniel stepped into his role as a property owner, and businessman with more energy and industry then ever. His ambition to succeed more than compensated for his lack of wealth and education.

• • •

Much was happening in the Plymouth Colonies during the early days as the little towns were growing and continued to flourish. One important event occurred in Plymouth that concerned everyone and Abraham recorded it in his journal.

A special council meeting was held in Plymouth on November 2, 1642 and when it was over Reverend Charles Chauncy was asked to leave the Plymouth church after 3 years of service. He had been causing much commotion throughout the colonies with some of his beliefs. Though he was well educated and admired by many it was decided that his services were no longer needed.

The mothers especially were concerned because of the way their children were being baptized by him. He believed in putting the whole body under water when he baptized them instead of just a sprinkling or pouring of water on the heads of the children. Reverend Chauncy would hold the young people's heads under water while saying such long prayers that they would faint with near drowning. He also wanted to hold baptismal services during the cold winter months and many people would catch horrible colds because of his misguided beliefs.

Patience Hurst Cobb, wife of Henry Cobb and the mother of two young boys, John and James, testified at the council meeting that she was extremely upset by his actions when he baptized her sons as babies ten years earlier. She reminded Governor Bradford in front of the council members that she had reported her own experience to him at that time. "I shall never forget that when the Reverend baptized James he was nearly drowned," she said. She told the council that when her son James was released from Mr. Chauncy's grip he went limp in the water. "I grabbed him from Mr. Chauncy's hand with such force that water poured from his mouth in a torrent," she said angrily. She didn't realize that if she had not done so the boy would have died by drowning. Being so afraid that her son was dead she had instinctively grabbed him about the belly forcing the water out of him thus saving his life. Henry and Patience Cobb moved to Scituate shortly after that and from there they moved on to Barnstable.

Mr. Chauncy was disgusted at Patience's actions at that time and made a big fuss saying, "You're just a doting mother and you will ruin your children's lives by coddling them." He was not concerned at all about the boy and said sharply, "If the children drown as I am baptizing them, they will surely go to heaven."

Now ten years later he was still baptizing children the same way and after watching a boy about the age of ten sputter and gag and vomit, the mother of a young girl caught her daughter to her breast and refused to let the minister touch her. Mr. Chauncy's hold on the young girl was so tight that he nearly pulled both her and her mother into the water. But the mother refused to let him take her little girl from her arms and she stormed off along with many of the other people who had been waiting to be baptized. That afternoon when so many people protested to Governor Bradford he promised to hold a special town council meeting the next day.

Now at this special meeting many witnesses testified before the Governor about Mr. Chauncy's unbecoming behavior and cruel actions. After Mrs. Cobb gave her tearful account of her son James' near drowning the council decided to request Mr. Chauncy's resignation. The Reverend was so irate that he stormed out of the meetinghouse and went straight home and packed his belongings and moved to Scituate.

• • •

Mr. Ralph Partridge of Duxbury was asked to replace Mr. Chauncy's position in Plymouth and he is serving his congregation well. In 1631 Reverend Partridge studied theology and graduated from Trinity College in Cambridge, England and served as a pastor there for three years. When he became an ordained minister in 1634 he moved to Kent and served as pastor of a church there until he decided to immigrate to Boston in 1636. He served in the Church of Boston as a lay preacher for two years and then moved to Duxbury in 1638 and had been the pastor there for four years when he was asked to replace Mr. Chauncy.

The Reverend Partridge had also studied judicial law and punishment and his views on these subjects were well respected by everyone. He believed in the death penalty to both parties committing sodomy; to both the woman as well as man for bestiality; and he believed that it was unlawful to inflict pain of any kind on anyone. He disapproved of such things as wringing the nose, pulling ears, or other forms of torture to extract a confession of a crime of any kind from an accused person. He was convinced that a magistrate was bound to extract a confession from the accused by force of argument alone.

Many times he had drawn an acknowledgment of the truth from men with only his words, but by no means did he ever inflict violence or threaten to inflict pain from any of the accused in fear they just might be innocent victims themselves. His motto was that if a man were guilty as accused, he would be compelled to be his own accuser sooner or later. Trying to force a confession was, in Mr. Partridge's opinion, against the rule of justice. He conceived that in the case of capital crimes, there could be no safe proceedings unto judgment without two witnesses, unless there was evidence produced or available to prove that only one witness would be all that was necessary to convict the accused.

Patricia Louise Blish Gould

CHAPTER TEN
1643

On April 18, 1643 the funeral of William Brewster was held in Plymouth. Abraham and Anne Blish traveled up the coast by schooner to Richard and Mary More's home in Duxbury and from there the four of them traveled by horse the rest of the way to Plymouth together. On their way to the church Richard told Abraham and Anne about William Brewster, the man that raised him, and the role he played in creating the Plymouth Colonies.

William Brewster was born about 1562 in Scrooby, Nottinghamshire, England and at the age of 20 he and several close friends organized a Separatist congregation in Scrooby. He preached in the name of the Lord Jesus in England and fled to Holland in fear of arrest when the English authorities began to search for the publisher of certain controversial books and pamphlets, which were being circulated in England. In Holland he taught Latin and set up a printing press and carried on with his religious beliefs until it became unsafe for him there. After a few months, he managed to get passage aboard the Mayflower when it sailed to New Plymouth. Mr. and Mrs. Brewster left three of their children behind in Holland.

When my parents died my younger brother, Thomas and I were assigned to William Brewster and his wife Mary to be cared for by them. So, of course, we came to Plymouth on the Mayflower with them along with two of their sons, Love and Wrestling. Two of the children they left in Holland came over to New Plymouth about the year 1627. Their daugh-

ter Fear married Bartholomew Brewster, a second cousin in 1629 and came to New Plymouth the following year.

When Mr. William Brewster came to Plymouth he was in his late fifty's and he suffered as much as everyone else did, often eating nothing but fish. He never drank anything except water and labored in the fields along with everyone else. He was a reverend elder of the first church service in New Plymouth and a dear and loving friend of Governor William Bradford."

"By the way Governor Bradford will give the eulogy today," Richard said interrupting him self. He cleared his throat and then continued, there were tears in his eyes.

"Mr. Brewster preached twice every Sabbath and brought many to God by his ministry. He was a wise man, discreet and well-spoken, having a grave and deliberate voice and a very cheerful spirit. He was very sociable and pleasant among his friends, and had a humble and modest mind and peaceable disposition, under-valuing his own abilities and sometimes over-valuing others. He would tell you plainly of your faults, both public and privately, but in such a way that it was usually well taken. He was a wonderful father to me.

He was tenderhearted and compassionate with everyone, but none displeased him more than those who were haughty and proud and exalted themselves. He preached wonderful sermons, ripping up the heart and conscience before God in the humble confession of sin and begging the mercies of God in Christ for the pardon of it. He thought it best for ministers to pray oftener and divide their prayers rather than have them long and tedious. He was careful to preserve good order and purity in the doctrine and communion in the government of the church, and to suppress any error or contention that might begin to arise. William Brewster must be about 81 years of age; no one is sure exactly, not even him, he died peacefully in his sleep they told me."

Richard was silent for a while and then he said, "He was sincerely loved by all that knew him."

Abraham said, "Amen."

Mary and Anne wiped tears from their eyes as they continued their journey to the church.

142

• • •

On May 1, 1643 Captain Myles Standish sent word to Governor Bradford that a conspiracy was in the making by Chief Miantinomo, the new leader of the Narragansett Indians, to cut off the English settlers from Plymouth. Since the Pequot war, all the Narragansett tribes had formed a hatred for the English in all parts of the colony. This feeling was mutual for many of New England's leaders and they were opposed to being friendly with the Narragansett Indians who lived near the Massachusetts colonies. They called them heathens and were prejudice against them because most of them did not want to conform to the white man's ways.

When several friendly Mohigan Indians living near the Connecticut Colonies discovered this conspiracy, they sought a means to prevent trouble and also to secure themselves their own safety with the English and notified Captain Standish. This discovery resulted in the writing of the Articles of Confederation between the Colonies under the Governments of Massachusetts, New Plymouth, Connecticut and New Haven, which was the official formation of the United Colonies of New England.

On May 19, 1643 Governor William Bradford made a decision that would benefit all Freemen of New England. In fact it was a very important day in the life of all peoples in New England, 'The Constitution of the New England Confederation' was written and signed by William Bradford. With the full consent of the all, he surrendered into the hands of all Freemen of the whole Court of the New Plymouth Corporation, all rights, title, power, authority, privileges, immunities and freedoms that had been granted to him. This Constitution formed the New England Confederation. (For a complete copy of these Articles, please see the appendix.)

Governor William Bradford gave the following speech and it was also written as part of the constitution. It was very impressive then and still is to this very day.

"Whereas we all come into these parts of America with one and the same end and aim; namely to advance the kingdom of our Lord Jesus Christ and to enjoy the Liberties of the Gospel in purity and peace.

And whereas in our settling by a wise Providence of God, we are further dispersed upon the Seacoasts and Rivers than was at first intended, so that we cannot according to our desires with convenience communicate in one government and jurisdiction;

And whereas we live encompassed with people of several Nations and strange languages which hereafter may prove injurious to us and our posterity;

And for as much as the Natives have formerly committed sundry insolence and outrages upon several Plantations of the English, and have of late combined themselves against us;

And seeing, by reason of those distractions in England;

And by which they know we are hindered from that humble way of seeking advise or reaping those comfortable fruits of protection, which at other times we might well expect.

We therefore do conceive it our bounded duty without delay to enter into a present Consecution amongst ourselves for mutual help and strength in all our future concerns.

That as in Nation and Religion, so in other respects, we be and continue One, according to the tenor and true meaning of the ensuing 12 Articles."

On July 29, 1643 Miantinomo, the new Chief of the Narragansett Indians, thought he was going to rule over all Indians around them since they had subdued the Pequot earlier that summer. But Uncas, chief of the Mohigan and the surviving Pequot were faithful to the English and would not submit to him, instead they swore they would remain faithful to the English in return for protection from the Narragansett.

This enraged Miantinomo and a month later on August 29, 1643 he tried to hire someone to kill Uncas. They conspired to try to poison him, or knock him on the head in the night by sneaking into his house while he was asleep or to shoot him in ambush while he was out hunting. However, none of these plots were successful so Miantinomo raided the Mohigan with 900 warriors without proclaiming war.

Though Uncas wasn't ready for a full-fledged war he had about 500 warriors who were always ready to protect their people and Uncas was the victor of this invasion. The Mohigan killed many of the Narragansett and wounded many more, but most important of all, Uncas captured Miantinomo.

Uncas kept Miantinomo prisoner until after the confederation was written and signed by all colonies. The commissioners saw that Uncas would not be safe while Miantinomo lived, so they concluded that the only justice for this bloodthirsty enemy was death. They advised Uncas that he should not torture Miantinomo, but should take his prisoner to the Mohigan territory and killed him with a blow on his head from a hatchet. On September 10, 1643 Miantinomo was killed in just such a way.

The Narragansett were not happy with this decision, but were not willing to fight the English and the Mohigan again so soon after so much blood had already been shed. They would have to bide their time and regroup their men.

• • •

At the June 6, 1643 Town Meeting, Abraham was appointed for another year as a Grand Juror or an investigator of crimes. He was one of the few men with the authority to bear arms. He had a flint-lock gun, powder, bullets and a powder horn that he had brought from England. He also took an oath of fidelity whereby he pledged to remain faithful to his obligations in the community of Barnstable and Plymouth Colony.

William Carsely was appointed Constable again at this same meeting. Some of the councilmen deemed that he was a loud bois-terous person when he was given to idleness and too much jeer-ing. He had been excommunicated from the church as punishment several times but he took it patiently, did his penance and was reinstated after promising never to be slovenly and drunk again in public. Abraham stated that he thought William was the perfect man for the job of Constable at this time because strangers were intimidated by his loudness. William was of the right age for this job also, he was 38, not too young and not too old. Everyone agreed that he completed his duties in the past without hesitation and after a few more minutes of discussion, most of it being in William's favor, he was unanimously appointed Constable again. His wife Martha was a year younger than he was and was never able to have children. She was however as gentle as William was strong. They were opposites in personality but they never quarreled and were always ready to help their neighbors.

• • •

On June 10, 1643 William and Elizabeth Bills had a baby boy they named Billy. Their baby daughter Sarah had died in her sleep from suffocation two years before and Elizabeth was terrified that the same thing would happen to her new son. Marie Dimmock assured her that if she made sure that Billy was put in his cradle on his back and she tucked the blankets tight under his arms he would be fine.

Five days later on June 15, 1643 Samuel and Henrietta Jackson had a baby girl. They name her Margaret. Marie and Jane helped her and her delivery was normal and the baby was healthy. This was her third child.

Marie and Jane gave a big sigh of relief after Henrietta's baby was born, glad that no more babies were due for a while and hoped that no injuries or sicknesses would occur for a while. They agreed they were tired.

• • •

Richard and Mary More of Duxbury had their fourth child she was born on August 10, 1643 they named her Rose. Richard called her his little rosebud because her cheeks were so pink and she puckered her mouth into a little bud when she was asleep. It being harvest season Anne and Abraham were not able to go to see the new baby immediately, but sent their best wishes along with a new little quilt that Anne made for her.

• • •

Summer and fall was a trying time for the men and women of Barnstable. Everyone felt that an Indian war would break out at any moment. A Military Discipline was established by the Colony Court embracing the towns of Plymouth, Duxbury and Marshfield on September 1, 1643. Myles Standish was chosen Captain, Nathaniel Thomas was Lieutenant, Nathaniel Souther was chosen Clerk and Dr. Matthew Fuller and Samuel Nash were chosen as Sergeants.

When the company met each month, the exercises were always begun and ended with a prayer. At the annual election of officers which was held on the first day of September, a sermon was preached. None but freeman of honest and good report were approved by the officers and by a majority of the company, were admitted. No servants were admitted.

No conversation was allowed while the company was on parade and the most exact discipline was enforced. If a soldier was absent without a sufficient excuse, a fine of two shillings was imposed and was to be paid within a month. If the party was delinquent he was summoned to appear before the company and a fine was exacted from him and he was stricken from the roll of the company.

For each defect in arms or equipment a fine of six pence was imposed and if their equipment was not repaired or remained defective for six consecutive months, his name was stricken from the roll of the company.

The arms and equipment required of each was an approved musket or piece, a pike or spear, a sword, a rest, which was a support for the butt of their muskets and a bandolier or red sash. Only 16 pikes were required, namely 8 for Plymouth, 6 for Duxbury and 2 for Marshfield. All of the officers of the company were forever after to be known by their titles. Each member paid six pence a quarter for the use of the company and at the decease of a member the company assembled with their arms and he was buried as a solider.

No person propounded for a member could be received on the day he was nominated, and before admission he was required to take the oath of fidelity. The fifteenth rule of the company required that all postures of pike and musket, motions, ranks and files, messengers, skirmishes, sieges, batteries, watches and sentinels always be performed to true military discipline.

This company was established on the same principle as the ancient and honorable Artillery Company of Boston, which has maintained its organization to the present time.

The freemen of Sandwich, Barnstable and Yarmouth provided they were men of honest and good report were granted by the Court liberty to form a similar company. In each town there was a military company, which included all men between the ages of 16, and 60 who were able to bear arms. The Military Discipline was not intended to supersede the ordinary training, it was intended as an honorable association of the freemen for the instruction in the art of war.

• • •

Anthony Thacher and his wife Lydia Gorham Thacher arrived from England on the *Griffin* on September 10, 1643 and moved directly to Barnstable. Anthony was a master weaver in Norwich, England and they were just recently married there on July 29, 1643. Before abandoning his homeland and his career he tried to convince the ecclesiastical court that he was a true believer in the Lord Jesus. But, because he did not bow down to the archdeacon's and the Bishop's court he was called a Blockhead, and his enemies conspired against him to take away his life. His wife hid him in the roof of their house, covering him with straw. Having become a marked man, he had no choice but to flee to New England.

Anthony built a new home that fall and winter making the sitting room especially large so they could set up several small looms in it. They made many yards of linen cloth from thread spun of the flax straw that was sent to them from Anthony's brother who still lived in England. They also used much of the flax that was grown in Barnstable. Their weaving skills were very much needed and they were welcomed to the town of Barnstable.

In the fall during the trading with the Indians Lydia was shown by some of the Indian women how to make a wonderful blue dye from several plants that grew wild in the meadows.

• • •

Nathaniel and Hannah Bacon had their first child on September 4, 1643. Marie Dimmock and Jane Annable helped Hannah with her baby's birth and it was an easy delivery, which was just as well as Jane was feeling poorly and had been for many months.

Hannah was also fearful that an Indian attack may happen and knew that she didn't have time to linger over of a hard labor, and little baby Hannah must have been just as anxious to see the world because her labor only lasted about three hours. Nathaniel named the new baby after her mother, he said she looked exactly like her and would not hear of any other name for his new child. However, she was called Baby Hannah for many years. Baby Hannah was baptized four days later on September 8, 1643.

• • •

Later that fall the Colony Court issued an order to Barnstable requiring its people to fortify a place or places for the defense of themselves and their families against a sudden assault from the Indians and three houses were built with palisades erected around them. Bernard Lombard, surveyor and measurer of land, was on this committee to enforce the court order from Plymouth and with the help of Henry Coggin and James Hamblen who were also on this committee the houses were built in a very short time.

It was decided that the homes of the three deacons of the Church would become fortified because of their locations. The fortification house of Deacon Thomas Dimmock was located on the hill just east of the church. The second fortification house was that of Deacon Henry Cobb and was located on the knoll northeast from the Church and that of Deacon William Crocker was on the northwest side of the old meeting house in West Barnstable.

• • •

Sadness befell the growing town of Barnstable, especially for the women. Jane Annable died on December 11, 1643. She had developed a nagging cough early in the summer and it had progressed steadily all fall until it was almost constant. Her friend Marie Dimmock did everything she could for her but nothing seemed to help.

Marie could not figure out why Jane was not getting better. Pneumonia was a horrible sickness to have and she and Jane had brought many people through it, but this time when Jane started coughing up blood she knew there was no hope for her dear friend.

Just after Thanksgiving Jane refused to eat and only sipped water occasionally between coughing bouts. Her body dwindled away to almost nothing and peace came to her on that cold December day.

Marie was deeply saddened to hear the news and told the young man that came with the message that Jane had passed away that morning, to tell Mr. Annable that she would come by his home in a little while. Marie had a special tea that would help them all through their grief and let them get some rest. She made a tea with a mixture of dried Valerian, Scullcap and Hops, added some honey and took it to them just after their noon meal and instructed Anna to see that they all drank at least one cup before they went to bed.

Anthony Annable mourned his devoted wife for many days. They were married for almost 24 years and had four daughters, Sarah, 21, married to Henry Ewell lived in Scituate, Hannah 18, Susannah 13 and Deborah age 6.

Sarah Annable Ewell came to Barnstable just before Thanksgiving, her father sent word to her that her mother was very sick and asked her to come and help him for a few days. They were a close family when they lived in Scituate, but since Anthony and Jane had moved to Barnstable they were not able to keep in touch with Sarah and her family as often as they would have liked.

Jane made the long trip by boat to Scituate when both of Sarah's two little children, ages three and eleven months, were born and helped her daughter through her labor.

Now Sarah brought the little ones with her and it seemed to cheer Jane up for a few days. Jane was so happy to see them and Sarah again. It was wonderful to see how much her little grand babies had grown.

Jane's second daughter Hannah, was 18 and in love with Thomas Bowman a young man not quite 21. They were planning to be married on March 10, 1644. Hannah wanted to change the date when her mother became so ill and get married December 1, 1643, but Jane told her that she should not change her plans, it might bring bad luck.

Sarah knew that her mother was not going to get over this terrible sickness and always believed that her selflessness toward others would cause her death.

Susannah and Deborah were devoted to their mother and took constant care of her during her last weeks. They did exactly what Marie Dimmock told them to do and made sure that their mother took her medicine and they did all they could to urge her to eat. Many townswomen helped the pretty girls as much as they could especially her mother's friend Anna Clark.

Anna Clark, 28 years old was called a spinster. She had never been married, she was too shy because of her disability. When she was a tiny little girl just leaning to crawl around her older brother accidentally stepped on her leg breaking her ankle. It had never healed properly and though she learned to walk she had a distinct limp. She and Jane were very good friends in Scituate and when Jane moved to Barnstable she invited Anna to move to Barnstable with her and hired her as a mother's helper.

At the funeral Anna Clark sat with the family. "You're just like a sister to Jane, Anna, please sit here with us," Anthony insisted. Anna was pleased and said, "Thank you Mr. Annable."

At the funeral Anna thought about what Jane had asked her during their last conversation, 'Could it have been only four days ago,' she wondered as tears filled her eyes.

When Jane became bed ridden just after Thanksgiving she asked Anna to take care of her family if anything ever happened to her. Anna promised her thinking only of the comfort that Jane seemed to get when she agreed.

"You must promise me you'll take care of Susannah and Deborah, after I'm gone Anna," Jane said between her gasps for air.

"Yes, Jane, I'll take care of your family," she said patting her friend on her shoulder. "I'll make sure they learn to do all the things they have to," she added.

Anthony could hardly believe that his lovely wife of twenty-four years was not getting better. "Oh, Jane," he said that same afternoon, Anna was still in the room when he came in from finishing his chores, "Please get better, I don't want to loose you." Tears filled his eyes as he said, "What will I do without you?"

"Anna will look after you for me," Jane said and closed her eyes. She opened them again and said, "I love you Anthony, please don't be sad, I'll wait for you in heaven." She closed her eyes again and took one last breath.

Anthony laid his head on her pillow and cried for a long time. The girls left the room and cried together until there were no more tears. Sarah's little ones needed attention pulling on their mother's skirt wondering what was happening, so she pulled herself together and said, "Your grandmother is breathing easy again and she isn't coughing any more, isn't that wonderful?" She picked up the little ones and said, "Thank you Jesus," and they all said, "Amen."

Anna said, "I'll send word to the Reverend and to Marie Dimmock. She has been very worried about her and has tried very hard to help her through this, she'll be so sad." Tears started again but she held her chin up and said, "We must also help your father get through this, too."

Marie arrived to find Anthony still crying on Jane's pillow. He had not moved since Jane took her last breath. She found five small mugs and poured some of her tea into each one and carried them into the bedroom. She handed the ladies theirs and then she went to Anthony and put her arm across his shoulders, "Anthony, you must stop now, Jane would not like to see you like this," she said kindly.

He sat up and looked at her, "I don't know what I'll do now," he said.

Marie handed him a handkerchief that was laying on the stand near the bed. "I know, Anthony," she said kindly, "but you have to pull yourself together, you have your daughters that need you, you have to be strong for them."

Anthony blew his nose and shook his head agreeing with her.

Then she handed him his mug and said, "Drink this Anthony and you'll feel better."

He took the mug and swallowed the tea in one gulp. He used the handkerchief again and then stood up slowly, "I'd better go and see Reverend Lothrop now and make arrangements." He hugged each of his sobbing daughters, one at a time and he gave Anna a pat on her shoulder.

Marie hugged each of the girls and then picked up her empty kettle and said, "You'll all feel better in a little while and remember, your mother would not like to see you like this. You must stay strong for your father," she added as she started to leave.

Anna said, "I'll walk you to the door Marie."

"Thank you Anna," she said.

"I've been wondering what you were going to do now without Jane's help," Anna said when they were out of hearing distance of the Annable girls. "The girls don't seem to be interested in carrying on where Jane left off," she added.

"I know, with Sarah living in Scituate and Hannah all excited about her wedding," Marie replied, "I don't expect them to."

"The other two are just too young, don't you think?" Anna asked.

"I've been thinking about it for a while, but was hoping that I wouldn't have to worry about it," Marie said quietly, "I think I'll ask Anne Blish if she'd like to help, she's helped several times and she was quick to learn about the herbs."

"That's a wonderful idea," Anna said, "in fact I too thought that Anne would be the perfect woman to help you."

"I'll ask her tomorrow," Marie said as she opened the door.

"Take care Marie, and thank you for all you did for Jane," Anna said.

"Good night, Anna," Marie said, "I'll see you soon."

'What will I do without you, Jane,' Marie thought to herself as she started down the lane. "Oh Jane, I'll miss you so much," she said out loud and sighed, "Go with God and be well again." She cried the rest of the way home.

The following day Marie called on Anne Blish and asked her if she would like to help her and learn her healing ways with herbs.

Anne was delighted to be asked and told Marie that she would do her best. It would keep her busy and she was sure that Abraham wouldn't mind.

• • •

Alice Goodspeed persuaded her husband Roger to go to church with her on December 31, 1643, when she joined Reverend Lothrop's congregation as a member in good standing. She wanted him there for their son Nathaniel's baptism and after much cajoling he put on his good clothes and the three of them went to church. She had been at him for several months to join with her on Sunday morning when she went to worship and he assured her that he would. But every Sunday he would find one excuse or another not to go.

On several occasions he made sure he was out of town on business, so Alice went by herself and sat on the side benches, members were the only ones that had a pew by themselves. Most of the women had already persuaded their husbands to join the church, or in many cases the husbands persuaded their wives to join. She wanted to join so she could have a pew of her own.

'Joining the church on the last day of the year is a nice way to end one year and enter into a new one,' she thought. After the service Roger was still convinced that he had no time to go to church every Sunday, but Alice was happy to have him with her this one day and now she too had a pew of her own.

Patricia Louise Blish Gould

CHAPTER ELEVEN
1644

The following week Anthony Annable, his daughters and Anna Clark went to church together and of course they sat in the same pew. Anthony could see no reason for Anna to move out of his home, she had lived there since they all moved to Barnstable. However, when they were seen later that day talking very seriously to each other, the rumors started.

Reverend Lothrop suggested to Anthony that he should marry Anna in order to stay in the good graces of the church.

Anthony agreed, but took his time in asking Anna; he wanted to wait until he knew he was over loosing his beloved Jane. After that day they kept their distance from each other in public, and were careful about being seen alone without the children, but they still sat in the same pew at church on Sunday making sure that they did not sit next to each other.

• • •

Nathaniel and Hannah Bacon became parents again on February 15, 1644 to a healthy baby boy that Hannah insisted on naming Nathaniel. Now they had Baby Hannah and Baby Nathaniel. Marie Dimmock and Anne Blish helped Hannah deliver her new baby. He was baptized on February 20, 1644 on a very cold and windy Sunday morning.

• • •

Hannah Annable married Thomas Bowman on March 10, 1644. Anthony walked her down the aisle and put her hand into Thomas' and said, "Her mother and I give Hannah to you to take care of for the rest of your life."

Thomas looked Anthony in his eyes and said, "I will, Sir."

The couple said their vows and after the service everyone was invited to the Annable home where a lovely meal was served. Hannah and Thomas moved to Scituate the following week.

• • •

On April 21, 1644 the Narragansett Indians under the leadership of a new chief named Weetowish, planned to attack the Mohigan in revenge for killing Miantinomo. It seemed that the Narragansett Indians told Governor Bradford that much wampum had been paid as ransom to the Mohigan in exchange for Miantinomo's life. But the Governor refused to believe this story of bribery and told them that it was they who were wrong and they who had broken the peace.

This acquisition made the Narragansett so angry that they gathered in great power and fell upon Uncas, Chief of the Mohigan, killing and wounding many of Uncas men. They did this without the knowledge and consent of the English breaking the formal peace agreement they signed the year before.

After hearing this news the people of Barnstable and other nearby towns lived in fear of Indian attacks. However, after several weeks passed and there were no more threats of war each town went about their business and meetings were held as usual. Barnstable held their annual town council meeting on June 5, 1644 and William Crocker was appointed as the new Constable of Barnstable. All other officials remained in their same elected office.

• • •

On June 16, 1644, about two months after they arrived in Barnstable, Sam and Jane Fuller had a daughter they named Mary. She was a healthy baby and seldom cried.

Marie welcomed the Fullers to town when they first arrived and told Jane that if she needed help when her time came to call on her and she would come right away.

This was Jane's fifth child and she said she would probably not need any help during the birth of her baby. It was like second nature to her now.

However, after breakfast Jane's lower back began to ache so much that she could hardly walk. She told Sam she was going to lie down for a while. Sam checked in on her a couple of times during the morning and both times he found her doubled up with severe cramping. He then decided that he would go and get Marie Dimmock.

"Jane, I'm going to go and get Marie," he said firmly, "I don't think this is normal," he didn't wait for an answer. It was about 10 o'clock in the morning when Sam left his house, he took his son Sammy and his two little girls and loaded them into the buggy and told them to hold on, "Hannah you hold Elizabeth tight," he said to his oldest daughter.

When he reach the Dimmock's home he knocked loudly and when Marie answered he didn't hesitate, "Jane's having severe back pain, Marie, please come and help her." Before Marie could say anything he said, "I know she told you that she would be all right by herself, but I don't think so."

"I'll get my bag and be right with you," Marie said.

"I brought the buggy," he said as they went out of the house.

"Good, I won't have to take the time to saddle my horse," she said.

When they were on their way back to his house Sam said a little sadly, "I was going to go and get my brother to help her but I know that Jane did not like the rough treatment she received from him last time." He silently blamed his brother again for the death of their last little baby.

"I'm more than glad to help her and I'm sure she'll be just fine," Marie said soothingly.

It only took a few minutes to get home; he had not been gone more than a half-hour when he pulled the horse up to his front steps. Marie was out of the buggy and into the house before Sam had barely stopped it. He helped Sammy and the girls out of the buggy and into the house and told them to sit by their bed and play quietly.

Jane was still in horrible pain; Marie could hear her moaning. "Jane, it's me, Marie, I've come to help you," she said soothingly. "Where are your pains dear?" she questioned her.

"Here," Jane said as she rubbed her lower back.

Marie said, "Let me examine you dear, can you roll over onto your back for me?"

Jane groaned and slowly rolled over and opened her legs.

"Jane, I can see that you're almost ready to have your baby, let me help you get into position," Marie said firmly. She reached for the birthing pad and put it under Jane and patted her leg, "It won't be long now, dear. I'm going to make you some 'new mother's tea.' I'll be right back."

Sam was standing in the doorway of the bedroom and she said "Sam, come stand beside your wife and hold her hand while I make her some tea." Then seeing his worried face she smiled at him and said, "Don't worry, she'll be just fine, the pains are just in a different place this time, no baby comes into this world the same as another."

Marie filled the water pitcher with hot water and then found a small pot to steep the herbs. It only took a few minutes to brew the medicine, the water was already hot and it didn't have to steep too long. 'I wish Anne was here, but there's no time to send for her,' Marie thought as she carried the pitcher of hot water into the bedroom and then went back to get the tea.

As soon as she finished getting everything ready Sam let go of his wife's hand and went to check on his children.

"Here, Jane, sip this tea, you'll feel better in just a few minutes," she said as she held the cup to Jane's lips. Jane took several big sips and then took the cup herself and gulped the rest quickly.

"Oh," she said, "I thinks its coming. Oh, wait a minute baby until the medicine works," she pleaded. But her baby didn't want to wait and she had to push.

Within five minutes Jane had another baby girl and everything was fine. Marie wrapped the baby in a clean cotton cloth and gave her to Jane and then she finished making the new mother comfortable and took care of the birthing pad. Then she cleaned the baby and put a new little gown on her. It was time for Sam and the girls to see their new baby sister.

Marie smiled when she left the Fuller's home, 'another baby,' she thought, 'I wonder how many I have helped bring into this new town. Jane could have had this baby by herself,' she thought, 'and that would have been better than having Dr. Fuller help her, but I'm glad I was there anyway besides she needed the new mother's tea.'

The horse and buggy were in the front yard where Sam had left them, but Marie decided not to bother him to take her home, 'The walk will do me good,' she mused.

• • •

On July 28, 1644 Roger Goodspeed joined the Barnstable Church. Alice had finally persuaded him to take an hour or so off to go with her on several special occasions and he went just to please his wife. He still wasn't able to attend every Sunday, but he went as often as he could and finally joined on this day.

• • •

Anne Blish realized she was pregnant again after talking to Marie Dimmock and couldn't wait to tell Abraham. She made a special dinner and lit candles and set the table with her best linen cloth and her china dishes.

"Well, now, is it my birthday?" Abraham asked when he came home that evening.

"No, but if you promise to mind your manners I have something to tell you," she answered.

"Is it another secret?" he questioned her.

"Only for another few minutes," she said teasing him.

He put his arms around her and kissed her on her mouth, "Please tell me now," he whispered.

"I'm going to have a baby sometime around Thanksgiving," she whispered back.

This time he held her closer and then they kissed again. "Our meal will be cold," she said.

Abraham only said, "Ummm," and picked her up and carried her to their room.

• • •

Serunk, a Mattakeese Indian, sold his section of land and meadows to the Town of Barnstable on August 26, 1644 for four coats and three axes. By Plymouth law no one could purchase Indian lands without the Colony's consent. This property was called the first purchase and Richard Bourne, a great missionary to the Indians stood by when the deed was signed, and made sure the boundaries were set properly. Care was taken that the Indian's rights were respected. Thomas Dimmock, Anthony Annable, Henry Cobb, Thomas Allen, John Smith and Lawrence Willis were signers of this deed. The settlers already occupied most of this land called West Barnstable.

• • •

Thomas and Marie Dimmock had a baby boy they named Shubael on September 15, 1644. She was glad that she had been teaching Anne Blish about herbs and the ways of childbirth. Anne helped her very much during the delivery of her baby. She stayed calm and knew exactly what to do when the baby came.

"A perfect way to teach someone to deliver a baby," Marie said smiling, "have one yourself and see if they know what to do."

Anne smiled back and said, "I have a wonderful teacher, and remember, you did most of the work."

• • •

On September 19, 1644 Uncas, Chief of the Mohigan called for help from the English and a Commissioner was sent to help him settle a dispute between him and Weetowish, Chief of the Narragansett. However, the Commissioner could not find any proof of this proposed attack although he assured Uncas that if an attack were made against him the English would be ready to assist him.

Uncas had planned to get the English to march against Weetowish and had convinced his men that with the help of the English they could destroy the Narragansett Indians forever. His plan did not work because the Commissioner did not believe his story and he was left to devise another plan.

Despite the rumors of Indian wars life continued with very few people upset over Uncas' problems, the people of Barnstable had enough of their own.

• • •

Sarah Blish was born to Abraham and Anne at 8 PM on December 2, 1644. Anne was in labor for about 16 hours, but most of the contractions were during the day while she was doing her chores. The little twinges of pain began in the early morning, about 4 o'clock. She stayed in bed until Abraham woke up about 5:30 and then she got up with him and told him she was having small contractions. He tried to make her stay in bed, but she insisted that she was all right, knowing it would be better to get up and go about her daily routine, she made breakfast while Abraham did his chores.

When he came back in from the barn Anne was making bread and had a nice pot of beef stew cooking in the stew pot. He asked her if she was going to be all right and if there was anything he could do for her. She asked him to make sure the large pots had plenty of water in them. It was about 10 o'clock in the morning by then and Anne's contractions were getting a little harder and lasting a little longer. Abraham was hovering over her like a mother hen over her chicks, he was in her way every time she turned, so she asked him if he would go and get Marie Dimmock.

When Abraham returned home with Marie about noon, Anne was relieved and relaxed a little. After Marie had warmed her hands in a pan of hot water she took Anne into the bedroom and examined her. Everything was going to be fine, the baby seemed to be strong and Anne was doing well. When they came back into the common room Marie told Abraham that everything was normal and that he would be a father before morning.

"Would you like some new mother's tea?" Marie asked Anne.

"That sounds wonderful," she said as she had another slight contraction.

Marie poured the new mother's tea for her and some nice English tea for Abraham and herself and then sliced some freshly made bread. Anne took a piece of cheese and some rose petal preserve out of her cupboard and they all ate a light meal.

Afterward they sat in front of the fire and chatted about a name for the new baby. Anne wanted to name it Sarah after her mother if it was a girl and Joseph after her grandfather if it was a boy.

Abraham sat turning his pipe over and over in his hands listening to them chat and wondering how they could be so calm. He wanted to smoke, but he didn't want to leave Anne's side for one minute. He hadn't lit his pipe in the house for months, since Anne complained of a headache and became nauseous whenever he would light it in her presence. She had not actually asked him to refrain from smoking in the house, but he knew she was grateful that he didn't. After about an hour or so when he was sure Anne was going to be all right, he went outside and tended to the animals and smoked his pipe for a while and tried to relax.

"Is Thomas with the children?" Anne asked Marie.

"Yes, but I think he plans to send for Susannah Annable about noon," Marie answered.

"Susannah Annable is sitting with little Abigail Coggin," Marie said. "She is sick with a very bad cold and the croup. Henry Coggin was afraid his little daughter's cold would turn into pneumonia so he sent for me last evening," Marie added. "I gave her some medicine and stopped by the Annable's house on my way home and asked Susannah if she would go to Henry's home and stay with little Abigail during the night."

"Mary Gaunt seems to be of no help whatsoever to Henry does she?" Anne said.

"No," Marie replied, "and I hear that she does not enjoy the roll of Aunt, either."

"I'm sure Henry will be happy to have Abigail home," Anne said.

"Susannah is more helpful to Henry than Mary will ever be," Marie said.

"She is very helpful to you, too, I'm sure," Anne said.

"Susannah is becoming very good with the herbs," Marie said, "maybe she'll be a natural like her mother was when it comes to healing people."

"Maybe," was all that Anne said as another contraction took over her belly.

Marie continued chatting to keep Anne's mind busy with conversation instead of the pain, "This morning when I went to check on little Abigail, Susannah was still with her. When Abraham came after me she offered to go to my house and keep Mehitabel and Shubael while I came to help you," Marie said.

"How nice of her," Anne said. "She will be a big help to you while I'm having my babies," Anne said smiling.

"It will be years from now before she'll be ready to help bring a baby into the world," Marie said grinning, "she's only 13."

Susannah Annable, being a bright young girl, had gone to sit with little Abigail with only a little reluctance, as Mrs. Coggin was not at home.

Abigail Coggin had recently returned to England to visit her sick father and left her children with their father and their Aunt Mary Gaunt, Henry's sister. They were in good care, as far as being fed and kept clean, but Aunt Mary was not very affectionate and showed no love to them.

Henry and his little ones missed Abigail more than she would ever know and they all hoped that she would be coming home soon. It seemed to them that their mother and father were hardly ever together, one or the other of them was always off to England for one reason or another.

Every evening since their mother left they could hardly wait to see their father return home from his business meetings. They would jump in his lap and hug and kiss him until he laughed and giggled. Then they would eat their evening meal with him that their Aunt Mary had prepared and afterward he would tell them a story from the bible. This whole scene was a little unusual because it was usually their father that was gone instead of their mother.

Henry Coggin was an adventurer and wealthy businessman and traveled often to England. He had three men and two women working for him as indentured servants as well as his widowed sister Mary and he was responsible for their welfare so when he was home he was busy trying to catch up on his personal responsibilities.

It was about 5 o'clock when Abraham came back into the house and Anne was walking back and forth in the common room, stopping every few minutes or so when a contraction would overtake her. Marie was walking beside her step for step ready to catch her if she fell. "Abraham, if you are hungry, there's a pot of beef stew ready to eat," Marie said as she guided Anne into the bedroom.

"I'm not very hungry right now," he said.

"Would you please get Anne a cup of the new mother's tea," she asked, "it's in the small pot."

"I'll be right there with it," he said quickly.

He came into the bedroom right away with a steaming cup and held it while Anne took a small sip.

"Thank you dear," she said taking a deep breath, "I hope I can keep it down."

"Is there anything else I can do," Abraham said a little worried.

"No, not at the moment," Marie said, "we just have to be patient, babies have a mind of their own you know." She smiled at him and patted his arm. "Why don't you fix us each a dish of stew and try to relax, we haven't had anything to eat since noontime, I myself am a little hungry, you must be too," Marie said trying to reassure him and find him something to do.

"All I want is a little broth," Anne said.

"All right," he said and went back into the commonroom. He helped himself to a dish of beef stew and served up a dish for Marie and carefully ladled out only a small portion of the broth for Anne, he sliced some bread for all of them.

"Do you want to eat at the table or would you like me to bring everything in here," Abraham asked Marie as he entered the room. Anne was sitting on the edge of the bed now.

"We'll eat out there," Anne said and got off the bed with Marie's help and they went to sit at the table. Anne had made a pound cake the day before and after they ate their stew Abraham served a slice with blueberry preserve poured over it. "I'll save mine for tomorrow," Anne said when Abraham placed the dish in front of her. It was now about 7 o'clock and Anne said she had to lie down, she couldn't stand up anymore. Abraham helped her into the bedroom.

"Thank you for your help Abraham," Marie said kindly, "but I think you should leave us now. Anne will be just fine, it won't be long now."

He kissed Anne's forehead and said, "I love you," he was glad to leave the room.

Anne had prepared her side of the bed about a week before with several layers of heavy cloth and then topped it with soft cotton to absorb her water if it broke in the night. Many women did this knowing that having a baby in bed could ruin a featherbed or straw mattress.

It wasn't long before Anne's contractions were almost constant and the pain was almost unbearable. She was determined not to scream, but she knew she would have to groan aloud as many women did, and it wasn't too long when she couldn't hold back any longer.

She groaned and panted when Marie told her to pant between each pain, "Don't hold your breath, Anne." After about the third time, the baby's head appeared and then just two more bearing down pushes and it was over.

Marie was so proud of Anne. "You did wonderful, my dear," Marie said to her.

"What is it, Marie?" Anne asked, sobbing a little when she heard her baby cry.

"You have a beautiful baby girl, dear Anne," Marie said as she wiped the baby's face and head with a warm cloth, wrapped her in a soft blanket and handed her to her mother.

"Sarah," Anne said, "her name is Sarah," then she prayed, "Oh thank you Lord for helping me through this." Sarah's cries stilled as Anne cuddled her to her chest.

"Marie tell Abraham to come in now please," she said.

"I will in just a minute, dear," Marie said, "as soon as I'm finished here."

Marie finished cleaning Anne and removed the birthing pad, washed Anne's face and smoothed her hair back. Then she went to the door and told Abraham that he could come in now.

As Abraham entered the bedroom he quietly approached the bed and dropped to his knees beside it. He could hardly believe his eyes. In front of him there were two of the most beautiful people in the world, his lovely wife and a little baby girl that looked exactly like her. He was laughing and crying and thanking the Lord all at the same time.

Marie had never seen such a happy couple; she gently closed the door behind her and set about putting the soiled bedding to soak and cleaning the dishes that had been left on the table. It was dark when Marie left but the moon and stars were bright enough so she could guide her horse home.

After Anne and Sarah were both asleep Abraham got out his pen and paper and wrote to his parents. He also made a note in his journal that there was another new little person now living in the town of Barnstable.

On December 5, 1644 Sarah was baptized with a sprinkling of water on her brow. Anne and Abraham were so proud of their beautiful daughter. They didn't stay long at the church after the service because a strong wind was blowing and the smell of snow was in the air. They wanted to get home without giving the baby a chill.

• • •

Abraham's house seemed to be full of little ones when Richard and Mary More came to visit during the Christmas holidays. Richard and Mary's four children, ages 7 and under and his own new little daughter Sarah filled his house full of holiday cheer. Mary would have her next baby in early summer she was pregnant again.

Anne and Mary talked about helping babies into the world and the men listened to their conversation lost in their own wonderment of childbirth. Dr. Matthew Fuller's name came up and the ladies wondered why he did not wish to participate in helping women have their children.

"I think I might know the answer to that question," Richard said.

"Oh, do tell us," Anne said. "Marie and I thought that he may have had a bad experience delivering a baby or something," she added.

Richard began his story.

"Dr. Samuel Fuller, his brother Edward Fuller and his wife Ann and their ten-year-old son Sam came to New Plymouth on the Mayflower in 1620. Edward and his wife Ann died in the first epidemic of sickness that took so many lives in February 1621 leaving young Sam an orphan.

I remember that Dr. Fuller was very distraught over losing so many people to the numerous sicknesses that plagued us when we first arrived. He could do nothing for them except bleed them from time to time.

Young Sam Fuller then became the charge of his Uncle Dr. Samuel Fuller and he lived with him until he was of age of 21. Dr. Samuel Fuller built a home in Scituate in the early years, I don't think that he was married, if he was his wife must have died, I never remember hearing about her.

When young Sam was only 24 in 1634 he was granted colonial land by Governor Bradford and was propounded a freeman of the Colony. Shortly after that he and Jane Lothrop, the Reverend John Lothrop's daughter, were married and in 1635 they built a house on Greenfield Street in Scituate where they owned twenty acres of land.

When his older brother Dr. Matthew Fuller came to the colonies in 1640, I remember that Sam was so happy to see him. But Matthew treated him as if he were a stranger. I suppose they may have been as it was almost twenty years since they had seen each other. Young Matthew had to stay behind in England with friends when his parents sailed to Plymouth because he was studying to be a physician and his parents wanted him to finish his schooling before he came to New England.

When Dr. Matthew Fuller moved to Barnstable in 1642 Sam and Jane visited them several times. Matthew is married to a lady named Frances; she came with him from England I never knew her maiden name.

Now, the three oldest children of Sam and Jane Fuller were born in Scituate, Hannah age 8, Samuel, Jr. age 6, Elizabeth age 4."

"Marie and I helped Jane Fuller when she gave birth to her fifth child this past summer," Anne said.

"Yes, a little girl, right?" Richard said.

"Yes, a very pretty baby," Anne answered.

"Sam and Matthew built their Barnstable homes near each other but are not what you would consider close relatives," Abraham said.

"That is true," Richard said and then continued his story.

"Two years ago Sam and Matthew purchased a parcel of land together called Sandy Neck from an Indian named Secunke.

Sam and Jane built their house in a secluded spot where travelers or others seldom have occasion to pass. He is very religious and does not engage in public business, he claims that he is too busy with his own property. He is, however, a juryman and has been on several committees to settle difficulties that might arise with the Indians.

Dr. Matthew Fuller is the only regular physician in Barnstable but always seems to be busy with official or military business whenever a doctor is needed."

"Since he became Captain of the Militia a few years ago I believe that he prefers to be called Captain, is that right Abraham?" Richard asked.

"Yes, I do believe so," Abraham answered.

Richard continued his story. *"I have heard him say that women were supposed to have babies by nature and they should be able to help themselves.*

Sam and Jane were visiting Captain Fuller here in 1641 when their fourth baby, little Sarah was born. Sam was very upset with his brother's treatment of Jane and his new baby and it disturbed him that Matthew, in Sam's opinion, was very unsympathetic during Jane's labor. It was as if he actually pulled the baby from Jane's womb before it was ready. He has always blamed his brother for baby Sarah's death; she was just six days old when she died. *She did not nurse well and she didn't move her arms and legs as normal babies do. Sam always blamed the baby's abnormalities on the rough treatment that Jane received from Matthew when her baby came.*

This, I believe, is the reason why he does not help women who are in need of care during childbirth. He may even feel guilty about little Sarah's death. I know that he does not talk about this subject. If a man mentions that his wife is going to have a baby, he will change the subject or walk away. No man that I know of has ever asked him to treat his wife during her pregnancy."

"I wondered why Dr. Fuller was not there to help her," Anne said, "but I didn't ask, I thought that he was probably away on official duty."

"I would suggest that you ladies keep on helping the women of Barnstable," Richard said, "and let the good doctor treat the soldier's wounds."

"I for one shall never call on him," Mary said, "though I don't dislike the man I have never felt that he was caring or compassionate enough to be a good doctor."

"We are so blessed to have Marie Dimmock living here in Barnstable," Abraham said looking at Anne. Then smiled and took her hand and added, "And my beautiful wife Anne, she's becoming quite the little doctor you know." He kissed Anne's hand and said, "I am so proud of you."

Anne blushed and said, "Thank you Abraham."

"That was a good story Richard," Abraham said, I think it wise to know why people act as they do. It prevents us from judging their actions to harshly."

"I agree, but I think its about time for bed," Mary said, "I'm tired."

Anne helped Mary take the older children up to the loft and they tucked them into bed.

The men finished their pipes and then they all said good night.

CHAPTER TWELVE
1645

The Reverend Lothrop was happy to perform the marriage ceremony for Anthony Annable and Anna Clark on March 3, 1645. The rumors stopped about them living together in sin and then everyone waited to see if she was pregnant.

• • •

Abigail Coggin had a baby girl she named Mary on April 20, 1645 while her husband Henry was at sea. When Business took him to England again on February 1, with his ship full of prime cattle he promised to be home before the baby was born. Abigail knew he wouldn't be, he hadn't been present for the others, but it didn't matter to her as much this time, because her love for him was less than she knew it should be. She also knew he would bring her many gifts and she would forgive him. His love for her had not changed and she knew it, it was just his way of life and she had to accept it, but she didn't have to like it.

On May 3rd Henry arrived home to find no one there. One of the hired hands told him that his wife and new baby were at the Reverend's house and he should probably go there as soon as possible. He found his grief stricken wife there sobbing; his new baby had died the day before, he never had a chance to hold her. He stayed home for three months and then business called him back to the sea, he promised that he would be home by Christmas. This time he kept his promise.

• • •

Richard and Mary More's fifth baby was born on June 1, 1645. They named him Jasper after Richard's little brother that died shortly after he arrived on the *Mayflower*.

Again Abraham and Anne were not able to visit them but promised to see them soon. Anne sent another small quilt embroidered with little blue ducks.

Richard and Mary sent word back that they would try to visit them during the winter holidays.

• • •

On June 4, 1645 at the annual town meeting of Barnstable Abraham and Nathaniel Bacon were chosen by several townships to be surveyors of highways. They were also Haywards, or official guardians of, fences, hedges and public pastures that impounded the cattle. They did much walking and horseback riding that year and were away from home for several days at a time.

William Crocker was appointed Constable again and he accepted the position, as it did not take up too much of his time and he was able to keep up with his own farming business.

• • •

Anne was lonesome that summer but tried to keep busy with Baby Sarah, helping Marie and doing her chores. During this time without Abraham she had the opportunity to become more acquainted with her neighbors. She had a wonderful garden and frequently shared many of her herbs and vegetables as well as her flowers with her friends. She was glad to go with Marie Dimmock and tried to learn something new every day about the herbs that Marie was always gathering.

Hannah Bacon, Nathaniel's wife, and Anne soon became close friends. Hannah's Little Hannah was almost two now, and Little Nathaniel was about five months old, just a little younger than Sarah was. They welcomed each other's advice about the little ailments that babies had during their first year and they found that they had much in common. They tended their children together as well as their gardens and they spent many hours helping each other get through the long days that their husbands were away surveying.

• • •

Roger Goodspeed and his wife Alice had a baby boy on June 5, 1645. They named him John. Marie and Anne helped Alice with her delivery and everything went fine with both the new mother and the new baby.

• • •

John and Hannah Barker moved from Duxbury to Barnstable on June 15, 1645. John built their home near the shore and then built a wharf with a small fish house at the end of it so he could continue his fishing business. He had three hired men, one took care of his small farm and the other two helped him with his fishing business.

Hannah loved her new home and she was happy to be living so close to her friend Anne Blish again. She was five months pregnant with her second baby and just a little apprehensive but Anne assured her that she and Marie Dimmock would be there to help her when her time came.

Hannah's daughter Deborah was six years old now and loved her new home, though she missed her friends, William and Samuel and Ellen More. She adjusted quickly and it wasn't long before she was watching over little Sarah Blish and Hannah Bacon's children like a mother hen.

• • •

Again the threat of war between Uncas, Chief of the Mohigan and Weetowish, Chief of the Narragansett hung in the air like a huge cloud close to the ground for many days. Then on June 29, 1645 the Narragansett gathered in great number and killed many of Uncas men and contrary to their agreement, they did this without the knowledge of the English. They were determined to continue the war in revenge for their dead chief Miantinomo.

The English were furious at Chief Weetowish for his lying ways so they sent forty men to the Mohigan fort on July 10, 1645 to help Uncas. The fort was located on the Pequot River and the English set up camp all around it to help protect Uncas until the commissioners could meet and take further steps.

Three days later on July 13, 1645 the English sent three messengers, Sergeant John Davis, Benedict Arnold and Francis Smith, to the Narragansett requiring them to come in person to council. If they refused, the messengers were to warn them that 300 Englishmen would be sent to help the Mohigan and that war would be declared.

The Narragansett received the messengers with scorn and contempt and threatened to lay the English cattle in heaps as high as their houses and that no Englishman should stir outside his door so much as to relieve himself or he would be killed.

When the messengers returned they reported the horrible threats that Weetowish made toward them and war was declared between the English and the Narragansett Indians to begin on August 12, 1645. Of course, Uncas' men would join the battle and maybe this would end the bloodshed between all Indians and the English forever.

But the commissioners didn't want any bloodshed on their hands, so on July 28, 1645 they thought it was only right before any hostile act was committed, to return a present which had previously been sent to the Governor of Massachusetts from the Narragansett Chief. The gift was a beautifully decorated sash of fine leather covered with red, white and blue quills and tiny shells and was fringed on each end with thin pieces of beaded thread.

This gift had not been officially accepted by the Governor, but had been laid aside, to be accepted or refused, depending upon the Indians behavior. So it was sent back by two messengers and an interpreter, who were further instructed to inform Chief Weetowish that the English army had already sent for Uncas and had given orders to him to stand ready for war

The message also stated that the English were desirous of peace and did not wish to harm any Narragansett Indian. Therefore, if, Chiefs Weetowish, Pessecuss and Mixano and his great warriors would go to Boston to council, they would come to no harm. But if on the other hand they would have nothing but war, the English were ready and would proceed accordingly on the set date of August 12, 1645.

Finally on August 8, 1645 only four days before the war was to begin the three Chiefs with a number of their warriors went to Boston. After two days of negotiations in the council they all agreed to a treaty between the United Colonies and the Narragansett Indians, thus avoiding the pending war.

Fall passed peacefully with only a few more rumors of renegade Indian attacks. No one in Barnstable was really afraid because most of the Indians nearby were friendly Nauset Indians.

• • •

Later that year on October 21, 1645 Mary Barker was born to John and Hannah Barker, their second child. Marie Dimmock and Anne Blish were with Hannah when her time came and everything went fine. Little Mary was a good baby and only cried when hungry or wet allowing Hannah to rest whenever she needed to. Deborah was a big help to Hannah, fetching this and that and doing small chores.

John and Hannah had Mary baptized on October 29, 1645 in the same manner as Sarah Blish had been, with a sprinkling of water on her head. Deborah was so proud of her little sister and so gentle with her. She and the other children just adored her.

• • •

On November 12, 1645 Samuel and Henrietta Jackson had a baby boy they name William. Marie and Anne helped Henrietta deliver her baby and they were both healthy.

It seemed that the little town was growing by five or six babies each year. Not to mention of course, people from other towns that found their way to Barnstable.

On December 5, 1645 Henry Coggin came home with several trunks full of gifts and presents for his lovely wife and children. Everyone in Barnstable seemed to have a wonderful time that holiday season.

Richard and Mary and their children came to Barnstable to visit Abraham and Anne at Christmas time and having traveled most of the way by boat were not bothered by any Indians.

Of course, the subject of Indians brought another of Richard's stories to light and after a nice evening meal on Christmas day they all gathered in front of the fireplace to hear it. Richard began with a date, of course.

"The sun came up warm and bright turning the first day of May in the year 1614 into an unexpected warm spring day. Squanto was a handsome young Nauset Indian boy, with a slight build and not very muscular about the age of 15. He was one of the first people to see the big ship entering the harbor that morning.

The trade ship 'Godspeed' had anchored off shore of the Virginia Colony during the night and by early that morning a longboat full of sailors with trunks and barrels full of trade goods came ashore. There was much excitement in the loud voices of both Indians and sailors bickering over the prices of tobacco, corn, beans, pots, kettles, deerskins, moccasins, and coats. Hundreds of items were piled in heaps with a guard standing over each one and with all the many gifts being passed around by the sailors it was easy for a young boy to become taken in by the white man.

Squanto had been told to be leery of these men because of their lying tongues and filthy ways. But on this particular day he was enthralled by the beautiful gifts of glass beads and the tall, hairy men in their handsome coats with silver buttons.

Captain Thomas Hunt befriended him by openly admiring his shiny black hair and the beautifully decorated deerskin shirt that his mother had made for him. Although Squanto was not afraid of Captain Hunt he was cautious of him, however, after a while he relaxed and tried using some of the English words that he knew. They talked and traded most of the day and the Captain told Squanto many stories about the beautiful treasures he had found at sea that he had hidden about the big ship.

Of course, Squanto couldn't understand many of the words, but he was fascinated by the great gestures and smiling face of the man.

The Indian women brought food to the men late in the afternoon serving wonderful vegetables, squash, beans, ears of corn cooked with the husk still on them, corn cakes and roasted venison and duck.

The white men had not eaten such wonderful food for many months. The sailors brought jugs of rum and kegs of beer to share with the Indians and by the time the evening meal was over many of the Indians as well as the sailors were drunk.

The Captain convinced Squanto and six of his Nauset friends to go aboard the longboat with him offering to pay them for the food with some of the treasures that he had in the ship's storerooms. Thomas vowed with a salute of his right hand held palm out toward Squanto that he would return him and his friends the next day along with twenty other young Indian men and boys from the Patuxet tribe that had been convinced by several other sailors the same way.

The young naïve Indian boys were promised that they would be given special trinkets and shells that had been found on the seashore of far away lands and they went willingly to see all the great wonders of the huge ship close up.

However, when the boys awoke the next morning they were way out to sea. The white men had betrayed and captured them. They all soon learned that this promise was just the first of many that the white men made but never intended to keep.

Captain Thomas Hunt treated Squanto badly whenever he was drinking. Making him do things that were disgusting and it hurt him and made him bleed whenever he had to use the chamber pot, at least that's what Thomas called it. But he also gave Squanto wonderful gifts of round silver coins and buttons that he sewed onto his shirt and taught him English and how to read the markings of the book he called the Bible.

Three months later the 'Godspeed' anchored off the coast of Spain and this time the young Indian boys were traded or sold along with the other trade goods.

Squanto was sold to a Spaniard by the name of Ferdinando Gorges where he was made to dress in frilly, lacy clothes and was sprayed with smelly water that made him sneeze. Ferdinando used him more frequently in the same bad way as Thomas Hunt had. Squanto quickly learned that the Frenchman was not as generous in giving gifts and he was actually robbed several times by Ferdinando's friends. It didn't take him long to learn the French man's language though and he was often asked to translate for him when he was dealing with the English. Eventually he learned to use his knowledge of both languages as a way to get what he wanted from Ferdinando. Which was money and independence.

Three years later in 1617 when Ferdinando tired of Squanto's haughtiness he sent him to live with a man named John Slany. It seemed that Ferdinando owed Slany some money and after a little persuasion Slany agreed to take Squanto in trade to settle the account. Slaney was nicer to him and allowed him to read books and gave him plenty to eat although he still abused him in his bottom.

After two more years of slavery John Slany sold Squanto to Captain Thomas Dermer. The Captain appointed Squanto as his cabin boy and took him to England and in May of 1619, Dermer and Squanto set sail to New England where Dermer was in hopes to settle a new colony with the help of Squanto's knowledge of the Indian language. Dermer counted on his loyalty to convince the Indians to sell him their land. Squanto was now a man, about the age of 19 and he was anxious to return home and agreed to do his best for Dermer. However, Thomas Dermer died almost as soon as his ship anchored in the harbor near the Virginia coast. He had been sick with dysentery for several weeks, but the ship's doctor had nothing to treat him with excepts sips of rum mixed with lemon juice.

After they dropped anchor Squanto convinced the first mate to allow him to leave the ship with several sailors to see if they could find help for the Captain among the Indians. Needless to say, Squanto never returned to the ship and the sailors were never seen again. Rumor has it that Squanto's friends murdered them when he told them how he had been treated after his capture. Captain Dermer died the same day.

Squanto found his village empty, every one of his people were dead from the white man's sickness called small pox.

The following year, in 1620 he greeted Governor Bradford in English. Squanto soon realized that Governor Bradford was different than the other white men he had known. He was a quiet spoken man and could keep the other men in check and they seemed harmless enough. In fact, Squanto told me once that we seemed on the verge of death and he believed that we were no threat to him or any of the other Indians.

Governor Bradford was extremely surprised that a heathen, as some of the men called him, could speak the English language. He was even more surprised to learn that Squanto could also speak Spanish and French and several Indian dialects.

In the spring of 1621 Squanto showed us many practical methods of fishing. Squanto and his friend Samoset helped us find food and taught us to fish that first year we were in Plymouth. The great Chief Massasoit of the Wampanoags was Chief over all the tribes from Plymouth to Cape Cod and Squanto was the interpreter between the Chief and Governor Bradford.

Squanto showed us how to catch Cod, Mackerel, herring, shark, bass, squid, mussels, and lobster weighting 25 pounds or more, some as long as six feet from antenna to tail, ugly creatures they were. Oysters were as large as a foot across and we used their shells for platters and plates. The Indians killed the fish in the brooks with clubs and the colonists scooped them up in frying pans. The terrapin birds were considered a luscious food and were very plentiful and easy to catch. A good-sized rock thrown with accuracy could sometimes kill two at a time.

He taught us how to use our feet to catch eels from the brook by treading about making much noise to scare them and then catch them with our bare hands. Each fisherman worked on his own hook and was usually accompanied by one of us young boys. Salmon and shad were not very well liked by us but in those days we ate almost anything.

Cod was the greatest staple of fish food although sturgeon and sea bass were just as plentiful. The dun colored codfish were usually big enough to last a small family three days.

Wild ducks, geese and swans were so plentiful that they were enjoyed often. The Indian women showed the white women how to stuff them with oysters and apples and cornmeal as well as wild sage and mustard seeds and then they placed them in huge tortoise shells and roasted them in mud ovens.

The Indian women showed us how to plant corn in early spring and in the summer they showed us how to tend it. Indian corn helped save our lives and altered our methods of living, especially in the manner of cooking and our tastes of food. They showed us how to grind it and cook it in many ways. Hominy, pone, suppawn, beans and succotash were dishes that we learned to cook. They soaked or parboiled corn in hot water for twelve hours then pounded it in a mortise or hollowed stone in the field until it was turned into grain or coarse meal. It was then sifted in a woven basket and then boiled again and served with thick syrup made from the sap of the sugar maple tree. It was one of my favorite ways to eat corn back then, and still is.

Suppawn was corn meal made into a very thick porridge. Succotash was corn and beans cooked together. The women picked corn, removed the tassels and then wrapped it in its own leaves and roasted it over the coals in the fireplace. Parched corn or popcorn was enjoyed by everyone some people sprinkled it with sea salt.

Hasty pudding was made daily and was a staple in all homes. It was a simple easy dish to make, all they had to do was mix corn meal with water that was slightly sweetened and then boil it in a cloth bag.

Nocake or Nookick was parched corn pounded into powder and put into clothe bags and was very nourishing when mixed with water and heated, it was used by the Indians when they traveled long distances.

In the early days we even used corn as legal tender and it was very valuable, it was also used to pay taxes to the King of England. We must have sent thousands of bushels to England over the years.

People still store corn in their attics and I am sure you have all helped gather the ears into hands and you see them every night when you go to bed hanging from the rafters. You young children still help to shell the corn from the cob in the evening and we use the cobs to smoke bacon and hams, and they are always kept handy for making fires.

The Indian women taught us how to dry pumpkins and apples by stringing them on long pieces of heavy thread and we still hang them in the rafters to dry. Apples were also made into apple sauce or apple butter and placed in barrels in the root cellars back then just as they are today.

Without Squanto, Samoset and Chief Massasoit we would have had a horrible time trying to survive those first few years after we came to New England.

Squanto died in 1623 at the young age of 25 of the white man's fever. We all were very much sadden by his death and many attended his funeral. Samoset died about five years ago, about the year 1640 he must have been about the age of 40 or so. Chief Massasoit died about the same time Squanto did. He was a very peaceful man and a great leader.

Richard ended his story with a note of sadness in his voice. He had good memories of Squanto and felt bad about the way the white men had treated his friend.

Mary recognized his expression and knew that his thoughts were sorrowful and that his story was over. "You tell such a wonderful story dear," Mary said yawning a little.

"Yes, you do," Abraham agreed standing up and stretching.

"Thank you all for listening," Richard said, "I think now that we should all go to bed."

"Yes, indeed, the baby will probably wake us up early," Anne said smiling.

"Good night and thank you for your wonderful story, Richard," Abraham said. He helped Anne out of her chair and they all went to bed

Richard and Mary stayed several days longer and while Abraham and Richard talked business, Anne and Mary huddled over baby Sarah.

CHAPTER THIRTEEN
1646

Samuel was born to Anthony Annable, age 46 and his new wife Anna Clark age 30 on January 22, 1646. He was Anna's first baby and Anthony's first son. Anthony's two daughters, Sarah and Hannah, ages 23 and 20, both married and living in Scituate were happy for their father, he now had a son. His two youngest daughters Susannah and Deborah were ecstatic about their baby brother. Anthony called on Marie and Anne to help Anna with her delivery.

It took Anna a few weeks to recuperate; her delivery was long and painful and Anna was a little older than most of the women having their first baby.

Marie Dimmock prepared her new mother's tea as soon as she arrived at the Annable's home. Anne Blish's kind words and soothing voice helped to calm Anna down and soon after little Samuel was born. Anthony worried about his new wife but Anne Blish assured him that she would be fine in a few days and so he went about his daily business as usual proud to have a son at last.

Several days later Anthony was on his way home from Abraham's house, after discussing some property lines that he and Abraham had been surveying earlier in the week. As he rode up the lane toward his house he thought he saw someone near his back shed. He casually dismounted his horse in front of his house, hitched it to the post and walked up his front walkway and into his house. He quietly told his daughters to go into his room with Anna and baby Samuel and stay quiet. He then went to the back door, stepped out and approached the wash basin that was on his left. He washed his hands then wiped them while he carefully eyed the back of his house, then he turned slowly toward the wood-shed. He could see a shadow moving through the openings of the boards so he quietly made his way toward the barn as if to check on the animals. The person making the shadow in the woodshed was also going toward the barn, he was inside the woodshed, and Anthony was outside. As Anthony neared the doorway of the barn he could see out of the corner of his eye that the movement had stopped, so he turned sharply and reached his long arm into the shed and grabbed the shirt of a very surprised man.

Daniel Russell almost wet himself as Anthony pulled him out of the woodshed and threw him on to the ground. "What are you doing here, and who are you?" He shouted.

"I ain't doin' nothin'," Daniel stammered. "I was jus' passin' by."

"What is your name, where do you come from?" Anthony re-peated.

"I'm Daniel Russell, " the dirty man answered shakily.

"If you were just passing by, what are you doing in my shed?" Anthony asked reaching down and pulling the dirty man to his feet.

"I weren't goin' to hurt nothin'," he stammered.

By this time the Annable girls who had been watching from the door came out and were standing in back of their father. They had never seen him so angry before and were astonished to hear him speaking so loud.

Anthony noticed that Daniel's shirt had a bulge in the front of it. He instinctively reached out and grabbed the front of the very ragged dirty shirt and pulled the bottom of it out from Daniel's breeches. A green article of clothing fell to the ground with a thump.

"What's this? Where did you get it?" Anthony questioned.

"It's mine, I found it over yonder," Daniel lied.

As Anthony picked the cloth up a pewter plate fell onto the dirty snow. Susannah let out a gasp. She recognized the plate as one of their good pieces of pewter; and the green cloth was Anthony's new waistcoat with red trim that Anna had just fin-ished making for him.

"Why you scoundrel," Susannah fumed. She was so furious that someone had actually dared to sneak into their house while they were home alone. It was unheard of. Even the Indians had the decency to knock and wait for an invitation to come in.

Anthony picked up the articles and shoved Daniel back down onto the cold ground again. He said, "Susannah," who was standing next to him with her fists doubled, "go to the barn and get some rope."

"Yes, Papa," she said angrily, anxious to be a part of this unusual event.

Anthony was so upset that he didn't dare touch Daniel, he just stood over him and said, "Don't say anything else and don't even move a finger."

When Susannah came back, Anthony tied Daniel's hands together and hitched him to a post like a horse. The foolish man was still pleading in his horribly uneducated language that he didn't do anything wrong.

"Watch him," he said to Deborah and looked at Susannah motioning her to come with him.

As they walked to the barn to get his horse he said, "Susannah, while I'm gone I want you to make sure you and your sister wash every dish in the house and clean the floor wherever you think that filthy man may have stepped with his dirty feet."

Susannah said, "Yes Papa," and immediately went to the well house to get a pail of clean water.

When he came back he said to Deborah, "I'm going to take this dirty creature to Constable Crocker's house."

"Can I go with you Papa?" Deborah begged tugging on his sleeve.

"Not this time my dear," he answered patting her head, "I want you to help your sister while I'm gone."

"Yes, Papa," Deborah said pouting a little. She had been with him almost constantly since her mother died.

"This terrible man shall spend the night in the stockade if I have anything to say about it," he continued, as he rode off pushing Daniel ahead of him with his foot in the middle of the ragged man's back.

When he arrived at Constable Crocker's home he tied Daniel to the hitching post and knocked loudly on William Crocker's door.

William opened the door a little surprised to see Anthony Annable. "What brings you out on such a cold day," William asked his friend.

"A dirty thief," Anthony said as he stepped back and pointed in the direction of Daniel.

"Well, now where did you find him Anthony?" William asked.

"I caught him red handed in my woodshed and found his shirt stuffed with my new coat and a pewter platter, he says his name is Daniel Russell and," Anthony said in a loud voice, "I want you to arrest him please."

"Well, let's take him to the barn," William said, "we'll tie him in with the cows."

"That would be too clean for the rascal," Anthony said, "maybe you should put him in with the pigs."

"We could do that, but then we wouldn't be able to tell one from the other when we take him to the courthouse," William laughed.

Daniel stayed tied up in William's barn for about two weeks. Alice kept him fed and William led him to the outhouse once a day. It was February 24, 1646 before a special town meeting could be called as several of the jurymen were in Plymouth on colony business. The dirty man Daniel Russell was brought before the court and within twenty minutes he was sentenced to receive 20 lashes with a wagon whip at the whipping post for stealing. His punishment was carried out on March 2, 1646. Alice Crocker applied a comfrey salve to his back and gave him some clean used clothing and Constable Crocker escorted him to Plymouth and told him never to come back again or his punishment would be many times more painful.

Someone said that several months later he was seen in Boston begging on the street.

• • •

The first real church or meeting house in Barnstable was completed on May 31,1646, the men had been working on it since early spring. It was large enough to seat 200 people and it was filled to capacity at the first meeting held June 4, 1646.

The Reverend's house that had been used as a church was beginning be very over crowded and most people had to take turns sitting during the services. There were only about ten small pews and several long benches along the walls. It was time to build a real meeting house.

The new building was built opposite the Lothrop Hill burial ground and was to be used, of course, as a Courtroom and a Meeting House, or Church. It was a wood framed building with a stone foundation and a huge fireplace on the north wall, its roof was shingled with cedar and the windows were covered with oiled paper. Like most of the houses the outside walls were covered with weather boarding and then clapboards. The inside walls were sheathed with boards molded at the edges in an ornamental manner and the space between the walls was filled with clary to keep out the cold. It had a raised pulpit in the middle of the south wall for the magistrate or the minister with side chairs for jurors or deacons. There was a small platform in front of the pulpit for the accused criminal to stand. On Sundays a small table was placed there as a place to put a vase of flowers that the women brought for decoration.

Each family could have their own pew now and visitors would occupy the side benches that were placed along each wall. The fireplace was used in winter but only to take the chill off so the women would bring quilts with them for covering their children and themselves. Many times the Sunday church services would last for several hours or until Reverend Lothrop would start to shiver, on these cold days people knew the church service would be short. He was known to be quite unaccustomed to the cold, he liked nothing better than to sit before a nice warm fire and read the gospel.

The men did not always resort to covering themselves with quilts because the winter dress for most of them consisted of wearing two of every article of clothing they had. In winter they wore two pair of stockings one pair made of Hampshire Kersey lined with fine skins the other made of fine red or green Gilford linen. Two pair of drawers under two pair of breeches, one pair made of white linen the other of fine tan colored leather. Their undershirt was made of Gedlyman white kersey and over that they wore another heavier white linen and covered their shirts with a waistcoat made of green or red cotton trimmed with colored tape. A leather girdle dyed a bright red was worn around their waists. Some men still wore sleeveless leather doublets that were usually red with hooks and eyes up the front that made them seem like a close fitting vest with a high neck. A Mandillion, or great cloak type coat, usually black, dark blue, dark green or deep brown in color, lined with heavy cotton, covered all. On their hands they wore a pair of fine leather gloves and a tall black beaver skin hat with a wide brim and lined in the brow with soft leather completed their wardrobe. Of course they never wore a hat in the church, but the collars of their shirts came high upon the back of their necks and under their ears. They wore their hair long and tied at the nape of the neck with a black ribbon.

Their shoes were made of welt-neat's leather crossed on the outside with a seam for sturdiness and silver or pewter buckles adorned the front. There were two soles the innersole was made of good soft leather, the outer of thick tallowed leather. The heels were made of wood. Boots were made exactly like the shoes except that the upper part of the shoe extended up over the calf of their legs.

Magistrates always wore their white wigs, which helped very much to keep their heads warm in winter, but in summer you could see the beads of perspiration run down their cheeks.

The clothing that the women wore was not quite as warm, thus needing the warmth of quilts when setting still in church. Their wardrobes worn about the house were long dresses with several petticoats under them for warmth and were made mostly of cotton and heavy linen. They wore high collared dresses with wool shawls over their shoulders. The high collar protected their skin from the rough wool of their coats and shawls.

Their bonnets were made of cotton or linen and trimmed with embroidery. A silk hood attached to a cloak was worn over their hair on special occasions. They usually wore their hair pinned on top of their heads with combs made from tortoise shells or whalebone or pulled back into a bun at the nape of their necks. Knitted scarves and hand muffs and gloves kept their shoulders and hands warm.

Women tatted lace of all kinds and used it as decorations for their collars, petticoats and bodices, even putting it on some of their husbands dress shirts. Tortoise shell or whale bone combs, lace fans and veils were treasured as well as silver, pewter and steel buckles. Making gimp buttons from silk thread using thin slivers of wood for stiffness was tedious work. Therefore buttons were only used on clothing made for special occasions. Their dress shoes had French heels made of stacked leather shaped into curved forms and silver buckles adorned the front. Everyday work shoes for everyone were usually two layers of leather, soft on the inside and thick and durable on the outside with no heel. Many people went barefoot in the summer especially the children, their shoes were for church and only worn in cold weather.

They dressed all their children age 5 and under in long shapeless dresses and long cotton or woolen stockings covered their legs. The older boys were dressed in breeches and shirts like their fathers and the older girls wore dresses with little collars sewn on them and many petticoats to keep them warm. Full aprons were tied around their waist and decorated at the bodice with embroidery and lace. They wore little knitted shawls over their shoulders and bonnets covered their hair.

The children wore knitted caps and mittens in winter to keep their ears and hands warm. Wool was used in making warm frocks for men, women and children and worn over their good clothes to protect them from soiling. They also wore them in cold weather or to cover up an untidy appearance. Making clothes for their families was something most women enjoyed; it allowed them to sit still for a few hours in the evening.

• • •

Preacher John Eliot and his wife Ruth built a nice home in Barnstable. John was a scholarly man interested in learning languages. He could speak French fluently and was also able to speak enough of the Dutch language to be understood. In early January 1646 he acquired a grant from the Governor to obtain a young Pequot Indian captive named Mintopa as a bondservant for the sole purpose of learning the Pequot Indian language. John being a fair man gave Mintopa his food and board and a shilling a day to teach him the dialect. His intentions were to release him from service in the summer as soon as he had learned the young man's language. However, Mintopa became extremely homesick within a few weeks so John took him back to his people's village.

A few days later John found a new teacher, a young man a little older than Mintopa, named Job Nesutan who remained many years with him as his servant, teacher, and assistant missionary. John Eliot's college training in linguistics in England enabled him to master the Algonquian dialect of the locality, and get a clue to the intricacies of its grammar, as the Indian tongue was highly inflected and exceedingly complicated.

Later in the year John visited the Nonantum Indian village on the Newton bank of the Charles River. It was a beautiful October day, bright and sunny and the trees had not yet been stripped of their gorgeous foliage by the autumn rains. The local chief Waban made John Eliot welcome and invited him to smoke with him.

John preached a sermon for an hour and fifteen minutes in the Indian language, and his audience declared that they understood every word. Then he distributed apples and biscuits to the children and tobacco to the men, an excellent method of holding audiences that John always followed although it proved a heavy burden for the cost of conversation.

Costly or not, by the following year John had converted many great chiefs, Kutshamakin of the Neposet, Nashobah of the Nauset, and Passaconaway of the Pennacook tribe, to believe in just one God. John was considered the Apostle of the Plymouth Colonies and on May 2, 1646 was escorted by a guard of 20 sub-chiefs to the Quabaug village whose people were hungry for instruction about the Lord Jesus.

John believed that his converts should be prosperous and self-respecting and he insisted upon one-family lodges, no scalping of their enemies and urged them to give up their mutual and friendly changing of bed partners. He did not insist that they change their habits of bathing or way of dressing, they were in most cases, much cleaner and better dressed than some of the white folks he knew. Sometimes, having received gifts of the Indian clothing he dressed as they did when he was preaching in their villages.

John Eliot tried to teach the women to spin and weave without much success, they were set in their ways and continued making their husbands clothing from animal hides as they had done for hundreds of years. A settled life for some of the Indians meant a loss of both aptitude and opportunity to procure the fur garments they needed to keep them warm in winter. John did however, get some support from his English friends who furnished blankets and coats and winter type clothing to them as gifts and trade goods.

John Eliot was away from home much of the time, but Ruth understood his needs. Many times she would go with him so that she could learn more about the Indian ways. She was as well liked by the Indians as John was.

• • •

Henry and Abigail Coggin had a son they named Henry, Jr. on October 11, 1646. Henry was home when their baby was born because the weather was bad, the high seas caused him to postpone his business trip to England for several days. Abigail was happy to have him home to help with the older children so she could rest several days longer than usual. Young Abigail, now nine was able to help also.

Mary Gaunt did not help as much as Henry thought she could have, she complained that the more she did the more she was expected to do. This was not true because Abigail had two servant girls that did the cooking and cleaning. Mary was suppose to watch over one child or the other and take care of their needs if Abigail was busy with one of the other ones. Lately Mary was busy going to meetings and socials with her new friend Francis Crocker. She told Abigail that she hoped he would ask her to marry him soon and said, "Maybe during the holidays I will be able to persuade him that he is in need of a good wife."

Abigail agreed with her that the holiday season was a wonderful time to convince a man that he was in need of many things.

CHAPTER FOURTEEN
1647

Winter passed quickly with no unfortunate happenings for the people of the town of Barnstable. The lambing was successful and spring planting was almost over.

On May 1, 1647 Francis Crocker proposed marriage to Mary Gaunt, however, Henry Coggin first cousin and guardian of Miss Gaunt, did not think Francis was worthy of being a husband to anyone. He had a kind of spell that made him start to shake uncontrollably, become light headed and turn very pale then faint and fall to the ground. He was always able to get up after a few minutes but it frightened some people.

Henry refused to give Mary permission to marry him so Francis petitioned the town council to give him their permission. The council decided after weighing the circumstances, that if he were given a certificate by Captain Matthew Fuller stating that he did not have the falling sickness, then they would grant him permission to wed Mary Gaunt.

After Captain Fuller examined Francis thoroughly and could find nothing wrong with him that might cause his problem he signed a letter to the address of both the town council and Mr. Coggin.

Several days later Francis had another spell while visiting Mary. She did not dare call on Captain Fuller; instead she went directly to Marie Dimmock to see if she could help. She loved Francis and wanted to marry him she did not care if he had the falling down sickness or not, but she didn't want him to die either.

Anne Blish happened to be visiting at Marie's home that afternoon conferring about another sickness that had been giving the children of Barnstable the diarrhea. After Mary described Francis' symptoms to the ladies, they talked between themselves for a few minutes and concluded that if Captain Fuller had found nothing wrong, then Francis probably had sick blood or anemia. They decided to give Mary some Red Raspberry Leaf, Dandelion Root, Nettle Blossoms, Oats and Yellow Dock Root and told her how to make them into a tea.

Mary made sure that Francis drank his 'tea' everyday for the next few weeks and when he had not fainted during that period of time she told her cousin, Henry Coggin that he was well and Henry changed his mind and gave Mary permission to wed Francis. Of course the letter from Dr. Fuller was also influential in his decision. Henry Coggin gave Mary and Francis his blessing at their wedding that was held at the Barnstable church July 2, 1647.

Neither Henry Coggin nor Captain Fuller knew anything about this treatment that Marie and Anne gave Francis, and no one was about to tell them.

Abigail was sorry to see Mary leave Barnstable she had been a wonderful help to her. Mary, however, could not wait to leave she wanted her own home and family. "Who could blame her," Abigail said to her husband. Henry and Abigail gave her a wonderful gift of silver candlesticks for a wedding present.

• • •

The annual town council meeting was held on June 6, 1647 and everyone continued in the same office except for Constable William Crocker. He asked to be excused from his duties for one year and then if all went well with him and his family he would accept the office again the following year. The town council agreed and appointed William Carsely to the office of Constable again. He had been Constable for five years from 1639 to 1644 and he agreed to the appointment for one year only, he said he was getting too old to go to Plymouth every week.

• • •

On July 10, 1647 Mary was born to Roger and Alice Goodspeed. Marie Dimmock and Anne Blish assisted Alice in her delivery and it was becoming only natural for family members to call for one or both of the ladies whenever a child was born.

• • •

On September 19, 1647, early in the morning, William Crocker called on Marie Dimmock. His wife Alice was about to deliver her baby. Marie left immediately for the Crocker home while William went to Anne Blish's house. Marie thought it best to have both of them at each birthing if it was at all possible. One of them took care of the new mother while the other took care of the new baby. It was an easy delivery and Marie and Anne were back at their own homes before noon.

William and Alice named their son Josiah and it being a Sunday William took his baby directly to Reverend Lothrop's church to be baptized the same afternoon. He was only about three hours old. He had suckled at his mother's breast soon after he was born and then his father carefully checked him over from head to toe. He was perfect William thought as he dressed him in a little gown and warm blanket and smiled at his tired wife. "I'll be back soon," he said quietly, "you get some rest," and he patted his wife's arm. He believed that his babies should all be baptized as soon as possible after they were born. He was especially happy if they were born on the Sabbath and could be baptized on the same day.

• • •

In 1647 William Baker with his knowledge of the Indian ways and language, became very helpful to the new settlements that were still springing up. Sandy and William moved to another Indian village near Yarmouth shortly after he recovered from his whipping and they started a new life. After a while many of the men that had convicted him of treason regretted their decision. Many of them asked his forgiveness and he gave it willingly, he held no grudges. William and Sandy sent Elisha to the English school as soon as he was old enough to walk the three miles between their village and the Yarmouth school. He studied hard and was a good student. The teachers were happy to have Indian children in their classrooms it was easier to convert them to the Christian way when they knew how to speak English.

Their second son, Adam became a medicine chief and was well thought of by both the Pequot and the English, he was said to have magical powers because he had blue eyes like the sky and could heal almost any living creature. As a boy he always had an injured bird or squirrel that he was caring for.

William's oldest daughter was named Molly after his mother and followed him everywhere. When she was of age she married a Pequot warrior and had twin sons, which was quite a rare event. Their youngest daughter died at an early age from the white man's fever.

Sandy's two older children learned to speak English and traveled back and forth between the English and the Indian tribes trading and speaking of peaceful ways to live among each other. All five of Sandy and William Baker's children were well behaved and knowing both languages made it easy for them to become friends with everyone.

• • •

Hannah and John Barker's daughter Anne was born on October 29, 1647, their third daughter. Mary was two years old now and Deborah was eight. Again Deborah helped with the new baby, fetching this and that, changing her diaper and tending little Mary. She was always happiest when she was doing her part to help her mother with her chores.

"I want to name her after you Anne," Hannah said, "but we will call her Annie."

"I'm very flattered," Anne said. "She's so sweet and tiny, the name 'Annie' fits her perfectly." She kissed the little baby's head and then kissed her friend on her forehead, she had tears in her eyes.

Anne Blish was about three months pregnant again. Both she and Abraham were very happy, as Sarah was almost three years old now.

• • •

On Sunday, November 20, 1647 Daniel Russell returned to Barnstable. People commented that evidently he was a glutton for punishment because he was caught stealing again. This time he stole from John Crocker. John and Joan were on their way home late in the afternoon after visiting his brother William when they saw a man squeezing himself through the palisade near the south side of their house.

"Stay here," John said to Joan, "I'm going to try and catch the weasel," and he went as quietly as he could through the gate and out toward the back of his house.

"I'll not stay here, I'm going in and see what's missing," she said adamantly and followed John through the gate and walked bravely up to the door, opening it as if she knew nothing of what was happening.

John saw Daniel just ahead of him with a large grain bag thrown over his shoulder. The thief was trying to hurry but his burden was too heavy.

John quietly followed him until he was within an arm's length and then he reached out and grabbed the bag pulling Daniel backward onto the ground. "Daniel Russell," he shouted, "I thought that you were never to show your face in Barnstable again."

Daniel curled himself into a ball and started whining like a small child. "I didn't do nothin'," he whimpered.

"What have you got in the sack," John shouted pulling the sack open.

"That's mine, I found it," Daniel said and tried to grab the stolen goods.

"No you don't," John said yanking the sack further away from Daniel's reach.

Joan came up to the two men and seeing Daniel on the ground she kicked him in the leg, "You again," she shouted, "You've been in my pantry and took some meat, cheese and bread, and I don't know what else yet, you bloody thief,"

Daniel pulled his leg back and tried to stand up, but John grabbed his shirt collar and pulled him back onto the ground while Joan looked into the bag.

"You stay right there," John said and then put his foot on Daniel's chest.

"Here's some of your tobacco, John," Joan said, "and my newly made dish of butter. Do you know hard it is to churn butter and make bread," she asked the ugly man. "I didn't make any of it for you and you will not have any," she shouted as she put the stolen food back into the sack.

"I'm going to tie him up and lock him in the shed," John said, "then I'm going to go and get Constable Carsely."

"Okay," Joan said, "I'll keep an eye on him and if he tries to escape I'll shoot him."

John pulled Daniel to his feet and practically dragged him to the woodshed. He was furious with the man and decided that he might just whip the ornery bugger himself. After he tied Daniel's hands behind his back he hitched him to the large post near the door of the shed and headed for the Constable's house.

It was late by the time he arrived at William Carsely's home, he could see a lamp shining through the window so he rapped on the door and called, "Constable, it's me, John Crocker."

William opened the door still rubbing his eyes; he had been sleeping in his chair with his head on the table. "What is it, John," William asked sleepily.

Martha Carsely had tried to wake her husband up when she went to bed, but he shrugged her hand off his shoulder and continued snoring. This had been a habit of his for as long as she had known him. He would eat his evening meal, finish his second mug of beer and smoke his pipe, then lay his head on the table and sleep for a while. He wouldn't go to bed until the fire died down and he started to get cold. This annoyed Martha because he would put his cold feet on her and wake her up, then he would snuggle her neck with his whiskers and make her giggle. She tolerated him doing this to her only because she liked his arms around her when she slept and even though he was cold when he came to bed she would always cuddled up closer to him and go back to sleep.

"I'm sorry to wake you Constable, but I have a thief at my house and I want you to arrest him," John said loudly.

"Who is it this time," William said grumpily, he was cold and wanted to go to bed where he could warm his feet.

"It's that scoundrel Daniel Russell again," John said as if the name left a sour taste in his mouth.

"What's he doing back in town," William said as he sat down at the table and pulled his boots on. "Guess I'll have to go get the wretched man," he muttered to himself.

"I caught him coming out of my house with a sack full of food and my wife will attest to it, she saw him too," John said.

"Yes, yes, John, I'll go get him," William replied as he put his coat on and pulled his hat down over his ears then stepped out of the door that John was still holding open letting the cold air in.

"I want you to put him in the stocks tonight, let him stay there until morning," John said hatefully.

"Cold out tonight," William said ignoring the man, "guess I'll have to put him in the barn, don't want him to freeze to death before he has a fair trial." The wind was blowing freezing sea mist into his face.

"I'd like to whip him now and send him on his way," John said.

William went to the barn and saddled his horse while John started down the lane. William didn't have any differences with John Crocker, but sometimes he was a surly and demanding man and it made William angry. "Trying to tell me how to do my job," William muttered to no one as he rode off following John.

William caught up to John and said, "Did you do bodily harm to him when you found him with your property?"

"No, I didn't lay a hand on him," John replied, "I only pushed him to the ground and put my foot on his belly to hold him from running."

They reached John's woodshed and found Daniel moaning that his hands were asleep and he was freezing. When he realized that the Constable was loosening the bonds that tied his wrists he said pointing to John, "That man hurt my belly and he threatened me."

"Now, now Daniel, you know that he did no such thing," William said. "He caught you trespassing and stealing, you were on his property and I have no choice but to put you in jail for the night."

"Barnstable don't have no jail," the dirty man said.

"Yes, you're right about that but we're building one for the likes of you," William said as he led the man out of the woodshed, wishing the jail was finished. He had tied Daniel's hands in front of him so he could lead him along side his horse on the way home.

"Where you takin' me then," Daniel asked meekly.

"I'm going to put you in my barn in the pig pen," William said looking at John and smiling.

"It would serve him right," John said smiling back at William, "but you wouldn't be able to tell him apart from the pigs and we might take the wrong one to court tomorrow."

William laughed out loud as he mounted his horse and said, "You're right about that, John, I'll see you in the morning at the court house." He nudged Daniel in the back with his foot and said, "Come on piggy lets put you in your pen," and laughed again.

He made Daniel trot all the way back to his house, he was cold and wanted to go to bed, he knew Martha would be nice and warm. He went directly to the barn and tied Daniel to the cow stanchion next to his best cow. "You can suck her teat if you get hungry," William said, "but you better not hurt her or you'll get whipped for that, too."

"I don't want to stay here," Daniel whined.

"Would you rather me put you in the pig pen like I said I would?" William asked him.

"No, I'll sleep here," he said as he sat down on some hay near the cow's head. She looked at him and then licked his face. "Oh, blast it you bloody animal," he sputtered pushing her head away and slid closer to the wall of the barn.

"I'll see you in the morning," William said as he went out the door and closed it.

"I'm hungry," he heard Daniel yell after him.

"Too bad," he muttered knowing Daniel couldn't hear him. "You should have thought of that before you took to stealing food." Beggars were always fed by most all of the women in Barnstable. 'All they had to do was ask,' he thought. "No sense in stealing," he said out loud shaking his head as he went into his nice warm house.

He put another log on the fire and then got undressed and climbed into bed beside his nice warm wife. He put his feet on hers and then snuggled her neck, "So warm," he said as he put his arm around her; she snuggled closer to him.

The next morning in court the jurors heard John Crocker's story as well as William's and asked Daniel if he had anything to say in his own defense. He shook his head and said, "I was hungry and it was late and no one was home so I helped myself."

John Crocker stood up and said, "There, he just admitted his guilt, I would like to inflict his punishment myself."

Magistrate Thomas Dimmock said firmly, "Sit down Mr. Crocker, the jury has not decided on a verdict yet." Then he said, "Daniel, do you admit your guilt of the crime you have been accused of?"

"I was hungry your Honor, I rapped on the door but no one answered so I opened it and asked for the woman of the house. I didn't hear anything so I went in and found food in the pantry and helped myself." He bowed his head in shame and then said as he looked back up at Judge Dimmock, "I would have paid for it, I would have worked two days for food, but no one was home." He bowed his head again and sighed. His shoulders sank into his body and the skinny, dirty man looked as if he were melting into the chair.

Judge Dimmock shook his head and then asked the jury to deliberate. They went one by one into the jury room each looking at the poor thief, first with disgust then with pity as they left the Courtroom.

It only took about 15 minutes to reach a verdict. When the jurors were all seated and the courtroom had quieted Judge Dimmock asked, "Has the jury reached a verdict."

Abraham Blish rose and said, "Yes, your Honor, the jury finds the defendant guilty as accused."

"What do you propose as punishment," Judge Dimmock asked.

"Your Honor," Abraham said, "we propose that Daniel Russell be given 10 lashes with a cat-o-nine-tails by the Constable and then escorted to Plymouth and turned over to the Governor. He has been of no use to anyone or himself for many years. A list of his many crimes should be given to the Colony Court allowing them to consider further punishment."

Judge Dimmock looked at Daniel and said, "Daniel Russell, please rise." Daniel stood up shakily and looked at the Judge.

"Daniel Russell, I believe that you would not live if you were whipped again and dying would not be punishment enough for you," Judge Dimmock said. "So I propose that you will be given a good meal and then first thing tomorrow morning you will be taken to Plymouth and," he said adamantly, emphasizing each word, "you will be made to walk every step of the way. I will let the Governor deal with the likes of you when you get there. Constable Carsely please see that my instructions are carried out." Judge Dimmock struck his gavel on his bench and adjourned the court.

Abraham Blish followed William Carsely out of the meeting house and stopped him on the steps. "I'll be glad to accompany you to Plymouth, William," he said as he put his hand on the dejected looking Constable's shoulder.

"I would much appreciate the company Abraham, I shall probably be ready to go at first light," William said smiling and looking quite relieved. Plymouth was twenty miles away and the trail was narrow and there were many brooks and streams to cross. It was not a trip that William looked forward to unless he went by boat.

Walking always took him at least two days to get there and another two days to get back; the boat only took a few hours each way and he could make the round trip in one day if the weather was good.

"I'll meet you at your house at daybreak then," Abraham said. "I have business to take care of in Plymouth and Anne has been after me to take her to see Richard and Mary More, she'll be happy to go."

"It's mighty cold to be taking your wife and child on a trip to Plymouth isn't it," William asked wondering if it would take him even longer than two days.

"The weather doesn't look like it will be changing any time soon," Abraham said, "and there's no snow yet." He looked up at the sky and said, "I'll make sure we dress warm." He patted William on the arm and set off quickly down the road toward his house.

When Abraham got home Anne was making bread and Sarah was helping her. They both had flour on their faces and hands and he laughed at them. "You have more flour on you than you do in the bread," he said to Sarah as he picked her up and swung her around the room.

"You look mighty pleased with yourself Abraham," Anne said. She patted the loaf of bread she was kneading into a round and placed it on the wooden board she used to slide the bread into the oven. "What have you been up to?" she asked him as she reached up and gave him a kiss, she held her hands out so that she wouldn't get flour on his coat.

"I have good news for you," he said picking her up and swinging her around almost as easily as he had Sarah.

"Put me down you big oaf," Anne said giggling. "What good news," she asked as he sat her down gently.

"Do you feel well enough to go to Duxbury?" Abraham asked her.

"Yes, of course," Anne said, she really did feel wonderful she had not been sick in the morning at all during this pregnancy.

"Can you be ready to go to Plymouth by tomorrow morning?" he asked as he took his coat off and hung it up by the door.

"Yes, of course, you know I'm always ready to go with you," she said kneading another loaf of bread. "Why are we going and whose going with us," she asked.

"We are going to go overland on our horses," Abraham said. "William has to take Daniel Russell to Plymouth, part of the pun-

198

ishment that Judge Dimmock gave Daniel was to walk every step of way. William has to turn him over to the Plymouth court," he continued as he sat down at the table and picked Sarah up and sat her on his knee. "Do you want to go to Plymouth," he asked his little girl. She is so beautiful he thought as he kissed the top of her head, just like her mother.

"Yes, Papa," she said, "are we going to see Uncle Richard, Aunt Mary and my friends," she asked excitedly.

"I'm sure we will," Abraham laughed. "I think we might go from Plymouth to Duxbury by boat," he said to them, "we can leave the horses in the stable at the Inn."

"Oh yes, Papa," Sarah said, "maybe Uncle Richard will tell us a story."

"I'm sure he will, and maybe we can think of one to tell him," Abraham said.

"Oh, good," Sarah said, "I'll tell him about my pony."

"He'll like that story," Abraham said smiling.

"I'll go get my satchel ready," she said excitedly. She jumped down off his lap and ran to her room.

"I have some things for Mary that I would like to take to her," Anne said, "and I must pack a basket of food, too."

"I'm going to let Sarah ride Star, she's almost four years old and its time to let her ride alone," Abraham said.

"I've been teaching her and she does very well, and we'll be right beside her," Anne said. "I could ride by myself when I was her age. You ride on one side, I'll ride on the other."

The next morning they were all awake before dawn. Abraham went directly to the barn to get the horses ready while Anne finished packing her satchel and took her picnic basket out of the cupboard. Then she helped Sarah, making sure that she had her wool leggings on under her long petticoat and skirt. Anne carried her things to the door and then she packed her basket with bread, cold roast beef, cheese and apples, 'I think I have enough for everyone' she said to herself.

When Abraham came back he said, "Are you lovely ladies ready for a wonderful journey?"

They both said yes at the same time and then laughed. They sounded just alike to Abraham and he smiled at them as he picked up the satchels and the basket of food. Anne helped Sarah on with her wool coat and pulled her knitted hat down so that it covered her ears and then tied her new green bonnet under her daughter's chin.

Sarah loved the coat that her mother had made for her, it was green like the pine trees and her bonnet was a lighter color green, like the grass Sarah said when her mother gave it to her. She didn't much care for the knitted hat that her mother made her wear under her bonnet but it was warm and if she didn't wiggle too much it stayed on. Her mittens matched her coat perfectly and she put them on before she put her coat on, they stayed on nice and tight that way.

Anne had just finished putting her own warm coat and boots and mittens on when Abraham came back. He picked Sarah up and carried her out of the house and sat her on her horse and handed her the reins, then helped Anne into her saddle. Anne and Sarah both rode astride their horses, sidesaddle riding was out of the question, it was too uncomfortable for such a long trip.

When they arrived at the Constable's house he was just coming out of the barn leading Daniel with a rope tied around his waist. He decided that it would be easier for the thief to walk if his wrists weren't tied together, he did however tie a rope from one arm to the other across Daniel's chest and around to his back, pinning his upper arms to his sides at his elbows. Daniel couldn't reach the knots to untie them because William had brought the two ends of the rope together in the middle of his back and knotted it there. The lead rope was tied around Daniel's waist and then it was brought up under a section of the rope that secured his arms. If he tried to get away by running forward the rope would pull his arms tighter together in back of him. If he stopped quickly he would be pulled off balance and fall. William had learned this way of securing a prisoner from Judge Dimmock who thought it a more humane way of taking prisoners from one town to another.

"Are you ready," Abraham asked William.

"Yes, you're right on time," William said smiling. "And I see you have persuaded your lovely wife and daughter to accompany us."

"Good morning Constable," Anne said, "I think it'll be a lovely adventure," she said smiling at him.

"Good morning Constable Carsely," Sarah said happily.

William mounted his horse glad that the wind had stopped blowing, and started off down the road with the Blish family following him. He didn't feel as if he was being punished any more.

When Judge Dimmock gave Daniel his sentence, William felt as if he were a criminal. He didn't mind taking the thief to Plymouth, but he would have much preferred to take him by boat. He hated traveling alone with a prisoner; he never got much sleep and hated the fact that the prisoner seemed to enjoy the trip better than he did. 'This time it would be a pleasure,' he thought as he turned to look back at his friends.

The trip was uneventful the sun came out and warmed them up during the day and they found a nice shelter under some hemlock trees and spent the night. Abraham and Sarah cleared the leaves away from a small indentation in the ground and then she helped him find some stones and they placed them in a circle to make a little fireplace. Then she gathered some small twigs while Abraham looked for some dead branches. They had a nice warm fire going by the time Anne had their evening meal ready. Anne put thinly sliced roast beef on a slice of bread, added a slice of cheese, two or three thin pieces of apple and then covered it with another slice of bread. A large pot of water was heating over the fire and Anne put a small cloth bag of tea in it to steep while they ate. They all enjoyed their lovely cold meal and hot tea as they warmed themselves in front of the fire.

"I should bring you all with me every time I have to travel," William said laughing.

"Can I have some more to eat, please," Daniel asked Anne.

"Yes, of course, Daniel," she answered the poor skinny man. She fixed him two more slices of bread with meat and cheese between them and also offered Abraham and William an apple.

When everyone finished she put everything back into the basket and then she and Sarah lay down on a heavy wool blanket and covered up with a quilt. They were both fast asleep in minutes.

William took first watch and woke Abraham up about one o'clock in the morning to take the second watch. Daniel didn't complain or try anything and it took them only two days to get there.

When they arrived in Plymouth William took Daniel directly to the jail and then went to look for the Governor to give him the papers that Judge Dimmock had sent with him.

Abraham left Anne and Sarah at the Inn while he went to the harbor to make arrangements to go to Duxbury. Sarah was a wonderful traveler, she wanted to go with him to the wharf but he told her she should stay with her mother and then patted her head and told her how proud he was of her.

Anne ordered a hearty meal for all of them and by the time it was brought to the table Abraham was back. They would leave for Richard and Mary More's home in about an hour.

The More's were happy to see the Blishs' even though they arrived unexpectedly. Everyone was always happy to have guests; news had no other way of traveling than by word of mouth. The five More children were as happy to see Sarah as she was to see them, especially the girls.

Mary was making candles and the smell of the hot tallow made from boiling bayberries and goose fat, filled the house with a wonderful fragrance, like balsam, Anne remembered.

Mary started using the bayberry to make her candles and soap when she first arrived in Duxbury. The berries helped cover the smell of the animal or goose tallow she used and they also added more tallow from the berry itself to the pot. Soap made washing clothes much easier; the dirt was dissolved away. Olive oil imported from Italy and France was preferred by all of the women when they could get it. It made a much softer soap for cleaning oneself, but unless it was mixed with the bayberries or honeysuckle it did not have a very pleasant odor either. Mary also found that using rendered goose fat or chicken fat mixed with fine potash and rose petals created a nice smelling soft soap and she often gave away little pots of it to her friends as gifts. Adding petals from the bayberry, honeysuckle or roses made both kinds of soap much more pleasant to use.

Anne also made candles and soap with these same recipes and shared them with many of the women in Barnstable.

The women worked together dipping the candlewicks until they were of good size and then hung them from a small rod that Richard had attached to the ceiling near the door. It was always colder above the door and the candles were safely stored there out of the way.

Anne helped Mary make a wonderful evening meal while the men talked business. Sarah and Ellen helped set the table and William and Edward finished bringing in the firewood that would be needed for the night.

When their meal was finished and cleaned away the children sat quietly by the fireplace playing their numbers game while the men smoked their pipes. Anne and Mary talked about all of the new babies that were recently born and those that were about to be.

After an hour or so Mary decided to make parched corn for everyone. She put several handfuls of the small kernels of corn into her big iron pot and hung it over the fireplace. Then she sat a small pot of butter near the hot coals to melt. When she heard the first sound of popping corn she pulled the big pot away from the fire and covered it with a shallow basket. The smell was wonderful and the children played their game quietly on the floor near the fireplace knowing that a treat would be ready in just a few minutes. When the popping stopped Mary poured the corn into a large wooden bowl and then sprinkled the melted butter over it and added a few pinches of salt.

"Come children," she said as she sat the bowl of popped corn on the table, "we'll all have a treat." She scooped out a clamshell of the parched corn for each of them and then one for each of the adults.

When there was a lull in the conversation that the adults were having Sarah asked, "Did you have parched corn when you were a little boy Papa?"

The adults all laughed at the same time, "No, Sarah," Abraham said, "we didn't know about this wonderful food until the Indians showed us how to make it."

"That's a good story," Richard said, "I was there the first time the Indians made it for us Pilgrims."

"Oh, Uncle Richard please tell us about it," Sarah said excitedly.

"Hum," Richard said smiling at her, "let me think for a minute." Then he began.

"I remember a time almost twenty-seven years ago when I was just a small boy in this new land. As you all know it was on December 20, 1620 that the Mayflower landed at Plymouth. I was 8 years old and my brother Thomas was 6. We lived with Mr. Brewster and his wife Mary and his two sons whose names were Love and Wrestling. My sister Ellen was 4 years old and lived with Mr. Edward Winslow and his wife Elizabeth. They also had two servants living with them; their names were George Sowle and Elias Story. My youngest brother Jasper was only 2 years old and he lived with Mr. John Carver and his wife Desire, they had two men servants named John Howland and Roger Wilder. They were also in charge of a young boy of about the age of 4 named William Lathan and a maidservant to help Mrs. Carver; I don't remember her name." Richard paused for a moment sorting out the good memories from the bad.

"Why did you live with other people Uncle Richard," Sarah interrupted, "where were your Mama and Papa?"

Abraham was about to reprimand Sarah for interrupting, but Richard put a finger near his lip and with his eyes he silently told Abraham that it was all right.

"That would be another story my dear Sarah," Richard answered the curious little girl, "and I'll tell it to you next time I see you."

"All right," she said, knowing that he would keep his promise, and she made a little mental note to remind him that he was to tell her about his Mama and Papa.

"The first winter we were here most of the women stayed on the ship. It was thought to be better for them there, but I know first hand that it was not. The people left on the rocking boat became very seasick during the first three weeks after we dropped anchor. There was much hunger and many of the women and children fought over scraps of food those first days. The men ashore tried to bring as much meat and fowl back to the ship as they could, but my brother Thomas would tell me whenever I had a chance to see him that he was hungry all the time. The smaller children developed scurvy and then high fevers and then we would have to bring their little bodies back to shore and bury them on the knoll where the Plymouth cemetery is now. The women grew weary and complained that the smell of the human waste was unbearable, still the men on shore did not allow them to leave the ship fearing Indian attacks.

My two brothers and my little sister were among the dead that first month. Mrs. Bradford was so distraught that she jumped overboard and drowned. She begged Mr. Bradford to let her go ashore, but he thought it best for her to stay. By February 1621 forty-six people had been brought ashore to the burial ground. It was a very sad time."

Richard paused for a moment and then pointed to his son and continued.

"I was about your age Edward when I came to this new land, but I worked as hard as any man. Those of us that were in reasonably good health did many chores from dawn to darkness for those that were not able to fend for themselves. It was a very hard time in my life, but I do believe that it has made me a better person, I have learned to appreciated what I have, no matter how meager, and to love everyone that I have contact with.

One day as I was gathering wood I was frightened almost out of my wits when an Indian appeared directly in front of me. He said, "Welcome

English boy." I was stunned and I could not move. I know that my mouth fell open and I could not speak for a minute or so. And then the strange man put his hand up with the palm facing me and said again in very plain English, "Welcome English boy." I did not know what to do, I was shaking and did not know if he was going to kill me or not. I had only heard bad things about the Indians. Instinctively I put my hand up in the same manor as he did and said, "Greetings."

"My name Samoset," he said.

I said with a shaking voice, "My name is Richard More.

The Indian smiled at me and said, "Samoset come to see Chief. I come by North," he said as he pointed in a northerly direction. "I come see English Chief."

All I could do was shake my head yes as he pointed toward our settlement. I turned slightly toward the village making sure my back was not turned completely toward him and started walking slowly toward the nearest house, Mr. Hopkins house. The lone Indian followed me and walked boldly beside me into our settlement; it was March 26, 1621. As we neared the walk in front of Mr. Hopkins house I decided that I should not allow the Indian to go any further, I didn't think I should take him to the Governor's house without warning. So I said, "Wait here, I will go and get him," and I pointed to his feet hoping he would know that I wanted him to stay where he was while I went to find Mr. John Carver, he was the first elected Governor of Plymouth.

Samoset was dressed in soft buckskin trousers trimmed with a fringe down the side of each leg. His shirt was of a lighter deerskin and it had fringes of red and white fur decorating the front and the sleeves. He wore his hair pulled back and twisted into a braid with feathers tucked into it, several of the feathers stuck up above his head. He had a red fox fur over his shoulder with the tail hanging down his back. His shoes were made of soft hide and had a thick leather like sole, they were trimmed with red and white fur, too. He stood tall with his shoulders back and appeared to be unafraid. He smiled broadly and his teeth were clean and white.

When I found the Governor he was with Mr. Bradford in the sick house. I rudely interrupted them and was in fear of being punished, but I was so excited I could not help myself. With fright and excitement both mixing in my stomach I hurriedly explained what I had just seen and done.

He said, "Stay here," and he picked up his hat and almost pushed me down as he ran out of the door.

You know that I did not obey him, I couldn't help myself, and I followed him back to Mr. Hopkins house.

Samoset saluted Governor Carver in the same Indian fashion that he saluted me and said, "Welcome."

The Governor was quite surprised by the man's knowledge of the English language and after introducing himself, Mr. Carver invited him to a nearby bench to sit and talk. Though a little frightened, many people gathered around the Governor and the strange and fascinating Indian, anxious to hear everything that was being said.

Samoset told us that he came from the north and lived in a place called Maine. He had learned English from the captains of fishing vessels that frequented the coast off the Monhegan Island there. He said that four years before our big ship came here the white man's small pox had killed all of the Indians that used to live here. That was why there was no one to hinder our possession of the new land or lay claim to it. No Indian would ever want to live there again, they believed that the place was possessed with evil demons. He told us that a young Patuxet Indian named Squanto was the only one of his tribe that was left and he had been in England when the white man's sickness killed his people. He said that Squanto was devastated when he returned and found not one of his people alive.

He told us that Squanto could speak better English than he could and he promised Governor Carver that he would bring him with him the next time he came to visit.

He also told us that the Nauset tribe and his tribe, called the Wampanoag, occupied the territory between Narragansett Bay and Cape Cod and they numbered about sixty people. The Nauset tribe to the southeast was about one hundred in number. His Chief's name was Massasoit and he was overlord of all of the Nauset Indian tribes in the territory.

Samoset explained to us why the Nauset Indians had bad feelings against the English stemming from the time when Captain Hunt deceived them a number of years ago. The Captain and several other sailors had bribed twenty Wampanoag Indians, five Nauset Indians and two Patuxet Indians with rum and trickery and empty promises into going back to the ship with him and then sailed away during the night while they were sleeping and sold them into slavery. Squanto was one of them."

"The story of Squanto is another wonderful story that I have told your father Sarah," Richard interrupted himself this time. "Maybe someday he'll tell it to you, or we can save that one until you're a little older." He smiled at Sarah and the other children and said, "Now where did I leave off," as he winked at Abraham.

"Several hours passed and after much questioning the Governor allowed Samoset to stay the night. Mr. Hopkins house was built with an extra room attached to the back and he agreed to let Samoset stay with

*him. Samoset was gone when we awoke the next morning; Mr. Hopkins
was quite distressed at first, but could find nothing missing.*

*It was early afternoon that same day, Sunday March 28, 1621 when
Samoset came back and brought five other members of his tribe with him.
They brought several nice skins with them but Mr. Carver would not
allow any trading because in was the Sabbath, however, they accepted
our invitation to eat with us and told us many things about our new
land.*

*After everyone had eaten their fill and the men were all smoking their
pipes several of the Indians nodded to each other and left our table. We all
thought that they were going to leave without thanking us as they disappeared back into the forest, but several minutes later they came back with
the tools that they had taken during the past months when we all were
asleep.*

*Later that evening just after dark they all left except Samoset, he en-
joyed our company so much that he asked to stay with Mr. Hopkins for a
few days; he didn't leave until Wednesday, March 31.*

*I remember that he had a pleasant voice, it was deep and loud so that
everyone could hear him. His accent was thick but we could all understand what he was saying. He very carefully listened to us and we all
knew that he was trying to learn and understand our language better.*

*It was on this evening when Samoset asked if he could use an empty
pot that was sitting near the fireplace. Mr. Hopkins shook his head yes
and the Indian took a small pouch that was hanging from his belt and
dropped its contents into the pot and pushed it closer to the fire. Everyone
watched him wondering what he was doing, he looked at me and winked,
it startled me a little and I looked down at the fire and then at the pot.
Suddenly we all heard a funny sound. Samoset saw a small basket near
the hearth and he covered the kettle with it as he pulled the heavy pot
away from the fire with a long stick.*

*After a few minutes when the noise stopped Samoset carefully re-
moved the basket and tipped the pot of parched corn that had turned all
fluffy and white out into the basket. He ate several kernels and then handed
the basket to me. I carefully smelled the strange food and then took one
piece from the basket and slowly put it into my mouth. It was wonderful.
I smiled at Samoset, took a handful and then handed the basket back to
him. He passed it around to everyone and a new discussion began. This
food was wonderful and very easy to make. It has been an evening treat
for me ever since.*

Richard looked at Sarah who seemed mesmerized by his story,
"So that's how I learned to make parched corn, Sarah."

"Is that the end of the story?" the little girl asked and then not waiting for an answer to the first question she said, "What happened to Samoset?"

"Well, Sarah," Richard said smiling, "from that day on Samoset was allowed to come and stay in Plymouth whenever he pleased."

"In fact, the next day Samoset returned with Squanto and they reported that Massasoit, their great sagamore, or Chief as you know him, and his brother Quadequina was nearby and all of their men were with them. They were quite frightening to us dressed in their buckskins, furs and feathers. They carried spears in their hands and bows and arrows on their backs. They wanted us to send Mr. Carver to talk with them, but our leaders decided that he should not go alone because of the great number of them, over sixty I do believe there were. Chief Massasoit did not want to come into our village either, probably for the same reasons.

Our settlement was beginning to look quite large when one stood at the top of the hill where they were standing and although they outnumbered us, I'm sure they were uncertain about our number of weapons. So Samoset and Squanto went back up the hill to talk with them and returned with the message that their Chief wanted to parley with our chief near the town brook. Most of their men would stay on the hill and most of us were to stay in the settlement.

After a discussion lasting several minutes our leaders decided that Mr. Edward Winslow, Captain Myles Standish and six other armed men would go and meet with them near the brook in a partially built house. They came back and related to Governor Carver and the rest of our leaders that they wanted to have trading and peace with us within a quarter hour.

It was agreed that we exchange several hostages with them; in other words, several of our men went to their location on the hill and several of their men came into our village.

A house that was being built near the town brook was still without a roof and they agreed that it would be a good place to parley, so we took them there, put a green rug on the thatch floor and gave them each a nice cushion to sit on. After the many greetings, introductions and assurances of friendship the first diplomatic agreement in New England was made, it was called the Massasoit Treaty and has been faithfully observed by both parties from that time until this very day.

We re-elected John Carver as Governor on April 5, 1621 but only two weeks later on the 19th of April the good Governor Carver passed on. I remember that day very clearly. The Governor had been plowing and plant-

ing in a great field. It was very warm that day and when he came back to his home in late afternoon he complained of a terrible headache and he lay down on his bed. His wife Desire was at a loss as to what to do for him. She bathed his head in cold cloths and tried to get him to drink sips of water. She could not wake him at all during the night.

In the morning when Mr. Bradford went to see him, he could not speak all he could do was open his eyes, although we do not think that he was able to see us. All of his senses failed that day but he did not die until four days later. It was April 23, 1621. We buried him on the hill with great ceremony and care and those that bore arms sounded a volley in his honor over his grave.

Mr. William Bradford was chosen to be Governor in Mr. Carver's place and is still to this day our esteemed Governor. Now, at the time Mr. Bradford was still not fully recovered from his near death sickness so Mr. Isaac Allerton was chosen to be his assistant and is also still the Governor's assistant.

Just before our Governor Carver passed on, it was April 15th the Mayflower left our shore to return to England. The good Captain Christopher Jones was sorry to leave us, but he promised to send help to us. He also took messages back to England for Governor Bradford and others that had loved ones still there.

It was a very lonesome sight to see the ship leave the harbor, many of us felt a great loss, and we all felt stranded, I believe that at that very moment it came to most of us that this was to be our new home forever. I dare say that many have never returned to our homeland, I for one have not, and I do not wish to do so.

By the time Richard's story was over the children were all yawning and ready for bed, the adults soon followed, it had been a long wonderful day for everyone.

Patricia Louise Blish Gould

CHAPTER FIFETEEN
1648

The following spring, on March 7, 1648 a second parcel of land, on the north side of the town between West Barnstable and Yarmouth, was purchased from Nepoyetum, Chief of the Mattakeeset Indians for the sum of two coats and one-days plowing. The town also agreed to build a fence from Stony Cove to the area of land that Nepoyetum was living with his people. Thomas Dimmock, Isaac Robinson and Thomas Hinckley represented Barnstable.

Abraham agreed to see that the plowing was completed as soon as the weather would allow.

The new burying place was laid out directly east of the meetinghouse on March 28, 1648 but because of the weather the Barnstable Cemetery was not officially dedicated until May 1, 1648 after the ground had thawed.

Patience Cobb, wife of Henry Cobb, was the first person buried there on May 4, 1648 just three days after the dedication. Her new baby Eleazer born on March 30, 1648 was just one month old.

Patience was a small woman and shortly before her baby was born she caught a terrible cold and it developed into a persistent cough that racked her little body severely until she had no more strength to hold on to life. She died on May 2, 1648.

Sarah Hinckley stayed with her every day helping with the children and the new baby.

Hannah Barker shared her mother's milk with Patience's new baby and several of the other nursing mothers helped to keep little Eleazer fed.

Every day Sarah would take the little one to each neighbor that could spare some of her own baby's milk for him.

Marie Dimmock tried to relieve Patience's coughing by giving her an extract made from Wild Cherry compounded with Lobelia, Slippery Elm, Marshmallow Root and Red Clover Blossoms. It helped her, but couldn't cure her consumption.

Before she died, Patience had long talks with Sarah about her illness, she knew she wasn't going to live. She asked Sarah almost daily, "Please Sarah take care of my children for me and see that Henry marries again."

Sarah would say, "Yes, Patience I will take care of your children," tears would fill her eyes and she would always add, "But, you will be up and around in no time, everyone is praying for you."

The day before Patience passed away, she said, "Sarah, I think that I will rest in peace if you promise me you will marry Henry and be a mother to my children."

"Oh, Patience, please don't talk that way," Sarah said kindly, "you know that I will be here until you are well." She smiled and added, "You know that I will probably never be married, and I'm sure that Henry will be keeping you as his wife for a long, long time." She tucked the clean sheets and quilts around her friend's frail body and kissed her on her forehead, "You get some rest now and please don't fret anymore, it is wearing you away."

Patience reached her cold, thin hand out from under the covers and held on to Sarah's arm and said tearfully, "Sarah, please promise me."

Sarah looked down at her sick friend and said, "Yes, Patience, if anything happens to you, I promise to take care of your children and marry Henry." She just knew that Patience would be well very soon, she had seen a number of women in her condition recuperate within two or three months, but if it would make Patience get better she would promise her anything she thought as she left the room.

That was the last thing Sarah said to Patience because when she returned a few minutes later Patience was gone.

Everyone in Barnstable attended Patience's funeral service.

• • •

Joseph Blish was born to Abraham and Anne Blish on April 1, 1648. He was baptized on April 9, 1648.

Early in the morning on the day Joseph was born Anne felt restless and depressed so about 8 o'clock, shortly after Abraham left for the meeting house, she decided to take little Sarah and walk to Marie's home. Her house was only about a half-mile down the lane and she thought that the walk and the fresh air would do her good. It was a little chilly but the sun was out and it was warming up. 'Spring is almost here,' Anne thought.

Anne also wanted to get some herbs that would make her child bearing easier and she wanted to talk to her friend about women things. She took her knitting basket on one arm and taking little Sarah's hand she headed down the lane. About a half-hour later she knocked on the Dimmock's door and then leaned against the house, the walk had made her more tired than she thought it would.

Marie answered the door almost immediately, a little surprised to see her friend so early in the morning. She noticed that Anne looked a little pale and quickly helped her into the house to a chair by the fireplace. "Are you all right my dear?" Marie asked quite concerned.

Anne quickly replied, "Oh, yes, I just came to visit. I wanted to talk with you for a while."

"Well of course my friend," Marie said with a worried look, "Let me get you a cup of tea."

"That would be lovely," Anne said removing her frock. "Come here Sarah, let mother take your frock," she said to her pretty red headed daughter, "then you can go play with Mehitabel."

Mehitabel Dimmock was Marie's oldest child; she was almost six years old, about a year older than Sarah was. The two of them were friends and when Marie suggested that they go out and feed the chickens and gather the eggs, Sarah put her frock back on and they both skipped off toward the chicken coop together holding hands.

Shubael was almost four and was busy being helpful by bringing in wood from the woodshed, one log at a time.

Thomas Dimmock was at the meetinghouse with Abraham and several of the other councilmen.

Marie poured tea for both of them and sat down on a short chair in front of Anne. "Is your baby moving hard?" she asked putting her hand on Anne's belly.

"Well, he was earlier this morning before I got up, but I think he's resting now," she answered in a smiling voice. "He's probably tired from our walk over here," she laughed at her own little quip.

Marie smiled, too. "Well, you sit for a while and then when you're rested I'll show you the new quilt that I just finished. It's on my bed upstairs."

Anne sipped her tea and closed her eyes, why was she so tired she wondered she walked everywhere. Lately Abraham did take her to church on Sunday in the buggy, but she still walked to Marie's home or one of the other neighbors quite often. "Umm, this tea is wonderful Marie," she said sleepily, "what a dear friend you are."

"Why don't you lean your head back and rest," she said patting Anne's hand, "if your baby is sleeping, so must you while you have the chance."

Anne sipped the last of her tea and handed the cup to her friend and closed her eyes again, she was asleep within a few minutes.

Marie put a shawl over her and put a little pillow under her head. She knew very well that there would be a new baby in the community in a little while.

When Anne woke up about a half-hour later she was quite embarrassed. She apologized to Marie and started to get out of the chair. "Where is Sarah?" Anne asked, "I'm sorry, I didn't mean to leave her in your care."

"Oh no, dear don't get up," Marie quickly calmed her friend down saying, "Sarah and Mehitabel are still in the barn gathering eggs and I have some more tea ready for us to sip."

"I think I really must be going home," she said. "Abraham will be home soon. I have no idea why I felt that I must see you today," she continued.

Marie smiled and said, "Your baby will be coming very soon. Look how low he is, walking over here was the right thing to do."

Anne felt a twinge in her lower abdomen. "Oops," she said in a lowered voice, "Marie, I think I just felt the first sign of labor."

"Let me make you comfortable in the side bed, Anne," Marie said.

"Oh, no," Anne said firmly, "I will have this baby in my own bed, just as I had Sarah. Besides, my birthing bundle is already prepared. All I need is a packet of herbs for new mothers tea."

"Then I shall get my medicine bag and I will walk you home and stay for a while," Marie said just as firmly. "Are you having any contractions yet?" she asked.

"Yes, I think so, little ones," Anne replied. Another twinge nagged her lower belly.

Every married woman kept a birthing bundle in her wardrobe or cupboard. It was made of several layers of wool tightly woven into a thick pad and then covered with soft cotton. After childbirth the cover was removed and washed and the wool was thrown away and another pad would be woven and covered with the clean cotton cover.

The bundle also held coarse thread for tying the umbilical cord and some women kept a small pair of scissors or a small knife in their kits to cut the cord with. There was a clean linen cloth to clean the new mother and clean cotton cloth to use as a bleeding pad after the baby was born. There was also a soft cotton cloth to wash the baby, a little gown for the baby and cloth to be used as a diaper.

Marie and Anne always gave pregnant women a little packet of herbs to be made into a tea to ease the birthing, if there was time, and a salve that soothed the womb after their babies were born. The herb packet contained Blue Cohosh Root that helped to stretch the neck of the uterus to make delivery easier. Golden seal killed infection and reduced swelling of the hands and feet. Red Raspberry, high in iron, enriched their breast milk, and prevented hemorrhaging and reduced birthing pains making childbirth easier. Queen of the Meadow soothed the nerves in the uterus and reduced water retention. Ginger was always added to help in distributing the herbs to needed places throughout the body, and Capsicum which stimulated the other herbs to do their job.

After the baby was born Marie used Blessed Thistle to increase mothers' milk, control fever, stop excessive bleeding and ease cramping of the legs. Marie called to the girls and Shubael, who had decided that it would be more fun to help his sister with the chickens, they were on their way back from the barn with a basket full of eggs. "Hurry children, we are going to go back to the Blish's now," she said as she took the basket of eggs from the girls and sat it on the table. Then she knelt down in front of her little daughter and pulled her coat collar up around her neck and said, "Mehitabel, please go to the meeting house directly, and don't dawdle, tell Mr. Blish and your father that Mrs. Blish will be having her baby very soon. I'm going to walk back with Mrs. Blish, you come over with your father, I'll take Shubael with me."

"Yes mother," she called back, "I'll go as fast as I can."

"Tell him that we will be at the Blish's house," she added.

"Yes, mother," she said, "and I won't dawdle."

"Take Sarah's hand Shubael," she said to her son. "I'll carry your knitting basket Anne, we'll go slowly," she didn't want to sound too excited, it might hurry Anne's contractions.

"Umm," Anne said and stopped walking for a minute.

Marie held on to her arm supporting her. "Sarah, you and Shubael can walk on ahead if you'd like," she said evenly. She didn't want them to be frightened if Anne groaned too loud. The children skipped along ahead looking back every few minutes to make sure they could see their mothers.

It took about thirty minutes to get to Anne's house; the children were sitting on the front steps waiting for them.

Marie helped Anne undress and get into bed and then went back into the commonroom to set the water kettle over the hearth. She coaxed a small fire from the coals that were still hot by adding a few splinters of wood to them and then she added some small sticks to the little blaze.

When she went back into the bedroom to see if Anne would like some tea, Anne was using the night pot.

Anne said, "Marie, I think the baby's coming already."

"Oh my dear," she said with alarm when she saw Anne.

Anne's water had broken as she had started to sit down on the pot, then she was seized with a hard pain; she grabbed the bedside table to keep from falling.

"Can you get back into bed?" Marie questioned quietly.

Anne could only nod her head yes as she tried to stand.

"Let me help you Anne," she said as she lifted Anne's legs into the bed.

As Anne lay back on the bed another pain took over her lower body and this time a loud moan escaped from her mouth. Her whole body shook as she took a deep breath, lifted her head and held on to her knees; then she began to pant quickly and said between clenched teeth, "It's coming, I have to push."

Marie moved around to the end of the bed and grabbed the clean pad that was ready for birthing and slid it under Anne's body. Anne was pushing again and Marie could see the baby's head. "I guess we got here just in time Anne," she said.

Anne moaned and pushed her baby's head out of her body.

Marie reached for the soft cloth to wipe the baby's face, Anne pushed again and the little shoulders and body slid into Marie's hands, another push and it was over.

"What is it?" she asked Marie.

"A boy," Marie answered her. "This baby was in a hurry, he could hardly wait to see the world," she said more to herself than to Anne. The baby gave a healthy cry before Marie could finish her part in helping Anne, she quickly tied and cut the baby's cord then she found the little blanket Anne had made laying on the dresser and wrapped him up.

"You have a perfect little boy Anne," she said softly as she put the baby into Anne's arms.

Anne held her baby close to her breast and said with a tearful smile, "I'd have ten babies if they were as easy as this."

Marie chuckled, "It sure didn't take very long did it?" She finished cleaning Anne and removed the birthing pad and put a clean nightgown on Anne.

They both heard little Sarah saying, "Papa, Papa, Mama's in bed." Shubael was saying, "We're going to have a real baby to play with Mr. Blish."

"Are we now," he said smiling as he hung his coat on the peg by the door.

Marie went to the bedroom door and said, "Abraham, you have a son and everything is fine."

He couldn't believe what Marie had just said. All he could do is repeat her words, "A son and everything is fine?"

"Yes, everything is fine," she said again, "come and see."

As he entered the room he could see Anne holding their baby, her red hair was scattered over the pillow. He had never seen her look more radiant. "So soon?" he asked her. "Why?"

Anne just smiled and said, "He was in a hurry, I guess."

Abraham reached for the baby and then unwrapped the blanket slowly to check him out. Then he looked at Anne and smiled and gave her a kiss. "I think we should call him Joseph," he said.

"I think that's a perfect name," she said and closed her eyes, she was so tired. Little Joseph had other ideas though; he was sucking his fists.

"I think he's hungry," Abraham said.

Marie helped Anne sit up in bed with her back to the pillow and it didn't take long for Joseph to learn that his mother had something better for him to eat than his hand.

Anne thought that she had never seen Abraham happier than he was at that moment as he watched his tiny son take his first drink of his mother's milk.

"Joseph," Abraham said, "with red hair just like your mama's." 'I have a son, I have never been so happy, I'm in love,' he thought and he leaned down and kissed his beautiful wife.

Then he said to his little daughter, "Sarah, come and see, Joseph your new little baby brother."

"You can kiss him on his cheek if you want to, Sarah," Anne said.

"He has red hair like me, father," she said looking up at Abraham with her big blue eyes.

"Just like yours," Abraham said and hugged his little girl.

• • •

Abraham Blish, Anthony Annable and John Eliot, along with three other councilmen, were in deep discussion with Paupmumuck, Chief of the South Sea Indians regarding the purchase of more land when Mehitabel quietly entered the Meetinghouse. She approached her father and whispered to him that Mr. Blish was wanted at home. After Abraham left the meeting the men postponed their discussion until the next day. Not everyone was happy about it, but most of them understood. Abraham's wife was having her baby.

The property the town council wished to purchase extended from the South Sea, abutting Yanno's lands on the east, and Nepoyetum's and Seaquanck's lands on the north. The Chief intended to reserve for his village 30 acres and now they were bargaining again for a higher price. The Chief had changed his mind and wanted the sum of two brass kettles, one bushel of Indian corn and a wood fence to enclose half of the thirty acres of land that he reserved for his people. The fence was to be built by the townsmen of Barnstable.

Several of the men on the council did not want to help supply the fencing and suggested building the fence with stone, but Paupmumuck said that a stone fence was not what his people wanted. The Indians liked the staggered look of the wooden split rails that the Barnstable farmers built around their pastures to mark their own property lines.

John Eliot did not think the idea of a bushel of corn was a good one either. The farmers needed the seed to plant their own crops and the Indian women were said to have plenty of their own seed. In fact, Yanno's wife recently told his wife Ruth, that they had already planted some of their fields.

The Chief also wanted to reserve the right and liberty to hunt on the land he was selling. The council agreed provided that if he set traps, he would watch out that the cattle were not injured or become caught in them. So after much discussion, Chief Paupmumuck agreed to settle for one great brass kettle of seven hand spans in width and one broad hoe. The Chief requested help from Abraham and John to build the fence and they agreed to allow their hired hands to show the Indian men how to build it. The Indians themselves, however, were to split the rails and do the labor.

The actual boundaries of this land were defined by Chief Paupmumuck to reach across over the sea to Nope Island, which is now Martha's Vineyard. This was not a reasonable boundary as far as the townspeople were concerned; it was not possible to own the sea. Several town committees were named to settle and adjust these boundaries with no avail. John Alden and Captain Josiah Winslow were called down from Plymouth to iron things out by obtaining another deed amplifying disputed clauses of the boundaries. Many of the Indians were fearful of the Captain because of the burning of the Pequot village eleven years earlier in 1637. However, the Chief was not intimidated and the differences over the boundaries of this land were not completely settled yet. The Barnstable town councilmen never tried to exercise control of the Island lands; they used only the mainland for their crops and homes.

Several weeks later, on May 17, 1648 the bounds of this land were still not clear even after the purchase price of the large kettle and the broad hoe had been paid and the agreement was signed by the town council and the Indian Chiefs. Some of the rails for the fence were split but it had not been set yet for lack of specific boundaries.

• • •

At the annual town council meeting held on June 3, 1648 William Carsely was re-appointed Constable. He was reluctant to accept, but William Crocker promised him that he would make himself available to help him whenever possible. Abraham Blish and Henry Cobb were elected as Surveyors and Hayward for the following year.

• • •

Marie Dimmock was called to help Hannah Bacon deliver her baby girl on Sunday, August 20, 1648. Anne Blish was there to help and Hannah welcomed the new mother's tea that made childbirth easier. Nathaniel and Hannah named their new baby girl Mary and she was baptized on the same day.

• • •

Fall and winter came and went with nothing unusual happening. Abraham and Anne went to Duxbury for the holidays and visited Richard and Mary. Richard's story this year was about the first duel ever fought in New England.

"It might have been the last, to my knowledge anyway," Richard said before he began.

"I haven't heard of any," Abraham said, "I believe the punishment for such is extremely severe."

"I think that if a man is caught dueling he would wish that his opponent had killed him, as his punishment would most likely be a slow death," Richard said.

"I'm glad the children are in bed," Mary said, "they do not need to hear about killing and such."

"So true," Anne replied.

"Now you ladies know that I would not tell our children about death and dueling," Richard said. "I came across this story when I was looking through my journals the other day and thought that it would be one that would interest Abraham."

"Yes, I haven't heard this story, Richard, and I will listen intently," Abraham replied smiling.

The ladies just looked at each other and smiled and continued sewing.

"Well, now the first duel in New England was held on June 28, 1621. It was held at high noon so that the sun would not be in either man's eyes causing a disadvantage for one or the other. I of course, was not suppose to be there, but having heard some of the men talking about the settlement of a great argument I could not help myself. I carefully hid in the bushes and lay as quietly as I could; I really had no idea what a duel was. I soon found out.

Edward Dotey and Edward Leister were very disgruntled with each other about the killing of a large deer. Dotey claimed that he shot it first and tracked it for about a half-mile and when he finally came upon it Leister was claiming it as his, he was cleaning it. Dotey was furious with Leister and accused him of stealing. Leister denied that the deer was dead when he found it and declared in a loud voice that he had shot it himself before he slit its throat. Dotey said that he never heard a gun shot and he had been close enough to the deer at all times, if Leister had fired at the deer he would have heard it.

Another man that had been hunting with them that day, John Langmore said that he did not hear a gun shot either. Dotey decided that the only way to settle this account was to challenge Leister to a duel.

Now dueling was not yet against any law that the people had agreed upon, but Dotey did not want to be denied his revenge, so they arranged to meet at a secluded place near the south end of town early the next morning. They were each to bring the weapon of their choice, however, there was to be no firearm. They also had to bring another man with them as their second, as they called him.

I was at the clearing before anyone else that day. Edward Dotey was the first to arrive, he had Langmore with him and he carried a dagger and a sword. Edward Leister came into the clearing shortly after and he was also carrying a dagger and a sword, Richard Gardner was with him.

As far as I can tell there were no rules to this duel, Dotey said en guard and they both proceeded to advance toward one another and swing their weapons. This went on for about twenty minutes before they made any contact with each other. I think that they were both afraid that if they were wounded they may not heal and would die a horrible death of infection or blood poisoning.

Anyway, Dotey finally struck Leister on his thigh with the pointed tip of his sword drawing blood and almost at the same time they were close enough so that Leister drew his dagger across the top of Dotey's hand.

Langmore and Gardner both held up their hands to stop the duel so they could check on the wounds of each man. Langmore told them both that they should have their injuries tended to immediately, both wounds were sufficient enough to cause serious problems if they were not dressed promptly. Dotey and Leister both agreed and though they did not shake hands they decided to call this confrontation a draw.

Dr. Fuller put a poultice of plantain weed on each wound and then questioned them privately as to how they came about their injuries. He felt it his duty to report this incident to Governor Bradford and a meeting of the entire company was called to settle this dispute once and for all.

Governor Bradford reprimanded these men and explained to them that dueling was not the way for Godly men to act, in fact he said it was barbaric and would bring nothing but sadness to those involved as well as their loved ones. After his lecture he asked the company for suggestions as to what kind of punishment should be given these men. Someone suggested, I don't remember who, that they be branded with a 'D' on their foreheads, another suggested they be flogged. Mr. Brewster suggested that they be tied together at head and foot and left to lay that way for twenty-four hours. Governor Bradford decided that he would let the entire company vote as to which of these punishments should be invoked.

The women being able to vote chose the latter; they voiced that enough harm and blood shed had already fallen upon these men. Governor Bradford agreed with them and Captain Myles Standish placed the men on the ground back to back and tied their heads together and wound the rope around the length of their bodies to their feet. They were completely unable to move. The tying up of the men was completed about 11 o'clock in the morning and they were to stay that way until 11 o'clock the next morning.

Well now, it was about 3 o'clock in the afternoon when the Governor went to check on them and they were both suffering greatly, in fact they were crying and moaning and pleading to be released. They both promised the Governor that they would not carry their disagreements to the extent of dueling ever again. They also promised that they would act as gentlemen and go to all prayer meetings if he released them.

Governor Bradford relented and shortened their punishment to time served and Captain Standish was ordered to cut the rope and the men were released from their bonds. Dr. Fuller helped them sit up and told them they must go to the brook and wash themselves in the cold water and then rub their bodies briskly so that the prickles in their arms and legs would go away. It was several hours more before they were able to stand up straight and walk without limping. I believe that washing themselves in the brook was almost more punishment than being tied together.

By the time our evening meal was served both men were able to walk about and they had no trouble eating, they had had nothing to eat since the morning before. Needless to say, Edward Dotey and Edward Leister never had any conflicts with each other or anyone else for that matter, again.

"That was a wonderful story, dear," Mary said.

"It wasn't as violent as I anticipated it would be," Anne agreed.

"Thank you ladies," Richard said.

Abraham chuckled and said, "You have such a way with words Richard, I am privileged to know you, I will never tire of hearing your stories."

"And once again you have kept us up past our bedtime my dear husband," Mary chuckled, "I'm going to bed."

"Me, too," Anne said, "the children will be up before you know it."

Patricia Louise Blish Gould

CHAPTER SIXTEEN
1649

Ezekiel Annable was born on April 20, 1649 to Anna and Anthony Annable. Anna's labor was much easier this time and she was up and around in no time. However, Ezekiel was a sickly baby and did not eat very well, he died on May 20, 1649 when he was just one month old, about three weeks after he was baptized. Many of the townspeople were sadden for the Annable's, they knew that Anna had done all she could for her little infant son.

Marie Dimmock gave Anna special herbs that would enrich her milk hoping that it would help the little baby, but it did not.

God must have needed another angel Anne Blish told Anna trying to console her while she cried in Anne's arms.

• • •

On May 6, 1649 Benjamin was born to Roger Goodspeed and his wife Alice. There seemed to be a baby born almost every month or so. Marie and Anne helped Alice and there were no complications.

• • •

Another sad event occurred on August 3, 1649 when William and Elizabeth Bills' little boy Billy died in a boating accident, he was just 6 years old.

Little Samuel Crocker and Billy were playing in an old rowboat near the dock with several other young boys, taking turns rowing with the heavy oars. When Samuel and Billy took their turn they were not paying attention and rowed out into water that was quite deep.

Two men on the dock getting ready to launch their fishing boat called to them that they should come back to the shore. At the same moment a wave caught the little boat broad side and tipped it sideways spilling Billy into the water. Sammy managed to hang onto the oar and stayed in the boat.

The men jumped into their boat and rowed as fast as they could to Billy, put he was floating face down when they got to him, he was dead. He had a big gash on the top of his head where the side of the boat had hit him.

William and Elizabeth were devastated; this was the second child they had lost. Elizabeth vowed there would be no more, her heart could not stand to lose another child she said. They laid Billy to rest beside his sister the next day. The whole town grieved for William and Elizabeth.

• • •

Elder Henry Cobb married Sarah, daughter of Samuel Hinckley on December 12, 1649. His first wife Patience had been gone just over a year now and he was trying to raise his seven children by himself. His oldest son John was 17, he was born in Plymouth on June 7, 1632. Then James, also born in Plymouth on January 14, 1634 was 15. Mary born on May 24, 1637 in Scituate was 12, and Hannah also born in Scituate on October 5, 1639 was 10. His three youngest children were born in Barnstable; Patience born March 13, 1641 was 8, Gershom born January 12, 1644 was 5 and Eleazer born March 30, 1648 was not quite 2 years old.

Sarah had been helping Henry almost every day since the death of his lovely wife Patience on May 2, the year before. She loved Henry's children and he was kind to her; she could probably learn to love him she told herself. After all she had promised Patience that she would take care of her family and marry Henry, now here she was, Henry Cobb's wife.

Sarah's father was Samuel Hinckley and her brother Thomas and her two sisters, Susannah Smith and Hannah Lewis all lived in Barnstable. They all approved of the courtship and her father had discussed many times with her the advantages she would have if she married Elder Cobb. He was well respected in the community, a Deacon in the Church and he was wealthy. His children were of an age to be very helpful to her and she was not getting any younger. Her father was usually right about matters of this nature and he convinced her that she should marry Henry Cobb and stay respectable in the eyes of the church. She had been extremely careful not to be seen alone with him and was not aware of any rumors about her helping him with his children.

Sarah agreed with her father knowing that she would be 22 her next birthday and if she were not married she would be considered a spinster. She decided she would have to lock away her dream of marrying a tall young man and going back to England to live with him in a beautiful Manor, have four children and live happily ever after.

Henry Cobb was just the opposite of her dream, he was 40, sometimes when he was sad and quiet he seemed even older than that. He was still quite attractive, though his hair was thinning in front it was still dark brown with no gray in it. His dark eyes were sad most of the time, except when he was playing with his children. He was just a few inches taller than she was and though he had gained a few pounds around his middle during this past year he was by no means fat.

Although Henry was good to her and cared about her welfare he was not in love with her and she knew it, and she was not sure if she could ever love him.

Sarah was not considered pretty, she was quite plump and her teeth were crooked. Her hair was her best asset, it was blonde and she wore it pulled back into a bun at the back of her neck, little unruly tendrils were always coming out from under her bonnet and hung about her face. On humid days or if she was cooking near the hot fireplace it curled softly onto her round face and she became quite attractive. On one of these days Henry told her that he thought she was pretty. She had blushed and smiled then tried to cover her teeth quickly with her hand and turned back to her chores. She didn't know what to say, she could feel herself blush.

Shortly after that Sarah told her father that she would agree to marry Henry Cobb if he asked her. Maybe Mr. Cobb did find her attractive. The children all liked her even the older boys never disobeyed her if she asked them to help her with any of the chores.

Since she had been taking full care of them, she had lost enough weight so that her clothes had begun to hang on her; she had taken the seams in on several of her better dresses. The older girls had mentioned that she looked nice on Sunday when they all went to church.

It was on Thanksgiving Day evening after a wonderful dinner at the Hinckley's home that Henry asked Sarah to marry him.

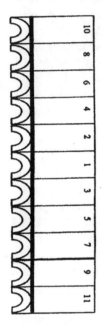

The children were playing a numbers game called 'Trollmadam,' a game that children of all ages could enjoy playing together inside with a minimum amount of noise. The game consisted of a board with thirteen round notches cut along the bottom, each notch was randomly numbered and each number indicated an amount of score when a round stone was rolled through the notch. The board was balanced on the floor or table with a small block at each end with a slot in it; after each child rolled a small round stone five times through one of the notches the one with the highest score won the game. Even the younger children could win at this game and would often win higher scores than their older siblings or parents. Each child took turns adding the scores making this an educational game as well as entertaining.

The women cleaned the table and took care of the food while the men were sitting by the fireplace with their pipes.

Henry had been watching Sarah all day and thought that he could see a change in her. He quietly asked Samuel, "Do you think it would be a good time to ask Sarah to marry me?"

"I do believe that the proper waiting time of six months, before you marry again, has come and gone, Henry," Samuel Hinckley answered him with just a hint of a smile.

Henry watched as Sarah wiped her hands on a towel then he walked across the room to her and whispered, "Could we go outside for a few minutes Sarah, I would like to talk to you."

Sarah looked quickly at her mother and then at Henry and shook her head yes and said, "I'll get my shawl Mr. Cobb."

As they went out of the door the children looked at each other and smiled. They were wishing that Sarah would be their new mother.

Henry Cobb took Sarah's hand and helped her down the steps and he didn't let go when she reached the ground, he turned her toward him and said, "Sarah, I think it's been long enough now since my dear wife has passed on."

She didn't know what to say so she lowered her head to hide her trembling lips and the blush on her cheeks. She knew what he was going to say.

He lifted her chin with his finger, looked into her eyes and said, "I do believe that I have made a decision that will benefit both of us." He let go of her chin and touched her cheek with his finger. "I want you to marry me," he said without any emotion.

She blinked her eyes, as tears started, she hoped it was too dark for him to see them. "I think that would be a good thing for the children, Mr. Cobb," she said as she lowered her head again to look at her feet. She was hoping he would say that he loved her, she would let him kiss her if he did.

"Does that mean you will accept my proposal Sarah," he asked.

"Yes, Mr. Cobb," she answered, "I will be your wife."

"Good," he said, "I think we should be married in two weeks, on December 12th."

Sarah wanted to say that she would do her best to make him happy and be a good mother to his children, but he was so matter of fact about this subject that she couldn't think of anything to say except, "That will be fine Mr. Cobb."

"You should probably start calling me Henry now Sarah," he said and he took her arm and turned her toward the steps.

'This conversation is over, maybe I should not have been so quick to say yes,' she thought as she followed his lead and went into the house.

The children, all smiles, looked at them hoping to be able to read their faces, when they came through the door.

Sarah shivered, 'It was cold out,' she thought, 'or was it just the coldness of Mr. Cobb's heart that chilled her.' She looked at her mother and smiled weakly, her mother nodded and then went back to her knitting. Sarah sat down on a stool near the hearth and little Eleazer crawled over to her. She picked the little boy up and hugged him and he cuddled into her neck. She kissed the top of his head knowing she would be fine as long as the children loved her that was all she needed.

December 12th came and went as any other day for everyone except Sarah Hinckley Cobb. She and Henry were married about 2 o'clock in the afternoon. The children were present as well as her parents and several friends of each family. Her mother made a light dinner for everyone and her parents and friends all left directly after they had finished eating.

After their meal Mary and Hannah helped the younger ones to bed and then put the food away and cleaned the table. Henry lit several candles and sat them on the long table and then told the four oldest children it was time to do their studies. Henry took his bible from the mantel and than sat down in front of the fireplace in his cushioned chair and began reading as he did every evening.

Earlier in the afternoon Sarah had moved her things into Henry's room and John and James helped her with her heavy trunk and satchels. Now she wasn't sure just what she should do next. When she looked over at the children studying quietly she caught Mary's eye and started to ask her if she would help her unpack, Mary put her finger to her lips and shook her head no.

'So,' Sarah thought, 'this is quiet time, no one is suppose to say anything until Henry gives him or her permission.' She turned and went into the bedroom and was almost of a mind to call to the boys to help her move her things into another room.

"What shall I do," Sarah whispered under her breath as she sat down on the chair in the corner of the room and looked around at all of the things hanging on the walls.

Most of the clothes were Henry's. Several pair of trousers, five or six shirts and other pieces of men's clothing hung on pegs. On the wall opposite her were two or three dresses that she had seen Patience wear when she was alive. They were still hanging there. She of course had not entered Mr. Cobb's bedroom after Patience died it was unheard of for an unmarried woman to enter a widow-ers bedroom even if she was looking after him and his children. Henry had not touched anything in this room either except his own clothes since Patience died.

Sarah had loved Patience like a sister and had cared for her when she was sick in this very room. "Dear God, I don't want to take her place, I just want to help her family," she prayed quietly.

She got up and opened her trunk and removed all her things placing them on the bed, then took Patience's clothes off the pegs and carefully folded them and placed them in her trunk. She then placed all of Patience's personal things that were on the bureau and in one of the dresser drawers, in the trunk with the dresses. She hung several of her own dresses on the empty pegs and put her undergarments in the empty drawer and laid out her wedding nightgown. She also found a clean nightshirt for Henry and laid it on top of the nightstand near his side of the bed.

She found clean sheets and another quilt in one of the drawers of the large bureau and quietly changed the bedding, sprinkling some talcum powder scented with rose petals on the sheets before she put the clean quilt on the bed. When she was sure that the room looked presentable she went to the kitchen and filled her commode pitcher with warm water and took it back into the bedroom. She found her bayberry soap jar and a clean towel she had brought with her and took a nice sponge bath and put her lovely white cotton nightgown on. She put some of her water from her pitcher into the wash bowl on Henry's side of the bed, 'I hope it isn't too cold by the time he comes to bed,' she thought as she climbed into bed.

"Dear God, help me to be the best wife I can be," she prayed again as she snuggled under the warm quilt, "I will make him love me, Patience, I know you did not want him to be unhappy," she whispered to her dead friend. She and Sarah had talked about him and the children everyday from the time little Eleazer was born until the day she died a month later. Sarah would do her best to make him happy but she would not allow him to make her unhappy. She was going to make this house a wonderful place to live, whether Henry Cobb wanted her to or not. She closed her eyes and dozed off to sleep.

Sarah opened her eyes as soon as Henry touched the bed, his back was to her and he was undressing. She did not hear him enter the room and she wasn't sure if she wanted him to know she was awake, so she did not move. A small candle sat on the top of the nightstand giving off enough light so that she could see his naked back as he pulled his shirt off over his head and then she quickly closed her eyes as he took his trousers off. She knew what a little boy looked like naked, but she wasn't sure if she wanted to know what a grown man looked like. Then she heard him splash some of the water and then smelled the clean soapy smell of the bayberries and opened her eyes just enough to watch him wipe his face and arms. Then she watched him as he put on the clean nightshirt she had laid out for him. She had taken the one that had been lying on the bed and put it in a pile of clothes that she intended to wash the next day. She smiled to herself wondering if he had noticed that the room was tidier before he blew out the candle and climbed into bed beside her.

Henry Cobb was surprised to see that his room had been straightened, it smelled better, too, he thought as he undressed. He looked around for his nightshirt trying to be quiet but he couldn't see it. 'It was on the bed this morning,' he thought grumpily. Then he noticed a clean one laying on the nightstand and pulled it on, he was cold. When he pulled the covers back he could smell roses, 'That's a nice pleasant smell,' he thought as he climbed into bed. He wasn't sure if he should wake his new bride or if he should just forget the needs of a man and go to sleep. He lay flat on his back with his thigh touching Sarah's knees; she was lying on her side facing him with her knees slightly bent. 'She's so warm and she smells so good,' he thought and his manhood stiffened. He turned slightly and put his hand on her hip, she didn't move, but he could sense that she was tense, he moved his hand over her hip toward her bottom and pulled himself closer to her. She moved closer to him at the same time and he sucked in his breath as his emotions carried him almost beyond reason.

"Henry," she whispered, "I will do my best to be a good wife to you and make you happy." She inched closer feeling his manhood against her belly, "All I ask is that you let me love you."

"Oh, Sarah," he sighed, "I am happy that you are my wife and I do want you to love me." He put his leg over hers and pulled her closer and kissed her mouth. 'Her breath is so sweet,' he thought and then he could feel her wanting him as much as he wanted her. He tried not to hurt her too much when he entered her warm place and when she stiffened and moaned he lay still for a minute. When he felt her start to relax he couldn't help himself, it had been so long since he had made love he shuddered and groaned and then let himself melt into her beautiful soft warm body.

Sarah knew the ways of a man; women talked about these things and shared their feelings with each other. She was told that when a man was without a wife for a long time that he would complete the act of lovemaking in just a few seconds after starting. However, he would often start again if the woman let him know that she would allow it.

Sarah kissed his face and his lips hoping that he wouldn't think bad things about her, she wanted him to move his body against hers again. She moved her hips under him and after a minute or so she felt his manhood thicken and he moved with her, she held him close and she put her legs over his holding him to her. She wanted to love him so much.

This time they became as one person and shuddered at the same time holding each other tight. He kissed her lovely mouth and she kissed him back, they fell asleep in each other's arms in the nice soft warm bed.

• • •

At the annual town meeting held on June 6, 1649 William Carsely was once again chosen to continue as Constable for another year. Abraham Blish told the council that he would help William if he needed assistance in taking a prisoner to Plymouth. The other elected officers stayed in their positions for another year.

• • •

John Crocker was licensed to keep an Ordinary, or what is now called a Tavern. He and his wife Joan had no children, probably because he did not treat Joan very well and they argued constantly about his behavior, especially when he was drunk. He was illiterate and always associated with an entirely different class of people than she approved of. He did not belong to the church and was very seldom home, except to sleep or eat. Earlier in the spring he sold about half of his land because he was tired of the hard work and applied for a license to open an Ordinary. Joan agreed knowing that she would probably be doing most of the work, but it was better than trying to run a farm by herself. At least she would be doing the things she liked to do, cooking and cleaning.

Joan was well respected in Barnstable and it saddened many of the women in town to think that she had to put up with such a husband. Then again the old saying was that when she made her bed in his home she had to lay in it. No one knew that her father had arranged her marriage in 1637 when she was only 17 years old, John Crocker was 39 at the time.

Joan believed that having no children of her own was just as well, she was free to help her sister-in-law Alice with hers. John's brother William and his wife Alice lived nearby and their children were always eager to visit their Aunt Joan. Uncle John on the other hand was a man to stay away from unless their father or mother was with them.

The Tavern soon provided the Crocker's a decent living. This was the kind of work that appealed to John; the land that he still owned was mostly haying property and he left most of the labor of caring for it up to his servant Roger Glass, a very worthy young man. However, he treated Roger with less respect than he had for his horse.

The only thing that Joan did not like about the Tavern was the fact that some of the men that visited the tavern often drank too much and indulged in low and vicious conversation. She complained that such company never improved the temper or moral character of a man or added anything to his respectability in the community. If these men became too rowdy and boisterous she would throw them out and send her husband to bed. He usually did as she suggested because she threatened to close the Tavern to all of his friends if he did not do as she asked.

William Crocker was the younger brother of John and came to Barnstable with Reverend Lothrop. He had a large estate and built his house on the lot next to Henry Bourne's. He was considered the richest man in town. Owning one hundred and twenty-six acres of upland and twenty-two acres of meadow in West Barnstable and also forty acres of upland at the Indian Ponds. The easterly side of his farm was bounded by John Smith's farm and by Samuel Hinckley on the southerly side, by the commons on the west and by Mr. Bodfish on the north.

William lived an exemplary and pious life. He did nothing dishonest and though he acquired a great wealth he never made any enemies or was the envy of any one, he was respected and beloved by all. When he moved to West Barnstable, the lands had only a nominal value, but he was industrious and a good manager, teaching his sons his same ways. Many families considered their wealth increased 100 pounds for every son born to them and 50 pounds for every daughter. William Crocker was no exception to this idea. He had five children, four sons and one daughter.

William and Alice's two oldest children, John, born May 1, 1637 and Elizabeth, born September 22, 1639, were born in Scituate before they moved to Barnstable. Samuel was born on June 3, 1642. Job was born March 9, 1644. Josiah was born September 19, 1647. His sons were getting older now and were able to assist him on their farm.

By the time the boys reached the age of seventeen they were able to do the work of a man. The girls were also brought up to do more than earn their own living. Young girls assisted their mothers with all household responsibilities. They spun and wove flax and wool and made their own clothes as well as their brothers clothes. In hay time and at harvest time the whole family assisted one another in the fields. From his farm a good farmer would obtain an abundance of the prime necessaries of life and any surplus was sold to pay for the foreign articles that every farmer required. The Crocker children were no exception to this upbringing and William considered himself a very fortunate and rich man.

• • •

Robert Davis moved to Barnstable from Yarmouth in June of 1649 with his wife Elizabeth and their two small children Deborah, age 4 and Mary age 1. He was the younger brother of Dolar Davis who was the owner of many acres of land. Robert was given a small house to live in as payment for helping Dolar run his properties. He was an ambitious young man and never complained about the hard work that he was asked to do. He was noted for his honesty and integrity and was trusted by everyone. He was also trusted as one who could bear arms.

• • •

Notice came to Abigail Coggin that her husband Henry Coggin had died at sea on June 16, 1649. His body was never recovered. Henry left her financially well off, but she was more lonesome now than ever, she was left alone to raise their four children without a father. Henry would never be coming home to her again. The Reverend suggested she have a headstone placed in the Barnstable Cemetery so that she would have a place to go and grieve for her husband. Most of the time she went there to be angry with Henry, for never being home when she needed him and then never coming back again to help her with the children.

1111 1 1

It didn't take long for word to get out that she was a rich widow. She was still quite beautiful and most men didn't mind the children that came with a new wife. Most women were careful though about marrying a man that didn't like her children and they usually stayed away from them or at least questioned their reputation with the Reverend.

• • •

Henry and Sarah Bourne had a new baby on August 26, 1649, they named her Dorcas. She was not a healthy baby and could not keep anything in her tiny belly, she vomited almost everything that she ate and she cried constantly.

Marie and Anne did everything they could think of to help the tiny girl but to no avail, she died on September 9, 1649.

Henry and Sarah laid her to rest the next day.

"Another tiny angel in God's heaven," Anne said holding Sarah tight while they both cried.

• • •

Samuel and Henrietta Jackson had a son they named Horace on December 28, 1649. He was healthy and Henrietta recovered quickly. Marie and Anne tried to make her stay in bed for an extra day or two but she refused.

"No," Henrietta said adamantly, "I have too much to do and my other five little ones need me."

"Some women manage better than others," Marie said to Anne on their way home after delivering Henrietta's baby.

"I won't mention Abigail Coggin's name," Anne said smiling.

Marie laughed and put her finger to her lips and said, "Me either."

CHAPTER SEVENTEEN
1650

Nathaniel and Hannah Bacon had another son they named Samuel on February 15, 1650. Hannah said she just liked the name. Nathaniel named the girls and Hannah named the boys. Marie and Anne were with Hannah and both her and baby Samuel were healthy.

• • •

Andrew Davis son of Robert and Elizabeth Davis was born May 2, 1650 their third child. Robert was elated that he now had a son. His family was growing steadily and he was able to save a little money each year and would be able to buy some land one-day soon and now he had a son that would some day inherit his property. Marie and Anne helped Elizabeth deliver her baby. Elizabeth was having a hard time relaxing and Marie had to give her two cups of new mother's tea before little Andrew was born.

Anne reported to Abraham that both mother and baby were in good health and he recorded the event in his journal.

• • •

At the annual town council meeting held on June 1, 1650 Nathaniel Bacon was appointed Constable. He replaced William

Carsely who claimed that at age 45 he was getting too old to be traveling so much and he was neglecting his duties to his farm.

John Mayo was elected to become full time record keeper. Thomas Dimmock was appointed full time teacher for the 40 children of all ages that were in need of schooling.

The town of Barnstable was now the home of over 150 people and John was not able to teach the children and keep the records that were needed to manage a town government.

Abraham relinquished his duty as record keeper to John Mayo and offered to help John if he needed his assistance and informed the council that he would continue with his own personal journal.

The other officials all agreed to hold their same offices for another year.

• • •

Thomas Dimmock, 48 years old was failing in health and unable to run his farm and earlier in the year he was forced to sell part of his land, he did not have the strength to do hard laborious tasks. However, though Elder Dimmock was not well he was able to teach the children their lessons. He was good with them having a friendly manner and kind words and the children enjoyed learning from him; he had two children of his own.

Abraham knew that Thomas would make a good teacher and was skilled in his knowledge of the bible, historical facts and his reading and writing were impeccable. Abraham and Thomas were good friends and they enjoyed each others company; their wives were together most of the time healing the sick and delivering babies. If Abraham had to be away on business and was unable to attend a town meeting he often asked Thomas to take notes for him so that he could keep his journal up to date. In fact, there was a story in Abraham's journal that Thomas helped him write having been a part of the story himself. Abraham told him once that he liked to tell the story about a young man that endured great pain and suffering when he was young and why he limped. He thought it was a good story that taught strength of character. It was titled:

"Thomas Rowley"

"Thomas Rowley grew up in a poor but happy family setting. His father Randall and mother, Prudence, led a simple life having moved to the Colonies in 1627 as indentured servants of a wealthy farmer in Scituate. They moved to Duxbury in 1634 when their servitude had been fulfilled. Thomas was about 6 years old at the time with two younger brothers, Stewart age 4 and Allen age 2. His parents managed to buy a half-acre of land with the little money they had saved over the years and they built a small two-room house on it.

Not having the means to buy an iron trammel-bar for the inside of the chimney, Randall made a wooden one, the bar was used to hang pots and kettles on over the fire. Prudence was always careful to keep an eye on the burn marks and to keep the trammel wet. It would be replaced with a new one whenever it began to burn through to a dangerous width.

Young Thomas was 10, Stewart was 8 and Allen was 6 when tragedy struck late one night in the winter of 1638. The Rowley children were asleep on their pallets near the hearth and their parents were asleep in their bed in their room opposite the fireplace. Prudence watered the trammel after the evening meal as she always did, however, Mr. Rowley built the fire a little bigger than usual before he went to bed because he was cooking a kettle of wort.

Wort was a type of beer that was made regularly by many townsmen. They boiled malt grain with water for several hours, usually overnight and then in the morning they added other herbs and roots for flavor and then poured the brew into jugs, corked the tops and let it set for a week or so. Everyone drank it, even the children if it was not left to ferment too long. It was very bitter when that happened and the children did not like it, they would drink water or milk instead. The bitter wort usually made their mothers giggle and their fathers loud.

About 1 o'clock in the morning a loud snap, a great crash and then the splashing of water followed by loud screams from the children woke the Rowleys. The trammel had caught fire and burned through causing the scalding kettle of brewing wort to spill over onto the sleeping children.

Randall reached the children first and pulled the two little boys away from the scalding water. Prudence took Thomas' arms and pulled him out into the middle of the room.

Randall's littlest son Allen was scalded to death almost immediately and Stewart died a little later that morning. Thomas was lucky to receive only severe burns on both legs. Being the oldest he allowed his little brothers to reap most of the warmth from the fireplace by letting them sleep in front of him.

It was about 1:30 in the morning when Randall pounded on Jane Annable's door. He could hardly speak he was so upset and out of breath, *he had run all the way to her house. Finally Jane understood what had happened and dressed as quickly as she could. She sent Anthony to tell Marie Dimmock to meet her at the Rowley's home as soon as she could.*

While Jane gathered her herbs Anthony went to the barn, hitched up a horse to Jane's buggy for her and was saddling his own horse by the time Jane and Randall were ready to leave. Randall was shaking and crying and could hardly breathe so Jane quietly questioned him in a calm voice for the details of what had happened as they rode back to the his house in Jane's buggy.

Randall told Jane that his son Thomas was unconsciousness when his mother pulled him away from the fireplace. He also told her that little Allen was dead, Stewart was still breathing though he had not opened his eyes at all his chest was still moving.

When they arrived at the Rowley house Jane was shocked by the mess that Prudence was still trying to clean up. The pallet and quilts were sopping wet and were lying on the back steps holding the door open. The house reeked with beer. Prudence was sobbing and trying to sweep the smelly liquid out of the back door. She hardly knew what she was doing, she kept saying, "Help me, God, oh help me God," with every sweep of her broom.

Jane immediately checked on little Allen and was certain that he was dead. Then she touched Stewart's scalded neck and felt only a faint pulse. She was sure there was nothing she could do for him; she knew that as long as he was unconscious he would not realize the pain. Then she turned her attention to Thomas.

She touched his forehead and said, "Thomas, can you hear me."

He opened his eyes and moaned, "My legs," took a deep breath tried to move his legs and then fainted again.

Jane gently pulled the ragged quilt away from Thomas' legs that Prudence had covered her shivering son with and then lifted his still wet nightshirt that was clinging to him.

Marie came into the house at that same time and seeing Jane standing over Thomas she ran to her asking, "What happened Jane?"

"There's been a terrible accident," Jane said quietly, "The little ones are gone."

Prudence screamed when she heard Jane, and Marie went quickly to the poor woman. "Not Stewart, too," she said questioningly to Marie.

"Now, now Prudence, you must calm yourself for Thomas' sake," Marie said gently patting the poor woman on her back. Then she went over to the little ones lying on a pallet near the door where Randall had gently laid them.

Randall was on his knees looking into the fireplace trying to understand what had happened. The big kettle and the other pots and pans were scattered in the ashes, little puffs of smoke curled here and there through the mess.

Jane said, "Randall, I think we should get a wagon and move Thomas to my house, I can tend to him much better there."

Marie looked at Jane and knew that she was thinking about the cleanliness that was needed when it came to burns of this size. "It will also be easier for me to help you at your home," Marie said knowingly.

Prudence said sobbing, "I can tend him Jane, will you let me, I'll help, too?"

"Yes, Prudence," Jane answered, "I will need you to help me too."
She hugged the poor distraught lady.

Marie shook her head in agreement and said, "Yes dear, your help will be needed too." Then she looked at the little bodies of Allen and Stewart and said, "We will send for Reverend Partridge to help you make arrangements for your little boys." She went back over and touched Stewart's neck as Jane had done. "He's gone," she said, and couldn't help the tears that started to fall.

Randall went to the barn to hitch his horse to his lumber wagon while Marie coaxed Prudence's help in fixing a pallet, covering it with a quilt so that the ride would be as easy on Thomas as they could make it.

Jane was busy preparing cold compresses that she had dipped in English tea, they would keep the dirt out and soothe his pain on the ride to her house. She hoped that he would stay unconscious until they got there.

When Mr. Rowley came back he put the pallet into the back of the wagon and then gently lifted his son's limp, almost lifeless body, carried him out into the cold night and carefully laid him on the back of the wagon. Thomas never moved all the way to the Annable's home.

Jane got to work immediately after they arrived. While he was still in the wagon and even though it was cold she removed all of Thomas' clothes. Then Mr. Annable, Mr. Rowley, Marie and herself carried him into the house and laid him on a pallet covered with a clean white linen sheet.

Jane quickly made a salve from Honey, Comfrey Leaves, and Slippery Elm Bark and applied it to Thomas' legs as carefully as she could without disturbing the burned skin.

Prudence and Marie helped Jane change the bandages every day. Thomas suffered great pain and dreaded this time of the day but he was very brave. Jane would make him drink a bitter brew made with Wild Lettuce and Capsicum about a half hour before his bandages were changed, but sometimes even after taking the pain medicine it would hurt so much that

241

he would faint. The women would then hurry and finish with the dress-ings before Thomas regained consciousness.

Jane and Marie made sure that he was able to walk by making him exercise his stiff legs every day. As his legs were healing Jane rubbed a salve that she made from St. Johns Wort Oil compounded with Comfrey, this mixture helped to keep the skin soft so that his legs could move easier.

Thomas would cry silently every time they moved his knees but he endured it. It took several months before his burns were healed and he could walk, and though he was left with just a few ugly scars and a slight limp he was able to walk without any pain. He was never able to run very far as his legs were weak but Thomas considered himself very fortunate to be able to walk.

The Rowley's were grateful for the kindness that Jane and Marie showed their son. Mary More and Sarah and Anne Pratt helped Pru-dence clean her house thoroughly to rid it of the horrible smell of beer.

The burial of the two little boys was a sad day and many a tear was shed. The people of Duxbury helped them through their ordeal by praying for them every day. Mr. and Mrs. Rowley were never the same after that horrible night, though they did take pride in Thomas for having the strength to endure the great pain and his long recovery. After that day they seemed to just plod along in their daily routines and they stayed to themselves most of the time.

Abraham made an iron trammel for their fireplace and was sorry that he didn't know they were using a wooden one. He vowed he would make it a point from that day forward to see that all fireplaces in Duxbury had iron trammels. He and Richard More forged several of them, loaded them into a wagon and went to each new home being built in Duxbury making sure that the new owner had an iron trammel to put in his fireplace.

Thomas did his studies while he was in his sick bed at the Annable's that winter. Marie thought it best to keep his mind on other things after the tragedy so she requested that her husband Thomas teach the young Thomas Rowley his lessons each week. The Annable girls helped him study as well.

When Thomas Dimmock moved to Barnstable in 1639, he invited the Rowley's to move there with them and hired Randall to work for him and help him build his house. He gave Randall an acre of land and the means to build a small house on it.

Randall Rowley was glad to leave his terrible memory behind and accepted Thomas' invitation.

Elder Dimmock tutored young Thomas for seven years and then the Dimmock's paid his way to England and for his education at Cambridge

*University where he studied theology. He is a wonderful preacher in Bos-
ton now 12 years later and has taken care of his parents since he graduated and returned to New England. He never forgot his first teacher and
recently visited the Dimmock's when he came home to see his parents.*

Thomas was grateful to Abraham for having nominated him as
teaching elder and knew that this story would be helpful in teaching the children about strength and fortitude. God works in mys-
terious ways he thought on his first day of school. He loved teaching Thomas Rowley twelve years ago, now he had 40 young people
to teach. He was going to really enjoy this new experience.

• • •

Abigail Coggin was quite a beautiful widow and since her husband died a year ago, she had been pursued by many, but for reasons only she was aware of John Finney of Plymouth was the man
she chose for her second husband. He was a wealthy businessman
owning three cargo ships that traveled to and from England four
or five times a year. Maybe she was secure in the fact that he was
not after her children's inheritance

Some people believed, that Mr. Finney did not love Abigail,
they thought that he was too much in love with himself to love
anyone else. All he really wanted was to be successful in winning
her hand in marriage. This he did by bestowing lovely flowers
and lavish gifts upon her and promising her the world, they were
married on June 10, 1650.

Abigail was in love with the tall, thin handsome man with a
well-trimmed mustache and she dismissed any complaints about
Mr. Finney that she heard as jealous lies. When she had questioned
Reverend Bearse of Scituate about Mr. Finney's reputation, he assured her that Mr. Finney was a man of honor and a sound businessman.

However, it was also well known that he did not like children
and had vowed that he would never have any of his own. He even
suggested to Abigail several times that she should send her children to England to live with their grandfather, Mr. Bishop, Abigail's
father.

Abigail wouldn't hear of such a thing and made sure that her
four children did not bother her new husband. Whenever he took

her to one of the many social gatherings he would not allow her to take her children with her. If they held a party at their home he made sure that her children remained in their rooms.

Mr. Finney also owned a home in Boston and whenever he and Abigail went there for a few weeks he would send the children on ahead or leave them behind with a nanny.

They moved to Plymouth in July but Abigail did not sell her property in Barnstable, she rented it out and hoped that one day one of her sons would move there. She and her children often visited in the summer time, spending several weeks there. She loved the little town where her children were born and Henry was buried. She and the children seemed to be happiest in Barnstable.

• • •

Alice Crocker woke her husband William up early in the morning on July 21, 1650 and told him to send their oldest son John to get Marie Dimmock. She was in great pain; much different than that of any she had had with her other five children.

When Marie arrived about a half-hour later, Alice was pacing about the room clutching William's arms. When each contraction came upon her she would practically fall to the floor and William had to stand in front of her to keep her from falling on her knees. He had never happened to be home when the other children were born, except when Elizabeth came into the world and it seemed that Alice gave out only two or three moans and the tiny baby girl was in his arms. He was the only one there to help Alice with Elizabeth's birth and he obediently did as he was told. He never knew that having a baby was as painful as this labor seemed to be.

He was trembling when Marie arrived and was very happy to hear her suggest that Alice get into bed, he hated to see his wife in such pain.

Before Marie examined Alice she asked William to get her a pan of hot water and some clean cloths. She asked little Elizabeth, now age 11, who was standing near the doorway almost in tears to bring her a cup of hot water and took her packet of herbs out of her satchel.

Elizabeth said, "Yes ma'am," and quickly left the room, happy to be helping.

Alice was covered with perspiration and panting almost constantly. Marie had to give her something to calm her down and knew that a tea made from Red Raspberry Leaves, Squawvine and Hops flavored with Licorice and Ginger would help her relax. She had used it many times in the past on women who were overly anxious and afraid to give birth.

Elizabeth came back into the room almost immediately and handed Marie the hot water. "Will mother be all right?" she asked in a scared little voice.

"Yes, my dear Elizabeth she will," she said and poured the contents of her packet into the hot water. Then handing Elizabeth a little cloth pouch filled with Comfrey Leaves she continued, "Please go and tell your father to put this little pouch into a small kettle of cold water then heat it over the fire."

When Elizabeth left the room Marie said, "Alice," shaking her shoulder lightly, "you must calm yourself and try to relax a little, I have to examine you."

Alice blinked her eyes several times as if to obtain a clear vision of the soothing voice she could hear. "Ohhhh, Marie" she moaned as she looked at her, "help me, please."

"Yes dear, I will but you have to lay still so I can see where your baby's head is," she replied as calmly as she could. Marie was feeling Alice's lower belly when another contraction took hold, and she held Alice's body as firmly as she could so she could feel the baby's head. When the contraction ended she knew what had to be done. She wished Anne Blish was here to help her but there was no time to send for her.

"Alice, you must relax and try and sip this tea for me," Marie said and held the warm cup to her lips.

Alice took several long sips knowing that it would make her feel better.

When the warm liquid was gone Marie said quietly, "Alice, you will have to turn over onto your hands and knees for me, we have to let your baby get into a better position so he can be born." She didn't want to scare Alice, but she had to get her to relax as much as possible so that her muscles would allow the little baby to fall forward in the womb so she could turn him over. He was facing the wrong way and Marie was afraid the cord would strangle him if she could not help him move.

William came into the room with the water and cloth as Alice was trying to turn over. Marie was on one side of her and said,

"William help me turn her over onto her hands and knees, I have to turn the baby over if I can."

William sat the pan of hot water on the nightstand and gently helped his wife turn over and then helped her raise herself up onto her elbows and knees and then he held her there with his strong arms braced under hers.

Alice moaned and held on to William as another contraction tried to take over her body. The tea was helping and this contraction was not as strong as the previous ones and as she relaxed her muscles loosened.

Marie put her hands on Alice's belly and pushed up with one hand and felt the baby's body move to the left. The little head was not very far into the birth canal and as she gently pushed on him again he wiggled himself over and Alice let out a surprised groan.

"What happened?" she asked surprised.

"I turned him over so he can come out right side up," Marie said smiling.

William looked shocked to think that anyone could do what she had just done. "You are amazing," he said.

"Your little baby did most of the work, I just helped him to get in the right place," she said smiling.

"Now, Alice lets get out of that bed and see if we can't walk that little baby right into this world," she said kindly helping Alice out of bed.

Alice was shaky but the next time she had a contraction it felt like a normal one, the pain was mostly in her lower back and not in her lower belly.

Little Eleazer Crocker was born about 8 o'clock that evening and Marie was there to make sure he was all right. "How did you know he was a boy," William asked Marie.

Marie smiled happily and said, "William you and Alice only have boys."

William chuckled, "I guess you're right there, Marie," he said.

"Besides he was too curious to be a girl, a little girl would never have done that to her mother just to see the world a little sooner," Marie added smiling.

• • •

Fall and winter passed as usual for the people of Barnstable. No new babies were born and no deaths occurred.

There was however, a great snowstorm that started about December 22 and lasted for six days leaving about six feet of snow. The towns were isolated from one another and they could not communicate until after the middle of January.

When the snow started all of the animals were herded into the barn or the barnyard so they could be fed each day, they would starve to death if left in the pastures. Each good farmer knew there would be no way to reach his animals during a great snowstorm if they were not close by.

Abraham did not hear of any cattle or sheep being lost during the storm and there were no injuries of any kind reported to him.

Patricia Louise Blish Gould

CHAPTER EIGHTEEN
1651

John Barker, Jr. was born to John and Hannah Barker, on March 3, 1651, their fourth child and only son. It snowed all day with gusting winds and John had just returned from the dock, about 5 o'clock after checking his boat line when Hannah started her labor.

"I think its time for the baby to come, John," Hannah said as he came into the house. "Would you please go and fetch Anne Blish for me, I'm going to need her help. I think it may be a little early for this child to be born," she added.

Concerned that Hannah had asked to have Anne help her so early in her labor, he said, "I'll go this minute, will you be all right?"

"Yes," she said and sat down near the fireplace. Hannah was a strong woman and had had no trouble delivering her three girls, but this pregnancy had been different since the first month.

Deborah now 12 years old listened to her parent's conversation and went to the fireplace to make sure there was plenty of water heating. She remembered watching Anne and Marie while they took care of her mother when her little sister Annie was born.

Hannah had seen Deborah check the water kettle and smiling to herself she said, "Deborah, if you would please get the birthing bundle from the cupboard in my room and lay it on the bed for me, it would be a big help."

"Yes, mother," she replied obediently and went into the adjoining room which was her parents bedroom. When she came back into the commonroom she put her hand on her mother's arm and said, "It's done Mother, is there anything else I can do for you?"

"You can feed your sisters their evening meal dear." Hannah said.

Deborah filled their bowls with several spoons of soup from the stew pot on the hearth. There was fresh baked bread on the table and Deborah sliced thick slices for each of them.

"Would you like something to eat Mother?" Deborah asked.

"No dear," she said with just as slight intonation of pain in her voice, "I'm going to lay down now, please keep the little ones entertained for me," she said. "When your father gets back he'll be hungry too," she continued.

"I'll feed Papa, too, mother," Deborah said and went to her mother's side and helped her up and across the room into bed.

"I'll be all right now, dear," Hannah whispered as she sat down on the bed, "Please see to the girls for me." She really wanted to groan loudly, but she knew she had to wait for Anne before she could let go and push, as her body wanted her to. She undressed and put on a nightgown and then pulled the covers back from the bed so she could cover the sheets with the birthing pad.

As she rested nagging little pains danced about her lower belly and she remembered how easily Anne had delivered little Joseph. She wanted this baby to be a boy and be happy to come into the world, too.

The front door opened and John and Anne came in with a big gust of cold March wind. Anne went directly to the bedroom and saw that Hannah was in no serious pain although she was very pale. She said, "Hello, Hannah, is everything coming along as it should be?

"Yes, Anne, I don't think this baby is in as much of a hurry as your Joseph was though," she said.

Anne smiled back saying she was going to warm her hands in a pan of hot water and then she would examine her. When her hands were warm she poured herself and Hannah a cup of tea, carried them into the bedroom and sat them down on the nightstand. She noticed that Hannah had become even paler in the last few minutes and her eyes were closed. She touched her arm and said, "Hannah, I think I'd better see how things are coming, let me move the quilt back."

Hannah only nodded her head.

As Anne pulled the quilt back she could see that Hannah's water had broken but she wasn't having the hard birthing pains that normally occur after the water breaks. Something was wrong. She wasn't sure exactly which herb in Hannah's packet was the Blue Cohosh Root that would induce her labor, so she decided to send for help.

She covered Hannah and went quickly back into the common room to ask John to go and get Marie Dimmock. "Tell her to bring some herbs to make Hannah's pains stronger," she said to John as he left the house.

She went back into the bedroom and found a heavy linen sheet and replaced the birthing pad with it. She tried to keep Hannah talking while doing this and coaxed her into sipping her tea. Then she made Hannah get out of bed and they walked about the room for a while.

Hannah was having little uncomfortable pains but nothing very serious. They were coming several minutes apart and lasting only a few seconds.

Anne had known babies to be born hours after the water had broken, but it had always been extremely hard on the woman and some had never really recovered fully from dry births. They were still walking back and forth across the room when John came back with Marie about a half-hour later.

"Hello, my dear Hannah," Marie said entering the room, "John said you might need my medicine that induces better labor pains?" she continued.

"I guess so, I think my baby's asleep, I haven't felt him move for a while now," Hannah answered.

"This new baby thinks it's too cold to be born?" Anne chuckled.

"I must agree with him," Marie said smiling. "I'll make some of my special tea, and we'll see then how stubborn the little tyke is," she laughed. "Just keep walking until I get back," she said and patted Hannah on her shoulder.

Marie made Hannah sip the hot tea as fast as she could and then gave her a second cup. It was very bitter and it made Hannah's tongue pucker, but she obeyed her and drank it all. After a few more minutes of walking, Marie suggested that Hannah get into bed where it was warmer. She knew that within fifteen minutes or so after taking this herbal tea a woman's pains would begin.

Sure enough, the first pain was hard but bearable and Hannah was relieved that this birthing would be over soon. Within an hour after drinking the bitter brew, Hannah was panting and Marie could see the baby's head. Several minutes later little John, Jr. was born, it was just before midnight. He was a small baby but healthy and hungry.

Hannah was so happy that she had finally given her husband the son he was hoping for.

When Anne and Marie left the Barker's early the next morning, the wind had died down and the sun was just coming up.

The Barker's were indeed a very happy family when they entered the church the following Sunday to have little John Barker, Jr. baptized by Reverend Lothrop.

• • •

About six weeks later, on April 16, 1651 Reverend Lothrop was unable to attend to his ministering any longer. He became very sick about the end of March, but continued to go about his daily routine and his weekly visits to his growing flock. But his Sunday he could not get out of bed and was unable to preside over the Sunday meeting. He was very weak and his breathing was labored.

Marie Dimmock was convinced that he had developed pneumonia after coming down with a chill several weeks before. She made an elixir of Comfrey, Fenugreek, Marshmallow, Slippery Elm Mullein and Lobelia. Marie found that a combination of these herbs was extremely helpful in bringing a person out of the coughing sickness.

At the end of a short sermon given by Elder Thomas Dimmock the members of the congregation were asked to go to Reverends Lothrop's home. The Reverend had requested that a day of humiliation be held there for him after the church service.

Reverend Lothrop asked the town councilmen to also be present at the humiliation and asked them to start searching for a new minister to replace him. He was too frail and sick to carry on the duties as their minister anymore. The council agreed and promised to supply him with everything he would need for the rest of his days. Everyone prayed for a new and Godly minister or teacher to replace the Reverend that day. Elders Cobb and Dimmock filled in for the Reverend, following his instructions and suggestions for appropriate sermons.

• • •

The following month on April 10, 1651 Thomas and Lydia Dexter's son Richard was born. This was Lydia's first baby and she had quite a hard time delivering him. She was in labor for about two days before she finally gave birth to him, but it wasn't long before she was up and around doing her chores. However, by the time little Richard was three months old her breast milk was diminishing, and she had a problem trying to keep her baby fed, he seemed to be hungry all the time.

Five weeks later on May 18, 1651 Samuel and Jane Fuller had their sixth child, a son they named Thomas. He was a very small baby and he seemed to be very listless. He didn't cry very much and several times during the day Jane would have to wake him up to feed him, he would eat for just a few minutes and then fall asleep again.

Marie Dimmock gave Jane the same herbs that she had given Lydia that produced richer breast milk knowing that both she and the baby would benefit from them, but it didn't seem to help. Baby Thomas died on July 19, 1651. Thomas was Jane's seventh child but she was devastated, her breasts were full and her heart was empty she told Marie several days after Thomas died.

It was about this time that Marie decided to suggest to Jane that little Richard Dexter would probably like to have a good meal. The next day Marie went to Jane's home and asked her if she would consider feeding Lydia's baby mid morning and early evening, maybe this would give Lydia's breasts more time to fill with milk and it might also help Jane get over the loss of her son.

Lydia was extremely saddened by the death of Jane Fuller's baby. She worried about Richard not getting enough to eat and she took the Blessed Thistle, Alfalfa, and Fennel Seed mixture that was boiled in barley water, three times a day. She drank a tea made from the Red Raspberry and Marshmallow herbs that Marie had given her. These herbs helped her body produce more milk for him, but he still cried a lot. She didn't think she would be able to stand it if her baby died too.

Both women were agreeable to the idea and talked for a long while trying to decide what the best arrangements would be for each of them. It was finally decided that Jane would go to Lydia's home in the morning and Lydia would take Richard to Jane's home in the evening. This routine lasted for about six months or so.

Lydia became pregnant again during this time but it did not seem to make a difference, she still didn't have enough milk for her growing baby.

Jane's milk helped keep him quiet during the day but she wasn't able to feed him every time he was hungry.

So when Richard was about eight months old Marie suggested that Lydia start feeding him barley meal mixed with goats milk twice a day, he stopped his crying and he grew into a healthy baby.

Many women nursed their children as a method of birth control. Usually as long as they nursed their babies they didn't have their menstrual cycle. But in Lydia's case when she wasn't able to produce enough milk for her baby, her cycle started and she became pregnant again.

Jane however, did not get her cycle back and she was thankful. She needed time to grieve for her baby and wanted to make sure her body was well healed before she became pregnant again.

Many of the Indian women used the Blessed Thistle plant as a method of birth control. They steeped the whole plant for days making a strong and bitter brew.

The Barnstable women did not agree with the Indian women regarding the subject of birth control and therefore would not hear of taking such a terrible concoction into their bodies.

• • •

At the annual town meeting held June 5, 1651 Abraham was a freeman again. He owed no one and was considered a well-to-do and upstanding citizen of Barnstable. His generosity was one of his greatest assets along, of course, with his love for his family.

However, he was intolerant of sin and was adamant about giving the proper punishment for a specific crime. As a member of the jury and town council, Abraham had a hand in sentencing several men for crimes they committed against the community. In fact several people found their way to the courthouse during 1651 for one crime or another.

One man in particular found his way there once again. His name was Matthew Graves and he was a Tinker, or mender of pewter pots, mugs, spoons and other utensils. The last time he was in Barnstable, which was ten years earlier, he was given ten lashes for cheating Reverend Lothrop's wife and told never to come back.

This time he was presented in court for cheating Nathaniel Bacon's wife Hannah. Nathaniel was no one to cheat unless you desired severe punishment.

The first day he was in town he mended a large pot for Hannah using one of her good spoons for a patch and then charged her for it as if it belonged to him. Hannah remembered that this was the same way he had cheated Mrs. Lothrop and she went immediately to her husband and insisted that the tinker be arrested.

When Matthew explained that he had made a mistake Nathaniel requested that he make restitution to his wife then and there. Matthew gave Hannah a new and larger spoon as compensation and Nathaniel released him.

The next day Roger Goodspeed accused Matthew of fraud. Roger was not considered a pleasant man but he was not a liar or a cheat and would not tolerate unthinkable behavior from others.

Matthew sold Roger two tankards that he had made of pewter. Thinking that the young man looked honest enough and maybe down on his luck he agreed to pay 2 shillings for them. That evening when he was having his supper he decided to use one of the new tankards. The first swallow he took left a foul taste in his mouth, he knew that his beer was fresh, it could only be the tankard.

He drew the bottom of it across the top of the table, and it made a very black mark. Roger knew that the best pewter was made of tin, brass, and copper so he realized immediately that he had been cheated, these tankards were made from tin and lead.

He left his supper unfinished, went to the mantle and took the other tankard, grabbed his coat and went directly to Constable Bacon's home. Roger accused Matthew of fraud and presented the evidence to Nathaniel allowing him to taste the beer that he had poured at his table.

Constable Bacon went to his front door and spat out the horrible tasting liquid.

The next day Matthew Graves was summoned to court and within several minutes after the jury heard the case, he was found guilty of fraud and was fined 20 shillings. He was also made to destroy the unusable tankards with a mallet in front of the court.

The next day Matthew had dealings with Elder Henry Cobb's wife Sarah. Sarah accused him of taking several small spoons from her to use to repair her large pot and he never gave her any pay for them. Henry was so angry that he told Nathaniel Bacon that if Matthew Grave's punishment were to be run through with a pitchfork it would not enter his heart. The court decided that giving Sarah three spoons and paying a fine of 10 shillings would be ample punishment.

Several days later after he had finished with all of the repairs of the village he was heard calling Hannah Bacon bad names. When Nathaniel heard about it he immediately confronted Matthew Graves and the Tinker confessed to the name-calling and was sent to the stockade. While he was there, Mary Cobb, Henry's 14 year old daughter was seen giving him food and water. When her father, for this unheard of act of kindness admonished the girl, she admitted that she was enamored by his charm and had let Matthew kiss her while he was at their house mending their pewter.

This seemed to be a bad habit of Matthew Grave's because the court remembered that he had tried to seduce Reverend Lothrop's daughter Agatha ten years before.

Henry was furious and wanted Matthew whipped immediately as punishment for molesting his daughter. In court Matthew said he was in love with her and would gladly take her for his wife but Mr. Cobb would have no tinker for a son-in-law and refused to let his daughter become involved with him.

Mary's punishment was almost as severe as Matthew's was. She was made to sit in her father's room on a straight chair for five days. She was not to move anything except her eyes. She was allowed to eat her meals at the table and go to the necessary, but she was not to talk to anyone and no one was allowed to talk to her. Henry was very strict with this punishment and none of the other children dared to interfere with his orders.

Sarah looked in on her to see if she was all right two or three times each morning and afternoon, but she said nothing to Mary.

Henry came home periodically throughout the day to check on her as well. Needless to say, after this punishment Mary vowed that she would never let anyone else kiss her until she was married.

When his second trial in less than two weeks was over, Matthew Graves was sentenced to the whipping post and given fifteen lashes and two more days in the stocks. After he recovered he left Barnstable and was never seen in town again.

• • •

Not a month had gone by when Constable Bacon was called upon to arrest Samuel Morton. Samuel was an unsavory character whose reputation preceded him by several months. He roamed from town to town in the colony expecting a handout at every turn. Today, Nathaniel thought, it's once again Barnstable's turn to deal with the scoundrel.

It seems that Robert Linnet had given Samuel permission to sleep in his barn the evening before. Robert owned the best bull in Barnstable and 30 head of milking cows. He was known as a pleasant sort of fellow, a little on the quiet side, but always spoke when spoken to.

Robert's wife had passed away many years before and he never remarried. For this reason he may have been overly hospitable because he never refused to open his door to anyone; and always enjoyed the company of his neighbors and passersby. So, when Samuel stopped at his gate and asked for a place to sleep, Robert told him there was plenty of room in the hayloft, but he had no room in his small two-room house. Samuel accepted the arrangement and Robert banked the fire in his fireplace and went to bed.

As the night wore on Samuel sipped heavily on the jug of rum that he always seemed to have with him; and about midnight after he gathered up enough liquid courage he entered Robert's home intending to confront him about his lack of hospitality.

When Robert heard a commotion in his front room he got out of bed quietly and pulled on his breeches.

Samuel, drunk and disorderly was standing in front of the fireplace with his jug.

Robert still half asleep, asked, "Just what do you think you're doing in here Samuel?"

Samuel said, his speech slurring, "I've decided that I should not be treated like an animal. It's cold in the barn and I'm not going to stay there with a big old bull drooling all over me."

Robert said, "I told you I didn't have any room in here and if you want to stay on my property you'll have to stay in the barn. So go on back out there now," he continued in a louder voice.

Samuel cursed and raised his arm and swung his jug at Robert.

Robert raised his arm to protect himself and tried to back away but the blow to his arm was hard enough to cause him to loose his balance and he fell to the floor.

Samuel fell on top of him hitting him several times in the head and face with his fists.

Robert was knocked unconscious and lay on the floor for several minutes before he awoke and realized what had happened. The broken jug with what little rum was left in it lay near him. He carefully lifted his head and saw Samuel sleeping on the floor near the fireplace. He quietly put his boots on using only one arm, his right one was throbbing and he couldn't use it without severe pain. He took his frock off the nail by the door and went directly to Constable Bacon's home.

Nathaniel Bacon did not like to be awakened in the middle of the night because of a deadbeat like Samuel Morton. He helped Robert to a chair and asked his wife to get a pillow so Robert could rest his arm on it.

Robert told his story while Hannah made tea, putting a small pinch of herbs in it that Marie Dimmock had given her for pain in her back. Robert seemed to relax after he explained what had happened to him and he dozed off to sleep.

Hannah covered him up with a blanket knowing that the pain medicine would make him sleep for several hours. The Bacon's went back to bed but were up before dawn.

At day break Constable Bacon, Abraham Blish and Anthony Annable went to Robert's house with him and found Samuel still asleep on the floor where Robert had last seen him.

Nathaniel pulled him roughly to his feet, bound his hands behind his back and practically dragged him to the courthouse.

Samuel hardly knew what was happening to him, he was still drunk and thick tongued. He had wet himself before they reached the jail but he was unaware of it.

The jurors were summoned and after they took one look at Robert's face and arm they found Samuel guilty as charged. His arm was very badly bruised, although not broken.

Marie Dimmock put a Plantain poultice on it and wrapped it up tightly. She changed the bandage every other day or so and the horrible bruise healed well.

Samuel was sentenced to sit in the stocks for a week with only bread and water to eat. He was also not allowed to use the outhouse. People threw stones at him during the first few days, but after the third day they stayed away from him as far as possible, the smell was horrible.

Hannah held her breath whenever she gave him his bread and water.

Robert was very upset with this punishment because he was still carrying a black eye when the week was over. The councilmen heard Robert's complaint and reconsidered Samuel's punishment. They allowed that Constable Bacon should administer 10 lashes upon Samuel Morton's naked back before he was released from the stocks.

Robert watched Samuel receive his punishment and finally felt justified.

The councilmen also ordered Nathaniel to take Samuel to the Sheep Pond and make him bathe.

Hannah gave Nathaniel a big piece of soap and an old rag so the dirty man could scrub himself.

Samuel Morton cried big tears all the while he was washing his crusty body. It was covered with feces and scabs from flea bits and welts from the whipping and the strong soap stung every part of his body that it touched. He blubbered that he was surely going to die now from taking a bath. He had never had one in his life, his poor old mother never believed in it and neither did he.

Nathaniel gave him a clean shirt and an old pair of breeches and then found an old pair of shoes that he couldn't wear any more and took him to the edge of town and told him never to return or his punishment would be one hundred times worse.

Samuel Morton kept his word to Constable Bacon because he was never seen in Barnstable after that.

CHAPTER NINETEEN
1652

The lambing was successful in January with many farmers going without sleep for several nights at a time. When they did sleep they usually slept in the barn on cornhusk pallets and wool blankets until the last lamb was born.

• • •

Samuel and Henrietta Jackson had another daughter on January 12, 1652, their seventh child. They named her Mildred. Marie and Anne helped her deliver her baby and though little Milly was very small she was well formed and ate well. Marie tried to persuade Henrietta to take Blessed Thistle in her tea each day, she did for a while, but she didn't really like the taste, so she stopped after two or three months.

• • •

Robert and Elizabeth Davis' son John was born March 1, 1652. Another son and a little less money to save each month, but Robert and Elizabeth were happy and their new baby was healthy. Marie and Anne were with her to help with her delivery.

• • •

Baby Mehitabel Cobb, age 6 months old and daughter of Henry and Sarah Cobb died in her sleep on March 8, 1652. She was Sarah's first child and Henry's eighth child. Sarah was devastated and cried for several days.

Two days later on March 10, 1652 Thomas & Lydia Dexter's son Mitchell was born. Lydia allowed Sarah to hold him whenever she needed to. Every mother in Barnstable felt Sarah's heartache caused by the loss of her child.

• • •

The spreading of manure from the piles near the barn was done early in April. This was the time of year that the women dreaded most. The men would come in ill smelling for their meals and no matter if they left their boots on the steps their husband's clothes still reeked of wet manure. It would take the women days of scrubbing their clothes in bayberry soap before the smell would be gone.

Anne followed her same routine of putting a water tub in the shed so Abraham could bathe before he came into the house. A few of the women also adopted this routine and many of the husbands grumbled but none of them refused.

• • •

A month later on April 10, 1652 Roger and Alice Goodspeed had a baby girl they named Ruth. Alice was also generous in sharing her baby with Sarah.

Henry helped Sarah too, by holding her at night while she cried, sometimes he even cried with her, silently, both their pillows would be tearstained in the morning. She had the other children to keep her busy and they consoled her whenever they noticed her sad face. They all loved their new mother and had cherished their new baby sister. "God needed another angel," they would say, "and Mehitabel was the most beautiful one He could find."

Sarah would smile and take a deep breath and go about her many chores, thanking her new children.

• • •

A happy event was held on April 22, 1652, Elizabeth Fuller, daughter of Captain and Mrs. Matthew Fuller married Moses Rowley of Yarmouth; he was Randall Rowley's younger brother. Every one in Barnstable attended the wedding and stayed until almost dark enjoying the food and cider that was served at the Fuller home. The women insisted that they go home before dark, there were still puddles in the roads from the spring thaw and they all had their best shoes on.

• • •

On May 28, 1652, Henry Coxwell, a sailor hired by John Willis, owner of the Barnstable shipyard, was seen kissing Gracie Gent near Blish Point. Mr. Willis happened to be on his way to prepare his schooner for a trip to Plymouth and noticed them standing very close to each other. Henry bent down and kissed Gracie full on the mouth and then pulled her closely to him.

"Coxwell," John shouted, "there will be no more of that on my ship."

"Sorry Sir," Henry said and jumped away quickly.

Gracie almost fell when he let go of her so abruptly. She looked at Captain Willis and then turned and ran as fast as she could toward home.

"I have no recourse but to take you to the Constable and have you arrested," John said. "You know very well that Gracie is under age," John said disgustedly.

"I wasn't going to hurt her," he finished lamely.

"When this is all over I'll take you to Plymouth and you will never work for me again," John said, shaking his head.

In court Henry confessed his guilt saying that he was in love with Gracie and wanted to marry her. The court fined him 10 Shillings, stripped him naked and covered him with tar and feathers, and then put him out to sea in a rowboat with only one paddle and told him that if he ever returned, he would be hanged.

"Your honor," Henry said trying to bargain with Judge Crow, "Captain Willis told me he'd take me to Plymouth."

"I can't allow that, Henry, the jury has already decided your punishment," Judge Crow said.

"Please don't put me in the rowboat, I'll never come back to Barnstable," he pleaded.

"No you won't Henry Coxwell," Judge Crow said, "and you may never get to Plymouth either." He rapped his gavel and said, "Courts adjourned."

Several weeks later it was learned that Henry Coxwell was accused of playing shuffleboard, a wicked game of chance in a Salem tavern, but somehow this case was never proven.

Gracie was also punished for her part in this sin. She was given only bread and water for five days as her punishment by her employer, Mrs. Foxwell, and was not allowed to look anyone in the eyes for a month. She was also made to confess her sins in front of the whole congregation at Sunday's service and had to sit, without slouching, on the repentance stool in full view of the church members for the entire service. This punishment was not as severe as some young people were given because she was a servant girl and could not read or write and just new from England; she was considered ignorant of the Colony laws.

It was only two days later, on May 30, 1652 that David Linnell and Hannah Shelley were also seen kissing and fondling each other in the woods just off the highway near Henry Bourne's property.

Abraham happened to hear a rustling of bushes in the woods as he rode by Henry's house on his way to a meeting with Anthony Annable. He couldn't believe his eyes when he peered into the woods and saw David and Hannah cavorting in the fashion of two wild animals.

"What are you doing," Abraham shouted.

David stood up quickly and pulled his breeches up, "Nothing," he said his voice shaking. Hannah rolled over onto her hands and knees and then crawled behind a big tree.

"David Linnell," Abraham said as he walked up to him, "don't tell me you were doing nothing."

David hung his head and pulled his pants closed tying the strings, then straightened his shirt. "Mr. Blish," he said stuttering, "I'm going, we're going, we want to get married."

"Well, now that's all fine and dandy," Abraham said, "but you should be keeping your breeches on until you are married."

"Yes, Sir," was all that David could say.

"Hannah come out from behind that tree right now," Abraham said loudly.

Hannah appeared slowly, her clothes were all proper but her face was as red as an apple. She walked slowly up to David and Abraham with tears streaming down her cheeks.

"I am ashamed of you, Hannah," Abraham said. "You now have nothing to look forward to on your wedding night." He shook his head in disgust, "You children will have to be punished and I have no other choice than to take you before the court."

Abraham felt a little sorry of them, but he had to do his duty as a citizen and he took them by their arms and pulled them both onto the road and they headed for Constable Bacon's home.

When the young couple was brought before the jury they confessed in tears. They told Constable Bacon that they wanted to be married and were sorry they hadn't asked permission from the Reverend Lothrop.

After a lengthy discussion about this obscene matter, the jurors decided that they would both be excommunicated from the church for a period of three months and dunked four times in the dunking chair on June 8, 1652 following the annual town meeting.

Goodeye Shelly, Hannah's mother, was so angry that her daughter was to be dunked that she confronted the town council openly in court immediately upon hearing their punishment.

The councilmen whispered among themselves for a few minutes and then agreed that Hannah would be dunked only twice.

Hannah was given two dunks and fainted after the first one, she had to be revived before the second dunking else she might have drowned.

David was dunked all four times with only a couple of seconds between each one which allowed him to take only about two great gulps of air before being dunked again; he managed to hold his breath during each dunking. He was so concerned for Hannah, thinking she might have drowned that he ignored his own bursting lungs and tried to concentrated on watching her when they pulled him out of the water, trying to see if she was breathing.

Goodeye was also excommunicated for the same length of time as David and Hannah because she made such a fuss over the unreasonable punishment. She had approved of the relationship between them and did not feel that it was anyone's business if they stole a few kisses here and there. After all, David was 21 and Hannah was 20. They both knew what they were doing. Circumstances had not been right for the two to be married yet. David had no money and Hannah had no dowry. There were too many people in David's household to bring another person into the Linnell house.

265

Goodeye was a widow and she had no one to rely on for help to support four children. Her only income was the mending and stitching she did for her neighbors. Hannah helped her mother with the sewing and tended their vegetable gardens. There was not enough money for a dowry.

On the day of the dunking Goodeye told Mrs. Fuller and Mrs. Coggin to their faces that they were proud and jealous of her because she had such a beautiful daughter. She told them that their daughters would never find a man because they were ugly and snobby and fat. She was just as happy to be cast out of the church, as the women in the society group never invited her to join them in their social gatherings anyway. Well, some of them did, but she felt bad for her daughter and it was her way of protecting her. Goodeye would not speak to Mrs. Fuller or Mrs. Coggin during the whole time of her excommunication, but at the end of three months all was forgiven and Goodeye was back at church.

Hannah and David went to Yarmouth when their excommunication ended. They were married at Robert Shelly's home, Goodeye's brother-in-law, on July 2, 1652. Robert gave David a job at his sawmill and helped them build a small house on a piece of land that he owned.

Robert welcomed his nephew and his help. Robert Shelly's only son had died of exposure when, at the age of three, he had become lost in the woods for three days. He had gone to look for his father one afternoon without telling his mother. Everyone in Yarmouth had gone looking for him, but he was not found for three days, by then it was too late.

• • •

On June 7, 1652 at the annual town meeting Abraham Blish, William Crocker and Dolor Davis were propounded freemen again and Abraham Blish and William Crocker were chosen as surveyors of highways for Barnstable for the ensuing year. Nathaniel Bacon was re-appointed Constable.

Captain Matthew Fuller was elected Lieutenant of the Militia Company of Barnstable. The Company included all men between the ages of 16 and 60 that were able to bear arms. His duty was to train these men in the art of war following the Military Discipline principles.

• • •

Summer passed with no mishaps of any kind and as the harvest season approached everyone joined together. Many hands made the numerous chores of harvesting seem easier, and all of the townspeople went from farm to farm helping each other until all of the fields were empty and the barns were full.

On Sunday afternoons in the fall the entire congregation gathered on the hill above Indian Pond. They brought their lunch pails or basket lunches and watched the children play in the cool clean water of the shallow pond.

The children as well as some of the adults also played games, one of their favorites was Nine Pins. The children set up a square of nine pins, 3 pins wide by 3 pins deep, each about a pin's width apart. Each player took two turns rolling a ball made of wood toward the square of pins. They received one point for each pin they knocked down and then they reset the pins for the next player. When their scores were tallied the first player to earn 31 points was the winner.

September and October were months that many prepared for winter. Fruits such as apples and grapes and blueberries, cranberries and blackberries were picked and dried by the women and young girls. Families spent many evenings stringing these fruits on long cotton thread while listening to stories of the great adventures that their parents had experienced.

Woodsheds were filled. The children gathered small dry branches from the woods that were used as kindling to start early morning fires. Last years logs were cut into four-foot lengths for use in the fireplaces on cold winter nights. Smaller one-foot lengths were cut to use in the small side ovens for baking.

Abraham, Anthony and other town council members were obligated to see that everyone was set for the winter, especially the widows or widowers or families with many children. If they needed anything the councilmen would see that their needs were met.

The days passed without too much happening in Barnstable except the usual bustling about of the people and their daily routines. This was the time of year when many stone walls and rail fences were put into place during late fall and early winter, that is when the weather allowed. Every one planned well for winter and there had been no unforeseen catastrophes until the year was almost over. Then came the worse early winter storm anyone in Barnstable had ever seen. It came blowing in from the northeast with no warning whatsoever.

It was during this storm on December 14, 1652 when John Barker drowned at sea leaving Hannah Williams Barker a widow with 4 children. John was a good provider and a good farmer, but he was happiest when he was fishing. The women in town knew they could count on him to have fresh cleaned fish hanging in his little fish house near the small pier where he docked his fishing boat whenever they wanted it.

That December morning the sun was shining and there was no sign of a storm coming so he set out to sea about 6 o'clock. He kissed Hannah goodbye with a lingering kiss, rarely given in the rush of their busy life. She could still feel it on her lips as she stood by their cottage door watching him paddle out of the harbor. She had a melancholy feeling in her heart as he hoisted his sail and disappeared from her sight. She sighed, she had to tend to the children they would be up soon and want their breakfast. She closed the door softly shivering a little and went to the fireplace, added some kindling and stirred the coals into little flames. Then poured water into her kettle and settled it over the flames. Hot porridge would be welcomed on this chilly morning. She shivered again.

As the fire grew warmer Hannah went about getting ready for the day. She brushed her hair and washed her face and hands, put on her apron and poured the oats into the hot water for the children's morning meal. Little John was nine months old now and he too would be crying for his breakfast soon. What a good baby he was she thought and she smiled to herself, he looked so much like his Papa.

About 7 o'clock the two older Barker girls left for school. It was warming up outside, but Hannah made them wear their scarves and mittens. She knew they would probably take them off when they got down the road and out of sight of the house, but they were good girls, they'd be careful not to loose them.

About noon Hannah had a shivering chill come over her. She looked at the fireplace to see if a down draft had put the flames out, but it was still blazing. She went to the baby's cradle to check on him. He was sleeping peacefully with the quilt tucked under his little chin. She kissed his forehead.

Little 4 year old Annie was playing with her cloth doll near the fireplace, she had dressed herself but had not tied her apron properly and the ties were hanging below her dress. Hannah tied it for her and kissed her little girl on the top of her head, telling her that she was growing up too fast.

She sighed again and straightened her shoulders and set about preparing a stew for their supper. John would be hungry when he came home; he had only taken a few biscuits, some cheese and a couple of apples with him.

The girls came home from school about 4 o'clock with their scarves wrapped tightly around their necks and their mittens tucked high under their coat sleeves, the wind was blowing mightily and it was just starting to snow. 'Where did this storm come from?' she asked herself.

About 5 o'clock there was a knock on her door. When she opened it Abraham Blish, Thomas Dimmock and Constable Bacon were standing there. When she saw their solemn faces she knew something was wrong. The wind was blowing fiercely, almost gale like, so she motioned the men to come in out of the cold. Only Abraham entered and closed the door behind him. He quietly asked her to please get her coat and come with them to the dock.

"Hannah, we found an empty boat that looks like John's washed upon the shore near the dock," Abraham said in a low voice.

When she hesitated for a second, her eyes filling with tears, he said, "The mast and sail are missing, so we're not sure if its John's."

"Oh," she said gasping for air. She felt as if someone had hit her in the stomach. "Yes, Oh," she took a deep breath through her nose and reached for her cloak on the peg near the door. "Oh, God no. Please, God no," she said in prayer.

Hannah's feet felt like lead and it seemed to her that it was ten miles to the dock though it was only a few yards. The sleeting snow stung her cheeks but she didn't feel it. It was almost dark when they reached the pier and the men held lanterns so she could see the boat.

She nodded her head yes and then she screamed, "John, John Barker, can you hear me?" The wind whistling eerily was the only answer she received.

Hannah slowly slid down onto the sand beside the boat crying and praying aloud, "Oh, God please keep John safe," she sobbed.

She opened her eyes and pleaded to God to let her see him walking up the shoreline, " Where are you, John?" she said sobbing.

Thomas Dimmock put his arm about her shoulders and lifting her up he turned her away from the blowing wind and, half carrying her, he led her home.

The other men set out along the shore to look for John. He may be washed upon the shoreline or he may have been able to climb into the little dingy that he always towed behind his fishing boat if it came to be that he had somehow fallen overboard. The men decided that it was too bad a gale to go out to sea to look for John, they would set out in the morning at first light.

There were many dangers in the ocean and a man that went fishing alone was sometimes never seen again. John Barker had never asked anyone to go with him except his hired men, but on this day he had decided to go by himself for reasons unknown to anyone.

This was not uncommon for him to do if his men had other business or if he didn't need a big catch, and though he was well liked and respected, some of the men thought he was foolhardy when he went alone like he did this day.

By the time Hannah and Thomas Dimmock reached the house, Marie Dimmock and Anne Blish were already tending the children. When Deborah saw her mother's face as she entered the house, she knew that something had happened to her father and she ran to her mother and threw her arms around her neck. They held each other tight, locked in each other's arms, sobbing. Mary and Annie were hanging on to them too, all crying.

Marie gently pulled the little girls away from their mother and helped her off with her coat. Then she led her to the settee in front of the fireplace and poured her sobbing friend a cup of hot Chamomile tea.

Deborah took her little sisters by their hands and led them to their pallets in the far corner of the common room comforting them as best she could all the while crying quietly to herself.

After a while Hannah's crying stopped and she was left with only a few hiccups now and then. She had to calm down for the children's sake and it was time to feed little Johnny, he was whimpering in Anne Blish's arms, upset that his mother was not where he could reach her. Hannah put her cup down and took him into her arms and he nestled down after a few minutes eating hungrily.

Hannah leaned back and closed her eyes while her little son nursed remembering John's last kiss. 'God why did you take him now,' she asked silently. Then she realized that there were little signs that her husband was going to leave her that God had given her, but she hadn't noticed them until now. John had finished putting all of the wood into the woodshed; all of the fish he had caught were cleaned and hanging in the fish house ready for sale.

John had helped his hired hand clean the stables and new straw was laid down for the horse and cattle. They had boarded up the chicken coop for the winter and the pigsty was covered to protect the old mama sow.

The night before he helped her put the children to bed giving them big hugs and kisses and he told each child that he loved them. Then later when they were snuggled down in their warm bed they had made sweet passionate love.

Had John been given a sign; or did he somehow know in his subconscious mind that he was going to meet the Lord?

Marie took Johnny out of Hannah's arms, he was asleep, and she put him in his cradle in Hannah's room.

Anne sat down beside her friend with another cup of Chamomile tea for them both and held her hand.

Marie came back and poured herself a cup and they just sat there being still and praying silently sipping their tea.

Abraham and Thomas came back about midnight. They had found nothing but they promised they would all go out the next morning at first light.

The men all had their own theory about what might have happened to John. He could have been knocked out of the boat by a whale or dragged from the boat by a huge shark or other creatures of the sea.

There were many tales about eight-armed sea monsters that could reach into a boat like John's and pull him into the sea. Some men told stories of sightings of huge fish with razor sharp teeth big enough to swallow a grown man. Or the mast could have hit him when it broke knocking him into the sea where he would have frozen to death in a mater of minutes. No matter how it happened it was a horrible way to die.

Poor John they would say aloud every now and then and shake their heads, poor John. And poor Hannah, what will she do now.

Marie and Thomas Dimmock left shortly after the men came back leaving Anne to care for Hannah the rest of the night.

Abraham went home to be with his children knowing that Hannah needed his wife more than he did this night.

The townspeople would gladly help her with anything she needed, but she would still be left a widow with four young children. How sad everyone was for Hannah and their sorrow lasted the rest of the winter.

CHAPTER TWENTY
1653

A little happiness came to the growing town on January 11, 1653, Thomas and Lydia Dexter's son Thomas, Jr. was born, their third son in less than three years. Richard their oldest would not be three until April, and Mitchell would not be two until March

Just a little over two weeks later Nathaniel and Hannah Bacon had their fifth child. She was born on January 28, 1653 and Nathaniel named her Elizabeth.

Then sadness came again when Abigail Coggin Finney passed away suddenly on May 6, 1653 leaving her four children, ages 16, 14, 11 and 7 with their very cruel stepfather, John Finney. Many said that Abigail died just to rid herself of Mr. Finney. He certainly was not as kind to her as Captain Coggin had been. He resented the attention that she gave her children and accused her of minding their needs instead of his. He was a very selfish person caring nothing for the children who were sick with grief over the death of their mother. Some thought that maybe foul play occurred.

Marie and Anne thought that Mr. Finney had something to do with Abigail's death but could not prove anything. When they were called to her bedside because she had taken ill suddenly they thought they detected a faint odor of Lily of the Valley on Abigail's breath. They knew that Abigail grew them in her garden and was very fond of them. In fact they were in bloom now and a few of them had been picked and were in a small vase on the nightstand by her bed. They looked at each other curiously but didn't say anything because Mr. Finney was in the room.

Abigail's eyes were open and she was staring at the ceiling. Anne Blish put her ear near Abigail's chest listening for her heart beat. Then she put her fingers on her neck trying to feel her pulse. Anne closed Abigail's eyes and patted her hair away from her face, looked at John Finney and said, "I'm sorry sir," she had tears in her eyes.

"I'm afraid she's gone, Mr. Finney," Marie Dimmock said kindly and left the room. Anne followed her.

Mr. Finney buried Abigail the next day and by the end of the week he had moved to Plymouth taking the children with him. When he laid a small bouquet of Lily of the Valley on her grave he did not look as sad as most loving husbands would have been, Anne and Marie looked at each other knowing the truth, they hated Mr. Finney at that moment.

Anne and Marie talked about Abigail's sudden death with their husbands but there was no way to prove their thoughts that Mr. Finney had somehow fed his wife the berries from the Lily of the Valley flower. They had to trust that God would see that he was punished somehow.

No one knew that just a few days later another sadness would come to the people of the town of Barnstable. On May 23, 1653 Anne Pratt Blish, at the young age of 31 was killed in a tragic accident. Leaving Abraham unable to make any sense of why God would take away his precious loving wife and the mother of his two little children. Sarah was only 8 years old and Joseph had just turned 5. What would he do without Anne he wondered?

Anne was laid to rest on May 26, 1653 in the Barnstable Cemetery. Every resident of the little town was at her funeral. The church was so crowded that many of the children were made to stand quietly on the steps and in the yard. After the service everyone walked with bowed heads to the cemetery following the pallbearers in quiet procession.

So many flowers were placed upon Anne's grave that the turned earth was unable to be seen; it was covered completely.

Abraham held his children's little hands tightly so that he wouldn't be tempted to pull Anne from the ground and hold her close to his heart one more time. Tears streamed down every face and many sobs were heard as Reverend Lothrop finished the lengthy service.

Hannah Barker could not believe that just a few days ago Anne was helping her plant her vegetable garden. They had finished the last row of beans and were starting toward the house when a gunshot rang out from the nearby forest. A second later Anne grabbed Hannah's shoulder as she slowly fell to the ground face down. At first Hannah thought that Anne had tripped and called her a clumsy oaf, but as she bent over to help her get up she saw blood coming from the side of her neck. Anne coughed as Hannah turned her over and blood gushed from her mouth. Anne blinked once and gurgled and then she was still. Hannah could not understand what was happening and then she realized that the gunshot had missed its target and hit Anne.

"Oh Lord, Oh Lord, Oh Lord," Hannah screamed and ran toward the house to find her oldest daughter.

"Deborah, hurry run and get Mr. Blish," she shouted.

"What's wrong mother?" Deborah asked shakily.

"Hurry, something has happened to Anne," she said lowering her shaking voice.

"Mary, please keep the children inside, don't let them into the garden," she said trying to calm herself and her voice as she hurried to the water pail. Grabbing some linen towels from the cupboard she ran out of the door and back to Anne with the pail of water in one hand and towels in the other.

When she reached Anne she knew that her efforts were going to be of little use. Anne's blood was soaking into the ground and she was as white as the towels Hannah was using to cover the gapping wound in her neck.

She closed Anne's staring blue eyes and cradled her head in her lap and let the tears fall down her cheeks and onto Anne's beautiful red hair. "Oh, God. Why?" she asked aloud, over and over as she sobbed, "Why couldn't it be me? Why couldn't it be me?"

Abraham was planting corn in the field that joined the Barker's hay field and was nearly finished when he saw Deborah running toward him waving her arms and shouting. As she came closer he heard her words and realized something was wrong at the Barker's house again.

"Mr. Blish, mother needs you, please hurry," she was shouting. He yelled across the field to his hired hand to come and take the horse to the barn and ran toward Deborah.

"What is it?" he called to her as she came nearer.

"I don't know, but mother says for you to come at once," she gasped, "hurry."

He knew that Hannah would never ask him for help unless it was absolutely necessary. She had become very independent since John had died. He started running toward the Barker's house following closely behind Deborah and then passed her quickly as she slowed down to catch her breath.

When Abraham was almost there he saw Mary Barker pointing toward the back garden. He could not comprehend why Hannah and Anne would be sitting in the middle of the garden and then he saw Anne's white face and heard Hannah sobbing.

"What happened?" he asked Hannah. She was holding Anne's head in her lap and her apron was covered with blood. He stared for just a moment and then fell to his knees in front of the lifeless form of his beautiful wife.

"I don't know, but I heard a gunshot in the woods and then Anne fell and the blood started gushing from her neck, I think she's been shot, Oh, Abraham, why Anne?" she sobbed, "Why not me?"

Abraham felt Anne's face and knew as his fingers touched her cold skin that she was gone. He moved the towels and saw the gash in her lovely neck. Her jugular vein had been torn apart by the bullet and she had died in just a matter of seconds. He lifted her out of Hannah's lap and into his arms as if she were a feather and turned toward his house. He was crying softly and the tears were running down his face onto her lifeless body as he walked slowly home.

Hannah watched him leave the garden and knew that he should be alone for a little while and she put the towels into the pail of water, and slowly, as if she were a hundred years old, stood up and walked up the garden path toward her house. She left the pail and the bloody towels near the steps and opened the door to a room full of frightened children. Deborah, Mary and Sarah stared at her in wonderment. The other children gazed at her with big eyes of fear. They could see that she was covered with dirt and blood and tears and the little ones started to whimper while the older ones tried to comfort them. Hannah took off her apron and wiped her face and hands on the corner of it and then her legs started to shake and she sat down on the warming bench near the hearth.

"Where's mother?" Sarah asked, her voice shaking.

"Oh my dear Sarah," she said in a soft voice as she pulled her onto her lap and hugged her tightly. Then quietly she told the children what had happened.

Sarah's little body was shaking with sobs by the time Hannah finished.

Little Joseph looked bewildered and lost; he couldn't understand why his father had to carry his mother home. He had watched them go across the field through the open door as Hannah told them what she knew. "Is mother going to be well?" he asked innocently looking up at Hannah.

"Oh little Joseph, come here," she said, hugging him close to her side and repeated, "Your mother has gone to heaven where she'll be watching over you forever."

His eyes were filling with tears, but he looked at her bravely and said, "We have to go home and help Papa now, he'll want his evening meal." Then he touched his sisters face and said, "Don't cry Sarah," as he tugged on her arm.

Sarah obediently got out of Hannah's lap and followed Joseph out of the door toward home.

This gallant gesture from little Joseph brought Hannah back to reality and she hurriedly pulled herself together as best she could. She had to make a meal and see that the neighbors where informed of this horrible mishap. She also knew that the Constable would have to be told what has happen and maybe he could find out who fired the gun that had killed her best friend.

"Deborah, go to Constable Bacon's home and tell him as best as you can what has happened, tell him to meet me at Mr. Blish's farm as soon as he can," she said.

Then taking a deep breath she said, "And Mary dear, you go to Reverend Lothrop's and tell him to meet us there as soon as possible."

She went to the table by the back door and took off her bloody apron and washed the blood and dirt from her arms and legs as quickly as she could. Then she went to her room and put on another dress and apron. As she cleaned herself she asked her littlest daughter Annie to put biscuits into a basket. She had baked them fresh early this morning before Anne had come over. She went to the cupboard and found another basket that she filled with cheese and cold baked ham and a small crock of jam.

She couldn't help but think of all the wonderful times she and Anne had had together. From giving birth to their children, to silly frolicking with them in the green fields, from happy times to sad times.

She thought of John, her wonderful husband, gone just five months now. "Oh John," she whispered, "beautiful Anne is coming to help you watch over us." The tears flowed again, but she continued cutting the ham and cheese into slices and put them into the basket.

Then she went quietly to the crib in the corner of the room where little John was still taking his afternoon nap. It seemed impossible that he could still be sleeping. 'How could such a tragedy happen in so short a time?' she asked herself.

Then she put her baby into her back cradle and with Annie's help they managed to carry everything. They started out toward Abraham's farm; the sun was still shining. 'Why was it such a nice day,' she thought, 'it should be raining and storming, she wanted to scream to God to make it rain and thunder and lightening outside like she was feeling inside. But no time for such nonsense, her little ones would be unable to understand her actions and she had to get to Abraham's house,' her legs were beginning to shake again.

Deborah and Mary had seen her coming up the lane and went to meet her to help her with her heavy load.

When she came through the door the men stopped talking and just stood looking at her. It made her very nervous. She sat the baskets on the table and pulled her arms from the shoulder straps of the baby basket and handed Johnny to Deborah. She thought, 'I must look a sight,' as she realized her hair was hanging down in her face, she quickly turned away from them and wiped her eyes on her apron and pulled her hair back into the bun where it had been snugly tucked early that morning. Tears came to her eyes again as she turned back toward them and hurried to the dining table near the fireplace and started taking food from the baskets, laying it out with shaking hands.

Abraham had laid Anne on the pallet in the front room and was sitting next to her.

Nathaniel went to Hannah and said to her oldest daughter, "Deborah, please finish preparing the table and feed the children. Keep them in here while we talk to your mother," he said.

"Yes Mr. Bacon," she replied politely.

He turned to Hannah and put his arm across her shoulders and gently led her to the warming bench near the hearth in the commonroom where the Reverend was standing.

278

"Dear Hannah," Nathaniel said quietly, knowing she was terribly upset and probably acting in a state of shock, doing things out of habit and not realizing it, "tell us what happened if you can."

Hannah looked up at the Constable and asked, "Could I please have some water?" Her voice was gruff as she spoke; her throat was dry from crying.

The Reverend went to the water pail on the stand near the back door, got a dipper of the cool water, brought it over to Hannah and said quietly, "We know how upset you are dear lady, but we have to know what happened."

"Please try to tell us everything you can remember," Nathaniel added as she sipped the cool liquid.

"I'm so sorry I asked her to help me," she started. "If she had not been at my house she would still be here," she continued.

The Reverend patted her head as if she were a small child, in fact her daughter Deborah, only 14 was already a little taller than she was. 'How sad she looks,' he thought to himself.

Then Hannah took a deep breath and said, "We were walking back toward the house, having just finished planting the peas. We were going to have some tea."

She paused as if she could see the whole scene happening again, "I heard a gunshot in the forest, I think it came from the woods near the wheat field, toward the east," she pointed with her finger as if looking into the forest trying to see someone. She continued slowly, "Then Anne grabbed my shoulder and held onto me for a second, I thought she had tripped so I turned a little to steady her and she just slowly fell to the ground face down."

She paused again for a few seconds remembering that she had called her a clumsy oaf. She would never tell anyone the very last words she had said to her best friend. She looked over at Abraham wondering if he could read her mind, he nodded for her to continue.

She closed her eyes and said, "Blood was spurting from her neck when I turned her over. She was gasping and she blinked her eyes and then she gurgled and blood came out of her mouth and she opened her eyes and stared at me."

Tears were rolling down her cheeks again and her nose was running. She started to use the bottom of her dress to wipe her face then notice that the Reverend was handing her his handkerchief. She thanked him and blew her nose, then breathing deeply she continued.

"I wasn't sure what had happened, I knew I had to help her, so I ran to the house and told Deborah to go and find you Abraham. Then I grabbed some towels and the water pail and ran back to Anne. I tried to stop the bleeding, but I couldn't, and then all of a sudden it did stop. I looked at her face and I knew she was gone. I closed her eyes, her beautiful blue eyes they couldn't see me any more. I waited for you Abraham. I tried, but I couldn't help her, I didn't know what else to do. I didn't know a bullet could kill anyone so quickly," she finished. Hannah was crying silently.

Abraham was crying, too.

Both the Reverend and Nathaniel were silent for a few minutes, and then Constable Bacon said in a gruff voice, "I'm going to the woods to see if I can see where the shot may have come from."

By this time several men having heard about this horrible accident, were headed toward Abraham's farm. Nathaniel hailed to them and asked them to help him, telling them what had happened as they walked toward the forest. It was not quite dusk and if they hurried, they might find something, he didn't know what, but he had to do something. He felt useless. 'How could such an awful thing happen to such a nice family,' he thought. He remembered wondering the same thing last winter when John Barker never came home from fishing.

Abraham sat with his head bowed as Hannah told her story, when she was finished he turned to his wife's still body and picked her up again and cradled her in his arms.

After a few minutes Hannah willed herself to get up and see to the children. Deborah had given them a biscuit and they had helped themselves to some cheese and ham. She pored them a dipper of milk and they all took turns drinking from it.

She sat down on a chair near the table and took a small piece of cheese and nibbled on it. When she thought that her children had had their fill she asked Deborah to take them home and put them to bed. She told her she would be home in a short while it was almost dark.

Hannah took Joseph by the hand and they went to the pallet where Abraham was holding Anne's body. Sarah followed them.

"Abraham," Hannah said, "your children need you."

Hannah turned and walked to the door, she knew they would be all right, well maybe not all right, but they would continue on as she had done for the last five months.

She shivered and through the last of her tears she made her way home in the moonlight. Her children needed her. "Good night, John," she whispered as she looked up at the stars, "Good night, Anne."

Abraham looked at his little boy and then at his beautiful little girl, she looked so much like her mother.

He laid Anne's body back on the pallet and wiped his eyes. "I'm sorry Joseph," he said, "I'm sorry Sarah," and he pulled them both to him. "I will do all I can to help you through this, and I hope you will help me, too." Abraham put the children to bed after a while and then got out his pen and paper, he had to let his parents know about Anne.

May 23, 1653

Dear Mother, Father, John & Molly,

I am writing this letter with a heart so full of sadness that it will never be completely emptied no matter how much joy my future holds.

My beloved Anne died today. A horrible accident occurred that no one would ever have thought possible. I will try to explain briefly and as well as I can so that you may understand how it happened.

She was at her friend Hannah's house helping her plant her garden when a stray bullet from an unknown hunter's gun struck her in her neck. She died instantly. Hannah tried to help her but there was nothing she or anyone else could do.

Our Constable has tried to find clues as to who would be shooting so close to our town, but we will probably never know who's bullet caused the death of my Anne.

Sarah and Joseph are doing well, and as the days pass I will try to explain more thoroughly to them that sometimes only God knows the real reason why such things happen. I have to help them through his and I know they will be my only reason to live from now on.

I hope that this letter finds you all well and in good health, I will write to you again soon.

I leave you with my prayers and in God's hands and I will always be your loving son,

When Marie Dimmock learned of Anne's death that afternoon she cried for hours. She went immediately to the Blish home to see if there was anything she could do, there was not. She went back home crying all the way, as Hannah Barker had done. It took Marie

Dimmock a long time to go to sleep that night. She missed Anne already.

Her thoughts wandered, she had no one to help her now except her daughter Mehitabel who was only 11 and way too young to be delivering babies. She would have to see if she could find some one to take Anne's place. Marie wished Mary More lived in Barnstable instead of Duxbury.

'Maybe Martha Bearse would help me, she is a wonderful lady,' she thought. 'No, probably not, she has 7 children now under the age of 13 and another baby due in a few months. Granted, she knows much about childbirth, but still, what would she do with her own children while she was helping someone else give birth.'

She smiled to herself thinking, 'Hannah Bacon might help, but with her husband, Constable Bacon away much of the time on town business it would be hard for her, she also has small children, five of them under the age of ten.'

'So many babies have been born here during the last 14 years and I've helped almost every one of them into this world,' she felt a flash of pride and then directed her thoughts once again to the situation at hand.

She poured herself a cup of tea, and then said, "Sarah Bourne might be just the person that would help me."

"She just might be," Thomas said, "you should ask her."

Marie blushed a little, she didn't realize she was thinking out loud. "She has no children and her husband Henry is involved with town government much of the time," she said looking at Thomas to see if he notice her pink cheeks.

"He is also a deputy to the Plymouth colony Court now and he'll be gone much of the time," Thomas added.

"I like Sarah and everyone knows her as a kind and gentle lady. I'll call on her as soon as I can," she said sighing. She got up and put her cup on the shelf by the water bucket and said, "Thank you for your help dear." She walked to the fireplace where her wonderful husband sat and kissed him on the top of his head. "I'm going to bed now, I feel so sad for poor Abraham," she said tears filling her eyes.

"I have been praying for him all evening," Thomas said. "I'm going to bed too," and he laid his bible down and put his arm around his wife and they both went to bed.

Marie Dimmock cried herself to sleep that night in her husband's arms.

The next morning she called on Sarah Bourne to see if she would be willing to assist her in helping her. Sarah agreed and was a wonderful help and learned how to mix the herbal medicine quickly.

Sarah even found a way of making the new mothers tea less bitter, she added honey to it. The women liked it much better, too. Sarah also helped Marie cope with the loss of her dear friend Anne.

Nathaniel Bacon went back to Hannah's house the following morning to question her again as to where the shot had come from. He asked her to re-enact the scene as best she could, telling her that he needed more information as to where to look for clues.

Nathaniel found evidence that someone had been in the area because there were several moccasin footprints. He was unsure of whose they were because many hunters had adopted the Indian way of dress, especially on their feet. He felt helpless there was nothing more he could do.

• • •

Roger Goodspeed and his wife Alice sold all of their land to Henry and Sarah Bourne and moved his family to Marstons Mills on June 8, 1653. Roger had been on the outs with several of the town councilmen over the lack of punishment to the criminals that seemed to be arriving in Barnstable weekly. He was a severe man and on several occasions was accused of being too harsh with his own children.

In one instance Abraham Blish was irate with him for whipping his son John with a leather strap.

John Goodspeed was only ten years old at the time and was late getting his chores done making him late for his evening meal. When the young boy came in he hurried to wash his hands and then sat down at the table.

Roger said, "You will have no meal tonight young man, you have been dallying all day." He lifted John out of his chair by his arm and took him to the barn and gave him ten lashes with a leather strap leaving his back covered with horrible welts.

John's mother didn't go to the barn to tend him until after Roger had gone to sleep that night.

She found her son on floor of the barn curled up into a fetal position, she thought he was dead for a minute. She whispered his name, "John."

He opened his eyes and looked at her. "I'm sorry Mama," he said and tears rolled down his cheeks.

"I know, dear," she said sadly. She got the salve that was used to heal the cow's teats and spread it on his poor little back. John shuddered with every touch and moaned quietly.

After putting a clean shirt on him she gave him sips of water and helped him stand. She carefully helped him into the house and into bed.

The next morning Roger acted as if nothing had happened and no one said anything to him about it. Roger often drank too much of the beer that he brewed and Alice knew that it was the beer that made him do the mean things that he did to her and the children. She always had an excuse for his actions whenever anyone confronted her about them. John's brother Nathaniel did his chores for him that day.

Needless to say, Abraham was one of the many townspeople who didn't mind Roger Goodspeed's move. He did worry about Alice and the children though and he called on them whenever he went to Marstons Mills.

• • •

On October 10, 1653 Anthony and Anna Annable's third baby was born, they named her Desire. She was a healthy baby and smiled before she was a month old. Marie and Sarah helped Anna with her delivery; she was Sarah's first patient.

• • •

Things happen in threes, so they say, and in less than a year three prominent people in the small town of Barnstable passed away, John Barker, Anne Blish and now the Reverend Lothrop.

Reverend John Lothrop died on November 8, 1653 he was 73 years old. He left behind his young wife Elizabeth she was 39 years old and 15 children ranging in age from 38 to 4. His oldest son, James 38, was only a few months younger than his stepmother was.

The Reverend was a wise leader and during the past 14 years that he lived in Barnstable he was a staunch believer that church and government should go hand in hand. He served Barnstable as both judge and jury in many instances during those years.

John's first wife was Hannah Howse whom he married in 1610; they had nine children together. Hannah died in 1633 while John was still in prison in England.

The Reverend was 58 years old in 1638 when he married his second wife Elizabeth she was 24. Their son James was born in Scituate on August 5, 1639 just before the Lothrop's moved to Barnstable, James was now 14. Catherine was born July 9, 1641; Joseph was born on September 8, 1643 and died a month later on October 10, 1643. Samuel was born April 4, 1645, Madeline was born on July 15, 1647 and little Rebecca was born August 12, 1649.

One by one his older children by his first wife Hannah had gotten married or gone off to school in Boston or England. His second son Matthew, 37, was living back in England and had a family of his own. His four oldest daughters were married, Rachel was living in Boston, Elizabeth lived in Yarmouth, Ellen lived in Scituate and Jane was married to Samuel Fuller and lived in Barnstable.

Adam, 19 and Robert 18 had chosen to help their father run the farm after he had become ill two years earlier. His daughter Mary, 17 was a great help to her stepmother and they had become close friends.

The Reverend had been sick for almost two years with lung problems. Marie Dimmock had treated him with her wonderful herbs, but in the end, all she could do was relieve his congestion with a special tea made from Comfrey, Marshmallow and Mullein. It helped him to breath a little easier and eased his pain and helped him sleep, sitting up of course.

He made Elizabeth promise him that when he died she would lay him out with only a very small pillow for his head. He wanted to lay down flat on his back for eternity, as it had seemed to him that he had not been able to ease the soreness of his lower back for years. He could not stand and he could not sit up for very long, he could only recline sitting with most of his weight on his tailbone, though by this time he was skin and bones. He was never hungry; he didn't have the strength to eat any way. He had been ready to die for several weeks.

In fact, Reverend Lothrop had been ready to be laid to rest about the same time Anne Blish had been killed.

Anne's funeral was the last service that he performed. 'If there was such a thing as a beautiful funeral, it was hers,' he thought. It was late spring and the flowers were so plentiful that the children had gone into the fields and picked hundreds of daisies and daffodils and violets and even some of the lilacs were still in bloom.

It was as if Mother Nature knew she had to produce an abundance of beauty just for Anne Blish.

His will to live had left him forever after her service and he grew weaker by the day. He wished he could have spoken longer. 'Yes, yes,' he smiled to himself, 'I know everyone used to think I was long winded.'

He was proud of his sermons, only the most obedient could stay with him through the entire sermon or service.

He chuckled out loud and this little gesture threw his body into a spasm of coughing. "Oh, please God; take me now," he prayed.

Elizabeth helped him through his coughing spell like she always did and when it was over she wiped his face, smoothed his hair back and kissed him on his forehead. "I love you," she said.

He made his lips move saying, "I love you, too," then he closed his eyes and went to sleep. He always did after these fits as he called them.

God must have heard his prayer this time because about twenty minutes later, it was a little after 2 o'clock, Elizabeth found him slumped over the edge of his bed. The tears rolled down her cheeks as she lifted his frail body back onto the bed. She removed all of the pillows and laid him down gently, flat on his back.

'It's all over, my poor dear man,' she thought and she said a silent prayer as she sent Adam to Constable Bacon's home to tell him that the Reverend had finally passed on. He wasn't suffering anymore.

Elizabeth was now left with the responsibility of raising and caring for nine children. She was a large lady and healthy, having her babies had not made her frail. She knew that with her stepson's help they would get by. After all, John had been sick for two years, and they had managed. She would miss him very much and had always loved him; even their age difference had not interfered with their relationship. He was a wonderful man and a dear father to all of his children. She knew she would survive.

'After all, if Hannah Barker could keep her farm going with only three daughters to help her, I certainly can,' she thought.

Elizabeth wondered what the town of Barnstable would do now without John's guiding ways. With slow transportation Barnstable was considered to be isolated and hard to get to, especially if the weather was bad making the sea an unsafe way to travel. She knew it was going to be a difficult task to find a minister to replace her husband because England was no longer a place for nonconformist clergymen to flee from, nor was New England a land of rainbows and promises. There was nothing but hard work here. They managed because of the farmland they planted and because of the help from their sons. A new minister would probably not be able to do his own farming and tend to his people, too.

She sighed to herself and felt a great sadness for the children of Barnstable. It had been a very bad year for them; twenty-one children had had to mourn the loss of a parent. Counting the Reverends older children of course. Two widows and a widower, too, she sighed again and started the sorrowful job of preparing John for his funeral.

After the death of Reverend John Lothrop a conflict of opinions forced town and church apart and there was a struggle of wills for control in the church. It caused a division among them making it harder to separate church teachings from town politics.

Barnstable was growing in population and it also began expanding westward and southward, and others came whose ties to the church were not so strong.

Reverend William Sargeant preached for a time, along with Elder Henry Cobb, Thomas Huckins and Reverend John Mayo. During that time the little town appointed lay preachers and many times Abraham was asked to give the sermon.

Abraham would always listen closely to Reverend Mayo whenever he gave a sermon, and tried to be as up lifting as he was. He liked to think his sermons would leave the congregation encouraged by God's love.

Many other townspeople also enjoyed listening to Reverend Mayo's services, he was Godly and an able minister who gave light in a glorious and resplendent manner. But John wasn't able to fill the duties of a full time preacher, he had his large farm to run and he was still the keeper of town records. John Smith was also called to preach several times, but evidently much too tolerant of the Quaker religion to suit some of the members.

Elizabeth Lothrop was allowed to stay in the parish house until she re-married or until another preacher could be found. She kept it clean and repaired with the help of the children and with her vegetable gardens she was able to keep food on the table. She allowed social gatherings that were usually held in the Reverend's home to continue as they always had. She still considered herself the Reverend's wife and went about her duties as usual.

• • •

On November 10, 1653 Samuel and Henrietta Jackson had another daughter they named Laura. Both mother and baby were well. Marie and Sarah helped her and she was up and around in no time.

• • •

On December 14, 1653 Thomas and Lydia Dexter's daughter Hannah was born, their fourth child, Lydia's second baby this year. Baby Thomas was born in January and now this one, they were 11 months apart, in fact all of her children were less than a year apart.

• • •

After little Hannah was born Lydia's strength did not return to her until almost summer and then she realized she was pregnant again. Marie Dimmock gave her a tea made from Schizandra Berries and made sure she drank at least a cup full every day. Lydia felt much better after a few weeks and was able to keep her house and babies in good order most of the time.

Thomas hired a man and his wife to help them that summer and Lydia was very grateful. Peter and Pauline James were newly from England and were in need of a place to live. Thomas Dexter hired them and gave them a small lot to build a house on. In return Peter was to help with the farm and Pauline would help Lydia in the house.

Lydia liked Pauline the first time they met and the children adored her. She had none of her own, yet, she told Lydia, maybe someday, she sighed.

• • •

Anne Blish's horse Penny had her new colt on December 31. Abraham was with Penny and she did just fine though the colt was a little small she looked healthy and she stood up as soon as Penny nudged her with her nose. She nursed soon after she was born and he thought that she would become a great little horse for Joseph.

As soon as Penny was settled in with her baby Abraham went into the house and helped Joseph on with his coat and hat, "I have a surprise for you," he said as he carried him out to the barn.

"Look what we have for you Joseph," he said tears filling his eyes. "This is your pony, your Mama told me when this pony was born it would be yours and you could name it," he added and he let the tears run down his cheeks. Joseph didn't notice them he was too busy looking at the little mare.

"Oh, Papa," Joseph said, "Mama said she would be mine, I remember."

"Isn't she beautiful?" Abraham asked his son.

"Oh, yes," Joseph answered, "I'm going to name her Bell, Papa, Blue Bell, like the pretty flower that Mama liked."

"All right," Abraham said, "I like that name and your Mama would have liked it, too." He wiped the tears from his face with his coat sleeve and then said, "Blue Bell it is then Joseph, want to go tell Sarah?"

"Yes, Papa, let's go get Sarah," Joseph said all excited.

Sarah helped Joseph take care of his horse, she had full charge of her own horse, Star, now and she told Joseph she would teach him how to take good care of Blue Bell. She hugged her little brother and patted the little colts head, "She sure is pretty isn't she Joseph," Sarah said.

Patricia Louise Blish Gould

CHAPTER TWENTY-ONE
1654

At Reverend Lothrop's funeral it was clear to everyone in town that Abraham Blish was seeing Hannah Williams Barker. They sat together at Church every Sunday and it soon become apparent to everyone that he was spending more and more time helping her at her farm. He was often seen escorting her and her children home in the evening just before darkness fell. Hannah had been bringing meals to him and his children, sometimes even preparing them at the Blish residence since Anne's death.

The hired hands had whispered for several months now that she was helping Abraham more than she really needed to. She never was seen alone with him though. She always had little John, now almost three, with her.

Abraham knew how hard it was for Hannah to be alone, many nights he would dream of Anne and wake up feeling empty inside. They were talking about combining their adjoining farms and land holdings and had decided that a marriage agreement would be the easiest way. On Sunday just before Christmas Abraham made the announcement after the Church service that he and Hannah were going to be married in early January.

Hannah was still pretty at age 34 with dark hair and brown eyes and she always seemed to have the energy of a younger woman. She even blushed when some of the women congratulated her when the church service was over that day.

Reverend William Sargeant performed the simple ceremony at the Barnstable church on January 10, 1654. Hannah had dressed all six children in their very best and they all walked the mile to church in their good shoes, being careful not to step on any ice or snow. It was a beautiful sunny day and many of the townspeople attended the wedding and everyone decided it was a nice way to start the New Year. After the wedding Elizabeth Lothrop requested that they all meet at her house for a luncheon. Everyone enjoyed the food that was made by the women of the church and the gathering lasted until late afternoon.

At dusk Abraham carried little John all the way home; it had been a long day for everyone.

Hannah made arrangements with Thomas Allyn to have her children's sleeping pallets brought to Abraham's house while they were at the church and put into the upstairs bedrooms. He also kept a nice warm fire going in the fireplace all day. The older children were excited about the new arrangement; they wouldn't have to be carrying things back and forth from one house to the other anymore.

After a light meal of bread and cheese and applesauce the children went to bed, Hannah tucked them in with a kiss and they were all asleep in just a short time; it had been a very exciting day for them.

When Hannah came down the stairs, Abraham was sitting in his big chair with his shoes off enjoying the warmth of the fire on his cold toes. His toes were always cold lately, he needed new stockings, heavy wool knitted ones, he knew Hannah would make him some as soon as she found out that his were full of holes.

He smiled at her.

Abraham was 38 years old but he felt like a young man on his first date. Maybe he drank too much cider this afternoon, a couple of the tankards were a little bitter he remembered.

Hannah smiled back at him and then disappeared into the bedroom.

Hannah also asked Thomas and Harriet to rearrange Abraham's room so that the bed faced the window. She wanted things to be different for Abraham tonight so that he would think only about her and not about Anne. She had dreamed of Anne several weeks ago, it was so vivid, it was as if Anne was in the room with her. In the dream Anne told her to go to Abraham and make him happy and then she disappeared.

Hannah promised herself she wouldn't think about anything or anyone else tonight except Abraham, so she squeezed her eyes tightly shut, said a small pray thanking God for this wonderful day and got undressed.

She slipped into a pretty yellow cotton nightgown she had made herself and was tying her hair back with a yellow ribbon when Abraham knocked quietly on the door. She was startled for just a second, then quickly finished the bow and went to the door.

At first glance he thought he was in a different room, but then as he recognized the furnishings he realized that they had just been rearranged. He smiled at Hannah and said, "When did you do all this?"

She cleared her throat, there seemed to be a big lump in it all of a sudden, then said, "I asked Thomas and Harriet to change it while we were at church today." She looked at him, her eyes pleading for understanding.

He smiled and said softly "I think it looks nice this way. And so do you," he added almost in a whisper. He touched her arm gently and she shivered.

'We have never even kissed before,' he thought as he pulled her toward him.

Her face tilted up to his and their lips met, softly at first and then as their passion grew they clung to each other as if they were both drowning. In a way they were, their bodies were as lonesome as their hearts.

Abraham picked her up kissing her neck and shoulders, and laid her on the bed, she was breathless. Then he quickly undressed and blew out the candle.

The next morning the children were up long before they were. When they entered the dining room there was a wonderful meal waiting for them to indulge in. All of the children were gone, even little John, Deborah had left him at Harriet's house on her way to school.

They looked at each other and smiled sheepishly. Neither one of them could remember the last time they had slept late. Both thinking that this really had been the right thing to do, they sat down at the table and ate and talked about what had to be done first.

When they were finished, Abraham said with a husky voice, "You know Hannah, there is something better we could be doing right now."

She looked at him and her mouth opened with a little gasp as she realized what he really wanted to do. She felt her cheeks redden as she lowered her eyes for just a second, then when she looked back at him, her eyes were flashing brightly and she reached across the table for his hand. "And just what is it that you would like to do my dear husband?" she questioned in an innocent little voice.

Abraham laughed out loud and almost upset the table as he lifted her to her feet, "Come with me and I'll show you," he said his voice even huskier as he led her to the newly arranged bedroom, their bedroom.

It wasn't long after they were married that Hannah discovered she was pregnant. A bit of gossip among the women in town was whether or not there was something going on between Hannah and Abraham long before they were married. Nothing was said to them of course.

At the June 2, 1654 Town Council meeting both John Crocker and William Crocker were appointed to the Grand Jury. Nathaniel Bacon was re-appointed Constable and Abraham Blish continued his duties as Surveyor.

• • •

Marie Dimmock was busy helping the women of the town deliver their babies, but she still had time to visit with Hannah. They both missed Anne Blish very much, but they were realistic and knew that life had to go on. The first baby of the summer was another son born to William and Alice Crocker, he was born June 10, 1654 and they named him Joseph.

• • •

On June 20, 1654 Captain Myles Standish appointed Captain Matthew Fuller Lieutenant to lead a company of 50 men on an expedition against the Dutch Colony at Manhattoes. The men were ordered to rendezvous at Sandwich on June 29, 1654 to embark from Manomet in the bark *Adventure*, belonging to Captain Samuel Mayo of Barnstable and join the force of the other colonies at the place appointed.

On June 23rd the news of the conclusion of peace between England and Holland was received and the preparation for the expedition halted. Peace had long been desired by the colonies and they opposed the war, but they were loyal subjects and were willing to follow orders.

Talk of the possibility of war was the topic of conversation all during the summer.

Thanking God for peace among the colonies was the topic of conversation all during the harvest season.

• • •

One evening just before dark about the middle of July, Abraham came home and Hannah was frantic, she couldn't find Joseph. His horse was still in her stall so he had not taken her for a ride like he did once in a while forgetting to tell anyone where he was going.

"What time did you realize he was missing?" he asked Hannah.

"I don't know, I think it was late afternoon, I thought that he might have gone with the other children to the pond, but he wasn't with them when they came home," Hannah said.

"He didn't go with you to the pond?" Abraham asked Sarah.

"No, Papa, he was with Blue Bell when I saw him last," Sarah said, "he told me didn't want to go with us, he just wanted to groom Blue Bell."

"Well then lets start looking for him in the barn, have any of you been out there since you came home?" he asked looking at the children.

"No," they all said at the same time shaking their heads.

Abraham took a small candle from the shelf and lit it with a fire stick from the fireplace, then went out of the door with everyone following him and headed toward the barn.

He opened the barn door and waited a minute for his eyes to adjust to the darkness.

He lifted the candle high enough so that he could see into the barn and walked toward the horse stalls.

He went first to Blue Bell's stall; Joseph was not there. As he approached Penny's stall she raised her head slowly and looked at him, he patted her head and she turned a little sideways and there was Joseph.

He had climbed up on her back and was fast asleep with his arms wrapped around her neck.

Abraham handed the candle to Hannah and then put his finger to his lips so that everyone would be quiet and he gently picked up his little six-year-old son.

Joseph put his arms around his father's neck and hiccuped it looked like he had been crying his face was dirty and tear-stained.

Abraham carried him into the house and sat down on the settee in front of the fireplace and held him close.

Hannah got a warm wet cloth and handed it to him and Abraham carefully wiped his son's face.

Joseph woke up when the wet cloth touched his cheek and he sat up, looked at his father and said, "Papa, I couldn't open the barn door."

"Why not?" Abraham asked him. "I put the latch down low so you could reach it," he said.

"I think it was stuck," Joseph said, "and I was afraid when it got dark."

"You shouldn't be afraid of the dark, son," Abraham hugged him tighter, "if you let your eyes get used to it, you can see by the light from the stars and the moon."

"I heard some noise, too, Papa," Joseph said.

"It was probably just a mouse or one of the other animals moving around," Abraham assured him.

"I saw my Mama, and she said you would find me," Joseph said, "she helped me get up on Penny's back and told me to go to sleep."

"She did?" Abraham said wondering if it could have been true.

"She was an angel and she was pretty," Joseph said knowingly, "I want to see my Mama again."

"I know Joseph, and you will some day when you go to heaven," Abraham said, "but you can't right now."

Joseph leaned back into this father's arms and said, "I miss her."

"Me too," Abraham said holding his son close.

Hannah quietly put the other children to bed and then she went to bed and waited for her husband, she knew he needed to be alone with his memories and his son.

• • •

Robert and Elizabeth Davis had another son, on August 24, 1654 they named him Robert, Jr. He was their fifth child in nine years.

Elizabeth did not recuperate very well and Marie and Sarah could not find anything seriously wrong with her except that she was exhausted most of the time.

Marie gave her Schizandra Berry herbs to make a tea with and she willingly took it for several weeks.

• • •

William and Alice Crocker's last child, Joseph, was born October 1, 1654. Alice's labor was not as long and tedious as it had been when she had Eleazer. Both her and baby Joseph were healthy. And of course, William was away on business. Secretly he was glad about that when he came home and found that he had a new son and that Alice had done just fine throughout the ordeal. He never wanted to see his wife suffer again like she had with Eleazer.

• • •

Samuel Cobb was born on October 12, 1654 to Henry and Sarah Cobb. Marie and Sarah helped her through her labor and everything went smoothly for both the new mother and baby.

Four days later Abraham Blish, Jr. was born to Abraham and Hannah Barker Blish. October 16, 1654 was a cold day, but no one seemed to notice, there was just too much happiness in the Blish home.

The gossip, which was considered a sin of course, did not become any louder than a whisper and after that October day it disappeared altogether. Abraham and Hannah had been married nine months and six days. Together they now had seven children to care for. Deborah being the oldest was now 15 and a big help to her mother. She was quite adept in sewing and cooking and was making her own trousseau. She had quilts and pillows, embroidered sheets and pillow covers and table clothes in her big trunk in the corner of her upstairs room. After her new little brother was born she realized that her mother did not have the energy that she once had and took over many of her mother's duties for several weeks giving her time to regain her strength.

Baby Abraham was a big eater and it was all Hannah could do to nurse him and care for him for the first three months. He was a big baby and Marie and Sarah made her stay in bed for a week after his birth getting up only when necessary. She was so thankful to have Deborah and Mary, 11 now, and Sarah 12, to help her with the cooking and cleaning and the younger children.

The winter was blustery and it snowed often leaving big snowdrifts against the fences in the little town. Wagons full of hay and corn were taken from farm to farm almost daily to feed the livestock toward the end of winter. The Haywards had a lot of hard work to do to make sure that no animals died of starvation or cold.

One morning when the children went out to do their chores Johnny Barker almost 4 years old now, heard a strange noise near the back of the shed. It had snowed a couple of inches the night before and he noticed that there were tracks leading from the shed toward the back of the barn.

He followed them carefully, he thought they might be made by a fox or young wolf. Then he saw a little pile of snow move and heard the noise again.

He picked up a small stick and knocked some of the snow away and found a little black and white puppy whimpering from the cold.

"How did you get here, little fellow," he asked the small dog. The puppy made no move to get up and laid its little head down in the cold snow.

Johnny reached down and gently patted the dog and when it didn't try to move he scooped him up and took him to the barn.

"Pa," he called to Abraham, "look what I found in back of the barn."

"What is it?" Abraham asked, as Johnny came toward him with his arms outstretched. He jumped back a little when he saw the black and white fur.

"Don't be afraid Pa," Johnny laughed, "its just a poor little puppy. I think he's lost and he's almost frozen."

"For a moment there I thought you had a skunk," Abraham said feeling a little silly.

"Can I keep him?" Johnny asked looking up with the same expression in his eyes that his mother had when she wanted something but wasn't quite sure if she should ask for it.

"I guess it would be all right," Abraham said, "but you might want to ask you mother if she approves."

"Oh, thank you, thank you Pa," Johnny said all excited, "I'll take care of him all by myself, like Joseph takes care of Blue Bell."

Abraham did not realize that Johnny felt slighted about having nothing of his very own for a pet. "You tell your Ma that I said we could use a good watch dog around here," Abraham called after him as he ran toward the house.

"Ma, Ma," Johnny called as he ran into the house slamming the door behind him.

"What is it dear," she asked concerned that the excitement in his voice might mean something was wrong.

"Look what I found," he said coming closer.

She jumped back a little too when she saw the black and white fur. Hannah said, "what do you have there Johnny?"

"It's a little puppy Ma," Johnny said laughing. "Pa thought it was a skunk too," he said holding the almost lifeless dog out to her.

"Oh, dear, Johnny, he looks like he's been injured or something," Hannah said gaining her composure.

"Can I keep him, Ma?" Johnny asked pleadingly. "Pa said we could use a good watch dog around here," he added quickly.

"I suppose we could," Hannah said, "but first lets see if he is hurt," and she picked the cold little puppy out of her son's arms gently. Hannah carried him over to the fireplace and sat down on the settee and laid the puppy in her lap. She petted him for a few minutes and then said, "Johnny why don't you get him some warm milk."

"Oh yes Ma, that's a good idea," he said as he ran out of the house toward the barn.

Hannah patted the dog and felt him all over to see if she could feel any broken bones, all she felt were ribs that seemed to be too close to his skin, "I think you're just about starved little dog," she crooned. The puppy tried to wag his tail a little but it was almost too much of an effort, he just looked at her with sad eyes.

Johnny came running in with some warm milk that Abraham had poured into a small pail from the big milk pail. He held it up to the puppy's nose.

"Let's get a small dish so he can reach it better," Hannah said to her son. She couldn't remember when she had seen him so happy. She held the puppy in one arm while she went to the cupboard and took down a small clamshell and dipped it into the milk. She sat the dish on the hearth in front of the warm fire and then sat the puppy down in front of it. The puppy stuck his nose in it and then his tongue. He drank every drop of it.

Johnny was so gentle as he patted the dog and rubbed its fur, "I think he wants some more," he said and picked up the dish and dipped it back into the pail. The puppy drank almost all of the milk that was in the little pail and then he started shivering.

"I think that she's just cold now, Johnny," Hannah said, "I'll get her a blanket to lay on."

Johnny was holding him when Hannah came back to the fireplace, "Here you are son, and I think she's going to be just fine, but I think she's a girl dog so you might want to think up a girl's name."

"I can keep him?" Johnny asked with big eyes.

"Yes, I think we could use a good watch dog around here, too," Hannah said smiling, "but remember it's a girl dog."

"Yes, a pretty black and white girl dog," Johnny said covering the little puppy up with the blanket. "I have to think of a girl dog name for you," he said to his new best friend.

Abraham came into the house a few minutes later and found Johnny still sitting in front of the fireplace holding his new puppy. "Have you thought of a name for him yet son?" he asked Johnny.

"Yes, Pa," Johnny said, "but mother said I should think of a girl dog's name."

Hannah came into the commonroom from the bedroom where she had just put little Abraham down for a nap.

"So it's a girl dog," Abraham said looking at her.

"Yes dear, I think she'll make a wonderful watch dog, don't you?" Hannah asked smiling at him.

"Yes, I certainly do," Abraham said.

"I'm going to name her Daisy because she has a white mark on her head and it looks like a daisy to me," Johnny said seriously.

"Well let me get a close up of this little creature," Abraham said as he bent down to pet the little puppy. "I think you might be right, Johnny, that little spot does look like a daisy and that's a very good name for her, Daisy it is."

Hannah said, "That's a wonderful name Johnny, but remember you have to make sure that she doesn't chew anything in the house and that she does her jobs out side, right?"

"Yes, Ma, I will," Johnny said smiling broadly, "I will take care of her all by myself, even in the night time."

Hannah looked at Abraham over her little boy's head and her eyes said, "I love you."

He smiled at her and winked and then went back outside to finish his chores.

• • •

The harvest was bountiful this year and food was plentiful for the people of Barnstable. Thanksgiving and Christmas were just around the corner and family gatherings were being planned by many of the women. They enjoyed cooking in their big fireplace ovens during the cold days of winter. Bread or biscuits were made daily and served at every meal.

Hannah, Deborah, Sarah and Mary and even little Annie shared the cooking duties that went with having a large family. Yorkshire pudding was made at least twice a week or whenever a roast of beef was being cooked. The recipe was easy and delicious. A cup of finely ground flour was mixed with a little salt, two eggs and one cup of milk and left to stand for about an hour. Then when the meat was almost cooked and the fat and juices started to drip from the meat, the pan of pudding was set under it to catch the flavorful drippings.

By the time the meat was finished the pudding would become a delicious side dish and was enjoyed by everyone.

Another favorite was cranberry pork chops. This was an easy meal that the women made for a large family. Six to ten pork chops were browned on each side in a hot skillet. Then they chopped about four or five cups of dried cranberries into very fine pieces and mixed them together with about a cup and a half of honey and a teaspoon of ground cloves. Then they alternately layered the pork and the cranberries into a large covered skillet and baked the meat for an hour or so.

This was a favorite of the Blish family.

With the left over pork roasts the ladies made pork and apple casserole. They layered dried sliced apples with slices of cold pork and bread stuffing, which was stale bread made into crumbs and flavored with sage and thyme and parsley, into a large skillet, added about two or three cups of cider and baked it for about an hour. Sometimes they topped this casserole with winter squash that they mashed with butter and a little maple syrup.

The women of Barnstable shared their family recipes as well as the recipes that the Indian women had given them. The Indian women had shown them in the earlier years of the settlement how to make maple syrup from the sap of the sugar maple tree, and how to cook meat with the sap. They also gave them many of their favorite recipes; especially the ones made with maple syrup, cranberries, beans, and corn or squash.

Sometimes mistakes turned out to be wonderful meals that they shared with each other, never admitting of course that they didn't intend the recipe to turn out as it did. For instance, Mary and Sarah were making a cake one cold afternoon and they found that there wasn't enough sugar in the sugar crock. Not wanting to go to the cold storeroom in the big shed for more, they decided to use maple syrup instead. Then after licking the spoon they decided that it needed more flavoring so Sarah added nutmeg and Mary added some ground ginger.

As the cake was baking the smell of spices permeated the whole house, needless to say it was mouth watering and Hannah decided she would taste this new cake before she did any scolding.

It was ready to come out of the oven just as the main meal was being finished and the girls served it warm.

Abraham spooned a little applesauce over his and thought it wonderful, Hannah put a dollop of heavy cream on hers, and Sarah and Mary were given well-deserved praise by everyone that evening.

They were often found experimenting at the cook table on cold winter afternoons after that. Keeping track of their recipes and making careful notes so they could pass the good ones on to the other girls in town.

Many Sunday evening meals were shared when neighbors got together. The women would bring food to share and after the meal was over they would sew or knit and listen quietly while the men talked about town government or told stories about the early days. Most of the families had everything they needed and the town was running smoothly, except for the fact that they didn't have a full-time preacher. The town prospered and was growing steadily and though there was an unusual amount of snow that winter there were no problems to speak of except that another family was left motherless.

• • •

On November 10, 1654 Elizabeth Davis, wife of Robert and mother of five children died. Their baby was only three months old. Marie and Sarah gave her a mixture of Black Cohosh, Squaw vine and Red Raspberry to help her recover after her baby was born but nothing seemed to help. She just never recuperated. Robert was left with five little children to raise by himself. Many of the neighbor women were there to help and several new mothers took turns feeding little Robert.

• • •

On November 12, 1654 Thomas and Lydia Dexter had a baby girl they named Eleanor, her fifth baby, her fourth baby, Hannah, was not quite a year old. Marie Dimmock tried to make Lydia take Blessed Thistle, the old Indian birth control treatment, but Lydia refused. She said that she was fine and a strong woman and besides if God wanted her to have a new baby every year, she would. But she did drink the Schizandra Berry tea each day it always made her feel better and it helped her gain her strength back.

• • •

On December 14, 1654 Sarah Fuller was born. She was the seventh child of Samuel and Jane Fuller and as usual Marie Dimmock was there to help Jane bring her new baby into the world. Her delivery was easy and she recuperated quickly. Being December it was easier to rest, there were not quite as many chores outside the home during that time of year.

• • •

Abraham and Hannah invited Robert Davis and his five children to Thanksgiving dinner and they all had a great time playing games and telling stories.

At Christmas Thomas and Marie Dimmock invited Robert and his children to eat dinner with them. Marie made sure that they all had new mittens and hats and wool socks enough to last them through the winter. Robert was very grateful and told Thomas to be sure and let him know if he needed anything done around his farm.

Patricia Louise Blish Gould

CHAPTER TWENTY-TWO
1655

Another cold wind was blowing off the ocean on the morning of February 3, 1655 directly into Barnstable bringing with it sadness for Sam and Jane Fuller. Little Thomas, not quite five years old died of pneumonia.

For two weeks Marie and Sarah gave him a tea made with Elder Flower, Golden Seal and Mullein three or four times a day. Jane kept him warm and held him as much as she could and propped him up on pillows in his bed while she was tending to little Sarah who was just a year old.

Jane gave Thomas his medicine about 10 o'clock the night before and got into bed with him holding him in her arms. She dozed off to sleep after a while and when she woke up just before dawn she realized that her little boy was not breathing. She laid her little boy down on the bed and went into her bedroom and woke up Sam.

"Our little Thomas has gone to heaven," she said crying softly.

Sam got up and ran into his son's room and picked him up. He put his ear to his little boy's mouth and could hear nothing, he listen to his chest and it was quiet, there was no heartbeat and no wheezing.

Jane was standing beside them and Sam put his arm around his wife and they both cried. The Fuller's had a service for him and then he was put into the crypt until spring. Another angel was needed in heaven.

• • •

Lydia Dexter was again unable to feed her newest baby. Eleanor was three months old and hungry most of the time, so several new mothers helped her. Alice Crocker, Sarah Cobb and Hannah Blish all had babies that were still nursing and between the three of them they kept little Robert Davis and Eleanor Dexter fed.

• • •

Mary Fuller, age 20, daughter of Captain Matthew and Frances Fuller married Ralph Jones on April 17, 1655 at the Barnstable Church and there was much celebrating. The weather was beautiful that spring day with just a slight breeze from the ocean. The wild seaside roses were just starting to bloom and the sun was warm and bright.

Mary and Ralph moved into their new home later in the afternoon and it was said that they didn't come out to see the sky again for three days. Whenever Mary and Ralph were seen together, even after many weeks had passed, the men still smiled knowingly at Ralph and the single young ladies would giggled behind their hands until their mothers hushed them. Ralph and Mary would just look at each other and smile, let them wonder their eyes said.

• • •

At the annual town council meeting in June William Carsely took over the duties of Constable again. Nathaniel Bacon declined the appointment because he had been Constable for five years. He did promise to help William if he needed him. Henry Bourne was appointed Surveyor and Abraham Blish was chosen as Hayward.

William Crocker was again elected a member of the Grand Jury for Plymouth Colony. He accepted the job feeling that it was an honor to serve his country. His farm was practically running itself now and this left him able to carry out his duties to the government. He now owned 126 acres of upland and 22 acres of meadow in West Barnstable and forty acres of upland near the Indian ponds.

William Crocker's house was one of the first fortification houses built and was made mostly of stone and located just a short distance from the Barnstable Church. He was also a Deacon of the church and both him and his wife Alice were loved and respected by everyone.

His six sons now ages 18, 13, 11, 8, 5, and 1 were his pride and joy. His only daughter, Elizabeth was the apple of his eye; she was 16 and already known as one of the best cooks in town.

Barnstable town ran as smoothly as many of the towns in the new colony did. The large amount of snow that winter had produced was gone from the fields by the early spring and the planting was completed about a week earlier than usual.

The weather cooperated all summer bringing just the right amount of rain and sunshine and the crops were large and plentiful. After the harvest there was an abundance of food for anyone.

Nothing out of the ordinary happen until on September 27, 1655 when Constable William Carsely was thrown from his horse. He was on his way home late in the afternoon from Yarmouth after meeting with several other town councils regarding town boundaries when a deer spooked his horse. His horse reared up unexpectedly and William lost his hold on the reins and fell heavily to the ground landing on his left shoulder and hip.

He must have been knocked unconscious because when he came to he couldn't remember where he was for a minute. When he gained his senses he realized he was laying on the ground and his horse was no where to be seen. As he tried to get up he realized that his shoulder must be broken or dislocated because the pain was excruciating and he thought he was going to throw up.

After a few minutes when the nausea subsided he decided that he had to do something no matter how much it hurt so he crawled to the edge of the road way where there was a big rock and used it to pull himself upright. His left leg was numb but he could put his weight on it so he figured he had no choice but to start walking.

He managed to take a few tentative steps before it gave out and he fell to his knees. This time his stomach churned and emptied onto the ground as if he had no control over it. He fainted.

It must have been a half-hour before he regained consciousness and opened his eyes again; it was getting dark. He thought he heard someone coming on horseback so he whistled, knowing the sound would carry better than yelling out.

Then as the sound came closer he realized it was his own horse, "Good old Jessie," he said softly, "You came back for me."

He soothed her nervousness by talking quietly to her and she put her head down toward his outstretched hand. He sat up still talking quietly to her and after a minute or so he reached for the stirrup and slowly pulled himself to his feet.

Using her to lean on he guided her closer to the big rock, crawled onto it and then carefully pulled himself up onto her back laying across the saddle.

Tapping her with his hand on her front shoulder and holding on to the reins as best he could, he turned Jessie still a little skittish, toward home.

It must have been an hour before he reached his house and how he stayed on his horse that long he will never know; he kept passing out every few minutes.

Martha heard his horse coming up the lane, and breathed a sigh of relief as she stirred the stew pot.

When several minutes passed and he had not come into the house she went to the door. William always rode up to the door and came in to say he was home and give her a kiss then he would promptly take Jessie to the barn and tend to her.

Martha screamed his name when she opened the door and saw his lifeless body lying over Jessie's saddle and ran to him repeating his name.

"William, oh, William," she said over and over. Her shouting startled Jessie a little and the horse jumped a bit causing William to lose his grip and he started to fall to the ground.

Martha grabbed him about the waist and held on to him as he groaned and tried to push himself the rest of the way off the saddle.

Being the strong woman that she was she practically carried him into the house and helped him to their bed in the corner of their big common room.

He woke up a little and realized he was home and that Martha was talking to him. He moaned, "Martha, help me."

"What happened to you William, where are you hurt," she soothed him as she took off his right boot. He moaned a little but didn't answer her.

When she pulled his left boot off he screamed a low deep groaning scream.

"Oh, William, I'm so sorry," she said tearfully, she expected to see his foot all swollen, but it wasn't.

Then as she lifted him a little by his shoulder to remove his frock his body went limp; he fainted into unconsciousness again.

"Oh dear God," she said aloud and ran out toward the barn to get help from their hired hand.

"Everett," she called as she ran, "Go and get Marie Dimmock and Sarah Bourne, William has been hurt, go quickly."

Everett James did not hesitate one minute, in fact noticing that William's horse was still saddled, he grabbed Jessie's reins and rode her across the meadow, a short cut to the lane, and headed down the road at a gallop toward the Dimmock's farm.

Martha ran back into the house and found William still unconscious but breathing regularly. She lifted him gently and took off his frock and shirt and then she removed his breeches.

His left shoulder was swollen and black and blue and it was hunched into an unusual position. His left hip was red and purple with blood very close to the skin.

She felt the rest of William's body gently and found that there seemed to be no other wounds anywhere else.

She took his dirty clothes to the back shed and put them in the wash tub, they smelled awful.

"What could have happened to you my dear man," she crooned softly as she wiped his face with a cold cloth. He groaned again and opened his eyes and looked at her.

"How did I get here?" he groaned.

"Jessie brought you home, dear," she answered. "Lay still now, don't fret yourself," she said softly, "can you tell me what happened?"

His pain eased a little as he realized he was in the comfort of his own bed with his loving wife caring for him. "I'm embarrassed to say I must have fallen off Jessie," he groaned.

"How could you have possibly done that, have you been drinking?" she scolded a little.

"No, no, dear Martha, I made a promise to you and I've kept it, I was not drinking," he defended himself with a little more gusto in his voice. "A deer ran out of the woods and startled her I think," he continued. "I'm not sure what happened. I heard a rustle in the woods, I saw a deer leap in front of us and Jessie reared up and then I was on the ground. Poor Jessie was running off toward home leaving me lying there in the road. I passed out I think, I don't know for how long, then I heard hoof beats and she was coming back for me," he finished moaning from the pain in his shoulder. "Where is she now?" he asked a little concerned.

"Everett rode her over to get Marie and Sarah," Martha replied, "They should be back any minute, can I get you some water," she asked him, tears were filling her eyes.

"Yes," he said trying to lick his dry lips with his dry tongue.

"I think I was sick after I fell, the pain made be vomit, did I get any on my frock?" he asked a little embarrassed.

"It's nothing that can't be washed out," she said patting his hand and going to the water pail.

"My shoulder hurts so much," he groaned again as he tried to lift his head to drink the water Martha was holding to his lips.

"Rest for a minute and try to relax," she said softly, "the ladies should be here any time now." Martha turned her head so he wouldn't see the tears of helplessness she had in her eyes.

Marie and Sarah arrived soon after Everett returned to tell Martha that they were on their way. They had of course brought their herbal medicines with them and within a matter of minutes after Marie's arrival she had a tea of Mullein, Lobelia, Hawthorn, Hops and Garlic brewing over the hearth.

As the herbal tea simmered they examined William with tender hands. The tea smelled quite potent but it always worked very well for pain and shock.

William was a little embarrassed with his nakedness, but the women didn't seem to be paying any attention to his anatomy, except for his shoulder and hip.

They asked him many questions about how he had landed on the road. If he hit his head, they could feel no bumps on it; the pain must have made him pass out they concluded.

Marie and Sarah discovered that he had dislocated his arm from the socket in the shoulder, they hoped that the collarbone was not broken.

They could feel no broken bones in his arm or leg, and his hip had not swollen, as was often the case when a person's hip was broken.

After they finished their examination and the tea had cooled a little they gave William small sips until he had consumed about two cups of it.

By this time he was much relieved of the pain and very sleepy and he relaxed and dozed off to sleep.

Marie took Martha aside so William wouldn't hear them and told her what they had to do. They would need Martha's help and she agreed.

Quietly the women lifted him into a sitting position, it would take all three of them to correct William's situation.

Marie took hold of William's arm just above his elbow with both her hands, Sarah held onto him under his arm with one hand on the front of his chest and the other on his back in a hugging posture.

Martha was instructed to hold him about his chest and to pull him against her when they were ready.

They moved him gently into position between them and Marie nodded her head said, "Now!" All three women pulled and they could hear his shoulder pop back into place.

William, feeling a sudden horrible sharp pain in his shoulder again yelled and even cursed and then fainted into a peaceful sleep. He didn't realized what had taken place, but Marie, Sarah and Martha had put his shoulder back into its socket.

All three women were shaking a little when they laid William back onto his bed, but they were smiling, being very satisfied with what they had done.

Marie assured Martha that her husband would be all right now. "His arm and shoulder will be very painful for several weeks," she said handing her an herbal packet. "You can give him tea made from these herbs about every two hours, or whenever he wakes up."

"He'll be up and around in no time," Sarah said as they gathered their things and put their frocks on.

"Keep an eye on his hip and if it starts to swell send Everett for us immediately, I don't think its broken but there may be a small crack in it," Marie said. "If it is broken it will swell during the night, if not it means that it is just very badly bruised," Marie continued. "It will still be very hard for him to walk for several weeks and he shouldn't use his arm to lift anything very heavy for a month or so." Marie continued in a calm voice. Then she patted Martha on her shoulder and said kindly, "But be sure to make him get up every day for a few minutes, even if he just stands by the bed it will help him to heal."

"I'll bring some comfrey when I come back tomorrow and we'll put some in his tea," Sarah told Martha, "and I have some salve that I'll bring for his bruises, too."

"Make him move his arm up and down two or three times each day," Marie said as she gestured her own arm in a waving motion, "don't let his arm become immobile or he won't be able to ever use it again."

"One of us will be back each day to see how he's doing, and bring him more medicine when he needs it," Sarah said as they both left quietly.

Martha was crying softly as the two most wonderful women in the whole town climbed into their buggy and headed for home.

When Everett heard them leaving he came out of the barn where he had been doing chores and tending Jessie. He waved to them and seeing Martha standing in the doorway he started toward the house calling to her to see if William was all right.

Martha walked out toward him and with a shushing motion, putting her finger to her lips, she told him that William would be just fine in a few weeks.

"Please go and tell Mr. Blish about William's mishap and let him know that we will be all right tonight," she said quietly, "but be sure to tell him that I expect that William will want to see him tomorrow morning."

"Yes, ma'am I'll get right to it," Everett replied courteously.

Martha turned and went back into the house, so grateful that her William was home safe, even if he was injured, at least he was home. She lit the candle that was on the table and took it to the bedside; she had to assure herself that he was really all right, Martha bent over and kissed her husband gently on his forehead.

'What would I ever do without him,' she thought wistfully, and sighed. "Thank you God" she whispered.

Abraham was asked to take William Carsely's place as Constable that following day. After William's injuries healed he declined his appointment as Constable and was appointed Hayward for the town. Of course, his duties didn't start until the middle of January when he was back on his feet again.

As Hayward he didn't have to travel alone very much and Martha was very thankful that the town council agreed that William had indeed been a great Constable for the town of Barnstable for many years prior.

• • •

On December 12, 1655 Robert Davis and his five children married Ann Oates, daughter of John Oates of Yarmouth. Robert was 33 and she was just 18.

Robert met Ann at church just after she and her parents moved to Barnstable from Yarmouth in June.

Reverend Mayo knew that Robert was having quite a hard time trying to bring his children up alone, and he suggested that Ann work for him during the day.

Robert thought it was a good idea, he offered to pay her a shilling a week and she accepted.

Ann loved the children and was often seen carrying little Robert to one of the nursing mothers with the other four tagging along after her.

She was a big help to Robert and he enjoyed her company during their evening meal.

He told her every evening before she left to go home how much he appreciated her help. She always smiled and said she was happy to be there.

One evening he put his hand on her arm and said, "Do you think you would be happy to live here all the time?"

Ann blushed and said, "I couldn't do that Mr. Davis unless I was married to you."

It was Robert's turn to blush, "Of course, I, you, we would be married," he stammered.

"If you talk to my father Mr. Davis, I think he would give you permission to marry me," she looked him directly in his eyes.

'He has nice green eyes,' she thought, 'and he's so kind, he's a good father, I'm sure he was a good husband to Elizabeth.'

Robert smiled and said, "I will talk to him tomorrow."

"I love your children Mr. Davis," Ann said, "they are very well behaved and I would very much like to be their new mother."

"Thank you, Ann," he said quietly, "you have been very good with them."

"Mr. Davis, did you just ask me to marry you?" Ann asked.

"I, well, we, well, yes, I guess I did," he stammered again.

"Well, good then, my answer is yes, as soon as you ask my father's permission," she smiled up at him and turned quickly, took her cloak off the peg and left his house.

The next day he gathered his courage and asked Mr. Oates for permission to marry his daughter. Elizabeth had been gone a year.

Mr. and Mrs. Oates agreed after discussing Robert's request and thought that Robert would be a good husband for their daughter even if he was quite a bit older. Ann Oates was a big girl and not very many young bachelors gave her a second look.

Ann told her parents that she would marry him and that he was a good man, she didn't tell anyone that she was in love with Robert Davis.

•   •   •

On December 14, 1655 Jane Dexter was born to Thomas and Lydia Dexter. She was born on her sister Hannah's second birthday and was Lydia's sixth baby in five years.

"We must try to get Lydia to take Blessed Thistle," Marie said to Sarah when they were on their way home after delivering Lydia's baby.

"I have never seen or heard of any problems with this medicine and the Indian women take it all the time to control the timing of the birth of their babies," she added.

"I'll work on making it taste better," Sarah said. "If she didn't know that she was taking a birth control formula maybe she would take it every day," she added.

"That's a good idea," Marie said smiling, "maybe more of the other new mothers would take it, too."

"Some of them have had more than their share of children," Sarah said.

"I don't believe that Elizabeth Davis would have died if she did not have so many babies so fast," Marie replied.

"I agree," Sarah said, "I'm kind of excited about making a new medicine, what shall we call it? Blessed Tea?" she added smiling.

"That's a good name for it," Marie said, "we'll call it our 'Blessed Tea,'

"Very good then, I'll start today," Sarah smiled.

"We'll take it to all new mothers that have lots of young children as soon as you finish with it," Marie said laughing a little, "but you'd better hurry or they'll all be pregnant again."

"Yes," Sarah said smiling, "I'll give it to Lydia first before we run out of nursing mothers to feed her babies."

A week later word came from Marstons Mills that on December 20, 1655 Roger and Alice Goodspeed had a baby boy they named

Ebenezer, their seventh child. No one had heard whether or not Roger was still cruel to Alice and his children, they hoped that he wasn't, they prayed for them.

• • •

Captain Fuller brought a letter to Abraham on December 26, 1655. It was from his brother John in England. The Captain had been in Plymouth and he often delivered mail to the people in the colony whenever he was going in their direction.

September 3, 1655

Dear Brother Abraham,

I hope this letter finds you and your family in the best of health. I do regret that the news I have to tell you is not good. Father passed away this morning. He was working in the mill as he always did every day and suddenly he fell to the floor. I saw him but could do nothing; I was too far from him to catch him. He did not hit his head on anything he just collapsed into a heap. I do believe that his heart just stopped beating.

Mother is doing well; she told me that she expected him to do this because his father had done the same thing many years before. Father always told her, she said, that when he died he wished to do so just as his father had. I do believe that he got his wish. Mother believes that he did not suffer and she is grateful for that, as am I.

We will bury him in the family plot here in Devon the day after tomorrow.

I must get to bed now. I have not been able to understand how he can be gone so suddenly. I will not be able to talk to him again. I am sorry that you will not be able to be here for his service, but I am sure that your prayers will be with us.

Mother sends her love to you and your family as do Molly and I. Our children are all growing and we are in good health.

I leave you in God's hand and I will always keep you in my prayers.

I will always be your loving brother,

John

Abraham called his young children to his side and told them that their Grandfather in England had passed away. He would be meeting their mother in heaven and then he would be able to see for himself just how beautiful she was.

Sarah felt very sorry for her father and hugged him tight thinking how awful it was loosing her mother and hoping that she would never have to feel the loss of her father, too.

Joseph hugged his father too and asked, "Did he have red hair like me, Papa?"

"No, Joseph, you got your red hair from your Mama," Abraham said, "your Grandpapa had dark brown hair."

Abraham took his journal down from the shelf in the commonroom where he kept it and gathered his pen and ink. He had an entry to make.

The children went about their daily activities and he watched them for a minute thinking about his own childhood.

Then he sighed and opened his book, 'Life goes on,' he thought and his eyes filled with tears as he started writing.

Hannah held him close when they went to bed that night and told him how sorry she was for his loss. She knew how he felt; she had lost her father, too, though it was many years ago.

CHAPTER TWENTY-THREE
1656

Sam and Jane Fuller had a son on February 9, 1656 and they named him Little John their eighth child. They had been married 20 years, Sam was 42 and Jane was 40. Marie Dimmock persuaded Jane to take a special tea that she had developed to help new mothers recover from childbirth, she called it 'Blessed Tea.'

Marie knew that most of the women did not realize that she was giving them Blessed Thistle Tea for their own good. Some of the women were getting too old to have more children and some of them had too many to take care of. She told Sarah that she did not feel guilty doing this and Sarah agreed.

• • •

Abraham was officially elected Constable at the annual town council meeting held June 3, 1656. He did a great job while William was healing from his injuries and the council members all agreed that he should be appointed Constable of Barnstable, Duxbury, Scituate, Marshfield, Yarmouth, Darby and Plymouth for the ensuing term of five years. The duties of a Constable had increased as the small towns expanded growing closer together. The roads between them were better and small bridges were being built each summer. The Governor and the Colony Court maintained that crime was less now and a Constable could easily cover a twenty-mile area. Of course, he was allowed to ask for help if there came a time when he might have to be in more than one place at the same time.

• • •

On September 3, 1656 Robert and Ann Davis had a son, Ann's first child, Robert's sixth, they named him Josiah. They were married almost nine months.

Josiah was very small and Marie and Sarah made it known that he was born about two weeks early.

Ann had been working hard in the garden trying to get all of her vegetables picked before they spoiled. It wasn't easy doing everything while big with child.

No one said anything after a week or so, after all gossiping was sinful.

• • •

On November 30, 1656 Thomas and Lydia Dexter's seventh child, a son they named Charles was born. They had been married for just a little over six years.

This time Marie Dimmock gave Lydia the new special Blessed Tea, as she called it. Telling the exhausted woman that it would make her healthier and she would be able to nurse her baby longer without help from her neighbors.

This time she did not refuse to drink her cup of tea every day, it was much better than the other tea that Marie used to try to get her to drink.

Sarah had flavored it with honey and a little touch of Lemon Grass.

• • •

Abraham received word from Richard More that Captain Myles Standish died on December 2, 1656 at the age of 72. His funeral would be held on December 4th in Plymouth and Governor Bradford would be there.

"I hope that you can bring your family and meet me there and we will attend his funeral together," Richard's letter stated.

Abraham made arrangements to go to the Captains funeral service and to visit Richard and Mary More. He needed to take his family on a holiday and this was a good opportunity to do so.

"Can you all be ready to go to Duxbury by tomorrow morning?" he asked during their evening meal.

"Yes," all of the children answered excitedly almost at the same time.

"I'm not sure," Hannah said. "Maybe with everyone's help we might possibly be ready," she smiled at him. "What time do we leave?" she asked.

"Our boat will sail about mid-morning," Abraham answered. "The weather is supposed to be agreeable so Captain Mayo says, and he is planning to leave then."

"Deborah, you help the older children each pack a satchel and I'll help the younger ones," Hannah said.

She was already organizing in her mind all the things that she needed to do in order to be ready in such a short time.

They were all at the dock by 9:30 the next morning ready to board. Abraham smiled to himself, 'What a great family I have,' he thought.

Abraham met Richard in Plymouth and sent his family on to Duxbury with Captain Mayo. Mary met them at the wharf and they were all settled in by the time Abraham and Richard arrived home after the funeral.

The children wanted to hear a story that evening so after their evening meal Richard told them a short story about his long time friend Captain Myles Standish.

"Myles Standish was born in Lancashire, England in 1584. In 1620 he joined the Pilgrims and sailed on the Mayflower to Plymouth.

I remember him well, he was a kind man, but he was firm in his belief of God and his duties as a soldier.

He became a great leader under the guidance of William Bradford and was successful in helping to establish peaceful relations with the Indians.

Before we disembarked from the Mayflower Captain Standish and a party of sixteen men rowed our small shallop to shore and then set out on foot on November 25, 1620 looking for a permanent settlement.

They had not gone far when they met a small party of Indians who were frightened and fled into the forest upon sight of them.

They followed the Indians for a few miles until it became dark and then they made camp for the night.

The next morning they explored for several hours and found some Indian corn and fresh water flowing from a small brook.

The men were extremely thirsty but Captain Standish did not allow them to drink until he tasted the water to see if it were tainted.

After several minutes and he was not sick, he allowed the men to all drink their fill while he marked the map that he had been making.

They saw many deer and great flocks of geese and ducks and killed three fat geese and six ducks and because they had not eaten much since they left the ship, they devoured every last bite of their first meal in the new land.

They also found many more signs of Indian habitation; they found heaps of sand and when they dug under them they found baskets of Indian corn of many colors and took some of it back to the ship.

This food helped to sustain all of us that were still on board the Mayflower while we completed repairs to our small shallop. It was leaking and needed to be sealed with rope and tar, we also cut wood and got our tools in readiness to make a permanent landing.

On December 7th Captain Standish set off on foot again with about thirty men and found more signs of Indian habitation and more corn and beans.

They brought the corn and beans back to the ship so we could use it as seed for the planting that we knew we would have to do in the spring.

They did not however, find a good place to harbor the Mayflower or a good place to settle permanently.

On December 16th Captain Standish and twelve men left the Mayflower again in the newly repaired shallop to find us a good harbor.

The weather was so cold that it froze the sea spray as it covered the men's coats and they looked as if they had been glazed.

They came upon about a dozen Indians near a small cove who were very busy cutting up a big black thing but they could not tell what it was.

They watched them for a while and then proceeded on for a short way, then they went ashore, built a barricade and built a fire.

In the morning they divided their party, four walking along the shore and eight cruising along side in the water.

The men on shore found the carcass of a small whale and realized that it was what they had watched the Indians cutting up the day before.

They found nothing else though and when they rendezvoused that evening they were all very hungry and ate what was left of the few cold biscuits that they had in their sacks.

On the morning of the 18th they had their first encounter with the Indians, there were about thirty or forty of them.

They were thankful of their barricade because the Indians shot many arrows at them but none of the men were hit or hurt though there were many holes in the coats that they had used as a roof.

They shot their muskets several times at the Indians and the noise must have frightened them because they all left, they did not think that any of their bullets wounded any of them.

When this skirmish was over they quickly left in the shallop and by afternoon a storm developed with gale force winds. The boat's rudder was broken and the mast splintered and they had to depend on their oars for steering.

It was dark when they finally managed to find the lee of a small island and remained there somewhat safely all night.

The next day they found themselves to be in God's good graces and He favored them with sunshine. They were on a small island that was uninhabited and they were able to dry their things and fix their shallop and it being the last day of the week they stayed there to keep the Sabbath.

The next day was December 20th and they sounded the harbor and found it fit for shipping and then they marched inland they found it had many cornfields and little running brooks, a fit place to live.

At least it was the best they had found and the season of winter would be presently upon them. Necessity made them glad to accept it and they returned to the Mayflower with the good news.

The Pilgrims had finally found a place to settle.

They named the new settlement Plymouth and several men engraved the numbers 1620 on a great rock that was on shore to mark the year of their landing.

In 1625 Captain Standish made a successful trip back to England to negotiate for supplies that we were in desperate need of. He convinced the men that financed our pilgrimage, a group of businessmen that incorporated themselves with the title 'Merchant Adventurers,' to send us tools and goods that would see us through another winter.

He was appointed the first Town Clerk here in the new colony and was in charge of keeping all records of marriages, births and deaths. Captain Standish was also a magistrate or judge, authorized to perform marriages and has married many prominent people of the colonies.

I remember when Captain Standish performed the marriage ceremony of Sam Fuller to Jane Lothrop on April 8, 1635 in Scituate, even though Jane's father was a Reverend the couple decided to have the Captain marry them. These marriages were acknowledged as legal in the Church and were entered in the Church register.

On November 7, 1636 he joined the Reverend Lothrop's Scituate Church after receiving a letter of dismissal from the Plymouth church of which he had been a member in good standing for sixteen years.

A few years later he and fellow colonist John Alden founded the town of Duxbury, named for the Standish ancestral home in Lancashire.

Needless to say Captain Myles Standish was a man of honor and has helped to lead us to where we are today in this new land we call New England. There are many other stories that I could tell you about the good Captain Standish but they will have to wait until another day."

Richard finished his story and as usual he received great praise for telling it so well.

The smaller ones were asleep in their mother's arms and they gently put them in their cradles and then tucked the older ones into their beds.

"It's been a long day for me," Abraham said when the ladies came back, "I think its time we went to bed too, Hannah," he said yawning.

Richard and Mary both agreed and they all said good night.

CHAPTER TWENTY-FOUR
1657

On March 6, 1657 Abraham took another oath of fidelity. Abraham, Indian Chief Messhatanpaine, and Elisha Baker Nauhaught all swore to keep the peace and saw to it that fair treatment was given to all of the Indians as well as the English.

William and Santumtanya Baker's oldest son, Elisha was now 18 years old, and had recently become a deacon in the Yarmouth church. He was called upon regularly to interpret many negotiations that were made between the white man and the Indians. Elisha was considered a man of both worlds.

Chief Messhatanpaine was a well liked and a respectable Indian and his village was only three miles from the edge of the Barnstable town line. Between the three men, the town council had no doubts about peace being kept in their growing community.

At this same meeting Robert and Ann Davis were granted land in the common field adjoining Mr. Cobb and Mr. Gorham's land.

Robert was still not a man of wealth or involved in town politics or ever called Mister, but he was an honest man and made a good living by laboring. His character for honesty and industry transmitted into prosperity for him and his family.

• • •

On May 8, 1657 Jeremiah Bacon was born the sixth child of Nathaniel and Hannah Bacon they had been married 15 years. Little Hannah as they still called her, was 14 now and a big help to her mother. Marie and Sarah gave her the Blessed Tea and she took it willingly, she was tired most of the time lately.

• • •

An urgent message came from Richard More to Abraham on the morning of May 10, 1657 Governor William Bradford had passed away on May 9, 1657. His funeral will be held on May 11. *"Please come as soon as you can,"* it read, *"I will be waiting for you at the Anchor Inn in Plymouth, and we will go to the funeral together from there."*

Hannah quickly packed Abraham's satchel while he went to make arrangements with John Willis to take him to Plymouth in his schooner the next morning.

He also instructed the hired hands to finish planting the wheat field and if he wasn't back by Monday, they should begin planting the corn, and to watch over his family and help them plant the vegetable garden if Hannah needed their help.

He really didn't have to worry, his people were trustworthy and he treated them respectfully and they in turn were loyal to him.

On his way to Plymouth Abraham thought about the Governor and considered himself lucky to have known him.

He didn't know him as well as Richard did, but he did know that he was the most respected man in New England and had been for almost 40 years.

Abraham arrived in Plymouth shortly after noon and went directly to the Inn.

"I've been asked to give the eulogy," Richard told Abraham after warm greetings between the two best friends were exchanged.

"I'm delighted about that," Abraham said. "You have the gift of story telling and of all people, I think that you knew him best."

Richard smiled and said, "I have known him since I can remember, he was like my own father."

Tears started to fill his eyes and he brushed them away with the back of his hand and said, "Enough of this, lets go to church."

They walked together into the beautiful Plymouth church. It was a solemn occasion with over three hundred people attending Governor Bradford's funeral.

Richard was wearing his best suit and he looked very dapper as he stood in front of the congregation, he was both humble and proud to be a part of the service.

Abraham knew that there wouldn't be a dry eye in the church by the end of the service.

Many people never knew about the Governor's early years, and they listened intently as Richard began the eulogy in his story telling fashion.

"William Bradford was born March 15, 1590 at Austerfield, Yorkshire, England the third child and only son of William Bradford and Alice Hanson Bradford. When he was only a year old his father died leaving his mother to raise him alone. She was a kind and gentle mother and William always spoke lovingly of her. She passed away when he was 15 and he went to live with his grandparents, the Hanson's, for six years until he finished his schooling.

Richard, the good storyteller that he was, always enjoyed an attentive audience and decided he would tell the congregation everything he knew about William. He recalled the very first months of their stay in this new land and he continued.

"I remember William's first wife Dorothy May she was a beautiful lady. William married Dorothy in 1613 in Amsterdam and they lived in Leydon for about six years. Dorothy was very much in love with William and was devoted to him and she agreed to follow him wherever he went. When they decided to come to this new land she was ready almost before he was. She stayed on board the Mayflower helping the other women cope with the cold and undesirable conditions those first days while he took part in the boat expedition.

I was just a young child about 8 when we landed here, but I was considered old enough to help the men and so I was allowed to live on shore with them. I like to believe that Dorothy was driven to her destiny by the cold and hungry days that plagued the women and children that had to stay on board the Mayflower. Dorothy wrote of the conditions they endured in the letters that were found in her trunk the following spring when William moved their belongings into his new home.

One of the letters she wrote told of how much she missed him and that she could no longer tolerate the filthy conditions and the constant rocking of the ship. She wanted to be with him, but no one would take her to him and she couldn't row the huge lifeboats alone. She even tried to bribe several of the sailors, but they didn't dare take her ashore. She wrote that they were probably afraid of the savage Indians.

When the men from shore came to bring what meager amounts of food they managed to gather for them she tried to persuade them to take her back to shore with them.

William thought that the living conditions on shore were worse than those onboard the ship. I don't think he realized just how bad it was on the Mayflower. I remember going with the men to take some meat to them one time. Dorothy asked me to tell William that she wanted to go ashore. I never did, I was afraid to talk to him then. I was just a child and no one would listen to me. Children were seen and not heard."

"Maybe that's why I talk so much now," Richard smiled. The congregation chuckled, then remembered where they were. He cleared his throat politely with his hand over his mouth hiding his smile and then continued.

"Dorothy wrote that she couldn't eat and she couldn't sleep. She wrote that she was always tired and the fighting and bickering among the women over food for their children, at least among those that were not sick, was too much for her to bear. Some of the women fought over the hard tack biscuits and spoiled bacon; no one ever had enough to eat.

She wrote that she prayed for the water to freeze so that she could walk to shore. She could see the fires at night and would stay on deck until the wee hours of the morning. She tolerated these conditions for six weeks, she was sick from a broken heart she wrote, and she couldn't stand being 'alone without her beloved'.

One morning very early she climbed from her filthy bunk, went up on deck, took off all of her clothes, except her undergarments, and 'fell' into the ocean and was drowned."

The congregation gasped and Richard paused briefly, cleared his throat and then continued. *"The Mayflower was anchored about a mile and a half off shore and it took several hours before word came to William that Dorothy had died. I'm sure she knew that many would find use of her shoes and coat and dress, and also the food she wouldn't be needing any more could be given to a child who still had the will to live. Her wish to leave this world was not entirely selfish. The Mayflower's Captain Christopher Jones instructed several of his sailors to take her body ashore to William. He was so grief stricken that he didn't eat for several days. He buried her on Burial Hill with many of the others that had died."*

Tears were streaming down many faces as Richard paused to take a sip of water. He took a deep breath and continued with his story.

"Three years later the widow Alice Southworth and her two young boys named Edward and Constant came to Plymouth. Alice's husband died of a fever in Holland about the same time that Dorothy passed away. She had been a friend of Dorothy's and a former member of the Leydon church in Holland, and she and William knew each other there. William and Alice were married in 1624 and had three children, all boys, young William, John and Samuel. William Bradford was now the father of five sons, Alice's two young boys and their three. Edward Southworth died at a young age but Constant Southworth is still very well and lives in Plymouth, he's a representative of the New Plymouth Government."

Richard looked at the four men who were setting on his left with their heads bowed reverently, and said, "Please stand and I'll introduce you." They stood proudly and Richard introduced William, John and Samuel Bradford and Constant Southworth to the congregation. The men bowed slightly and then seated themselves bowing their heads again as Richard continued his eulogy.

"William Bradford was Governor of Plymouth Colony from 1622 to 1656 except for a 5 year period when he was assistant to Governor Winslow and Governor Prence. William Bradford was the principal leader of the Pilgrim Fathers and never left New England after he landed here in 1620. He made the major decisions and exercised more plenary authority than any governor of any English colony in the world.

He was a most honored man and if he had been moved by the love of power and ambition he could have been lord and proprietor over all of the Plymouth Colonies.

You see when the Warwick Patent was signed in 1631 the Council of New England made out the official document in his name alone, William Bradford legally owned all of New England. But instead of keeping everything to himself he promptly shared his propriety rights with all the men, or other Pilgrim Fathers, that were alive and well in 1640, and surrendered the patent to the whole body of Freemen.

Freemen were all those men that had come to New England during the years after the Pilgrims and were in debt to no one. He knew that they had all worked hard to clear their land and build their homes and he felt that they were just as worthy as he was. He said that they too deserved their share of land.

In turn the Freemen gave the Pilgrim Fathers a monopoly of offshore fishing and fur trading providing them with an income to pay off the debt

327

Patricia Louise Blish Gould

to the merchant adventurers who had financed the Mayflower voyage some 20 years before. Still it was another 8 years before this affair was settled once and forever. It was finally paid in 1648, after William Bradford, John Alden, Myles Standish, Edward Winslow and Thomas Prence sold some of their own houses and plots of land, to settle and clear this account. The self-centered Merchants had shown no mercy toward the Pilgrim Fathers and had added interest upon interest on a yearly basis for over 27 years."

Richard looked around hoping that his anger about the past abuse of the Pilgrim Fathers wasn't heard in his voice. He knew that he shouldn't let it bother him as it did. 'If William could forgive them,' he thought to him self, 'I guess I can.' He pulled himself together and took a sheet of paper from his pocket.

"I would like to end with this beautiful poem that our wonderful Governor William Bradford lying here so peacefully before us wrote during his last year." He took a deep breath and quoted:

"FROM MY YEARS YOUNG IN DAYS OF YOUTH,
GOD DID MAKE KNOWN TO ME HIS TRUTH,
AND CALLED ME FROM MY NATIVE PLACE
FOR TO ENJOY THE MEANS OF GRACE,
IN WILDERNESSS HE DID ME GUIDE,
AND IN STRANGE LANDS FOR ME PROVIDE.
IN FEARS AND WANTS, THROUGH WEAL AND WOE,
A PILGRIM PASSED I, TO AND FRO."

Richard bowed his head wiped a tear from his eye and sat down. The Reverend Thomas Walley stood up and stuffing his handkerchief back into his pocket led the congregation in prayer. After the prayer everyone rose almost in unison and walked slowly toward the cemetery behind the pallbearers carrying William Bradford to his final resting-place.

William left his three sons, Major William Bradford, II, Major John Bradford and Samuel Bradford and a stepson, Constant Southworth, all of his possessions including several parcels of land, a house and an apple orchard.

Richard and Abraham left the Plymouth Cemetery about 2 o'clock and reached Richard's home in Duxbury just after dark.

Mary had a hardy meal waiting for them as well as many questions. She wanted to know all about Hannah and the children and then of course about everything that was said at the funeral.

The men answered her many questions with good humor and when she started to fall asleep late in the evening Richard told her that he would finish telling her everything in the morning and led her to their bedroom.

Abraham took off his shoes and lay down by the fireplace on a pallet that was neatly covered with a warm quilt and watched the glowing coals. His thoughts went back to Anne and then to Hannah and he went to sleep remembering their pretty smiles.

Abraham returned home in time for the annual town meeting and he was re-appointed Constable. The other town officials also stayed in the same offices and nothing unforeseen happened to anyone during the summer and fall.

Patricia Louise Blish Gould

CHAPTER TWENTY-FIVE
1658

Sam and Jane Fuller had a baby boy on February 8, 1658 they named him Edward. He was a very small child and cried for long periods of time. No one could calm him down except Marie Dimmock and then only when she gave him tiny sips of a special herbal tea that she made for him.

A few days later on February 16, 1658 a terrible tragedy occurred, Hannah Williams Barker Blish died of pneumonia at the young age of 38.

Hannah developed a horrible cold right after Christmas. Marie and Sarah gave her Elder Flower, Peppermint and Lobelia to bring out the congestion and infection in her lungs and she was feeling much better toward the end of January.

However, she had a relapse after she helped Abraham bring a new calf into the world on February 15th.

It was a snowy night, windy and cold and Abraham was having a hard time trying to keep their best cow still while he helped her deliver her calf. The children named her Tessie and were upset when she started having a hard labor earlier that day.

When Abraham came home that evening, the children told him that Tessie was not doing very well. He went directly to the barn and did not come in for their evening meal.

Hannah and Deborah put the little ones to bed and waited until dark and when Abraham had still not come in Hannah decided she would check on him.

"Deborah, I'm going to the barn and help Abraham," she said finally, "something must be wrong with Tessie. She usually has no problem with calving," she continued while pulling on her boots and coat. She tied a woolen scarf around her head and then went to the fireplace, lit a lantern with a fire stick and then picked up a warm stein of cider and headed toward the barn.

Deborah protested that she should not go out into the cold and tried to persuade her not to, but Hannah wouldn't hear of it.

"It's my place to help around here and I haven't been able to lately, I'll be just fine, now go to bed, it's getting late dear daughter," she said as went out of the door carefully so she wouldn't spill the hot cider.

The little calf was twisted and its head was not in the right position in the birth canal. Abraham knew that he had to keep Tessie calm and turn the little head or he would lose both the cow and the calf.

As he started toward the house to get help he saw the light of a lantern coming toward him so he waited a minute and then realized it was Hannah.

"Hannah, you shouldn't be out here in the cold, you're not completely well yet," he said with alarm in his voice, "I was just going to go and get one of the hired men to come and help me."

"I'll be fine dear, I brought some hot cider to warm you," she said as she stretched up on her toes and kissed his cold cheek.

"How is she," she asked with little puffs of warm breath freezing in the coldness of the night air.

He closed the big barn door and took the lantern from Hannah's hand and hung it on a nail by the stall where Tessie stood. "She's in hard labor and I can't hold her still enough to see if the calf's head is twisted," he sighed as he took a sip of the cider.

"Let me hold on to her while you try again, she like's my voice and I'll try to keep her still, she's panting again, hurry," Hannah said as she went to the back of the stall where she could hold onto Tessie's bridle and talk to her soothingly.

Tessie bellowed as Abraham slid his hand further into her reaching for the little head, he felt its ear and then cupped his hand under the calf's nose and pulled hard.

Tessie hunched her back as the contraction took over her body and as Abraham drew his hand from her the little head followed it, one more bellow and the baby calf was in Abraham's arms.

He laid it gently on the soft hay covered floor and Tessie turned around and nudged the little one, licked his face and shuttered, as if to say thank God that's over.

After about a half-hour or so when they knew that both Tessie and the newborn were going to be all right, Abraham and Hannah went back to the house.

Hannah had a bad coughing spell when she reached the house but convinced Abraham that she would be fine, she took a big spoonful of the medicine that Marie had made for her.

She fixed Abraham a bowl of stew and some biscuits and then she warmed the bed with the bed warming pan.

Hannah was exhausted by the time they went to bed but she didn't say anything to Abraham about it. She wanted him to think she was getting better each day, she didn't want to be sick any more.

She said her prayers to herself as she snuggled down into the warmed bed.

'Oh Lord why am I so tired? Please help me get better soon,' she prayed silently. She sighed out loud.

Abraham climbed into bed and held her close to him for a long time that night, making sure she stayed warm. Her breathing wasn't as soft as it usually was.

He prayed that she would be better soon.

What would he do without her? Hannah was first feverish and then she would shiver uncontrollably.

He fell asleep praying.

When Deborah got up she noticed that her mother was still in bed and tiptoed into her room to see if she was all right and found her covered with perspiration.

She told Mary to hurry and get dressed and sent her to get Marie Dimmock and Sarah Bourne. Then she sent Joseph to the barn to get his father.

She wasn't sure what to do next so she put Sarah in charge of getting little Abraham dressed and asked Annie and Johnny to help her get the porridge made for the children's breakfast. She wasn't hungry, but she knew they would be and thought that maybe her mother would like something hot to eat when she woke up.

Abraham had gone back to the barn at daybreak to check on Tessie, Hannah was still asleep.

Abraham came rushing into the house almost closing the door in Joseph's face. He ran into the bedroom and tried to wake Hannah up. She was as limp as a rag doll as he lifted her out of bed. 'She's as hot as a poker,' he thought.

Deborah gasped as she watched Abraham open the door and take her sick mother out into the cold air.

"Deborah, put clean sheets on the bed, quick, while I cool your mother down," he said as he went out the front door.

Abraham knew he had to get her fever down, he sat down on the step and while holding her in his lap he took a handful of snow and rubbed it on her cheeks, then down her arms and onto her legs.

When her body felt a little cooler he carried her back into the house and laid her on the clean bed. "Sarah wet a cloth with cold water and wring it out for me, please," he said as he covered Hannah up with a warm quilt.

Sarah brought the cold cloth to him and stood looking at Hannah's white face as Abraham put a dry nightgown on her. Sarah thought that Hannah looked like a big doll and was scared that she wouldn't wake up and she wanted to cry.

She held out the cloth and said, "Hannah is a wonderful mother, I don't want her to die like my real mother did."

Abraham took the cloth and pulled Sarah into his arms and hugged her tight.

Tears were still streaming down both their faces when Marie and Sarah came into the house a few minutes later.

Marie and Sarah did everything they could for Hannah.

When her fever was breaking she thrashed around and mumbled words that no one could understand.

Once in a while the words 'John' and then 'Anne' would be audible and then she would lie still for a while.

It was about midnight when she stopped muttering and moving.

Abraham was sitting in a straight chair that he had put next to the bed and had been holding her hand for hours. He laid his head on the pillow beside hers and was dozing off and on when suddenly he awoke.

Hannah had said, "I love you."

He raised his head quickly and looked at her in the candlelight. She was so pale.

He touched her face and whispered "I love you, too."

And then he realized that she was not breathing.

Marie and Sarah were still in the commonroom and heard him say something. They both stood up from the settee in front of the fireplace and went to the door of the bedroom.

He looked up and said, "She's gone," and laid his head beside hers and sobbed out loud for a long time.

Marie and Sarah went back into the commonroom and Marie stirred the ashes into a little blaze and added some wood. Sarah poured water into the teapot. They both knew that Abraham would be out to talk to them in a little while. He was such a good strong-hearted man and he would be all right but he would need some time alone to gather his composure.

Abraham was now a widower with seven children to care for. Deborah Barker 19, was the oldest, Sarah Blish was 16, Mary Barker was 13, Annie Barker was 11, Joseph Blish was 10, Johnny Barker was almost 7 and little Abraham Blish, Jr. was 3. Hannah's children had lost both parents now, and his children had lost two mothers.

Richard and Mary More were not able to attend Hannah's funeral because of the bad weather but they sent their condolences and promised they would visit as soon as the weather allowed.

Abraham was heartsick over the loss of Hannah; she had been a wonderful wife to him and was a loving mother to his children. The evening of her funeral he sat down and wrote his mother a letter.

February 18, 1658
Dear Mother,
I have more sad news to tell you, it seems that most of my letters to you are filled with sadness and I am sorry for that.
I have lost my lovely wife Hannah. I buried her today. She died from a lingering case of pneumonia. Marie Dimmock did all she could for her but she just wasn't strong enough to pull through the long bouts of coughing and fevers.
The rest of my family is fine and they are strong and healthy in both mind and body and they will get through this sadness. I however, do not think that my heart will hold any more grief. It must be at least half full from the loss of our little infant daughter that never took a breath, Anne, and father and now Hannah. I know I must trust in God during these times and I do, but my heart still remains sick.
I do not wish to put a burden on you about my sadness, but I have to let you know that we need your prayers.

As usual I have to make this letter too short, but I promise that the next time I write it will be only good news.

I leave you in God's hands and will always be your loving son,

• • •

Just a few days later Baby boy Edward Fuller died on February 23, 1658 he was only 15 days old.

The spirits of the women of Barnstable were low and many spent the rest of the winter at home, only going out side when necessary, except for Sunday Church services.

Abraham threw himself into his work and tried to avoid home until late in the evening. He wanted to keep so busy that he would be exhausted when he went to bed.

Day and night he found things to do, he had little time for pleasure.

He was up early and out to the barn tending his stock or off with Indian Chief Messhatanpaine, and Elisha Nauhaught keeping peace.

He came home late and ate whatever was left in the pot that Deborah had fixed for the children's evening meal.

Deborah was a good girl he thought as he sat down one evening at the table with a bowl of stew and cold biscuits in front of him.

He knew he should stay home more and help her with the children, after all he was the only parent they had left.

He went to the foot of the stairs and whispered her name softly, "Deborah," hoping she was still awake.

She answered him with a questioning, "Yes?"

"Come down to the table and talk to me for a minute, please," he said quietly.

She pulled her extra blanket around her shoulders and came quietly down the stairs to the table with a pair of wool socks in her hand.

Abraham motioned for her to sit and then he got up and put another log on the fire.

Deborah pulled her socks on and sat in wonderment while she waited for him to finish tending the fire. 'I should be the one fixing the fire,' she thought.

He came back to the table and said, "Deborah, I haven't been very attentive to you and the children these past few weeks and I'm sorry."

She didn't say anything; she wasn't sure what he was talking about.

He was in grief and she hadn't thought too much about how he had been acting. No one had been very happy these past weeks.

It had been cold outside and there wasn't too much for the younger children to do besides going to school and learning their lessons, coming home and eating and then doing their chores.

She kept busy with sewing and tending little Abraham and doing all the chores a woman had to do to keep her home in order.

She sat quietly watching him eat for a few minutes and then she said, "I know it's been hard for you, I love William the way you loved Anne and my mother."

Her eyes were filling with tears and she wiped them away with the corner of the quilt.

"The children have missed you very much, you're all they have now," she said softly. Then she asked, "Isn't there something you can have them help you do?"

Abraham sat back in his chair and looked at her. He wasn't sure if she was reprimanding him or if she was asking for his help in caring for the children.

"I do believe that I have put most of my grief behind me now Deborah and I will try to be of more help to you from now on," he said smiling sadly. Then he continued, "I have had a lot of time to think lately and your mother and I had many ideas about improving the land that belongs to you and your sisters and brother." He was silent for a minute and then he said, "I would like your permission to build a gristmill on Sandy Neck Cove, the water is swift and deep enough there to turn the grinding stones, it's a perfect place for a mill," he finished his sentence in one breath. He was excited about his new project.

Deborah wasn't sure what he was talking about so she just sat and listened to him. She wondered if William would talk to her about matters like this. She stilled her thoughts and listened to him.

He was saying, "I will give you half of the profits from grinding the wheat and corn and it will be your business when I pass on."

"But I don't know how to manage a business," she said, shocked that he would think that a woman could do such a thing.

"I'm sure that you could learn," he a said as he finished his meal. He got up and went to the fireplace and poured himself a cup of tea from the pot and then found another cup and poured Deborah one. He brought them back to the table and sat one of the steaming cups in front of her.

'And now he was waiting on her! She couldn't believe this was happening, men didn't wait on women or talk to them about business,' she thought.

'Her eyes are as big as saucers,' he thought and he smiled at her. "How are you with numbers," he asked.

"I know my numbers and sums," she stammered.

"Then there's no reason why you can't run a business," he said.

"I'm sure you can use the land, father," she said smiling, "I have no use for it."

"I plan to ask Thomas Dexter to help me do the construction and I'm sure the children will be very helpful when it comes time to do the grinding," he said as if he were talking to another man.

She took a sip of her tea and realized that he really meant what he was saying. 'If he thinks I can, then I guess I can,' she thought determinedly. 'I won't have to rely on William's family to support me if anything happens to him, I would be able to care for my children myself,' her thoughts were running away with her.

"Well, that's settled," Abraham said and he finished his tea in one gulp. "I guess its getting pretty late and I have to go to Yarmouth tomorrow morning, so I'd better go to bed," he said as he stood up and yawned.

Then he did something that he hadn't done for years; he leaned over her and kissed her on the top of her head.

She looked up at him as he turned to go to the bedroom and said in a soft voice, "Thank you, father."

He turned in the doorway and looked back at her still sitting at the table, "You're welcome daughter," he said and shut the door.

Deborah sat still for a few minutes and finished her tea. Then she picked up the dishes and took them to the dish bucket and rinsed them. She was still smiling to herself as she dried them and put them away. When she got into her bed beside little Abraham she shivered, not so much from the cold as from the idea of being a businessman. Or was it businesswoman? She giggled to herself quietly and then fell asleep wondering just how much work it would be to own her own gristmill.

The next morning Deborah could hardly wait until her chores were done and the children tended to. She wanted to run to William and tell him the good news.

William was an indentured servant to Thomas Boardman of Plymouth because Mr. Boardman had paid his way to the colonies when he was fourteen years old.

He would never forget the date he arrived, January 10, 1638 because it was so cold. There was a blizzard wind blowing so hard he was almost blown overboard into the harbor before his feet even touch the new land. He had to hold on to his only possession, an old trunk with both hands to keep his balance as he walked down the gangplank to the wharf.

He stayed with Mr. Boardman for six and a half years until his servitude as carpenter's apprentice ended.

In June of 1644 he went to work for Mr. James Barker of Marshfield to learn the trade of bricklayer, who happened to be Deborah's uncle, though she had never met him she had heard her mother speak of him.

William worked for Mr. Barker for six years. In 1650 he moved to the new settlement of Concord and helped build houses there for about four years

In 1654 Richard More employed William to build him a barn and that was when he first met Deborah.

She was 15 at the time and he was 30, he hardly dared to look at her for fear that his emotions would show. He did manage to find out from some of the other servants and housemaids where she lived and who her parents were.

After that first meeting, which Deborah was unaware of, William made sure he was in eyesight of her whenever she came to visit the More's. He often made sure that he went with Mr. More whenever his duties called him to Barnstable.

William watched Deborah from afar for almost five years. Now he was 34 years old and Deborah was 19.

Finally on the last trip to Barnstable he found the courage to talk to Richard about meeting her. Richard then relayed William's message on to Abraham.

William loved her so much and he hoped that she loved him. Now at last he found a chance to ask Abraham if he could court her.

Abraham reluctantly agreed telling him that she could not marry until she was 21.

William was very well liked by most and was recommended by all those that he had worked for over the years. Abraham liked the young man too, but felt that it was his fatherly duty to report any misdeeds to Deborah that William might have done.

Abraham also reported to her that William had been seen drinking too much and mixing it up with several other men, pushing and shoving each other. Several times a few of those men would show up the next day with bruises on their faces or black eyes. No one of any authority had every caught them so none of them had ever been taken to court for breaking the King's peace by striking each other.

Abraham often told Deborah that he thought she could find a better man to marry and on several occasions told her stories about William's scoundralous ways.

When he saw her face pucker up almost in tears he usually relented and would say that William would probably settle down once he was married.

Deborah would then smile and remember that Abraham was only trying to protect her from any harm that might come from a bad marriage.

Then her face would become all dreamy, she loved William's sense of humor, his dark curly hair and big blue twinkling eyes, she didn't care about his age, she knew he loved her and would give her a good home.

William always brought Deborah small bunches of wild flowers whenever he came to court her, and was always willing to go to church with her if he was in Barnstable on Sunday. They loved each other and everyone could see it in their faces.

They had been courting for almost a year now, seeing each other usually in Barnstable on holidays and Sundays.

The following week Thomas Dexter agreed to help Abraham with the construction of the gristmill having built one in Sandwich in 1650 and one in Yarmouth in 1654.

It was in early spring, on April 5, 1658 when Abraham, Thomas Dexter and John Scudder broke ground to build the Blish Gristmill across from Sandy Neck Cove near the Bridge where the creek water was swift enough to turn the wheel of the mill.

Deborah was at the mill site that day and watched as they dug the holes for the placing of the huge stones that made the foundation and she helped as much as she could when they used the long wooden lever to roll them into place.

Thomas and Lydia Dexter had moved to Barnstable from Sandwich in 1650. Thomas was a well-known stone mason and builder and had no problem finding work in the ever-growing town of Barnstable.

Abraham also hired John Scudder to help them and bought the stones from him. They removed many of the large stones that were on John's land by cutting them to the proper size with chisel and hammer. They then moved them to the site of the mill by loading them onto a large flat wooden sled-type boat that was pulled by Abraham's two large oxen.

John Scudder was a hard working man with a wife and three children. He came to Dedham in 1637 as an indentured servant at age 17. He had very little education or trade skills but he was a hard worker and honest. Michael Metcalf hired him as a hog yard cleaner. A job that he endured for seven long years. During this time John married a girl named Beatrice Bennett who was also employed by Metcalf as a dairymaid and they had three children by the year 1643. They managed to save enough money by working at odd jobs for Metcalf's neighbors and with the pittance that Metcalf gave them when they left his service in 1644, they bought eight acres of land in Barnstable.

The land that John and his wife purchased was very stony and it was hard for him the first year to grow enough food to feed his family. He spent most of his time clearing his land so he could plow it. Several times they had to petition the town council for food during those winter months and he was never refused. He would always find a way to pay for the food during the spring and summer. After using the field stones to build walls around his own fields he was called upon many times to help build stone walls to keep the cattle and sheep from getting into the hayfields. John had a way of knowing just where a stone would break if he hit it just right. After the Mill was built, John was asked to build many stone foundations for new homes and many of the stone walls used to fence in cattle and sheep were built by him.

As Deborah watched the men do the heavy work she thought about how well William had taken the idea of her owning the new gristmill someday. Then her thoughts wandered to her upcoming marriage. She smiled secretly as she remembered their last meeting at the church social when they had sat together under the big oak tree near the cemetery gate. They had secretly kissed for the first time.

She sighed and took some food out of the basket that she had made for Abraham, John and Thomas and then called to them that it was time to eat.

As the three men came toward the blanket where their lunch was spread Thomas smiled at her and said, "So, I hear that you are planning to be married."

"Yes, but, I haven't received permission yet, and William hasn't really asked me yet," Deborah paused and shyly glanced at Abraham, her cheeks turning pink. She poured ginger tea into large steins for each of them with shaking hands.

Abraham looked at her and smiled, "Don't hurry your life away, Deborah, it's much too short as it is."

Thomas tried to cover Deborah's embarrassment by pretending not to notice and said, "I had a hard time convincing Lydia's parents that I was a good man," he chuckled, "It took me over a year to get their permission to marry her."

Deborah knew the story of their romantic courtship, but she said, "Oh, Thomas tell me about it again while we eat."

Thomas smiled at Deborah and said, "You don't want to hear it now do you?"

"Oh, yes," she said.

Abraham looked at John and smiled and then they both shrugged their shoulders and nodded their heads at Thomas and he began his story:

"I met Lydia Kelly at a friend's home the year before we were married, it was 1649, and I fell in love at the first sight of her.

Every time I got the chance from then on I would try to talk to her. Her parents, Mr. and Mrs. Kelly knew my family; we are very reputable people.

However, we were not Quakers and Lydia's parents could not be reconciled to her marrying out of meeting and would not give her permission to see me, let alone marry me.

One Sunday evening shortly after Lydia got home from her Church meeting she headed for the barn. She had packed her belongings the night before and hidden them in her horse's stall and she put her plans into action. She saddled her horse and rode from her home in Yarmouth to Sandwich by herself. She had been planning to do this since I had men-

tioned to her the week before that I would soon be leaving for my new job there.

It was dark by the time she arrived, but luckily there was a full moon to guide her. She found the mill by following my description of the location where it was being built. She knew approximately where it was having been to Sandwich several times to Church Picnics with her parents.

She had very carefully memorized the directions I had inadvertently given her.

There was no one there that evening when she reached the mill and she was cold and hungry. She ate a biscuit, some cheese and an apple that she had packed in her bag and then curled up in a corner and wrapped her cloak around her to stop from shivering.

After a while she dozed off but kept waking up at every little noise she heard throughout the long night. It was early the next morning when she woke with a start, she sensed someone staring at her.

My helper and hired hand, Zenas Wood, was first on the job that morning and he found her sleeping on the hard stone floor.

When she realized who he was, she begged him to bring her to me.

Zenas was unsure of what he should do but when she started crying he finally consented to take her to the Reverend Bearse's home where she told her story of running away.

They sent for me and when I arrived at the preacher's home I was both surprised and happy to see her. I sent Zenas to Sandwich immediately to inform Lydia's parents of her whereabouts and to let them know she was well and in good hands with the Bearse family. Lydia stayed with them while arrangements were made for us to marry.

Mr. and Mrs. Kelly were very upset and blamed me for Lydia's immoral action of running away from home. But they finally gave their consent after I agreed to go to Quaker meetings in Sandwich with them every week for three months.

I left Yarmouth very early every Sunday morning and got back very late every Sunday evening, but I didn't mind because every mile I traveled brought me closer to my love.

We were married on May 6, 1650. We bought a small house in Sandwich and lived there until the following year.

The next summer, in 1651 with the help of our friends and neighbors we built our house here. We have been married now for eight years and we have seven wonderful children.

I guess Mr. and Mrs. Kelly have realized by now that we are very happily married!

Abraham smiled and said, "I think its time to get back to work, don't you John?"

John shook his head yes and threw his apple core into the woods, he was smiling from ear to ear.

"I guess it is," Thomas said as he mussed Deborah's hair, "it will be time to go home before we know it and we will have nothing accomplished today."

Deborah patted her hair back into place and picked up the food and put it back into her basket then she said, "I'm going home now to see to the children, Papa."

"We shall be leaving here at dusk, what will we be having for our evening meal?" Abraham asked.

"You just ate," John said smiling.

"I know, but I only have food to look forward to now you know," Abraham said.

"I'm going to make a pork and apple casserole," Deborah said pretending not to understand any of the bantering that was going on between the men.

"That sounds good, Deborah, I'll see you at dusk," Abraham said as he followed the men back to the mill site.

Deborah headed down the lane toward home smiling over the romantic story that Thomas had just told her, this time the story seemed even more romantic to her. Maybe it was because she too, was in love.

• • •

On June 1, 1658 at Barnstable's annual town council meeting Abraham was sworn in as Grand Enquest at the Court of Elections. He was the Investigator of death, or coroner, and handled other important matters that came about and he was also proclaimed a freeman again, all his debts were paid.

It was also announced that Thomas Hinckley was chosen as the new Governor of the Plymouth Colony. The men of Barnstable had all agreed to this and had signed their names to a letter that had been sent to Plymouth in May.

On July 17, 1658 Abraham bought a farm from Dolor Davis for 75 pounds. There was a house on the south side of the millpond, just a short distance southeast of the gristmill. The causeway that formed the milldam was renamed Blish's Bridge. The western side of the old common field where the land jutted out into the water was named Blish's Point. Abraham also owned 8 acres that he called "The Great Marsh." It had a creek on the northerly side and the southern side joined George Bowerman's land. Abraham was becoming quite wealthy; he now owned 11 tracts of land.

In 1643 when Dolar Davis came to Barnstable, he was a widower with a young son Nicholas who was about 10 years old. Nicholas was 25 now and considered a wise businessman. When he was 21 he bought three acres of land from Chief Yanno of the Cummaquid, with the permission of the town council and built a warehouse on the north side of the property. Individuals could not, by Colony law, purchase land from the Indians without permission from the town. Barnstable voted its consent to Nicholas Davis to quietly enjoy a parcel of land that Yanno sold him, called Sam's Neck, for the price of 10 shillings.

Nicholas did a considerable business shipping to and from the other towns. He shipped oysters, pickled in brine and packed in kegs, along with rum and other goods.

When he built his small house next to the warehouse he planned to marry and settle down to his new business. He was beginning to notice the young available girls at Sunday meetings and was thinking of courting Austin Bearse's daughter Martha. She was only 15 and a very shy young lady and Austin was not ready to allow his youngest daughter to be seen in public with anyone at such a young age.

About this time Nicholas seemed to have Quaker leanings, which was dangerous. Men were being fined and imprisoned for their Quaker beliefs and when Nicholas was in Plymouth one day on business he attempted to speak out that he was a witness for the Lord against their oppression and he was thrown into prison for two months. When he got out he went to Boston where he was again clapped into jail for his Quaker sympathies, this time he served two years. When he was released earlier this summer he was ordered out of the Bay Colony immediately and he went back to Barnstable where he belonged.

Many men of Barnstable believed as Nicholas did. It had not been so long ago when they themselves had suffered and been imprisoned for worshipping as they believed.

The Nonconformists or Puritans as they called themselves had suffered greatly. Had they forgotten in only 30 years why they had left England?

Many prominent men of Barnstable would not tolerate the harsh measures and bloody laws that were enacted and enforced against the Quakers and refused to enforce these laws and the town never adopted them.

George Fox in Britain founded the Society of Friends, which was the real name of the Quaker religion, several years before.

The nickname, Quaker came from a speech that Mr. Fox made. He said, "You should quake at the word of the Lord."

The main Quaker belief is that each person has an 'Inner Light' in his or her soul.

They do not have ministers or priests or have any rituals such as specific prayers and they worship silently until someone feels moved by the Holy Spirit to speak.

They have Meetinghouses instead of churches and they are known for their pacifism and charity work.

Dolar Davis welcomed his son back and implored him to keep shut of his beliefs.

In Nicholas' line of work word spread quickly from one town to another and his father was fearful that he would meet the same demise that his two friends did that were imprisoned with him in Boston.

They did not leave the Bay Colony immediately when they were released from prison and were hanged the next night on the Boston Common by a group of men declaring themselves protectors of the church.

Nicholas found that while he was gone Rachel Eliot had grown into a beautiful young woman and after convincing John Eliot that he was a true Christian and had no Quaker thoughts, he was allowed to court her.

They were married on October 20, 1658 in a quiet evening ceremony held at the Barnstable Church.

Later that year the Plymouth Government sent Marshal George Barlow of Sandwich to the Dolar Davis residence in Barnstable because rumors still persisted about Nicholas.

Marshal Barlow was requested to make search in any part of their houses or in any of the chests or trunks, or elsewhere for papers or writings that were false, scandalous and pernicious to the government.

They found nothing and therefore had no excuse to further apprehend Nicholas and they left the Dolar Davis farm with many apologies.

• • •

On the morning of November 2, 1658 Captain Matthew Fuller was elected one of the Council of War. Later that day he was brought before the Grand Enquest of the colony for speaking his mind about religious toleration.

Acting under strong feelings of excitement and indignant at the course pursued by a majority of the Court, he took a noble stand in the Quaker controversy. He said that the law enacted about minister's maintenance was wicked and devilish and that the devil must have been setting at the stone when it was enacted.

Captain Fuller was right in regard to the abstract questions underlying the Quaker controversy, but he expressed his opinions with such bitter language that the Court found his words unjustifiable under the circumstances in which they were uttered.

He held a high social position in the Colony but so did the other members of the court whose motives he so bitterly opposed.

To the honor of the court however, when the grand jury indicted him for speaking reproachfully to the slandered members, they disregarded their private grievances and looked only to the interest of the country and elected Captain Fuller as one of the Council of War.

Notwithstanding he continued to speak abusively about individual members of the government, but the court continued to confer on him offices of honor and trust, returning good for evil.

Abraham remembered the old saying, *'Men do not always thus heap coals of fire on their enemy's heads.'* It was so true in Captain Fuller's case.

The members of the Court knew Captain Fuller to be an honorable man and no matter how discourteous his words might be he would perform his duty to his country whole-heartedly.

In his private life and in his business relations, he exhibited a quarrelsome spirit, which was not commendable. He was often involved in lawsuits with his neighbors, which a more discreet man would have settled without an appeal to the courts. There is no reason to doubt however, that he was a man of sound judgment, of good understanding and faithful in the performance of all his duties.

In politics he was liberal and in his religious opinions tolerant, but unfortunately for his reputation he was very indiscreet.

This weakness in his character seems to have been well known to all and eventually his injudicious speeches were disregarded, and he was duly honored for the many good services that he rendered to his country.

Some thought that he held the Quaker religion in higher regard than he did his own Puritanism.

• • •

Robert and Ann Davis' seventh child, Hannah was born on September 9, 1658. Robert's seventh, Ann's second. Marie and Sarah were with her and when it was over Ann stayed in bed for several days letting her 13 year old step-daughter Deborah do much of the work, but then guilt took over and she again took up her roll as mother.

• • •

On November 22, 1658 Elizabeth Crocker age 19 died of pneumonia. She was the only daughter of William and Alice Crocker. Elizabeth was sick for five days before William sent for Marie and Sarah by then it was too late for them to help her. Her lungs were full and she could not breath, there was nothing they could do for her. Marie gave her small sips of Chamomile tea, but she could not swallow it, she just choked on it. William held her hand all afternoon and through the night, she died early the next morning. William and Alice buried their daughter the next day.

• • •

The Elder Thomas Dimmock age 42, Marie's husband for more than 21 years died on December 30, 1658. Their daughter Mehitabel was 17 and Shubael was 15. Marie tried for months to keep Thomas alive, but his heart was not strong enough. This was not a happy time for the people of Barnstable.

Earlier in the summer Thomas had collapsed on his way home from a town meeting and had never fully recovered. He would tell

Marie of the horrible pain in his left arm and he was so short of breath at times that he could not walk more that several feet without sitting down.

She gave him a combination of Hawthorne, Capsicum and Garlic every day, but though it helped with the pain somewhat he did not recover.

He left his estate to Marie and with her income from treating the sick and her medicinal herbs she managed her household.

She was glad that she only had two children.

Abraham knew Thomas Dimmock well and grieved with Marie and after his friend's funeral he went home and opened his journal and noted the many accomplishments that his respected neighbor had done in his short life.

"Elder Thomas Dimmock and Reverend Joseph Hull were the two main parties of which the grant for the land of Barnstable was given in 1639. They were also two of the original associates of Mr. Collicut in 1637.

Thomas was a leading man in Barnstable and was in some way connected with all acts of the first settlers. He was a deputy to the Plymouth Colony Court for six terms from 1640 to 1650 and in 1640 Thomas Dimmock and John Crow were the first two Magistrates chosen to hold court in Barnstable.

The colony Court appointed him to be one of the first Council of War members and he was elected lieutenant of the company of militia in Barnstable in 1642.

Lieutenant was then the highest rank in the local militia. In 1650 he was ordained Elder of the Church of Barnstable of which he had been a member for ten years.

The children loved him as their teacher. He made them enjoy going to school.

Elder Thomas Dimmock never forgot his duties to his God, his country and his neighbor. He believed as Reverend John Lothrop did and did not judge his neighbor if he was an Ana-Baptist or a Quaker.

His influence and advice for the people of Barnstable will be sorely missed. Thomas Dimmock was a very good friend of mine."

Patricia Louise Blish Gould

CHAPTER TWENTY-SIX
1659

Allice Derby's husband John Derby of Yarmouth killed himself in January 1658. He had complained of terrible headaches for as long as she could remember. Once while Elder Dimmock was in Yarmouth Allice asked him if he would ask his wife Marie to visit her husband.

Several days later Marie hitched up her horse to her small buggy and she and Sarah went to Yarmouth to check on him.

Marie gave him a tea made with Rosemary, Wintergreen and Wood Betony and showed Allice how to make the herbs into a tea and left a good supply of them with her.

John told Allice that the tea helped for an hour or so but then his headache would come back again.

Lately he was unable to get out of bed in the morning; the small amount of light from the sun shining through the small window of his bedroom was tortuous when he opened his eyes. He said it felt like needles being stuck into them.

He wore a hat with a wide brim and pulled it down over his eyes as far as he could whenever he went outside, and did as many of his chores as he could in the morning before sunrise or in the evening after the sun went down.

One day just after the new year he went to the barn late in the evening after dark to do his chores and afterward he laid down in the hay and cut his wrists with his hunting knife.

Allice went looking for him later just before it was time for bed and found him lying in a pool of blood; he was as white as a ghost.

There was nothing she could do for him, she knew he was dead, so she covered him with a blanket and left him there.

It was too late to help him and it was too late at night to disturb anyone.

In the morning at first light she went back to the barn and kneeled down beside him, she felt his face and thought that he was almost frozen, she said a prayer for God to take her poor husband's soul.

Then she sent one of her hired hands to Mr. Blish's home in Barnstable, 6 miles away and went back inside and sat down and waited for Abraham. As Grand Enquest it was Abraham's duty to see to the dead.

It was late morning by the time Abraham arrived at Alice's home. He found John Derby in the same position that Allice had found him the evening before and he pronounced the poor man dead after examining him. He determined the cause of John's death as self-inflicted knife wounds to the wrists.

Allice put John in the crypt in Yarmouth the very next day without a service.

The following Sunday after the Church service she asked Reverend Sargeant to say a prayer for her husband.

The town folks felt very sad for Allice, she had always been a hard worker and done more than her share to keep their small farm going.

She was a very plain faced lady with straight dark hair that she always wore pulled straight back from her face and twisted into a bun at the nape of her neck.

She was well thought of by everyone, although her shyness had many people thinking that she was snotty and aloof. She only spoke when she was spoken to and hardly ever smiled, except to the little children. Allice never had any children of her own.

A week later Abraham went back to Yarmouth to see how Allice was doing. She said that she was going to sell her property and move to Barnstable and stay with her cousin Sarah Fuller for a while.

Abraham was happy to hear about her plans and asked her if she would like to help him at his house. Deborah, Sarah, Mary and Annie needed help with the little ones, Joseph, Johnny and little Abraham.

Allice said that she would let him know as soon as she was settled.

A month later, her home was sold and she moved in with Sarah in Barnstable. She made it a point to talk to Abraham after church and told him that she had decided to take him up on his offer.

The children met her and seemed to take to her kindness immediately.

The girls were delighted to have her help and Allice especially liked little Abraham.

Abraham had moved into the Dolar Davis farmhouse in September and Allice started working for him soon after. He added another portion to the house that was almost as big as the original and after the addition was finished she helped him move and arrange the furniture into the spacious rooms. There were four bedrooms upstairs and one downstairs off the commonroom. There were two fireplaces back to back, one was used to do the cooking and faced into the large room with tables and cupboards and a large stone counter. The other fireplace faced the commonroom where Allice arranged two large settees to face toward the fire. She knew that the high backed settees would keep the children warm while they listened to stories their father read to them from his journal or the bible or told them tall tales about his life experiences.

The rest of the commonroom was filled with a long table with benches on either side where they all ate. It would seat a dozen people and there were two high-backed chairs, one at either end where Abraham and the honored guest would set. Abraham allowed each of the children to sit in the big chair apposite him, taking turns starting from the youngest, little Abraham to Deborah, the oldest. Allice always sat at his left on the end of the bench.

Allice made their new home quite comfortable, Abraham was very pleased and he felt at ease for the first time in a long while. Allice was quite lovely when she smiled and Abraham always complimented her cooking and sewing and her ability to mother the children.

Allice was a good cook but she insisted that the girls all share the responsibility with her. She also made sure that all of the Blish children were clean and presentable when they went to church and helped with the cleaning and running of Abraham's house.

Allice became a very social person now that she was not burdened with a sick husband and lately she was leaving a lot of the household chores for the girls to complete. However, all of the children were very fond of her and they soon became accustomed to the organized way she ran the Blish house.

After several months it seemed only reasonable that Allice and Abraham would marry and on Sunday, January 4, 1659 Abraham, now age 43, married Allice Derby age 40 in a quiet ceremony after the church service was over. Many of their friends stayed to wish them well. Afterward Abraham, his new wife and his children all went home to their new house near the Gristmill.

On their wedding night Allice was very shy. Lovemaking with her first husband had been very rare and one sided. She thought it only a matter of necessity for John Derby and was never asked by him to participate in any manner.

Abraham felt the tenseness of her body when he climbed into bed beside Allice. He lay still for a while with his arm around her waist until she relaxed a little. He quietly asked, "Are you happy dear Allice?"

"Yes," she whispered and sniffled a little.

"Are you crying?" he questioned.

"I'm afraid I won't be able to be a complete wife to you," she said and sniffled again.

He felt her cheek with his fingertips and wiped her tears away, "You already have been a wonderful wife to me," he said, "you have made our house a nice place to live and the children all adore you."

Allice was lying very still with her arms folded across her waist, but when Abraham finished telling her how much he appreciated her she moved her hands out from under his bare arm that was around her and touched his arm gently.

He whispered, "I love you Allice," as he pulled her a little closer to him.

Allice turned her face toward his and their lips met in their first kiss. "I love you too, Abraham," she whispered when he moved his lips down to her shoulder. That night Allice Blish found out for the first time the real reason why God made her a woman.

• • •

On February 28, 1659, Nathaniel and Hannah Bacon had another baby girl. Nathaniel named her Mercy. She was named more as a prayer than after anyone he knew. His loving wife Hannah was not as strong as she used to be. Their first child, whom they still called Baby Hannah, was almost 16 years old now and a big help to her mother, but this baby took a lot of her energy and it took her several months to get her strength back. He hoped Mercy would be their last child. Hannah willingly drank the new medicine that Marie gave her without complaining and never asked her what it was for; she didn't care as long as it made her feel better.

• • •

In June 1659 Robert Davis was admitted as a freeman at last. He had worked hard for twenty years and was finally free of debt to anyone. Robert and his wife Ann now had seven children.

• • •

Allice was a good wife, but she was much more social than Abraham would have liked her to be, she spent a lot of her time away from home. Deborah and the girls did most of the housework and cooking and though they never complained to Abraham, they were very pleased when he took them all to visit Richard and Mary in late August after harvest season was over.

Abraham sent word to Richard and Mary that they were coming by boat when he made arrangements with Captain Willis earlier in the summer. Mary had replied that she was delighted and was excited to meet Allice.

They were hardly settled when Sarah asked her Uncle Richard to tell them a story.

"Do you want to hear a sad story or a good story," Richard asked her.

"It doesn't matter, Uncle Richard as long as it's a true story," Sarah answered him flashing one of her pretty smiles.

She looks so much like her mother Richard thought. "Well, I have one that has just happened, you may even know the people that I will tell you about," he said smiling.

"Who are they?" Mary asked.

"Captain Henry Coggin's children," Richard said.

"Oh yes, we know them," Sarah said, "we haven't heard about them since they moved away with Mr. Finney."

"That was at least five years ago," Abraham said.

"Yes, I believe it has been that long plus a year," Richard said and began his story with the date.

"When Abigail Coggin Finney died six years ago John Finney took her three sons to Plymouth with him. He had no choice, being their step-father it was his obligation to care for them. Thomas was 14, John was 11 and Henry, Jr. was 7. He sent young Abigail, 16 to Billerica to live with Mr. John French and his family."

"By the way, she is planning to be married later this year to young John French," Richard said interrupting himself.

"Oh, how wonderful," Deborah said, and then she blushed. Everyone chuckled knowing how much she was in love with William Burden.

Richard smiled and then continued his story. *"Anyway, Mr. Finney married again and his new wife detested the boys. She was mean and cruel and convinced John, who hardly needed any more convincing, that the Coggin boys should earn their own keep. They were given one meal a day and they had only the clothes that they brought with them. They were forced to work unloading cargo from Mr. Finney's ships whenever they docked. He allowed them to go to school only if there was no work to be done.*

Now Mr. Isaac Robinson was about the only friend the boys had here in Plymouth, he had been a close friend of their father before he died and tried to see to their welfare when ever possible. But because they never complained to him there was not much he could do about how they were treated by the Finney's.

Earlier this year on January 16, 1659 Thomas Coggin, now 20 and his younger brother Henry, Jr. now 13, died in what was called an unfortunate accident, although their brother John who is 16 now, stated adamantly that they were murdered. He did not witness the scene, which was probably just as well, however, one of the men on the dock told him every detail of the horrible event.

On this very cold day in January the boys were unloading one of the ships when a dirty sailor of great girth approached young Henry. "Hey young laddy would you like to go below to my quarters with me," the horrible man asked him as he fondled himself.

Henry shook his head and said, "No sir," and backed away from him. "I'll show you something big that I have," he laughed bawdily.

356

"No, sir," Henry repeated, "leave me alone."

The horrible man then grabbed Henry by the arm and threw him onto his shoulder like a sack of grain.

Henry kicked the man and hit him in the back with his fists and yelled to his brother, "Thomas, help me," he screamed.

Thomas was on his way back to the ship for another crate and ran toward them screaming, "Hey you, unhand my brother."

He grabbed the dirty sailor by the back of his coat and swung him around and yelled, "What do you think you're doing?"

The giant of a man was furious and pushed Thomas away saying, "Tis none of your concern, go away."

But Thomas ran at him again and said, "That's my brother, you'd better leave him alone," and pushed him with one hand while he pulled on Henry's arm with the other.

This action made the sailor loose his grip on Henry and the young boy fell to the ground.

Henry was crying and the fall knocked the breath out of him for a minute and he couldn't get up.

The sailor then reached for Thomas, picked him up and threw him back onto the ground.

This action stunned Thomas for a second giving the smelly sailor time to reach for Henry again. He picked him up holding him with one arm about the slender boy's waist and said, "I just got me a new cabin boy," and laughed bawdily again.

Thomas got back to his feet as fast as he could and tackled the giant about his legs throwing him off balance. They both fell onto the wharf.

As the horrible man started to fall he threw little Henry into the water then kicked Thomas in his side.

Thomas was horrified as he watched his little brother flying through the air and splash into the harbor. Without thinking Thomas jumped in after him.

Henry of course was dead by the time Thomas reached him and within a minute or so he too was dead from the shock of the freezing water.

Several men who were watching the whole scene grabbed a big harpoon and fished the boys out, but it was too late they both had frozen to death almost instantly.

As he was coming back toward the ship young John Coggin saw a commotion on the wharf but by the time he reached the pier everything was over and his two brothers were lying on the dock both dead.

John stood there for a minute or so and then tried to wake his brothers up; he didn't know what to do he thought that he should try to find Mr. Finney, but all he could say was, "Oh, God, help us, Oh, God."

Then a hand touched his shoulder and Mr. Isaac Robinson helped him up. John was crying and saying that he had to get help.

Mr. Robinson put his arm around the small boy's shoulder and led him away from the horrible scene. "I'll get Mr. Finney for you, John," he said, "as soon as I get you settled into a warm room."

Isaac Robinson immediately reported to Governor Prence and Thomas Hinckley that the Coggin children had been suffering from neglect and abuse at the hands of Mr. Finney and two of them had just been killed.

John Coggin was alone now his sister Abigail lived in Billerica with her fiancee's family, he hadn't seen her for five years, since his mother died.

When Mr. Finney found out about the accident, he had the sailor flogged.

The flogging was for appearance purposes only, Isaac Robinson thought and he didn't hesitate when Mrs. Robinson asked if they should take John in until things were settled between the court and Mr. Finney.

Governor Prence agreed that it would be the best thing for John.

The bodies of Thomas and Henry, Jr. were taken to the crypt in Plymouth and were removed to the Barnstable Cemetery for burial this summer."

"I believe they were buried there about the first of June," Abraham said.

"Yes," Richard said, "you are right, they emptied the crypt about that time."

"Is that the end of the story, Uncle Richard?" Sarah asked.

"Well, no, my dear Sarah," Richard continued, "there is a happy ending to this story."

"Oh, wonderful," Mary said.

Richard cleared his throat and continued.

"On May 3, 1659 Mr. Isaac Robinson was appointed John's legal guardian and on June 7, 1659 all the lands of Henry Coggin, Sr. were transferred to John in care of his guardian until February 12, 1663 when he will be of legal age.

John Coggin gladly went back to school every day and is now one of the top students in his class.

Soon after the misfortune of the Coggin children Isaac Robinson was asked to leave the Plymouth Church where he was a member in good standing for many years. He was a prominent and influential man here in the colonies but he was also a great ally for the Quakers. The Plymouth Court decided that he and John Smith should attend a Quaker meeting to try and seduce the Quakers from the error of their ways of believing. However, after they investigated the Quaker religion Isaac wrote a manifest opposing some of the laws regarding them that the Church of Plymouth had enacted.

On June 6, 1659 the Plymouth Church disfranchised Isaac Robinson because of his written words and he moved his family, including John Coggin, to Saconesset, where he still continues to look upon the Quakers as a favorable and quiet people who enjoy the establishment of their worship.

Many of the members of the Plymouth Court have forgotten the reason why we are now living in New England. Less than thirty years ago we suffered many hardships so we could enjoy our own freedom of religion, Puritanism."

Richard shook his head sadly and said, "How soon we forget."

"That is why we have written our journals, Richard," Abraham said. "So someday when those that forget will be reminded."

"Yes, of course," Richard smiled, "and I have written of this matter many times."

"And so have I," Abraham said.

The young ladies had tears in their eyes when Richard finished his story and Abraham commented that he was glad for young John that Mr. Robinson has taken him in, otherwise there would certainly be another member of the Blish family.

Two days later Abraham told his children that he was sorry to spoil their visit, but it was time to go back to Barnstable, it was almost time to prepare for winter.

Patricia Louise Blish Gould

CHAPTER TWENTY-SEVEN
1660

On February 3, 1660 Deborah and William Burden were married at the Barnstable Church. The Reverend John Mayo performed the ceremony. Deborah's friend Lydia Dexter sent word to him just after the Christmas holidays requesting that the good Reverend come to Barnstable to perform the same wedding ceremony that she and Thomas had. The Reverend agreed and sent word back that he would be happy to officiate at Deborah and William's wedding.

Abraham walked Deborah down the aisle and all of the Blish and Barker children followed them and then sat quietly in the front row. Even little Abraham followed them holding the hem of her dress with his right hand and sucking the thumb of his left hand. Deborah wore her mother's wedding gown; it was made from thin white cotton and embroidered with little white flowers. She had sewn dried sea roses onto the brim of her bonnet and carried a bouquet of the lovely pink flowers tied with a blue ribbon.

Abraham told Deborah while they were waiting to walk down the aisle that he would miss her smiling face every morning. She hugged him and promised to help out as often as she could after she was settled.

Deborah and William were going to live in Abraham's old house until her new house was finished so she would still be close by. Sarah, Mary and Annie were very good cooks and he knew they would manage.

The gristmill was making money enough for both William and Deborah to live on now and William was planning to start a small farm. 'They would all be just fine,' he thought as he watched his oldest stepdaughter get married. A wonderful buffet followed the wedding and lasted until almost dark.

Deborah was overseeing the running of the mill whenever Abraham was away and was anxious to start managing the operation of it by her self. William was impressed and proud that she was proprietor of her own business and they decided that they would build a house on some of the Barker land closer to the mill. It would be finished by early summer.

On March 1, 1660 Abraham Blish settled his second wife Hannah's estate with Deborah in the amount of 10 pounds. This money helped Deborah and William put the finishing touches on their new home and it was completed enough for them to move into on April 1, 1660, earlier than they anticipated.

Another wedding was held at the Barnstable Church on April 4, 1660. This wedding was even bigger than Deborah and William's. Thomas Hinckley, Sr. married Mary Glover, of Dedham and all of their children followed them down the aisle.

Mary had three children and Thomas had eight, his youngest daughter Rebecca was just four. She carried a lovely bouquet of dried seaside roses just like the one her new mother carried, only hers was not quiet as large, in fact, all of the girls carried a bouquet of the lovely pink roses and the boys had a small rose pinned to their coat lapel.

Mary was the widow of the late Nathaniel Glover of Plymouth and was well to do, as Nathaniel had left her a comfortable fortune sufficient enough to rear and educate their three small children. Mary was 29 years old, Thomas was 40 but they were both very much in love with each other.

Mary's mother, and her deceased husbands parents, thought it absurd for her to wed Thomas, however, they finally gave in when he resigned all rights and interest to her estate. But they also insisted that Mary resign guardianship of her three children to them before they would agree to allow her to marry Thomas. She agreed to do so but only on the condition that they be allowed to visit her at least four times each year. After these agreements were finally made they were married and she moved to Barnstable to be with Thomas and his children.

• • •

On April 7, 1660 Lydia Dexter died. Abraham came home that evening after hearing this sad news from Thomas and went straight to his bedroom. Allice could not understand what had happened to him, so she waited for about an hour before she went to peek into his room.

They did not sleep together very often any more, she had moved her things out of Abraham's room and into Deborah's old room shortly after Deborah was married. In fact Allice had tried to avoid going to bed at the same time that Abraham did since they were married. Though she enjoyed their togetherness, she did not think it proper to have the feelings that their lovemaking gave her.

When Abraham questioned her about her lack of affection she insisted that she loved him and would allow him into her bed whenever he asked, but she would never think of going into his room. She never thought she was worthy of being loved even though Abraham told her that he loved her on many occasions. After all, she knew that she was not beautiful.

When Allice was young she would not allow herself to look into a mirror to do more than see if her hair was tucked properly into her bonnet. She was often told when she was growing up that she was the perfect picture of her father and she thought that her father was ugly to look at.

John Derby had rarely touched her after the night of their wedding. She didn't mind though, the experience was painful and she cried for hours afterward, thinking that there should have been more to a wedding night.

Other women had told her of their experiences but she never heard them complain about it.

The next morning John moved his things to another room and they never mentioned that night again during the next 15 years of their marriage. Once in a while he would enter her room and stay for no more than five minutes, all he left was a mess for her to clean up.

Abraham was much different than John had been and she knew he cared for her, he always showed her affection, and he would touch her shoulder and leave his hand there while he was talking to her.

On several occasions during the last four months he had put his arms around her and kissed her on the forehead.

She never backed away or moved when these brief touches of endearment occurred, but her body stiffened without her telling it to, 'What is the matter with me?' she wondered.

Abraham was sitting on the edge of the bed with his head in his hands when she peeked into his room.

"What's the matter Abraham," Allice asked quietly?

Abraham looked up at her with such a sad face that she instinctively went to him. When she was within arms reach of him he put his arm out and pulled her to him and buried his face in her skirts that were gathered around her waist.

She put her hands on his head and patted his hair and then she ran her hands down his neck and shoulders and pulled him closer.

Her heart beat quickened; this is a wonderful feeling she thought as she caressed him. "What happened, Abraham," she asked again.

His shoulders shook as he cried silently for another minute or two, then he pulled his head away a little and said, "Lydia Dexter died today."

"Oh, my," Allice whispered, "Oh, my, what happened, what ever will Thomas do without her," she said. "I thought that she was going to be just fine after her baby was born, at least she seemed to be," Allice continued, not expecting an answer from Abraham.

Rebecca Dexter was born just three days ago, on April 4, 1660 she was the Dexter's eighth baby in nine years.

She and Thomas were married not quite ten years. Their 10th anniversary was May 6th, one month away.

Lydia Kelly Dexter's parents were now more than ever convinced that they had made a horrible mistake in allowing her to marry Thomas. Mrs. Kelly blamed Thomas for her daughter's death, so many pregnancies in such a short time. It seemed to her that Lydia was pregnant from the time she married Thomas until the day she died.

Thomas was heartbroken and despondent for days. He had eight children to care for now with no wife to help him, the oldest Richard was only 10, Rebecca just three days. The neighbor ladies helped him as much as they could especially Deborah Barker Burden.

Deborah was heart broken too; she could hardly bring herself to go to Thomas's home, she saw Lydia in every one of the Dexter children. But she went there every day to help Dorothy Wells, Lydia's long time friend.

Dorothy did much of the cooking and cleaning and each child was given a chore that matched its age. Young Hannah Dexter, the oldest daughter, age 7 was put in charge of helping her younger siblings get dressed each morning. Little Charles age 4 was given the chore of bringing in as much wood as his little arms could hold, he made many trips to the woodpile each day.

Thomas' stayed busy with the many duties he had as town Hayward and Surveyor and was often called to Plymouth as a juror. He went as often as he was called leaving Mr. Wells and Thomas, Jr., age 10 in charge of running the farm and Dorothy in charge of his family.

The Well's had been married when they were in their forties and never had children of their own but Dorothy had helped Lydia with hers since they were born. Dorothy was like a Grandmother to the children and was very kind to them, but now that she was in her early fifties she could never seem to keep them under control. Deborah helped as much as she could.

Thomas managed though and when they were not in school he would take the three oldest boys to work with him. They helped him build chimneys and steps, carried stones and mixed mortar, they worked hard right along beside him, hardly ever complaining.

After Lydia died Thomas and Abraham had many long talks with each other and he gathered strength from Abraham. He also was grateful for the help that the generous townswomen bestowed upon him and his children, making sure that his baby was fed and Dorothy kept his housekeeping done and was always sure to serve their meals on time.

It was most difficult for him at night but he managed to survive.

The relationship between Abraham and Allice changed on that day. Later in the evening when the children were in bed and asleep, Abraham and Allice had a long talk.

Allice told him about her life with John Derby and her solitary life before him when she was growing up in Plymouth, England.

Abraham began to understand his new wife and he told her that he was not like John Derby and he never would be. At the end of their conversation Abraham asked, "Will you sleep in my bed with me tonight, Allice?"

She looked at him and shook her head yes, and then she got up and went into her room, put her nightgown on and then came back to his room. The only words spoken during the rest of the night were words of passion and love.

Allice got up the next morning smiling and happier than she had ever been in her life and after he left for work she moved all of her belongings back into his room.

Abraham whistled all day as he went about his chores, he whistled even louder when he came home that evening and found his wife where she should have been all along.

• • •

At the annual town council meeting held on June 6, 1660 Abraham was re-elected Constable of Barnstable again, a peace officer with powers and jurisdiction somewhat more limited than those of a sheriff were. His responsibilities took him away for several days at a time, but he was confidant that his children were well taken care of. Allice had become familiar with the routine that he had developed in order to keep his farm, gristmill and elected duties running smoothly and she made sure his many chores were carried out while he was gone.

He would get up early and eat his breakfast and then he would be out of the house to see about his farm hands. Making sure the planting or harvesting was going well. Then he would be off to the gristmill to see if Deborah needed any help and making sure the workers were there and all was in order. He cautioned the men to take care that they did not run out of grain while grinding it. Everyone knew that if the granite stones rubbed together without the grain between them sparks would be created igniting the flour dust and in turn the mill could be burned to the ground. This had happened in Sandwich to Richard Morgan's Gristmill just a few months earlier so Abraham cautioned Deborah and her hired hands routinely.

Deborah would always smile and pat him on the back whenever he came by to check on her, she knew he was more concerned for her safety than for the Mill itself.

Next he would walk to the meetinghouse to see if the town council was in need of him. In the past if he was needed in Duxbury or Plymouth he made sure he allowed the time to stop by Richard More's home for a visit with his old friend.

Allice wondered how often he volunteered to go to Duxbury even when he wasn't on official duty and she smiled to herself. 'His routine has become my routine,' she thought as she went about her chores.

• • •

The next month Abraham's duties did include a trip to Plymouth. David Mason had come back to town, people said he must be a glutton for punishment. He was in the stockade for three days and nights because he was caught taking a horse blanket from Laurence Litchfield's barn. He was a filthy man and never changed his clothes until they were nothing but rags.

As part of his punishment some of the councilmen wanted to have him scrubbed with lye soap and a horse brush, but no one was willing to get close enough to him to carry out that particular punishment.

After several other punishments were discussed the court decided to make him wash himself with hard soap in the sheep pond, brand him with a 'T' on the back of both hands and then make him walk all the way to Plymouth.

Abraham took him to the sheep's pond and tied ropes to one of his wrists and one of his ankles and held on to them while he bathed.

When he was finished he gave him an old pair of trousers and an old shirt.

Each town passed David Mason on to another town every time he was prosecuted as they did most of the other obnoxious beggars that roamed the colonies.

Abraham didn't think he looked much better after his bath, but he did smell a little less sour. The branding would take place in Plymouth and Abraham was thankful for that, he didn't want to have to treat burn wounds all the way there.

Abraham remembered when Samuel Morton was made to bathe as punishment for almost the same thing that this dirty man did. 'How he cried and carried on that he would probably die,' Abraham thought. 'No one has heard from him for a while, maybe he did,' Abraham smiled sadly to himself, 'he surely would be happier in heaven, poor man.'

No one had seen David Mason for over a year, but here he was again. He was well known all over the colonies as a beggar. But he was also lazy and would steal wood from everyone's woodpile so that he didn't have to hunt for any himself. He would sneak into people's barns late at night and help himself to a pail of milk, leaving the cow practically dry. When the milk maid or farmer's wife would go out to do the milking in the morning the cow would try to kick her.

He stole food from the women's gardens and eggs from the hen houses. Whenever anything was missing, everyone knew that David Mason was back in town. He even stole shirts and breeches off the drying racks.

No one ever made him give them back because he was so filthy they were afraid they'd catch their death from him, he had lice in his hair and flies hovered over him most of the time.

Once he built himself a shelter near the millstream during one of his visits to Barnstable and after he left Abraham had it burned because it smelled so bad.

In the past whenever Abraham caught sight of him he tried to get David to take a bath and come and work for him. He asked him several times to help out at the gristmill loading and unloading the bags of grain from the grinding wheel. But he was always too sick or too tired and would refuse.

Mr. Litchfield told the court that David Mason was such an evil fellow that if he died and went to hell the devil would send him back.

Abraham was thoroughly disgusted with David Mason and taking him to Plymouth was not what he wanted to do, but it was part of his job. He tethered David securely by the wrists and arms to a 20-foot rope that was tied to his saddle, and because he smelled so bad and whined so much, Abraham made him walk behind him at the end of the rope's full length.

He was never so glad to get to Plymouth than he was the next afternoon.

After depositing David at the jail under the courthouse he headed directly to Richard More's home arriving just before dark. He'd have his own story to tell this evening.

After the familiar greeting of hugging and hand shaking Mary served a lovely meal of roast pork, brown bread, succotash and Indian pudding. Older now, but still very beautiful and just as kind as ever, Mary More still had her laughing smile and a gentleness about her that put everyone who came in contact with her at ease. Every time he saw Mary he would think of Anne, they were such good friends, always helping each other in those times when they were still settling into their first homes.

Mary listened quietly to Abraham as he told Richard about David Mason and all the trouble that he'd been causing in Barnstable during the last few days. Abraham and Richard sat in front of the fireplace with a large stein of ale and reminisced for a while. Then Richard said, "I have another story to tell you Abraham, this one is different than the usual ones, it isn't about the distant past, it's about one of Duxbury's residents and it happened just two weeks ago."

"This should be good then, maybe I know who you'll be talking about," Abraham said. Richard's stories never ceased to amaze him; in fact he looked forward to them.

"You just might, but then again you might not," he smiled.

Richard started his story with a date as usual.

"On May 16, 1660 Jacob Perkins and his wife Julia left to go to Plymouth in the morning leaving the house in charge of Mehitabel Brabrooke, a sixteen year old serving maid, just here from England.

At about 2 o'clock in the afternoon she was taking tobacco in her pipe and went out of the house and climbed up onto the outside oven at the back of the house so she could be high up enough to see if there were any hogs in the corn. Seeing several of the hogs nosing their way into the field, she laid her right hand upon the thatch of the house to steady herself and with her left hand knocked out her pipe over her right arm. Ashes from the pipe dropped upon the thatch near the eaves of the house and not realizing that there were any live coals in it she jumped down and went immediately over to the cornfield to drive out the hogs.

About half an hour later when she was on her way back toward the house she looked up and saw smoke coming from the roof near the outside oven where she had tapped her pipe.

She ran directly to the water tub and grabbed a pail of water, climbed the outside oven as fast as she could and poured the water onto the smoke.

Then she jumped down, gathered another pail of water from the tub, ran into the house and up the ladder to the chamber and threw the water onto the floor under the still smoking thatch.

She quickly pried a floorboard loose and poked it up into the roof to push the smoking thatch away from the house.

Cinders from the burning thatch fell onto the wet floor and onto her as well, burning her hands and arms and several places on her face. She hardly noticed.

She pushed the thatch through the hole in the roof and onto the ground outside.

Mehitabel climbed back down the ladder, ran out to the water tub for more water and then climbed back onto the oven to douse the roof again.

She also filled her pail several times and doused the smoldering thatch that lay on the ground.

When there was no more smoke, she sat down and cried for fear of being sent back to England.

Her dress was torn and dirty and her burns were becoming blistered and red.

She was still crying and shaking when their neighbor, Justine Hall came running into the Perkins' yard.

She was carrying on and screaming that Mehitabel was just a no good tramp and that the Perkins' should know better than leave her in charge of caring for their home.

Mehitabel bathed her burned arms and face in cold water and was still trying to clean up the scorched thatch when Jacob and Julia returned home about an hour later.

They were furious over her carelessness and had her arrested immediately and taken directly to jail. They accused her of willfully setting their house on fire.

Mehitabel was horrified to think that the Perkins' would believe that she would do a thing like that. They were kind to her and she was faithful to them.

They had paid her way to Duxbury from Plymouth, England two years before. She was indebted to them as a serving maid for the next five years.

She didn't know there was any animosity between them, although Julia Perkins was on several occasions, quite rude to her after seeing her and Jacob coming from the barn after doing their chores in the evening.

Mehitabel had never really paid any attention to this rudeness, thinking only that Julia was tired after a long day of cleaning and cooking and caring for the children.

At the trial the next week Jacob brought several witnesses before the jury to testify that Mehitabel had deliberately set fire to his house. A young man, George Emory, who was a stranger to Mehitabel, testified that he and she had been in the meadow together earlier in the day before the fire and dallied for an hour or so. He told the court that Mehitabel had told *him that Julia, her mistress, was angry with her for accidentally breaking several eggs the day before. So to get even with her Mehitabel had put a toad in the milk kettle that morning and she must have also set fire to the house.*

Another false witness, Justine Hall, told the court that Mehitabel must have deliberately set fire to the house as there had been no hot coals in either of the fireplaces when she arrived to help put the fire out. The only smoke had been coming from the upstairs chamber and several floorboards were missing under the roof where the fire was. They were lying on the ground near the outside oven and were apparently used to set fire to the house. She told the jury that Mehitabel probably threw the water on them when she saw her and Mr. Emory running across the field to help.

When it was Mehitabel's turn to defend her self the jury was already prejudiced against her and only half listened to her testimony. Mehitabel told the jury that she did not know George Emory and had never seen him before this very day. He had not come running to the Perkins' house with Mrs. Hall after the fire was all out.

Mehitabel told the same story to the jury that she told the Perkins when they had returned home the day of the fire.

Mehitabel was petrified that she would have no place to live if they sent her back, as she had been an orphan since she was seven years old and had lived with an elderly aunt until she was fourteen. Her aunt had died of old age two years ago and left her nothing except a letter from the Perkins' that was a request for her employment as a serving maid in Duxbury. There would be a ticket waiting for her in her name at the "Wayside Tavern" on the pier where the big ships docked in Barnstaple, England.

The jury decided that the witnesses were more credible than Mehitabel, because of their positions in town, and they found her guilty.

Most of the jurors had no idea that Justine Hall and George Emory were brother and sister and very good friends of Julia Perkins.

The Court ordered her to be given 30 lashes, and fined her 40 pounds payable to her master, Jacob Perkins within the next six months.

The story over, Richard continued in a quiet manner, "Mehitabel is still at the jail under the courthouse recovering from her burns and the 30 lashes she was given. I don't know what's to become of her," he sighed.

"Is there anyone that can help her?" Abraham asked.

"There has been talk of sending her back to England, but I can't for the life of me think of how she will support herself there," Richard replied, and then added, "She has no one since her aunt died."

"Is there no one here that will loan her 40 pounds to pay her fine and give her another position as a maid to work it off," Abraham asked, this time appalled that this young woman had no one to turn to.

"I don't know where she'll find the money to pay her fine, Mrs. Perkins refused to allow her back into her home," Richard replied, "she had all of the poor girls meager possessions sent to the jail."

Abraham thought a moment and then said, "I'm going to the courthouse tomorrow morning, I believe there's a young girl there that needs a home and Thomas Dexter could use her help."

Richard smiled and said, "Now there's a story with a happy ending, and when you repeat it, be sure to tell about the part you played in it."

Richard stood up and reached out his hand to his friend.

Abraham took the hand of his best friend and pulled himself out of the chair.

They stood there for a minute looking at each other. "I knew you'd be able to find a solution to Mehitabel's problem," Richard said.

"Is that why you told me her story?" Abraham asked.

"Could be," Richard chuckled.

The two of them smiled at each other and they both said good night at the same time. Richard turned and headed for his bedroom. 'I know him like a book,' Richard thought.

Abraham went to the pallet near the back of the room and sat down on it. He thought about Anne for a few minutes, 'She'd be smiling about this,' he mused. Hannah would be shaking her head, 'always the Good Samaritan she would say.' He wasn't quite sure what Allice would say, but it didn't matter, Thomas would be happy.

The next morning Abraham was at the Plymouth courthouse shortly after dawn. He paid the magistrate the 40 pounds that Mehitabel owed Mr. Perkins and went downstairs to the jailer with her release papers.

Abraham helped Mehitabel up the steps; she could hardly stand up straight.

The jailer snickered and followed them into courtyard. He made a snide remark that Abraham didn't quite hear.

Abraham helped the burned and battered girl onto a horse that he had borrowed from Richard.

He glared at the jailer as he mounted his horse and stiffened his back as if to ward off the nasty sneer on the lewd man's face.

He asked Mehitabel if she was all right as he gathered the reins of Mehitabel's horse and she shook her head yes and together they rode away.

She was crying softly, who was this generous man she wondered.

As they started their journey Abraham told the frightened girl that he was taking her to Barnstable where she would be safe.

"I have paid the Perkins' the 40 pounds they claimed that you owed them, you are now free of them forever," he said.

"Oh," was all she said as she struggled to stay on her horse. Her back hurt with every step the horse made.

When they stopped for their evening meal that Mary had packed for them Abraham insisted that Mehitabel let him apply some soothing ointment to her back.

Mary had also given Abraham a small jar of healing salve and told him that he would probably need it for Mehitabel's welts. She had taken care of several criminals' after they were whipped and knew that the poor girl would be suffering. "It will be good for her burns too," she told him as he hugged her goodbye.

Mehitabel was reluctant to let him touch her at first but he explained to her that he was a decent man and only wanted to help her.

Afterward she put on one of the new waists that he gave her and then found a somewhat cleaner dress in her pack and put her coat back on.

He was very polite about applying the healing salve to her naked back and he turned his back to her while she dressed.

"I want you to know that I have a nice wife and I am the father of seven children," Abraham said kindly as she dressed, "and I do not intend any harm to come to you."

Mehitabel relaxed and said, "Thank you Mr. Blish, I guess I'm still not sure what is going to happen to me."

"I have a friend, Mehitabel, that has just lost his wife and he has eight little children to care for by himself," Abraham said quietly remembering the resent loss of Lydia Dexter.

"Oh dear," she said.

"I think that we should get some sleep now," he said yawning, "we still have another two days to travel. Have you ever been to Barnstable?" he asked her.

"No sir," she said trying to get comfortable, her wounds were still stinging but she didn't want this kind man to know.

The next morning Mehitabel was in better spirits. She felt better since he had applied the healing ointment on her whip lacerations and burns. The nice clean white cotton waists, or undershirt stuck to the salve but it felt like a bandage and made her wounds feel better.

Abraham said, "I'll put more ointment on your back this evening when we stop for our evening meal. We should not disturb your wounds until then."

Mehitabel only shook her head yes in agreement and went into the edge of the woods behind a tree for a few minutes. When she came back Abraham had the saddle on her horse and was tightening the cinch on his own horse.

He helped Mehitabel up onto her horse and handed her a slice of bread and cheese and an apple and said, "We can eat our breakfast as we ride."

Mehitabel smiled and said, "Thank you, Mr. Blish."

That night was a repeat of the one before and Mehitabel's back felt even better after Abraham applied the salve the second time. She put another clean undershirt on and she was able to sleep much more comfortably.

By the time they arrived in Barnstable she felt much better and Abraham couldn't help but notice that she had a beautiful smile, showing nice white even teeth. He would ask Sarah and Mary to teach her their washing habits and loan her some of their dresses until she could make some of her own.

"I believe that Mr. Thomas Dexter will appreciate your help," Abraham smiled at her, "he is a very nice person and I'm sure he will hire you as a maidservant."

Mehitabel smiled and said, "I hope he is as nice as you are Mr. Blish."

Abraham said, "I believe that everyone should act as if the eyes of the Lord were on him every minute of his life." Then he smiled back at her and said, "Mr. Dexter is a very kind man."

Abraham knocked on the Dexter's door and Thomas answered.

"Abraham, what brings you here," he asked as he invited them in.

"I have a surprise for you Thomas," he said smiling broadly.

"Well come in, please," Thomas said, "we were just about to sit down to our evening meal, won't you come in and eat with us."

"I'm sorry to disturb your meal, and I thank you for inviting me, but I can't stay right now, however I would like to introduce you to Mehitabel Brabrooke." He stepped aside, allowing Mehitabel to enter Thomas' house.

When Mehitabel smiled at Thomas he was stunned by her loveliness and all he could do was stare at the pretty girl with his mouth open.

"Mehitabel comes from Duxbury and has had an unfortunate accident and has no place to live," Abraham said.

"That's very sad," Thomas said, "what happened?"

Abraham suggested to Mehitabel that maybe she should sit down and eat with the children while he and Mr. Dexter had a short conversation. He helped her off with her coat and hung in on a peg by the door and Mehitabel went to the table and sat down beside Thomas' oldest daughter and smiled one of her charming smiles. The little girl smiled back and they became fast friends in that single little moment.

Quietly Abraham told Thomas Mehitabel's story as briefly as he could. "She is almost 17, and has been sold to me by the Perkins for 40 pounds. If you decide to hire her and she fulfills her obligation as your maidservant you can pay me back," Abraham said finishing his story.

It had been only five weeks since Lydia died, and it had been years since Thomas had admired another woman and he was a little ashamed of his emotions as he looked across the room at Mehitabel.

He hoped that Abraham could not read his mind, he hoped that God couldn't read his thoughts.

"Thank you for thinking of me," Thomas said, "and yes I certainly can use Methitable's help with the children."

"I have to go now, Allice is expecting me," Abraham said as he went to the door, "I'll see you tomorrow and I'll fill you in on some of the details as to why she's here."

"Thank you," Thomas said. "I'm sure we'll be fine. Look at that, the children have taken to her already," Thomas smiled.

"She has some salve that maybe Hannah could put on her back," Abraham said. Hannah Dexter was six now and he was sure that the little girl could manage to spread the healing ointment on Mehitabel's sore back.

"Yes, I'll see that her wounds are taken care of," Thomas said and then quickly added, "the girls will be glad to help her I'm sure."

Abraham knew that Mehitabel was in good hands, thinking Thomas is a good man, and he will not shame himself in front of the whole town by acting foolish.

Thomas gladly paid Abraham the 40 pounds the next day. The Dexter children took to her friendliness immediately and she adored them.

Abraham brought Sarah, Mary and Annie with him the next day and introduced them to Mehitabel, they knew all about the poor girl and they brought two of their dresses with them along with some cloth and needles and thread. They helped Mehitabel clean Thomas' house and then showed her several of their favorite recipes helping her make them for the Dexter family's evening meal. They all had a wonderful day.

Thomas was delighted with the wonderful meal when he came home and impressed with Mehitabel's appearance in her new clothes.

Dorothy Wells was very much relieved to have Mehitabel's help and after several weeks she was able to return back to her roll as grandmother again.

• • •

Robert and Ann Davis had another daughter that they named Sarah on October 10, 1660, Robert's eighth child, Ann's third. Their house was getting pretty crowded and Robert promised her that he would put an addition on to the back of it in the spring.

Ann took the Blessed Tea that Marie Dimmock gave for a few months until her strength returned and then she ran out and didn't ask Marie for any more.

The winter passed without any one dying or any more births, the Blessed Tea must be working. Marie Dimmock and Sarah Bourne were delighted with their secret.

• • •

Abraham received a letter from his brother John on December 29, 1660.

> *September 3, 1660*
> *Dear Abraham,*
> *I have sad news for you today and I very much regret that I can not tell you in person. Our dear mother died today. Exactly five years to the day since our father passed away. She was not sick but she was very lonesome for father. I went into her room this morning when she didn't come to the breakfast table and found her peacefully asleep forever in her bed.*
> *I am sure she did not suffer because her bedclothes were not disturbed and her sleeping bonnet was still tied neatly under her chin.*
> *I hope that knowing this about her death will give you peace of mind. She is now with father and they will enjoy eternity together in heaven. We will have her funeral the day after tomorrow and we will keep you in our prayers on that day as we do every day.*
> *Everyone else is in good health here and the children are growing so fast that I hardly recognize them from day to day.*
> *I trust that you are all well and pray that you remain in God's hands.*
> *I will always be your loving brother,*
> John

Abraham was heartbroken to learn this news and went to his room and cried for over an hour. He left the letter on the table so that Allice could read it.

Sarah read it too and after she thought that her father had spent enough time alone she knocked quietly on his bedroom door.

He told her to enter and she found him sitting in a chair holding his journal. "Are you all right, Papa," she asked.

"Yes dear daughter I am," he said. He held out his hand toward her and she went to him.

"I'm so sorry to hear about Grandmama," Sarah said as she kneeled down in front of him.

"I guess I should not feel sad," Abraham told his daughter, "your Grandparents were very much in love and had a wonderful long life together."

He touched his lovely daughter's cheek; 'she looks so much like her mother,' he thought. "I was hoping to have such a long and wonderful life with your mother, Sarah, but I guess God did not want that to be," he said and tears rolled down his cheeks.

Then he pulled his little girl almost all grown up now into his lap and they cried together for a while longer.

CHAPTER TWENTY-EIGHT
1661

On June 2, 1661 at the annual town council meeting, William Crocker and Thomas Huckins were ordered to take notice of intruders coming into the town. Their duties were to prevent people from residing in Barnstable if they were not of good standing and had no trades for which they would be able to support themselves and their families.

House lots were from 6 to 12 acres and if a perspective resident was not wealthy enough to buy one from a well established resident he was not welcomed in Barnstable. However, if he had a trade that was needed in town and he could find a resident in good standing that would hire him and give him and his family a shelter, he would be welcomed.

The little town was well settled and was almost self-sufficient. Everyone was busy doing his or her part in keeping Barnstable running smoothly.

In summer the women hung white linen, sometimes trimmed with tatted lace, in the windows. This kept the flies out and also created a breeze when the windows were open. The bare whitewashed walls, the brown roof timbers, floorboards and ceiling boards cast shadows of comfort into the room. The simple furnishings of the room and the dress of pewter plates, steins and mugs on shelves on the walls and over the mantle were enriched by the shadows from the glow of candle light and the room became a place of cheer.

The women did their best to make their homes a place of comfort where homesickness might be forgotten in the glow of the bright fire. Most of the families had everything they needed by now and they enjoyed their evenings sitting in front of the glowing flames of their fireplaces telling stories. On cold nights the short bench inside the fireplace was a place of choice for the children and the settee, a long seat made of boards with a high back to keep off the draft, was placed before the fire for the older members of the family. In winter the women made their homes cozy by hanging colorful quilts in front of the windows to keep the cold out.

Hot water was always at hand in kettles, some large enough to hold five or six gallons, were made of brass and copper and hung in the fireplace on iron trammels. Others kettles were used for daily cooking, the making of cheese, candle dipping and soap boiling. A long iron spit was fitted into holes across the center of the fireplace and gridirons were placed in the side ovens of the fireplace where roasts, bread, cakes and hasty puddings were cooked.

Small fires of specially prepared pine or birch wood that had been split and seasoned out of doors for a short time and then brought into the house to dry was used to heat the side ovens. When the fire died out the ashes were removed and the ovens were dusted out with a broom made of hemlock twigs.

The loaves of bread were then placed in the still very hot oven directly onto the bricks in the bottom with a peel, or long handled flat bladed shovel made for this purpose only.

Cooking meals was taught to girls at a very young age. Recipes were shared by many of the women. Corn meal was cooked into a mush for breakfast and served with milk and maple syrup or butter. A large pewter platter of boiled or roasted meat or fish was almost always served surrounded by boiled vegetables. Beans were served two or three times a week. Large sized beans were baked with bacon and maple syrup; smaller beans were boiled in kettles along with slices of pork and served with roasted lamb or mutton.

The most common bread was Indian Bannock, made by mixing corn meal with water and spreading it about an inch thick on a small flat stone and placed at an incline before the fire and baked. It was served with butter and was a staple at each meal. When rye meal was mixed with the corn meal and water it was called brown bread and was baked in the brick oven.

Hasty pudding was always on hand and it was made several different ways. One way was to mix corn meal and water, then slightly sweeten it with maple syrup or sugar and boiled in a linen bag until it was firm to the touch. Then when it was cooled slightly the bag was removed and then it was sliced or spooned onto each plate and served with butter.

Other delicious foods were also served, such as cabbages, carrots, Indian corn, English corn, hops, oatmeal, parsnips, peas, pumpkins, turnips and of course squash. Apples, berries, grapes, and raisins, made by drying grapes, were readily available year round because they were dried in the fall and stored in the attic or root cellar.

Sugar was used sparingly as it was imported and had to be brought in from Boston along with other spices that were highly valued.

Vinegar was made from apple cider and used for pickling vegetables and meat.

• • •

One winter evening when Richard and Mary and their children and Deborah and William were visiting Abraham and Allice everyone gathered around the warm fireplace to hear Abraham tell a story.

Abraham had his stories stored in his memory by titles and the children always remembered them that way. He wasn't as clever with dates as Richard was, but his stories were just as much fun to listen to.

This one in particular was a favorite of the Blish children and Abraham told it at least once or twice a year. It was titled, *"Aunt Beck."*

"Your Great Uncle Elisha Blish was a shoemaker by trade, a very honest and worthy man, and an exemplary member of the Church. In 1590 at the time of his first marriage he was 31 and his wife Rebecca Linnell was 46. Your Uncle Elisha was more in love with her money than he was with her, though he would never admit to that.

Now Rebecca had been married before to a man named John Linnell. She was his third wife. Mr. Linnell's first wife was Mercy Sturgis and his second wife was Ruth Linnell, Rebecca's sister. Now Mercy and Mr. Linnell had no children and Ruth and Mr. Linnell had no children, but Rebecca and Mr. Linnell had a daughter named Abigail. Many people declared that Abigail was illegitimate because under the English law no man was allowed to legally marry his deceased wife's sister.

So you see, when John Linnell died his brother James and his sister Dorothy wanted to claim the large estate that he left to Rebecca and Abigail. However, before any settlement was made Abigail died and Rebecca by law was left with nothing.

Then she married your Great Uncle Elisha. Soon after they were married however, the law was changed and Rebecca Linnell was indeed entitled to inherit a large portion of her late husband's estate.

About this time Rebecca changed her name and insisted that everyone call her Aunt Beck, even those who were not related to her were requested to address her as Aunt Beck.

Now Rebecca had always been a kind and generous person, and wanting to keep peace in the Linnell family she compromised with her late husband's brother and sister and gave them a large share of John Linnell's estate. But this compromise did not set well with the Linnell's and it left Aunt Beck with the fear that they would someday try to seize the rest of her property. This fear caused her to save everything from that day forward.

By early in the year 1610, twenty years later, everyone in Barnstaple, England knew of Aunt Beck's Museum. Of course I mean her home, but people called it a museum because of the way it looked. Her house was an old-fashioned, low double-house facing due south, with two front rooms, a cooking room with a pantry and a bedroom on the lower floor. The East front room, which was her sitting room, was about 14 feet square. The West front room was smaller, about 10 feet square.

Thanks to your Great Uncle Elisha, the outside of the house and the outbuildings were remarkably neat. The woodpile and fencing were carefully piled, the chips at the woodpile were raked up, and there was never any straw or litter to be seen about the barn or fences. It was an estate that the stranger would notice for its neat and tidy appearance. Your Great Uncle spent most of his time outside when the weather permitted.

However, the inside of the house was a sight to behold. Visitors to Aunt Beck's house were only allowed to see the East front room, though occasionally they would catch a glimpse of the curiosities in the adjoining rooms through the half-opened doors. A young lady who was a neighbor of Aunt Beck's and on excellent terms with her, almost always accompanied any of Aunt Beck's visitors. She would tell them not to look around the room when they entered, but to be sure to keep their eyes on the lady of the house, or on the fireplace. It was absolutely necessary to observe such precautions, because if the stranger who, on entering, should stare around the room, they would soon feel the weight of Aunt Beck's ire, or her broom-stick. Most everyone followed these instructions when they were invited to sit in one of the two chairs in the room.

One cool evening Aunt Beck was entertaining several people who were all sitting around the fireplace on the floor, except for one man named Amos. Now Amos was allowed to sit in the chair because he was the eldest, except for Aunt Beck of course, and his chair was placed just a little behind hers so that she may catch the heat of the fire better. This gave Amos the opportunity to appease his curiosity and examine the contents of Aunt Beck's room without her noticing his roving eyes.

He saw in the northeast corner of the room a bedstead with a few ragged, dirty bedclothes spread upon it. The space under the bed was occupied partly as a pantry. Several pans of milk were set there for cream to rise for the making of butter. In front of the bed and near the center of the room stood a common table about three feet square.

When Amos related the sight of the table to his friend and neighbor, Captain Ezra Hall, the Captain, who had been in Aunt Beck's house many times, assured Amos that to his certain knowledge, that certain table had stood in the same place for at least 20 years, how much longer he could not say.

On this table, for very many successive years, she had laid whatever she thought curious or worth preserving. When an article was laid thereon it was rarely removed, for no one would dare meddle with Aunt Beck's curiosities. Feathers were her delight, but many were perishable articles, and in the process of time they rotted and changed into a black mold, covering the table with a stratum of about an inch in thickness.

In front of the larger table stood a smaller one closer to the fireplace, from which the family partook of their meals. This table was permanently located, and Amos was informed by the neighbors that no perceptible change had been made in the order, or more properly disorderly arrangements, of the furniture and curiosities for at least ten years preceding Amos' visit.

The evening was cool, and though Aunt Beck was the owner of extensive tracts of woodland, covered with a heavy growth, she would not afford herself a comfortable fire. A few branches and two or three dead sticks, added after Amos and his friends came in, cast a flickering light over the room, but unfortunately the flames did not increase the temperature. Which was probably just as well because if the temperature had risen they would have all been overcome by the smell of mold and mildew.

The floor, excepting narrow paths between the doors, fireplace and bed, was entirely covered with broken crockery, old pots, kettles, pails, *tubs, and such. The walls were completely festooned with old clothing, useless articles of furniture and several bunches of dried herbs.*

In fact, every article named in the humorous song about 'The Will of Father Abby,' a funny song of the day, excepting 'a tub of soap,' could be found in Aunt Beck's house. The other articles named in the song were 'a long cart rope,' 'a frying pan and kettle,' 'an old sword blade,' 'a garden spade,' 'a pruning hook and sickle.' But in all justice to her, Amos said that she did actually, for many long years, contemplate making a tub of soap, too. Because for thirty years Aunt Beck saved all of her beef bones just for that purpose, depositing them in her large cooking fireplace and in other places about the room.

During the warm summer of 1620, these bones became so offensive that Aunt Beck reluctantly consented to have them removed, and Captain Ezra Hall, who saw them taken away, says there was more than an oxcart load.

Of the other rooms in the house Amos could not speak from personal knowledge, but the young lady that went with him informed him that in the West room there was a bed, a shoemaker's bench, flour barrels and chests containing valuable bedding, too good to use. There were also a nameless variety of other articles scattered over the bed and on the chairs. From the walls were suspended a saddle and pillion and many other things preserved as rare curiosities.

A pillion was a cushion that fit in back of the saddle for the comfort of women and children when they rode.

In time the room became so completely filled that it was difficult to enter it. The cooking room, bedroom, pantry and chambers were filled with vile trash and worthless items, all covered with dirt and litter.

This description may seem imaginary or improbable to the stranger, but there were quite a number of people living in Barnstaple, England in the late 1630's who could testify that what has been described here is the truth. The maxim, "The truth is sometimes stranger than fiction," applies in all its force to Rebecca Blish. Now it is true that she was a monomaniac, a person that acts in an irrational way, but to say that she was insane on all subjects in not true.

You see early in life Aunt Beck was neat, industrious and very economical, but after the death of her first husband, John Linnell, and the trouble she had with his family, her prudent habits soon degenerated into parsimony, or stinginess. Now economy is a virtue to be inculcated, but when the love of money becomes the ruling passion and a man saves that he may hoard and accumulate, he becomes a miser, and is despised. A miser accumulates money, or that which can be converted into money and hides it in every safe place that he can find.

Aunt Beck saved not only money, but also useless articles that others would throw away. These she would pick up in the fields, and by the roadside, and store away in her house.

So, for more than forty years she gathered up useless trash, and as she did not allow anything, except the bones, to be carried out during those years you can be sure that Amos was telling the truth. Therefore, it requires no great stretch of the imagination to form a correct picture of the condition and appearance of the place she called her home.

During the latter part of her life she seldom left home, she became a recluse. No one knows what caused her to become like she was unless it was the fact that she expected the Linnell's to take all of her possessions away from her.

Her estate, if she had allowed her husband, your Great Uncle Elisha Blish, to manage would have been much larger at her death.

She would not allow her great wood lots to be cut and sold and the proceeds to be invested. She lost by investing her money in mortgages on old houses and worn out lands, and loans to persons who never paid their notes.

She also had a habit of hiding parcels of coin among the rubbish in her house, and sometimes she would forget not only where she had placed the treasure, but also how many such deposits she had made. It is said that some of her visitors, who were not very honest, often carried away these deposits, unknown and unsuspected by her of course.

On the subject of saving, Aunt Beck was not of sound mind. She was, however, a woman naturally of strong will and no one could be captain over her. She knew more or less of almost every family in town, and was always very particular in her inquires respecting the health of the families of her visitors. She delighted in repeating ancient ballads and nursery tales.

In her religious opinions she was Orthodox and she hated the Puritans, not because they were innovators, but because the preachers called at her house, and because her husband contributed something to their support.

It is sad to say that not a dollar of the money saved and accumulated by her, during a long life of toil and self-denial, now remains. In a few short years it took to itself wings and flew away. Her curiosities, which she had spent so many years in collecting and preserving, were ruthlessly destroyed before her remains were even deposited in the grave.

On the Thursday preceding her death and unable to leave her sick bed her attendants started removing all of her possessions out of her house and all of her curiosities were either burnt or scattered to the four winds of heaven. She overheard them and asked if it thundered. They told the dying woman that it was the worst storm they had ever seen.

Aunt Beck died on Sunday November 7, 1630 at the age of 86. The old house soon lost all of its charm, and its doors ceased to attract visitors. Its interior was cleaned and painted, pictures adorned the walls and handsome furniture filled the rooms.

In fact just forty-five days after her death there was a wedding party at her house. Your Great Uncle Elisha Blish endeavored to correct the sad mistake which he made when he married Aunt Beck, and took himself a young woman as his new wife, she was only 29, and he was now 71.

His new wife happened to be a grand niece of your Aunt Beck with ironically the same name, Rebecca Linnell; however, she would not allow anyone to call her by any name except 'Rebecca' or 'Mrs. Blish'. Even more ironic is the fact that the new Rebecca Linnell Blish, was the daughter of Adam Linnell. Who was the son of James Linnell, who was the brother of John Linnell, Aunt Beck's first husband, and was indeed the person who inherited all of Aunt Beck's property that she so dearly possessed and feared loosing. It was as if all of Aunt Beck's efforts to obtain and protect her inheritance failed anyway.

For the next six years during the closing period of his life your Great Uncle Elisha Blish enjoyed all those comforts and conveniences of life of which he had been deprived of for forty years, and to which a man having a competent estate is entitled.

This great change in his mode of living did not, however, afford him much happiness. One remark, which he made during this time, is worth preserving. It showed the effect which habits of 40 years growth have on the human mind. Someone congratulated him on the happy change, which had taken place. His reply was, "Yes, I live more comfortably than I did, but," he added with a sigh, "my present wife is not so economical as my first."

Your Great Uncle Elisha Blish died on May 10, 1636 at the age of 77."

Abraham finished his story with the words, "Not quite a year before I came to New England," he smiled at the children, "but that's another story."

His family loved his tall tales as much as he loved telling them, he hoped that they would remember them. Most of them were written in his journal just in case they didn't.

The women put the little ones to bed after he hugged them all good night.

• • •

Word came that the great Chief Massasoit of the Wampanoag Indians had died. He was a great man and considered one of the Pilgrim Fathers best friends. Without him they all might have died that first year. The first peace treaty ever signed was called the Massasoit Treaty and Chief Massasoit made his mark on it in the year 1621, and for forty years he never went back on his word. Governor Bradford had always held him in the highest esteem. Many prominent men attended his burial Richard More included.

When Richard returned he reported to Abraham that Chief Massasoit's eldest son, Wamsutta was now in charge of the Wampanoag Indians.Abraham was sorry to hear of the Chief's death.

CHAPTER TWENTY-NINE
1662

Marie Dimmock gave her daughter Mehitabel away in marriage to Richard Child of Watertown on March 30, 1662. She was 20 years old. While Marie was away Sarah Bourne cared for the sick by herself and she was very happy to see her friend when she returned and grateful that no mishaps had occurred.

• • •

The population of the town of Barnstable on June 5, 1662 at the annual town meeting now numbered 65 freemen. They voted to admit to citizenship the sons of all inhabitants when they were married or turned twenty-four years old. The families were getting larger with at least four children each. If by chance the parents of several children in a family happened to die from fever or other mishaps, the neighbors would take them in. These matters were always discussed and considered by the town council, and helped to keep the welfare of the town healthy.

• • •

Abraham owned about one hundred and four acres of land in Barnstable at this time. His house was located on the south side of his sixteen-acre lot and was just a short walk from the gristmill. He had easy access to fresh water from the millpond and a wonderful view of the ocean. Deborah and William's house was also close by.

• • •

Everyone worked long hard hours on their farms and then helped each other with planting and harvesting. Every man had an occupation of one kind or another and they all worked together to keep the town sustained. The women were always busy with their everyday chores as well as their seasonal chores and they too all helped one another.

In early spring after the sheep were sheared the wool was cleaned, carded and then spun into yarn on a hand spinning wheel. By this time the weather was warmer and the yarn was woven into cloth on a handloom which was a ponderous affair and occupied a great deal of room.

Not everyone possessed a loom, but there were some weavers in each town that would weave for anyone who didn't have one. Weaving was hard work and five or six yards was considered a good days work. Several women sat up their looms in their woodsheds that were now empty because the cutting and stacking of next year's wood had not yet begun. When the weaving was finished, the cloth was cut and made into clothes.

The linen spinning wheel was about twenty inches in diameter and was operated by the foot resting upon a treadle. The finer fibers of flax were spun into linen and then the thread was woven into cloth to make into shirts, sheets, table covers, and dresses, handkerchiefs and strainer cloths. Ropes used on the farms were often homemade of linen and tow, the course and broken fibers of hemp and flax. In the summer men wore tow and linen clothes or a cloth made of cotton and linen called fustian.

Most of the women learned to spin yarn, sew and knit at an early age. It was one of the most relaxing jobs they had and they enjoyed it. Many cold nights it was delightful to sit by the fire and knit hats and mittens and scarves for their families.

When the yarn was to be knitted, it was generally colored first. The dye pot was made of earthenware and had its place in the chimney corner just inside the fireplace. It was covered with a piece of board or plank on which the children often sat.

The dye was made of indigo or other plants that were dissolved in urine. The yarn was put into this solution and remained there until it was colored.

When the yarn was wrung out, or the contents disturbed, the odor that arose had a rank smell and was one of the most unpleasant jobs women had. Women often took their yarn to dyers and weavers or traded it for already woven material. They were willing to pay or trade almost anything to have this dreaded job done for them.

Bernard Lombard's wife Evelyn was born without the sense of smell and had for many years found that she actually enjoyed dyeing the cotton and wool. Over the years she had learned to mix several kinds of plants and flowers together to make beautiful colors. One of her favorite colors was named after her it was called Evelyn Lavender.

Two of her daughters also inherited this unusual misfortune and by the time they were teenagers in 1658, the Lombard Dyeing business was in full swing. Unfortunately they had few visitors to their home except for the business of delivering the cotton and wool, and the smaller children of each family usually did that, every one of which considered it a punishment. However, the Lombard's were well liked and were always invited to their neighbors for quilting bees and other social meetings.

Jedediah Lombard's wife Suzanna, Evelyn's sister-in-law, was considered one of the best weavers in Barnstable. For years she made and taught other women to make many different kinds of cloth. The cloth they used for men's wear was called fulled cloth. After it was dyed, sheared and pressed it was made into coats, waistcoats and breeches. It was a very durable material and withstood the hard work that men had to do. It was also easy to care for.

After washing it was hung on rope to dry and did not wrinkle out of shape. The cloth that was used to make women's dresses and coats was simply dyed and pressed and called pressed cloth. Baize, a kind of cloth made without any filling and napping was also woven for women's use. Some women made clothes for each other's families but most women were skilled seamstresses and taught their daughters to sew at an early are.

• • •

William and Deborah Barker Burden had their first child on November 1, 1662. They named her Mercy. Deborah was in labor for about 14 hours, though the first twelve were merely twinges in her lower stomach.

William called Marie Dimmock to Deborah's bedside almost immediately; it was about 6 o'clock in the late afternoon right after their evening meal.

Marie hurried to the Burden's home assuming that Deborah was about to give birth at any moment, but after she examined the new mother-to-be she found that it would probably be several hours or so before the baby would come. "Your baby is not quite ready yet my dear," Marie told her trying to calm her.

"Is everything going to be all right?" Deborah asked Marie anxiously.

"Yes, Deborah, please don't get too excited," Marie said soothingly, "You know that sometimes these things can take a while."

Another twinge grabbed her belly and she winced, "That hurt," she said.

"Your body is trying to put your baby in the right position so you must help it by getting out of bed and going for a walk," Marie told her.

"I don't think I can," Deborah said. She knew she sounded childish, but the pain scared her, she hadn't realized how painful childbirth could be. She had seen many babies born but the mothers always seemed to clench their teeth and moan or groan and then they would pant like a dog a few minutes and then before you knew it a new baby was in their arms.

"Yes you can, Deborah," Marie said firmly, "William will help you and when the pain doubles you over he will send someone after me." She looked at William and motioned for him to help her get Deborah out of bed. "I know you are a strong young woman and I remember when your mother had your little brother Abraham, you were there. You must remember how brave she was, she hardly complained at all," Marie chided her.

"My mother was wonderful when she had Abraham, and she was strong then, but she was in so much pain," Deborah said, "I could see it in her face." Tears filled her eyes, she wished her mother was here now.

"You'll be fine my dear," Marie said as she patted Deborah's back and helped her walk across the small room. "I'll be back early in the morning dear, and William will send for me if your water breaks before then."

Another twinge made Deborah stop walking and she crossed her legs at the ankles, "Oh," she said, then she started walking again.

"When you get tired you can go to bed, but I want you to sit up with pillows behind your head and back and put one under your knees, you've seen how you should sit haven't you?" Marie asked her.

"Yes," she said and put her hands on the back of her hips, she felt heavy and fat, "I know what you mean."

"I have some Squawvine and Red Raspberry Leaves with me and I will make you some tea, it'll make you feel better," she said and went to the fireplace. She found a small kettle and filled it with water from the big hot water kettle hanging on the trammel, then she added the herbs and set the little pot on the hearth near the warm fire.

"William, you be sure to send for me if her pains get worse before I get back," Marie said touching his arm gently. She could see the worry in his face, "Don't worry know, Deborah is strong and she'll be just fine," she said gently.

When Marie left William helped Deborah walk back and forth across the room several times before he said anything. They both remained silent, deep in their own thoughts. "Do you want some of the tea Marie made," he asked her quietly.

Deborah looked at him and saw the concern he had for her etched in his face he looked so worried. 'He really loves me,' she thought and smiled slightly. "Yes, that would be wonderful," she said and straightened her back and reached for the back of the settee and stood waiting for him to get her the warm tea. 'I can't let him see me acting like such a ninny,' she chided herself, 'Marie is right, I am strong like my mother was.'

William handed her the mug of warm tea and she said, "Thank you, William," then took a little sip. It was a little bitter, but it made her feel better almost immediately. After a minute or so she said, "I feel better know, I guess I was just being silly, I've seen many women have babies and I've even helped a time or two."

William patted his wife on the arm and asked, "Do you want to walk some more?"

"Yes, I guess I'd better, I know it will make things happen faster," and she smiled up at him as she took his arm and put her hand in his.

William was relieved and wondrous at the quick change that had come over his pretty wife, he didn't understand her, but that was all right, he loved her and that was all that mattered right now. He smiled back at her and squeezed her hand.

They walked for about an hour, they discussed names for their baby, how the operation at the gristmill was going, how much they loved their little farm. They talked about William's life before he met Deborah. "I know how hard you have worked for others all of your life, William," she said softly, "I am so happy that your labors have finally brought you prosperity."

He kissed her cheek and said, "Now Deborah's labor is going to bring me a beautiful family," he said and then laughed at his own little joke.

Deborah smiled up at him and poked him in his side with her elbow, then her legs began to shake a little and she decided that it was probably time that she went to bed to try and get as much sleep as she could. "I think I should go to bed now, William," she said. She smiled at him and added, "would you help me arrange the pillows?"

William went to the large trunk at the foot of the bed and took out three big feather pillows and put them on the bed. Deborah arranged two of them so that they leaned against the headboard of the bed and then turned her own pillow the opposite way over them. She took off her robe and folded it neatly and laid it on a chair near the bed.

"Please get me my birthing pad and a linen sheet from the trunk, too, William," she asked, "I will sit on it in case my water breaks, I don't want to ruin my feather tick."

"You did a beautiful job making this wonderful bedding Deborah," he said.

She looked at him a little surprised at his words; he had never mentioned how comfortable their bed was or how clean she kept it. She had embroidered the top edges of the linen sheets with little flowers and had matched the edges of the pillowcases with the same design. The quilt she made was covered with the same little flowers stitched on little white patches placed randomly between the bright blue, green and red squares she had sewn together. It had taken her two years to make her quilt, and when it was finished she had put it away in her trousseau trunk. She never dreamed that a man would think it as beautiful as she had.

"Oh, William," she said, "I really never thought that you even noticed these things."

"I do notice the wonderful things that you do, I guess I just don't know how to tell you," he said a little self-conscious. Then he added a little braver now that he knew she was pleased at his remark, "I never slept in a more wonderful bed. I never knew a bed could be so comfortable." He was still standing at the foot of the bed near the trunk.

Deborah had not gotten into it yet, she had laid out the thick pad and left the linen sheet folded several times and was smoothing it out with her hands when he started talking, his words had stopped her from finishing her job. She was just standing next to the bed looking at him. "Oh, William," she said and tears filled her eyes. She reached her hand out to him and he went to her.

They wrapped themselves together holding each other tightly. "I love you," they both said almost in unison. Then they kissed a long kiss that fulfilled them both, almost as much as making love.

Deborah felt another twinge and jumped slightly, "Oh" she said a little startled and smiled up at William.

"Nice timing little baby," William said smiling back. Then he bent over a little and picked up his beautiful wife and gently sat her on the bed and helped adjust the pillows until she was comfortable. "I'll get you some more tea," he said a little flustered. Deborah's kiss had made him realize how long it had been since they had made love.

Deborah's heart was racing, she wasn't sure if she should be having these feelings when she was about to give birth. She took a deep breath and smiled a little, she felt almost giddy. She was smoothing the quilt over her big belly with her hands when William came back into the room and handed her the special tea. He sat on the bed beside her and they held hands while Deborah sipped the warm liquid. They both enjoyed the happiness of the quiet moment knowing that soon there would be a tiny baby that would take up much of their time. When she fell asleep William got quietly off the bed and undressed and then carefully crawled under the covers with her and held her as closely as he could without waking her. He lay there in the soft bed listening to the quiet sounds of the night until he finally fell asleep.

The next morning at dawn Deborah was jolted out of her sleep surprised to see light in the windows. She had been dreaming about pain in her back for several minutes until she finally realized it wasn't a dream. William wasn't in bed, "William," she called out. She sat up as much as she could and another pain came, this time it was in her lower abdomen, she couldn't help herself, "William," she called louder.

William came into the house with a warm pail of milk; he had been doing the milking and thought that Deborah would probably stay asleep for another hour or so. "I'm here Deborah," he said as he sat the milk bucket on the table and went to the bedroom door. "Are you all right?" he asked as he took off his frock.

"I, yes, I couldn't find you and I was dreaming," she stammered.

"I'm right here and I have some more tea ready for you," he said, "I'm sure Marie will be here soon," he finished hopefully, a little concerned for his still sleepy wife.

Deborah was sitting up on the edge of the bed sipping her tea when Marie came in. The wind was blowing and a cold gust of air came in with her. Deborah shivered slightly as the cold air hit her feet and she pulled them up onto the bed. "I'm so glad you're here Marie," Deborah said smiling. "I've only had three bad pains since I woke up about a half hour ago."

"That's good," Marie said smiling back at her, "has your water broken yet," she questioned.

"No, but I have to use the pot," Deborah said as she put her feet back onto the floor and stood up.

William had been standing in the bedroom doorway watching until Deborah said she had to use the chamber pot. He decided then that he probably wouldn't be needed anymore for a while and said, "I'm going out and finish my chores," but he knew they didn't hear him.

"Here, let me help you," Marie said as she pulled the chamber pot out from under the bed. "Hold on to my arm I'll help you hold your nightgown up."

Deborah was just a little embarrassed as she squatted over the pot; she had never peed in front of anyone before, except maybe when she was a little girl. When she was almost finished a real contraction hit her and she grabbed Marie's arm with both hands letting go of her gown. "Ohh," she moaned and a great gush of water escaped her body directly into the chamber pot.

Marie was quite surprised at such a happening, but was relieved to know that the fluid was clear and she said chuckling, "Wonderful Deborah, your water just broke and there is absolutely no mess to clean up,"

Deborah was still panting from the pain and held tight to Marie's arm as Marie helped her to stand up. She took a step or two toward the bed and sat on the edge, "I have to lay down Marie," she said as she tried to lift her legs onto the bed.

Marie was still holding on to her nightgown with one hand and said, "Let me help you take your gown off Deborah, I'm afraid I didn't do such a good job holding it up, it's a little soiled."

Deborah stood up and let Marie pull the damp nightgown over her head, "You'll be just fine without it Deborah," Marie said and she help Deborah into the bed and adjusted the pillows under her back and legs.

"Marie please get me my chemise on the chair, I'll feel better with something on," she said knowing that she was blushing a little. Marie picked up the little undergarment and helped her pull it on over her head. "That's better." Deborah said, "I felt strange being naked."

"You know that of all the babies I have delivered this was only the second time that I have seen any of my patients water break in the chamber pot," Marie said. She smiled at the modest girl and smoothed the folded linen sheet under Deborah's bottom, readjusted the pillows and made sure that the warm bedding was pulled tightly up under her chin.

"Are you warm enough dear?" she asked.

"Yes," Deborah shivered a little and then asked, "Who else had the good fortune of not making a mess?"

"Anne Blish," Marie said smiling a little sadly, "when Sarah was born."

Deborah smiled a little and then another pain rushed over her. "Oh, mercy, I think the baby's coming Marie," she said panting.

"Let me see," Marie said and she lifted the covers back sending cold air rushing over Deborah's sweating body. When she pulled the pillow out from under Deborah's knees she saw that things were moving faster than she had expected, being the first baby usually meant an all day labor. "You're right Deborah, it won't be long now." Marie knew that Deborah's contractions were real and only had about two or three more to go before the baby would be here. "Now Deborah when you feel the next pain try not to push very hard, I must get the water ready and get my hands washed, you are much faster than I thought you would be," she said and patted her leg leaving the quilt turned back and Deborah exposed.

"Hurry," Deborah said trying not to push.

Marie went to the fireplace and dipped hot water into the water basin that was on the shelf. She put her hands in it leaving them there for ten or fifteen seconds and then found a clean linen lying beside the basin and wiped them dry. Her satchel was still sitting on the table where she had left it and she poked around in it for a second until she found her birthing bag with the little bone knife and clean pieces of yarn. She carefully laid out her little pouches of birthing herbs and then went to the fireplace again and found the little pot of tea she had made the night before. There was still a little bit in it but she didn't dump it out she just added her fresh herbs and then more hot water. She went back to the basin and dipped the end of the clean linen towel into the still hot water and then she went back into the bedroom. Deborah was panting again, "Did you have another pain?" she asked.

"Yes, I tried not to push but I couldn't help it," Deborah said.

"That's all right my dear," Marie said and handed her the damp towel.

Deborah wiped her face and then said, "The baby's coming Marie, oh mercy," and pushed her baby's head out of her body. The pain subsided and then she leaned back on the pillow for a few seconds panting hard.

"It's almost over Deborah," Marie said soothingly, "you're doing just fine. Push hard when the next pain comes, I'll be right here." Deborah groaned loudly and as she pushed Marie helped the little baby from Deborah's body. "You have a beautiful baby girl, Deborah," she said as she cleaned the baby's face and made her cry.

"Oh, mercy," Deborah said and then smiled.

Marie laid the baby on the bed under Deborah's bent knees and said, "One more push Deborah, you'll have another pain and you must push again." This time the pain was bearable and the birthing was complete. Marie tied two pieces of the yarn around the umbilical cord about an inch apart then she snipped it. Deborah's crying little baby wanted the comfort of her mother's waiting arms and Marie picked her up wrapped her in a small cotton blanket and placed her there and said, "I must finish taking care of you Deborah, then I'll wash your baby."

Marie was satisfied that there would be no child birth problems for Deborah after she cleaned her womb and covered her with a clean linen cloth kept especially for these occasions. She removed the soiled linen sheet that had been folded under Deborah and found another one that was lying on the top of the trunk and spread it under her bottom. "Everything is just fine Deborah, you did wonderful, I'm very proud of you," Marie said and went into the other room to get a clean cloth to clean the baby.

Deborah checked her baby from head to toe, 'Her tiny fingers are perfect and her feet are beautiful,' she thought, and then laughed at herself, 'mercy,' she said to herself, 'how silly you are, feet are cute, not beautiful,' and she chuckled out loud to her baby and shivered.

Marie came back into the room then and took the baby out of Deborah's hands. "Where are your clean nightgowns Deborah, I'll get you one," Marie said, "Your Chemise is all stained from your baby, you'll want to look nice when William comes back."

"On the shelf over there, on the top shelf," Deborah said as she pointed toward the other side of the room, "there are new baby clothes that I also have ready on the second shelf."

Marie walked across the room and found the clean clothes and gave Deborah hers, "can you manage by yourself while I get this little one dressed?"

"Yes, of course," Deborah said smiling. "I'm so happy I think I could get out of bed and dance a jig."

"You may want to wait a day or two before you do any dancing my dear," Marie said laughing and quickly finished dressing the shivering baby and then wrapped her in a small quilt that Deborah had embroidered with little yellow daisies. Then as she handed the new baby girl to her mother she asked, "What are you going to name her?"

"Oh, mercy," Deborah answered, "I don't think William and I have decided yet. We talked a bit about it last night, but I think we decided to name a boy John after my father. My real father," she said quietly. "We couldn't make up our minds about a girls name, we were so sure we were going to have a boy."

"Well, my dear, I do believe that you have already named her," Marie said.

"What do you mean?" Deborah questioned.

"You have said 'mercy' several times since I've been here today, I think it's a lovely name, don't you?" Marie said.

"Mercy," Deborah repeated, "Mercy, I like that," she said and she laughed a little.

William came into the house quietly and as quickly as he could; the wind was blowing even harder now. Another gust of cold air sneaked in around him as he shut the door. He hung up his coat and went to the fireplace to warm his hands and check the fire, it was going good. He could hear the women talking so he went to the bedroom door and looked in; he was surprised to see his beautiful wife sitting up in bed holding his baby.

"You have a beautiful little girl William," Marie said as she saw his startled face, "And everything is just fine."

"Mercy," William said.

Deborah and Marie looked at each other and they both laughed. Deborah reached her hand toward William and he went to her side, "I think that will be a wonderful name for our little girl," she said.

William looked at her for a second and said, "What?"

"Mercy, I think we will name her Mercy," Deborah said pulling his hand down so that he was touching his baby's face, "do you like that name?"

Then William smiled and said, "Yes, but when did you think of it, I don't think we mentioned it last night."

"Marie told me that I said mercy several times during her birth," Deborah chuckled, "I guess maybe the good Lord was naming her." Then she looked at Marie and said, "Marie thought it a lovely name."

"Yes, yes, I do too, we'll name her Mercy," and then he laughed and said, "Mercy Burden, Mercy Burden, Mercy what a burden."

They all laughed then and Marie said several times at church the following Sunday at Mercy's baptism that she had not seen such a happy couple for a long time.

• • •

The holidays came and went along with the cold winter weather. The people of Barnstable enjoyed the peaceful season without any unforeseen troubles.

In late December Wamsutta, Chief of the Wampanoag Indians died leaving his brother Metacomet as the new Chief of the Wampanoag. Chief Metacomet, or King Philip as some of the English called him, formally renewed the peace treaty that his father had signed. The Wampanoag had always been friendly with the English and were seen as peaceful allies.

Patricia Louise Blish Gould

CHAPTER THIRTY
1663

Richard and Mehitabel Dimmock Child had their first son on March 30, 1663 they named him Richard, Jr. Marie was not able to be with her daughter, but the message she received from Mehitabel said that she and baby Richard were doing just fine.

• • •

Thomas Walley became the new Reverend at Barnstable church on April 1, 1663. He was a widower with a son, Thomas Jr. who was born in 1643 and a daughter named Mary who was born in 1644. The new appointed Reverend moved into the large house that had been empty for two years, since Mrs. Lothrop moved to Yarmouth.

The ruling elders had searched for ten years before deciding to hire Reverend Walley. He was a compassionate man about the age of 42. He was plain in face and very thin but his friendly manner made many women willing to care for his needs. His attention was always on his parishioners as a whole. His preaching was never about the fires of hell or the end of the world. His sermons were of joyful things that had happened to him or friends that he knew.

Everyone liked him, especially Deborah Annable, age 26, who had resigned her self to be a spinster, she was not a pretty girl, she looked very much like her father, and she had a large nose and was quite heavy. Her dark hair was straight, but she said that it was easier to keep tidy.

Although Thomas was much older than she was, Deborah was quite stricken with him and he with her. He was kind to her every time they met at church and she would not take her eyes off him during the service. It was only a few weeks after Thomas started preaching that rumors where being spread about Deborah and the Reverend. None of which were true. However, with Allice Blish's help Deborah found ways and reasons to invite Thomas to eat with her family. She would make him and his children pies and cakes and mittens and hats and find a way to present them to him discretely whenever she could. It didn't take long before the feelings between them became mutual.

Though Anthony Annable was strict with his daughters, and Deborah was his youngest by his first wife Jane he agreed to allow the Reverend to see her. Some people scoffed at the relationship, because of the age difference, but the courtship was open to the public and they were considered a respectful couple. Deborah helped at the church with the cleaning and polishing of the pews so that she could be near the Reverend Walley and after a while people realize that she would indeed make a good wife for a preacher.

• • •

Thomas Dexter and Mehitabel Brabrooke were married on April 5, 1663 and the Reverend Thomas Walley performed his first wedding in Barnstable. Thomas couldn't thank Abraham enough for bringing Mehitabel to him. The children were all dressed in their best clothes and were very well behaved at the wedding.

• • •

Elder Thomas Dimmock's son Shubael married Joanna Bursley on April 10, 1663. He was only 18 years and 7 months. She was 17 years and 1 month. They were considered by many to be too young for such a responsibility, but Marie said that she would rather they marry young and be happy than to marry old and be unhappy. Besides, she said, Shubael had been running their farm for five years since his father died and he was good at it, they were quite prosperous.

• • •

On May 7, 1663 Thomas and Caroline Huckins were granted a permit to open a village tavern provided that food would be served to every guest. The Lumbert Inn was on the west side of town near Sandwich, the Huckins Tavern was on the east near the Yarmouth town line. Thomas also was a remarkable man owning Barnstable's first packet, which was a vessel without regular sailing, connecting Barnstable to Plymouth and Boston and other harbors. He had served the town of Barnstable as a constable, selectman, and deputy to the colony court, surveyor of highways and a receiver of excise taxes. Each year he purchased 179 gallons of spirits, 43 for his tavern and the remainder for Nicholas Davis, Joseph Hull and Thomas Davis. He also fetched large quantities of powder and shot for the security of the town as well as for hunting.

His wife Caroline was actually the real caretaker of the Inn. She was a spotless housekeeper and a wonderful cook. Many guest were received during the first year they were open. Not only strangers passing from one small town to the next but local townspeople who came just to eat her wonderful food. In fact, it wasn't long before Caroline had to hire three young ladies to help her cook and serve the meals on a daily basis. She charged a nominal fee of two shillings for each meal and paid the ladies ten shillings a day for their help. Unofficially Caroline Huckins owned the first eating house in Barnstable.

Elizabeth Bills, Mary Barker and Samantha Hinckley worked for her whenever she called on them, which was quite often. The Huckins Tavern was open every day except Sunday and Caroline was not able to handle everything herself, there were just as many guests during the middle days of the week as there were on Saturday. Caroline refused to work on Sunday and any guest that might have stayed the night before was given only breakfast. That she had to cook anyway for her and Thomas.

Working for Caroline also gave the young ladies an opportunity to meet young men. However, the girls were never out of Caroline's sight for very long. If she had to leave the eating room, Elizabeth would be watching, and the young men knew they were being watched, nothing out of the ordinary ever occurred. But the young men always seemed to know the names of the girls and several of them were bold enough to seek out their father's permission to court them.

Samantha Hinckley, who was 18, met her husband, Nathaniel Fitzrandall from Duxbury at the Tavern shortly after she started working there. And though he was quite a bit older than she was, he was 32, they fell in love.

After that, Caroline was never in need of help as all the young ladies of marrying age were always willing to work for her in hopes of finding a husband. Samantha's sister Elizabeth took her place at the Tavern, but waited several years before she found her husband.

Though romantic ideas were always in the girl's minds, they worked hard and had to put up with a lot of nonsense from many of the older gentlemen. On several occasions, Caroline had to remove an unruly drunk from the premises by dragging him by the back of his neck and the seat of his breeches from the Tavern, telling him to sober up before he came back. This didn't happen very often because the word was quickly out that no mistreatment of the girls or drunkenness would be tolerated at Huckins' Tavern.

• • •

On June 1, 1663, at the annual town meeting, Abraham was chosen to be Grand Enquest again. The duties of a Grand Enquest were not as demanding as some of the jobs that the other town officials held, except when there was a death by unknown causes. Then Abraham might be busy for several days or even weeks.

He was 50 years old and was busy teaching Joseph, now 15, how to manage their estate.

Joseph loved his father and was always by his side. He loved the farm and the town of Barnstable and always had a smile on his face. He was getting very tall now and beginning to look very much like his father except for his hair. It was the same color as his mothers, golden red and curly, and he had her freckles, too, although they seemed to be fading, as he grew older.

The young ladies his age were always giggling and whispering about him. It disturbed him for a while until his sister Sarah told him they all thought he was handsome and were hoping to marry him someday. After that whenever he heard the giggling, he would look their way and flash one of his big smiles; the girls would always blush and turn away.

Joseph did not want to go away to Boston College so Abraham insisted that he read every book he could find in the town of Barnstable. He had a book by his chair every evening after supper and would read until he fell asleep. Joseph was very attentive to details and Abraham allowed him to make a few decisions on his own and included him in many of the important matters that concerned the farm and landholdings.

On December 2, 1663, Sarah turned 19. She was madly in love with Richard Orchyard of Boston who had visited her stepsister Deborah's house several times during the past year on the pretext of business. They were meeting discreetly during this time at Deborah and William's home and in July Richard had finally gathered the courage to ask Abraham's permission to marry Sarah.

Abraham finally agreed to the courting as long as Richard came to Barnstable. She was not allowed to go anywhere with him or to visit him in Boston.

Sarah realized that she could only push her father so far, then she must stop or lose all the ground she had gained.

Abraham was disappointed because when Sarah turned 18, he had wanted to send her to England to finishing school. She was a beautiful artist and could draw anything. She was also talented in music and sang solo in church and at weddings and funerals. Abraham thought that she might study music and art at Oxford, but Sarah wouldn't hear of it. She insisted that she was needed at home. Abraham relented. She didn't tell him about Richard.

• • •

Elder Henry Cobb's son James married Sarah Lewis daughter of George Lewis, Sr. of Plymouth on December 26, 1663. James built a house on a nice plot of land that his father gave him as part of his inheritance.

• • •

Abraham took his family to Duxbury during the Christmas holidays but they did not stay long. Allice had a social gathering planned for the last day of the year and wanted to go home.

It was a good thing they left when they did because on December 30 there was another great storm that came from the northeast.

It lasted three days. There was much to do when it stopped, everyone had to help pack the snow so they could get to the barns and tend their animals. It was almost a week before neighbors were able to check on one another. No one suffered any losses and everyone was thankful for that.

Allice's social was postponed naturally, and it was two weeks before she was able to hold her end of the year gathering. It was successful and there was much weather to talk about. No one had ever seen so much snowfall from one storm for a long time.

CHAPTER THIRTY-ONE
1664

Thomas Walley, Jr. married Little Hannah Bacon on January 15, 1664. Hannah Bacon, mother of Little Hannah did not want her daughter to marry Thomas Walley, Jr. He was, she said, a person with two faces one good, and one evil. She made Hannah promise that if he ever treated her in an unkind way that she would tell her and her father about him. Little Hannah said she would.

• • •

Richard Orchard and Sarah Blish were married on February 18, 1664, and moved to Boston. Abraham could not help but feel that Sarah was cheating herself. And on that cold day, although he outwardly appeared happy, he missed Sarah's mother Anne, more than he had for years. Maybe she would have been able to persuade Sarah to wait for marriage and go to school. He cried as he kissed his only daughter goodbye that afternoon.

Although Richard was good to Sarah, and they had everything imaginable, Sarah soon learned that he was not the type of man to stay home and help her with the children. She hired a maid and a cook and went with him whenever he allowed her to, but it seemed that only on rare occasions did he agree to take her to England. He had many properties that he needed to tend there and he would be much too busy to entertain her, she would be a distraction to him. She thought this was an insult, but he explained to her that in order to keep his businesses thriving he needed to keep his wits about him. He also told her that none of his friends in England allowed their wives to attend any of their meetings. She relented reluctantly and hoped that she was pregnant every time he left her.

Richard bought her a great house in Boston shortly after they were married. They were not poor by any means and so she went about filling her days with decorating her new home and entertaining her friends. In early fall after Richard left for England she cried for two days. She was not pregnant, but she rallied around and decided that she would decorate the room across from hers and make it into a nursery anyway, just in case she was the next time he left.

• • •

On April 15, 1664 Shubael and Joanna Dimmock had their first baby, they named him Thomas. Marie Dimmock helped her daughter-in-law deliver her baby and her delivery was easy.

• • •

The Reverend Thomas Walley and Deborah Annable wanted to be married by Reverend Ralph Partridge of the Church of Duxbury. Abraham had taken a message to the Reverend Partridge when he and Allice went to Duxbury during the Christmas season last year and Reverend Partridge had agreed to make the trip in the spring to marry Deborah and Thomas.

The wedding was held on April 30, 1664 and every member of the congregation was invited as usual and a lovely meal was served in the parish house after the ceremony. The town was happy to finally have a new preacher and the preacher was happy to have a new wife.

• • •

Samantha Hinckley and Nathaniel Fitzrandall of Duxbury were married in Barnstable on June 10, 1664 after a year long courtship, they moved to Duxbury shortly afterward.

• • •

Caroline Huckins hired Samantha's sister Elizabeth to take her place at the Huckins Tavern and she also hired Annie Barker at that same time. Both girls helped cook and serve the many people that were now coming into the Inn.

• • •

On July 19, 1664 the fourth parcel of land, now called Hyannis, Hyannis Port, Craigville and Centerville was purchased after much negotiation, from Yanno, Chief of the Cummaquid Indians, for the sum of 20 pounds and two small pair of breeches. Thomas Hinckley, Nathaniel Bacon, and Tristram Hull represented Barnstable and Abraham Blish and Thomas Walley, Jr. witnessed the signing of the deed. Other parcels of land, all negotiated with permission of the court were purchased by individuals from Chief Yanno. Nicholas Davis purchased a parcel on Lewis Bay from Chief Yanno for the sum of 3 pounds sterling and a pair of well made shoes so he could increase his warehouse business.

Yanno was quite old now, 'he must be about 85 years old,' Abraham thought, remembering the story that Richard told him, about the Chief finding a young boy that was lost in 1621, the first year of the colony. Yanno was still a wise and sensible man and knew that the land that he sold was of no use to his people except for fishing and hunting and the white men agreed that his people would still have those rights. His feelings were that he received 20 pounds sterling and two pair of breeches for his youngest son by simply making his mark on a piece of paper. Yanno's people knew that no one could 'own' land, it belonged to mother earth.

Yanno's village had been friendly with the white man for many years, and he had watched the small towns grow bigger every year. Most of the settlers were kind and friendly and well mannered. If they were unruly the town fathers always took care to settle any differences between the Indian and White man. His people liked to trade with the townspeople and the children of his village were treated well and always welcomed at the places they called Church and school.

• • •

Mehitabel Dimmock Child and Richard Child had a son they named Ephraim on October 9, 1664. Marie was overjoyed that she had a new grandson and was happy to hear that both baby and the new mother were well, but she was sad that she wasn't able to go to Watertown to help her daughter.

• • •

James and Sarah Cobb had their first daughter on November 24, 1664 they named her Mary. Marie and Sarah were with her during her delivery and both mother and baby were healthy and doing well.

• • •

Mary Goodspeed, daughter of Roger and Alice Goodspeed, married Samuel Hinckley on December 14, 1664. Everyone in town attended the wedding and enjoyed the lovely meal that was served by the ladies of the church after the ceremony.

• • •

Richard and Mary More and their family came to Barnstable for the Christmas holiday and they brought a wonderful surprise with them. John and Sarah Pratt came with them. John was now 75 years old and Sarah was 74. Abraham was so happy to see them. He had always made sure to stop in to see them every time he went to Duxbury and Joseph and Sarah had stayed over night with them once in a while when they visited the More's home. But John and Sarah had never been to Barnstable in all the years that Abraham had lived there. John was not a traveler, especially by water he would become very seasick. This time for some reason, maybe because he was only on board the small schooner for just a couple of hours it did not bother him.

Abraham was especially happy to see them and was glad that Sarah and Richard were planning to be there for the holidays too.

The Pratt's did not come to Sarah's wedding so they had never met Richard. Abraham thought that they might be impressed by him, he was very handsome and debonair, and very intelligent, and oh, yes, rich. However, he didn't flaunt himself and Abraham was happy for that.

They all had a wonderful holiday and when Abraham kissed his mother-in-law goodbye she whispered that she was sorry to hear about his parents.

He hugged her extra tight and thanked her. She still reminded him of his mother. The same name and the same kind face.

"Oh, by the way Abraham," Sarah said, "we think your son-in-law is wonderful."

Abraham beamed and kissed her again.

"They do make a handsome couple don't they," Abraham said proudly.

Patricia Louise Blish Gould

CHAPTER THIRTY-TWO
1665

On February 10, 1665 Thomas Walley, Jr. and Little Hannah had a baby boy and they named him Thomas, III. Sarah and Marie helped her deliver her baby and reminisced about the day she herself was born not quite 21 years ago. Had it really been that long they questioned each other.

• • •

On June 4, 1665 the councilmen of Barnstable appointed Selectmen to run the town for the first time. Barnstable was growing rapidly and there had to be better representation in order to meet the needs of the residents.

Abraham Blish, Joseph Hull, William Crocker and Nathaniel Bacon were those appointed that day and it was written in the records that the selection had been fair. There was a celebration of sorts after the meeting with everyone gathering for a picnic social on the church green.

• • •

Nathaniel and Hannah Bacon had another little boy on June 20, 1665. Hannah named him John and her delivery was easy and he was an easy baby to take care of. He looked exactly like his father. The bitter tea she had taken for five years worked as a birth control, however she had run out of the herbs for a while last fall and decided that she was feeling well and didn't need the body strengthening tea any more, then she realized she was pregnant again. She was 43 and her oldest child Little Hannah was 21, and she had a new baby of her own, five months old. Marie and Sarah made sure she didn't run out of the Blessed Tea again.

• • •

Abraham was happy to be busy with town affairs; his house seemed to get bigger every time he came home. Joseph, now 17, was busy with the farm. Johnny Barker's Uncle, Captain John Williams, his mother's brother, had been after him to move to Scituate. Johnny was a good boy and always minded whatever Abraham asked him to do. But Abraham knew it was probably just a matter of time before he would make his own decision as to whether he should stay in Barnstable or move to Scituate with his uncle. Allice was always busy with her friends and with church affairs. Mary and Annie Barker were still home, but they were gone much of the time, helping at the Huckins' Inn. Most of the time it was just himself, Joseph, Abraham Jr. and Johnny Barker. Of course, Mary and Annie prepared most of the meals and cleaned for them, Allice was always too busy lately to do house work or cook. He wasn't sure if he had made the right choice in asking Allice to marry him. Hannah had been gone over seven years but he missed her more lately than he ever had.

William and Deborah Burden's second child, a daughter they named Little Deborah was born June 28, 1665. This made Abraham's days a little brighter, he visited her often and made one excuse or another to see baby Deborah whenever he went to check on business at the gristmill.

In August Johnny Barker finally made his decision to go and live with his Uncle in Scituate. He was promised that he would receive wages and an education in return for any labors that he would be asked to do. He seemed reluctant to go when the time came, but his Uncle convinced him in several letters that he would gain a great inheritance when he turned 21 by making this move. He also promised Johnny that he would give him a good rank in the militia when he was old enough to serve.

Johnny had his trunk packed and was ready the day that his Uncle came to get him. Abraham hugged him goodbye that sad day and gave him ten pounds sterling in case he needed anything. Daisy was not allowed to go with him. His Uncle told him there were enough bitches on his farm and one more would just bring more puppies to feed.

Abraham assured Johnny that Daisy would be well cared for and she should probably stay where she would be happier. It might not be good for her to move she was old now, almost 12, 84 years in a dog's age.

Johnny had misgivings about his Uncle after only several miles had passed and this strange man had not so much as said one kind word to him. Johnny had always been a quiet little boy and even now that he was older he stayed to himself most of the time. Daisy seemed to be his only friend. Although he was included in family gatherings and functions and always ate his meals with them, he would go to his pallet to read or to the barn or shed and find a chore to do as soon as he was excused from the table.

By the time he arrived in Scituate he knew that his judgment of his Uncle was right. The Williams' farm was huge and there were over twenty people hired or in servitude to Captain John Williams. Johnny was treated not as a nephew, but as one of the servants. He slept in their quarters and ate when they ate. His Uncle hardly acknowledged him and paid him nothing. He did however, make sure that Johnny went to school everyday and bought him a new set of clothes once a year.

Every fall after harvesting Johnny managed to find his way to Barnstable to visit Daisy. He always stayed with Abraham and Allice. Abraham would question him about his well being and he would answer that he was fine and everything was going well. He always borrowed several books from Abraham's collection. His education was important and Abraham allowed him to take them home with him.

● ● ●

Toward the end of November Abraham learned the news that Joseph Hull, one of the founders of Barnstable, who had retired to the Isle of Shoals had passed away on November 19, 1665. It saddened him; he had always like Joseph Hull and thought that he would have liked to attend his funeral. The passing of his friend and the coming of cold weather covered him with a cloud of gloom. He hoped that come spring he would feel better, everyone seemed to be melancholy lately.

• • •

Robert and Ann Davis had a son they named Joseph on December 2, 1665, his ninth child and Ann's fourth. He did as he promised and added two large rooms onto the back of their house, this made his still growing family much more comfortable. Robert's two oldest daughters by Elizabeth his first wife were married now. Deborah married James Geere and Mary married Lawrence Dexter, they both lived in Scituate.

Ann now had seven young children to care for by herself including her new baby. Robert's oldest was Andrew, he was 15, then there was John, he was 13, then Robert, Jr., he was 11. Her own children were Josiah 9, Hannah 7, and Sarah 5. She really had no daughters that could help her with the meals and washing and making clothes.

Marie and Sarah left Ann a large amount of the Blessed Tea hoping that she would take it every day. She had enough children to care for.

• • •

Richard and Mehitabel Child of Watertown had a son they named Shubael on December 19, 1665. Marie Dimmock was not able to help her daughter deliver her baby but she had an easy delivery and she was fine and the baby was healthy.

• • •

Richard Orchyard left for England on December 30 and Sarah was pregnant and happy to stay home this time. She didn't tell him before he left, he would find out when he came home in three months.

CHAPTER THIRTY-THREE
1666

Shubael and Joanne Dimmock had their second child, a son they named John, on January 20, 1666.

James and Sarah Cobb had their second child, a daughter they named Sarah, on January 26, 1666.

Marie Dimmock and Sarah Bourne helped bring these new babies into the world as they had been doing for almost 25 years now. Marie was 49 years old and Sarah was 48, but they both were of good health and were always there when the women of Barnstable needed them. They were also there whenever they were called to help sick children and men, too.

• • •

Abraham was delighted to receive word from Boston that he was a grandfather, Richard and Sarah Orchyard's first child Joseph was born on May 6, 1666. A note at the end of the announcement read, *"See you soon, we may spend the summer with you."*

Richard Orchyard indeed was quite surprised when he came home in early March to find his wife had gained weight. He could see her waiting for him as the ship docked in the harbor. Maybe it was the new coat she had on. He waved to her and she waved back. 'How beautiful she is,' he thought, 'I don't care if she does gain weight.' He missed her very much. He promised himself he would take her with him next time.

When he kissed her hello a few minutes later, he was surprised at the way she kissed him back. In public most women turned their heads so that their husbands could kiss their cheeks. But today instead of turning her cheek to his lips she reached up and pulled his head down and met his lips with hers and they kissed each other full on the mouth in public for the first time. Several of the men with him chuckled and several women standing nearby gasped at the bawdy scene.

Sarah didn't care, and though Richard was a little surprised by his wife's behavior he reacted instinctively and pulled her a little closer. He grinned down at her when she let go of his head and she was smiling mischievously up at him. "What secret do you have for me this time little Sarah," he asked grinning broadly.

"You'll see when we get home," she said as she put her hand through his arm and they turned toward the carriage that was waiting for them.

Richard was delighted when she took her coat off and pulled her dress closely over her belly. He laughed and said, "When did you find out you were pregnant. You must be ready to have this child."

"I thought I was pregnant when you left but I didn't want you to worry about me," she answered knowing most of what she said was the truth. "I'm seven months now and you'll be a proud papa in May."

He pulled her gently to him and held her tight and said, "I'm glad you didn't go with me, you would have been miserable in a rocking ship."

"I suppose you're right Richard, but I really didn't get sick hardly at all during those first months," she said, "and I feel very well now, just fat."

He laughed and said, "You are not fat, you are beautiful."

She kissed him and said, "Come, I want to show you what I've been doing while you were gone," and she pulled him up the stairs to see the new baby things she had made.

It was an hour or so before he finally looked at the little clothes.

The next time Richard went to England was in July and tending her baby was Sarah's first priority and she couldn't go with him. She thought that he acted almost happy that she had stopped asking him to take her with him, but she knew that he probably was only happy that she wasn't alone now. Besides she had tentative plans of visiting her father in Barnstable during the summer. The ocean was so beautiful then and the air was so clean.

Richard made arrangements for her to go to Barnstable by schooner the same day he left for England. He held his new two month old son gently and kissed his cheek and then he leaned down to Sarah and they kissed each other goodbye the same way they had kissed hello four months before.

• • •

At the annual town meeting Nathaniel Bacon, Jr. was elected Constable. He had helped his father and Abraham many times over the years and being a much younger man and not married he would have no problem meeting the many duties of being Constable. Crime in Barnstable seemed to be more commonplace these days, but not as violent, they were mostly petty things that a Constable could take care of by himself.

John Mayo saw William Sutton take a Bible from the meetinghouse and took him to court on July 1, 1666. The court found him guilty and ordered him to return it immediately and fined him 1 pound for his transgression. William insisted that he did no such thing but after Constable Bacon searched his home and found the missing bible; the court fined him another 10 shillings for lying.

Several other misdemeanors happened that year.

Elizabeth Bills was accused of being a witch when her neighbor Dorothy Wells saw her disappear into thin air near the Blish Gristmill. Constable Nathaniel Bacon, Jr. took Elizabeth into court, with her hands tied behind her back and her mouth covered with a red bandanna. She would not hold her tongue, adamantly proclaiming that she was not a witch, so Nathaniel had covered her mouth to keep her quiet.

Elizabeth Lewis, born January 17, 1625 was only 14 when she married William Bills in 1639 in Plymouth England and they moved to Barnstable. William was about 15 years older than she was. They had two children both of whom died young. When her son Billy died in a boating accident she refused to sleep with her husband ever again, she did not want any more children taken away from her; instead she helped the other women in town with their little ones. She also helped Caroline Huckins' at the Huckins Tavern.

Constable Nathaniel Bacon, Jr. called the court to order when Magistrate John Crow entered the courtroom.

Henry Cobb was the prosecutor for the court. He tried to remain unbiased throughout the whole proceeding but he would have been the first to admit, if questioned, that Dorothy Wells was not one of his favorite people.

Dorothy Wells was first to testify in court and told many farfetched stories about Elizabeth. She accused Elizabeth of turning herself into a black cat. She told the jury in her prim and proper voice, "I saw her do magic tricks with candles." Some of the jurors chuckled behind their hands.

Judge Crow said, "Silence."

Dorothy Wells pursed her lips even tighter and continued, "I saw her lighting them without a fire stick and blowing them out only to have them re-light by themselves again."

Henry Cobb asked Dorothy, "What did you see Elizabeth do when you were at the Blish Gristmill."

"I saw her disappear completely into thin air," Dorothy said adamantly.

"Then what did you do?" Henry asked her.

"I ran home as fast as I could," Dorothy said her voice shaking.

"That was all?" Henry questioned.

"Yes," Dorothy said.

Henry said, "That's all Your Honor, the Prosecution rests."

Abraham Blish was Attorney for Elizabeth Wells and he called Caroline Huckins to the stand to testify on Elizabeth's behalf; they had been friends since moving to Barnstable.

"Mrs. Huckins, how long have you known Elizabeth Bills," Abraham asked her.

"I have known Elizabeth Bills for 25 years and she has worked for me since I opened the Huckins Inn and Tavern," Caroline said to the Jurors, "we are very good friends."

She looked at Judge John Crow and said, "I know that she is not a witch, although she is very shrewd in making a bargain." The courtroom buzzed with whispers.

Judge Crow rapped his gavel and said, "Please, Mrs. Huckins, no unnecessary comments."

"Sorry, Sir," Caroline said and then looked at Abraham.

"Please continue Caroline," he said.

"Elizabeth is known by everyone to be honest industrious and energetic and yes, sometimes a little eccentric but she is not a witch,"

Caroline said. "However," she added quickly, "Elizabeth out-smarted Dorothy Wells during last years trading with the Indians, and I personally think that is why Dorothy has made these accusations."

"That is speculation," Henry Cobb said quickly.

Judge Crow looked at the Jurors and said, "Please ignore that remark."

Abraham said, "Please answer only the questions that I ask you Mrs. Huckins."

"Yes, sir," Caroline said.

"How do you know that Elizabeth is not a witch," Abraham asked her.

"I have never seen Elizabeth do any of the things that Dorothy claims she has done," Caroline said. And then quickly added, "I am furious with Dorothy and I believe that she is nothing but a busy body and she has no right to accuse Elizabeth Wells of being a witch."

The people in the courtroom gasped in unison at Caroline's contempt, and though most of the jurors believed Caroline more than they did Dorothy the Judge rapped his gavel again and said to the Jury, "Please ignore that comment, too." Then he looked at Caroline and said, "Mrs. Huckins were you an eye witness to this case?"

"No your Honor," Caroline said.

"Then you are excused," he said. Then looking at Abraham he said, "Please call you next witness."

Abraham said, "Elizabeth Bills, please come to the witness stand."

When Elizabeth's turn came to testify in her own defense some of the jurors that were sided with Dorothy were apprehensive about being in her presence thinking that Elizabeth may indeed be a witch and turn them into toads or something. However, as she told her story they were all ears and full of laughter as she explained to them what had really happened to her near the Gristmill.

After Elizabeth was sworn in Abraham asked her to tell the court exactly what happened that day. Elizabeth started her story with some embarrassment, but she was determined to protect her reputation at all costs.

"I went to the Mill to get my cornmeal that Deborah had ground for me," she stated quietly. "I was walking fast because I felt that I was going to have a mishap in my bloomers if I didn't get home soon."

The jurors chuckled as she continued. "When I arrived Deborah and William were not there and no one was else was around. I called out several times, but I didn't hear anyone return my greeting."

She lifted her chin and looked at the jurors, "I decided to go in and look around to see if I could find someone, maybe Deborah's helper was sleeping, it was early. I didn't see anyone so I looked on the shelf where the bags of corn and flour are placed after it's ground," everyone knew where she meant. All the women had been to the mill at one time or another and picked up their meal from that shelf. "I found a bag of meal with my name on it after a minute or so and put it into my basket. I called out again that I had found my cornmeal and stepped out of the door. Just as I went to take the next step down the cornmeal started to fall out of my basket, and as I grabbed for it I lost my balance and fell to the ground."

The juror's snickered as they pictured the plump lady lying in a heap at the bottom of the gristmill steps. "Twenty pounds of cornmeal is heavy," she said haughtily above the noise.

She looked at the Magistrate and he rapped his gavel for silence, and nodded for her to go on. She wiped her brow with her handkerchief and continued, "I picked myself up and found that only my pride was bruised, then as I bent over to pick up the heavy bag of meal, my bowels moved without my approval."

This time the jurors laughed out loud, in fact most of the people in the courtroom could be heard chuckling.

'I am not a witch,' she told herself as the Magistrate quieted the courtroom again. She looked at Abraham and he nodded for her to continue. She knew her face was red but she was determined to finish her testimony.

"I then ran quickly behind the mill out of sight of any one that might be coming down the road, I was greatly embarrassed, but believed that no one had seen me fall so I stood there for a minute or so and tried to decide what to do. I realized that I had to clean myself up as best I could. After all, if I didn't my odor would attract flies all the way home and if I met anyone they would smell me and think I was unclean."

Another burst of laughter and Judge Crow banged his gavel several times before it became quiet enough for Elizabeth to finish her story.

Abraham said, "Please continue Mrs. Bills."

She took a deep breath and said, "So I removed my bloomers and my soiled petticoat and rinsed them out in the millpond. I wrung them out as dry as I could and put them on again. Dorothy Wells must have seen me fall, but she certainly didn't see me disappear. If she had been a kinder person she would have come to my rescue instead of accusing me of being a witch."

The jurors, though still smiling had to agree with her about Dorothy Wells and after only a few minutes of deliberation they found Elizabeth Lewis Bills not guilty of being a witch and requested that Dorothy Wells make a public apology immediately to Elizabeth before the court was adjourned.

Dorothy Wells did make her apology, but the two women never spoke to each other again. Dorothy, however, was also very careful about what she said about anyone from that day on.

• • •

A few days later William Burden and John Bates were fined 3 shillings and 4 pence each for breaking the King's peace by striking each other. William was drunk at the time and was fined another 5 shillings. Bates was ordered by the Court to pay William 20 shillings for abusing him.

Deborah was furious at William for embarrassing her and let him know in no uncertain terms just what she thought of his drinking with good-for-nothing no-account friends like John Bates.

Deborah berated William the evening of the fight after the children went to bed. "You are a grown man with a wife and two children and another one on the way," she said irately.

He was sitting on the settee in front of the fireplace with a cold cloth on his cheekbone; his head hung down in shame.

She continued, knowing that she should probably ask him why he would do such a thing as lay hands on another man in an abusive manner, but she wasn't sure if she wanted to know the answer. She said tearfully, "I'm embarrassed about your actions, and now everyone in church will shun you, and me," she said knowing she sounded selfish and unkind, "I am so ashamed for you."

William looked up at her pleading with his big blue eyes and said, "Please Deborah, let me explain."

She looked at him guiltily knowing that she sounded like a shrew and then sat down on the settee beside him and took his hand. "I'm sorry," she said, "I'm only thinking of myself." She gently touched the red mark on his cheekbone with her fingertips and said, "tell me what happened, I'll listen."

"John Bates is a very vulgar man," he said, "but I have no excuse for hitting him except that I lost my temper."

"And you also had too much cider," Deborah added.

"Yes, too much beer too," William said and then continued with his story.

"We worked all day helping Mr. Crocker fix his barn roof and I was getting cold as the sun went down so I asked John if he wanted to stop at the Tavern for a mug of beer, I thought it might warm me up. John said, 'sure, if you you're paying for it' and I said I would. When we went into the Tavern several of my old friends from England were there and before I knew it, I had drank four beers. Then I said that I had to go home, my wife would have my evening meal ready. John told everyone that I had a wife that was a wench and she did not allow me to have a mind of my own. He said that my wife told me what to do and when to do it. I told him that I took offense to such talk and he said that was because I couldn't stand up to you and your prissy ways. He also said that the only reason I went to church was because you insisted."

By this time Deborah was almost ready to put on her coat and head for Mr. Crocker's home, where John Bates lived as his hired hand and hit him herself. She was appalled that he had the audacity to insinuate that she was such a person. She could hardly believe what William was telling her, but she knew he would never lie to her. "How can he think such things," she asked William hardly able to constrain the loudness of her voice.

"I don't know, I have never talked badly of you and I have only said loving things about you in public," William said sadly. He was silent for a minute.

Deborah stood up and went to the fireplace and said, "Ooh," as she threw a log onto the fire as if she was hurling it at the head of John Bates. The sparks flew and she stepped back quickly and sat down beside William again.

"I do believe he is jealous of me," William said thoughtfully. "He came to the colonies with me and worked for Mr. Boardman during the same time I did. Mr. Boardman didn't always agree with the way John did things and would reprimand him from time to time. He hated it when Mr. Boardman gave me an extra shilling for the good work that I did."

"I think you are probably right dear William," Deborah said and put her arm around his back and laid her head on his shoulder. "The man is jealous of the things you have now and the things you've accomplished. Your family, the Gristmill and the wonderful work that you do for others," she said her voice growing softer.

William turned toward her and put his arm behind her and pulled her onto his lap. He loved to hold her like this. She was a little thing and even when she was pregnant she didn't weigh very much. He was a strong man with hard muscles that he earned from working with his hands, building homes and hauling bricks. He nestled his cheek into her hair; he loved the way she smelled. Like roses he thought. "I'm sorry that I embarrassed you by hitting that man and fighting in public like a heathen," he said. "I promise I will never do it again," he added and he kissed her cheek.

"I'm glad I wasn't there," Deborah said, "I think I would have had to hit him myself," she added with almost a chuckle in her voice.

"I'm glad you weren't, we wouldn't have been able to afford the fine," William said smiling.

"But maybe we would have been awarded 40 shillings," she laughed.

William laughed too, and then almost as if he just realized what she had said at the beginning of this conversation he said, "What did you say about another baby on the way?"

"I'm pregnant," she said and put her head back a little so she could see his face.

"Oh, Deborah, I'm so sorry I broke the law, you will never have to worry about anything like this happening again," he said sincerely, "I promise."

She couldn't say anything, he was kissing her lips, and all she could do was kiss him back.

He stood up with her in his arms as if she was light as a feather and carried her to their bedroom.

"I love you so much," she said as he laid her carefully on the bed and undressed her.

William and Deborah never mentioned this matter again and no one ever shunned them at church either.

• • •

Nathaniel Goodspeed, son of Roger and Alice Goodspeed of Marstons Mills married Elizabeth Bursley, daughter of John and Mary Bursley on November 11, 1666 and they moved back to Barnstable.

CHAPTER THIRTY-FOUR
1667

Richard and Mehitabel Dimmock Child of Watertown had a baby girl they named Little Mehitabel on January 2, 1667. She died within a few minutes, Marie Dimmock was there this time to help her daughter, but her baby girl was blue when she was born and Marie could do nothing for her little granddaughter. When Marie returned home every woman in Barnstable helped her through this horrible time in her life and they all grieved with her.

• • •

On February 15, 1667 Elder Henry Cobb and his wife Sarah had a baby they also named Mehitabel and she, too, was stillborn. Marie Dimmock told Sarah that she was too old to be having babies and that she should take some special medicine to help her get her strength back. Marie gave her Blessed Tea as well as the new mother's tea.

Sarah Cobb was now 40 years old and had had seven children. She already had several grandchildren and Marie was afraid that if she had any more children she would not make it through the ordeal. Elder Cobb was getting older too, he was now 58 years old.

• • •

429

On March 17, 1667 William and Deborah Burden's son John was born. Deborah was relieved that everything went easily for her during his birth and he was healthy. Little Johnny they called him. Abraham was delighted; he was a grandfather for the fourth time.

• • •

On June 1, 1667, Samuel Annable, now age 21, married Mehitabel Allyn, daughter of Thomas Allyn and was given a large portion of the Annable estate as his inheritance.

• • •

On June 4, 1667 at the annual town meeting Thomas Hinckley, Nathaniel Bacon, Sr., Abraham Blish, Thomas Dexter and John Chipman were appointed to represent Barnstable as members of the Council of War. The Commissioners of the United Colonies recommended raising a body of troops to convey a message to Chief Twacommatus of the Narragansett to compel him to desist from his hostile gestures. Each town was required to furnish five men. However, this turned out to be just a threat and there was no hostile encounter.

Abraham was elected Constable again, he thought that Nathaniel Bacon, Jr. had been doing a great job, but things were easier for him now as far as running his farm went. He had been Constable of Barnstable from 1656 to 1662 and he was now 54 years old and had not really wanted to take on the burdensome duties of overseer of the law. However, Joseph was managing the farm and his holdings quite well now so he decided to accept the position provided he was allowed to take a younger man with him if he had to accompany any prisoners to another town. Nathaniel Bacon, Jr. agreed to go with him whenever he was called upon. The Council agreed and Abraham became Constable of Barnstable again.

• • •

Robert and Ann Davis had another daughter on November 16, 1667 they named her Marcy. She was Robert's tenth child and Ann's fifth, and Ann was 44 years old. She had been tired during her entire pregnancy and could not seem to gain her strength back even by drinking new mothers tea at every meal as Marie Dimmock had instructed.

After the new year Marie Dimmock suggested that she take Blessed Tea for at least the next several years, her age was against her having a healthy baby and she would probably not live to see her next child grow up, Ann Davis agreed if it were kept a secret. Marie Dimmock seldom told anyone about her birth control tea. Sometimes not even the women she gave it to.

• • •

Richard and Mary More came to Barnstable for the holidays and stayed for two weeks. Sarah and Richard and baby Joseph came from Boston. Abraham was delighted to have his friends and family together on Christmas day and with all of the women cooking their dinner was spectacular.

Richard had a good story for everyone this year about the misfortune of a man by the name of John Finney. The adults could not wait to hear it, they remembered the mean man when he lived in Barnstable and knew how he had treated the Coggin children.

"On March 4, 1667 a horrible storm blew into Plymouth Harbor, a northeaster it was, and Mr. John Finney was standing on the wharf waiting for one of his ships to dock. He had been watching the big ship for about a half-hour as it slowly made its way to the pier.

Several dock hands were standing nearby ready to catch and secure the lines when the ship drew up to the huge pilings. They were all shivering from the cold and complaining about it taking so long.

Finally Captain Emerson signaled to his men to throw the lines and secure the ship and the frozen ropes were tossed to the sailors on the wharf. One of the men on the dock did not catch his rope and it hit Mr. Finney in the face and knocked him down. The blow of the heavy knotted rope stunned him and when he fell he landed with his left leg and his left arm hanging over the edge of the dock. The other men caught their ropes and pulled the ship toward them at this same time. The ship smashed Mr. Finney's arm and leg tight against the edge of the dock.

Mr. Finney screamed and fainted. The men on board the ship could see what was happening, but could not do anything about it. The men on the dock loosened their lines and the ship moved back enough so that one of the dock workers pulled Mr. Finney free. Blood was pouring from the end of his glove and his leg dangled uselessly as they laid him out on the ice-covered planks of the dock.

The Captain shouted for his men to secure the ship and then sent his First Mate to get Dr. Claymore, the ship's surgeon, then quickly ordered two of the sailors to set the gangplank.

One of the men on the pier ran to get Mr. Finney's carriage. Nicholas, the driver was inside trying to stay warm but after he understood there had been an accident he quickly guided the horse and carriage as close as he could to Mr. Finney's body.

Captain Emerson and Dr. Claymore helped Nicholas put the still unconscious man into the carriage and got in with him holding Mr. Finney between them as Nicholas took Mr. Finney home as fast as he could.

Mrs. Finney was so upset when she saw her husband that she fainted in a heap in front of the doorway. Her butler pulled her out of the way as Nicholas, Captain Emerson and Dr. Claymore carried Mr. Finney to his bed. They laid him on it as gently as they could then Nicholas went back to help Mrs. Finney while the doctor started to undressed Mr. Finney.

Dr. Claymore asked the Captain to get his bag from the carriage and by the time he came back with it Mrs. Finney had regained her senses and was helping the doctor undress her husband.

Mr. Finney's leg was almost flat were it had been pinned between the wharf and the boat and his arm was only attached by a small piece of skin. Dr. Claymore quickly took his knife and cut the skin and then bandaged the wound temporarily while he tended to Mr. Finney's leg. He had no choice but to cut the flesh where it was flattened and then he bandaged the leg too, there was little blood seeping from it so he went back to Mr. Finney's arm.

Mr. Finney was lucky he said because his shirt had kept the wound clean. He quickly took his needles and thread from his bag and prepared them so that he could suture the skin over the bone of Mr. Finney's arm. Mr. Finney was still unconscious. He was lucky there too, or the pain would have been unbearable.

When the doctor was finished with his arm he did the same thing to his leg; he pulled the skin over the bone and sewed it together. There were no jagged edges of bone sticking out so he left it alone. Mr. Finney's leg had been severed at the joint of the knee. His arm had been severed at the joint in his elbow. He was lucky there, too because there were no jagged *edges of bone to irritate the flesh and skin and less likely for infection to set in.*

He would heal he told Mrs. Finney when he was finished, but he would be in severe pain for a few weeks. If he lived for a month he would probably live to be a hundred years old the doctor said when he left.

Mrs. Finney was extremely upset and asked him if there was any medicine he could give her for the pain. The doctor said he never heard of any except a glass of rum now and then."

"He had never met Marie and Sarah," Abraham said, "they seem to be able to help whenever anyone is in pain."

"I've told her several times she's a better doctor than any I've ever seen," Sarah said.

"What happened when Mr. Finney woke up, Richard," William asked.

"Well, now when Mr. Finney woke up it is said that he was in a terrible rage for three days and it wasn't from fever, it was because he was missing his writing hand and his leg. "How will I ever work again?" he screamed again and again. Mrs. Finney tried to explain to him that the doctor had no choice but to amputate his useless limbs.

When he was over his rage the pain took over, Mrs. Finney wasn't sure whether she liked his crying from pain more than she like his crying from rage or not. She could at least pity him for his pain. She changed his bandages as often as he would let her and his wounds healed, but he is still a very irate person.

I happen to know that when Johnny Coggin was told about Mr. Finney's mishap, he smiled and said, "people like Mr. Finney usually suffer for their misdeeds by the hands of the Lord."

Mr. Finney is now hobbling around on a wooden peg like a pirate and has had to learn to write with his other hand. And I hear that Mrs. Finney will have nothing to do with him, they still live in the same house, but she will not talk to him."

"He must be quite old by now," Abraham said.

"I do believe that he is in his 70's," Richard said, "but when I saw him last he looked much older. He is not a happy man."

"Does he still have his ships and all of his money?" William asked.

"He's had to sell most of his property because he was not able to manage it and he does not trust anyone else to. I know that if he does live to be a hundred he will be feeble and penniless," Richard said.

"Which is exactly what he deserves," Joseph said.

"Well, now that was a very good tale Uncle Richard," Deborah said, "but I'm afraid that we will have to go home now."

"Yes, dear Uncle, you have once again keep the children as well as us adults up past our bedtime," Sarah said hugging Richard.

"Do you need help getting the children home, William," Joseph asked his brother-in-law.

"No, I'll carry Mercy and Deborah will carry Little John we'll be just fine," William said.

When the house emptied Abraham, Joseph, Richard Orchyard and Richard More all sat around the fire with their pipes while the women tucked their children into bed. It wasn't long before they all said good night and went to bed too.

"Thank you God for another wonderful day with my family," Abraham said as he got into bed.

Allice said, "Amen."

Abraham laid there for a few minutes trying to decide whether she was finishing his pray for him or grateful that his children and friends would be going home soon. He didn't bother to ask her, he didn't really care. 'Life is what you make it,' he thought and turned over and went to sleep.

CHAPTER THIRTY-FIVE
1668

John Goodspeed, son of Roger and Alice Goodspeed of Marstons Mills married Experience Holway on January 9, 1668 and moved to Mystic.

• • •

James and Sarah Cobb had their third child on January 12, 1668, a daughter they name Patience. Marie and Sarah helped her and she was up and around in no time.

• • •

At a special town meeting held on February 5, 1668 Abraham Blish, James Lucas, and James Cobb were all empowered to be Haywards for the ensuing year. Abraham had been Hayward in 1660 along with James Cobb and they both worked well together. He was still Constable but lately life in Barnstable seemed to be easier for everyone, there were fewer newcomers and less crime.

• • •

On February 10, 1668, John Crocker, Sr. purchased 40 acres of land from Abraham for 5 pounds 10 shillings. John Crocker wanted to use this land to grow barley.

• • •

Richard Stone died of exposure on February 20, 1668, after being lost in the woods just outside of town for three days. He was only 3 years old and had wandered off looking for his father who was out cutting trees. Jonas Stone worked for Robert Shelly and Samuel Mayo as an apprentice in their boat building business. They owned a large wooded acreage and often while they were out deer hunting they would tag special trees that they wanted to cut so they could use the lumber for the beams of their boats.

When Jonas came home that evening, his wife Isabelle was frantic, she had not been able to find little Richard all day.

"I sent word to Constable Blish early this morning," she told her husband. "Everyone in town has been out looking for him," she cried as he held her.

"Are you sure he's not in the barn hiding?" he asked her as he put his coat back on.

"I've looked everywhere," Isabelle said. "I think he followed you this morning, but I can't be sure."

"Why did you let him do that?" Jonas asked her not believing she would allow her son to do that, but not thinking he would do it on his own.

"He wanted to go outside so I helped him on with his coat and told him to go and gather the eggs," she sobbed. "I never believed he would leave the yard, he never has before."

Every able bodied person in town looked for little Richard from dawn to dusk for three days.

Abraham Blish found him about a mile away from home under a big tree on the morning of the third day; he was dead from exposure. Abraham carried his little body back to his mother and put him in her arms.

Isabelle held her little boy for a long time and then dressed him in his best clothes. She didn't cry, she had no more tears left. She was thankful that he wasn't killed and eaten by wild animals and that he was all in one piece.

When Jonas came home from looking for his son late that afternoon he carried his son to the Church and Reverend Walley blessed the little boy. The Stone's put him in the crypt and waited until May to bury him in the Barnstable Cemetery.

Robert Shelly was extremely upset about the death of Richard, he had lost a young son in much the same manner many years before.

• • •

On March 10, 1668 Shubael and Joanna Bursley Dimmock had their third child, a boy they named Timothy. Marie and Sarah helped Joanna and both her and her baby were healthy. Marie now had six grandchildren she was thrilled.

Joanna was so happy to have her baby because the past several months had not been easy for her. She was not happy with her sister Elizabeth and was relieved now that she had a wonderful excuse not to go to her house. Joanna often helped her sister whenever she could. Helping Elizabeth started out as a good deed on Joanna's part but lately it had turned into a habit, for Elizabeth that is, she expected Joanna to be there every day.

If for any reason Joanna couldn't go to help her, Elizabeth would cry and carry on and say that Joanna didn't love her any more. Joanna had suspected for quite some time now that Elizabeth had a drinking problem but did not say anything to anyone about it.

For several weeks she wanted to tell Marie, her mother-in-law, about her but had decided against it, but she might have to soon or else May and little Nathaniel might get sick in that dirty house. Joanna knew that Elizabeth would never clean it herself.

'Maybe she'd go and visit her next week,' she thought.

• • •

Later that year in early summer something quite romantic happened in Barnstable that made the tongues of the women wag uncontrollably. Mary Glover Hinckley's oldest son, Nathaniel Glover, now all grown up, had moved back to Barnstable to live with his mother. It was May 13, 1668 and spring and romance were in the air and Nathaniel age 21 fell in love the moment he saw his stepsister Hannah Hinckley.

Thomas Hinckley's oldest daughter Hannah, whose mother was Mary Richards Hinckley, was now 19 years old. They had known each other as children, of course, and had seen each other occasionally over the years but while Nathaniel was away at school during the last four years Hannah had grown into a beautiful young lady.

The women and the young people of Barnstable were all whispering about Nathaniel and Hannah when they learned that a romance was growing under the same roof. Nathaniel and Hannah were seen sitting together in church and walking hand in hand whenever they were together. Some people not knowing that they were not blood relatives considered this relationship to be incest and they were appalled. The women insisted that their husbands do something about it.

The Reverend Mayo questioned Mary Hinckley for almost an hour. He said that many people were gossiping about the relationship between her son Nathaniel and her husband's daughter Hannah. Mary insisted that nothing improper was happening under her roof and she approved of the romance.

Nathaniel and Hannah were called to the Reverend's home and they all talked about the young couple's intentions. They told him that they wanted to be married in July and by the end of the meeting they all agreed that because they were not immediately related he would approve their marriage and he apologized to Mary.

Immediately related meant brother and sister, father and daughter, mother and son or first cousins. Second cousins were not considered immediate relatives and were allowed to marry.

• • •

Nathaniel Fitzrandall and his wife Samantha moved back to Barnstable in early May and he was taken to court on June 5, 1668 and fined 42 shillings because he refuse to pay 21 shillings for his share of the ministers salary. Nathaniel did not like Reverend Walley and did not attend church. He willingly paid the fine as long as the Reverend did not receive any of it. The court promised him that his fine would be used for governmental purposes only.

• • •

Mary Barker married Samuel Pratt on June 10, 1668 in the Barnstable Church. Her sister, Anne Barker was seeing Samuel's brother John and they were planning to marry the following June. John and Samuel Pratt were brothers and Anne and Mary Barker were sisters, this was the talk of Barnstable for many weeks.

Abraham walked Mary down the aisle and placed her hand in Samuel's hand and said, "Take good care of this lovely young lady for the rest of your life."

Samuel said, "I will sir."

The Church was full of friends and relatives and a lovely buffet was served on the church lawn following the wedding.

• • •

Abraham Blish settled his second wife Hannah's estate with her second daughter Mary Barker Pratt in the amount of 10 pounds on October 27, 1668. Her husband Samuel witnessed the settlement and signed his name on the legal document after Abraham signed his.

Patricia Louise Blish Gould

CHAPTER THIRTY-SIX
1669

John Bursley died on February 23, 1669 he was 84 years old and was one of the first settlers of Barnstable in 1639. His wife was the former Mary Hull daughter of Rev. Joseph Hull she was 48. His farm was not large but it was substantial and he was a good provider to his family of two daughters and two sons.

He was in his early sixties when his youngest daughter Elizabeth was born and he spoiled her from the first day he held her in his arms. He was very seldom strict with her when she was growing up and gave her everything she wanted. He said she was pretty enough to be a princess in the Queen's palace he would tell her that a princess didn't have to work, all they had to do was play and do what ever they wanted to.

Mary would get very upset with him, but it was easier for her to do Elizabeth's chores herself than to argue with the two of them. At his funeral Elizabeth made a big scene about not wanting to live without her precious father. People felt very sorry for Mary Bursley and were glad that she had her lovely daughter Joanna to help her get through the loss of her husband. They knew that Elizabeth was too selfish to be of any comfort to her.

• • •

John Crocker died on March 5, 1669 at the age of 65. He left his wife Joan the Crocker Inn, and the rest of his estate he left to his nephews, his brother William's sons. The people of Barnstable attended his funeral out of kindness for Joan.

• • •

Several days later Henry Coxwell died in Salem a broken old man with only the clothes on his back, which was what he deserved as far as many people were concerned. He was Gracie Gent's lover and in 1652 was banned from Barnstable. No one grieved over his death.

• • •

Richard and Mehitabel Child of Watertown had a baby girl they named Experience born February 16, 1669. Marie Dimmock was there and this time the new baby granddaughter was healthy. When she returned home to Barnstable all of her friends were overjoyed with her good news.

• • •

Sarah Blish and Richard Orchyard's son Edward was born on April 12, 1669. She didn't feel like traveling during her pregnancy and she had only gone to England with Richard once during the year before. When she sent word to Abraham that he had another grandson she promised him that she would try to see him in late summer. If not then, she would definitely see him at Christmas time.

• • •

On April 15, 1669 Stephen Burden was born to William and Deborah Burden their fourth child. William was settled into his life as a family man and ran the gristmill now while Deborah tended their children and her daily chores at home.

Abraham was now the grandfather of four boys and two girls.

• • •

On June 10, 1669 Annie Barker married John Pratt. Mary and Annie Barker married Samuel and John Pratt. Abraham walked her down the aisle and put her hand in John's hand and told him to cherish her forever. He said, "I will Mr. Blish."

Mary and Annie looked very much alike and John and Samuel could have passed or twins. They often confused people when they were all together and many laughs were had between them, sometimes they tried to confuse people on purpose.

The church was full of family and friends and a lovely meal was served following the service on the church lawn.

Annie Pratt's real name was Anne and Abraham registered it in his journal with a note stating that she now had the same name that his lovely wife Anne had before he married her. Though Annie Pratt was a lovely girl she would never be as beautiful in his eyes as his lovely Anne was.

• • •

The first baby of Samuel and Mehitabel Allyn Annable was born on July 14, 1669. They named him Samuel Annable, Jr. His grandmother, Anna Annable was delighted to finally have a grandchild of her own. Anthony's grandchildren were from his first wife Jane's daughters. Anna loved them, but it just wasn't the same as having her own.

Anthony had a soft place in his heart for little Samuel, too. He was the first son of his only son. "You will inherit all of the Annable property," Anthony whispered to his new grandson, "you will be a rich man someday, Sammy."

• • •

After a court hearing Robert Harper was whipped at the post on May 2, 1669 for censuring Mr. Thomas Walley, Jr. Robert was a handy man about town and not very well educated, however he never refused to help any one and was very handy when it came to repairing furniture, broken door latches and anything else that gentlemen farmers or businessmen were to busy to repair. The widows and elderly often called upon him to help them do chores as well as repairs.

443

Abraham assisted Robert at the hearing and acted as Robert's attorney. Robert had helped Abraham many times in the past and he trusted him to be an honest man and had never known him to lie.

Robert knew that he needed assistance in this matter and although Abraham was not a lawyer, he trusted his judgment and knew that he would be treated fairly by the court if Abraham represented him.

Robert did not like the young Mr. Walley very much. The Rev. Walley's son was just the opposite of his father, he was a rotund and a pompous sort of man that many people disliked.

At the trial the first question that Abraham asked Robert was to tell the jurors why he was at Widow Mary Bursley's home on April 20.

Robert cleared his throat and said, "Mrs. Bursley's sent word to me that she needed me to go to her home to do some chores."

Abraham smiled at Robert to ease his nervousness and said, "Please continue, what happened next?"

Robert took a deep breath and tried to sound calm and said, "As I was coming from the woodshed at Mrs. Bursley's home with a big armful of wood for her fireplace I met Mr. Walley coming toward me down the path and I greeted him politely."

He glanced at Mr. Walley who was seated in the front row of the courthouse with his walking stick in front of him between his knees, both hands were placed over the shiny gold knob and he was using it as a leaning post.

Robert cleared his throat and said, "Mr. Walley grunted at me and said a few words that I didn't catch."

Abraham asked, "Was Mr. Walley's tone pleasant."

Robert looked at Abraham and said, "I don't think it was, I couldn't understand the words."

"You may continue," Abraham said.

"Just as we met it seems that Mr. Walley accidentally bumped into me," Robert said cautiously and looked at Abraham.

Abraham nodded for him to continue and the twinkle in his eyes told him he was doing fine.

"The bump made me lose my balance and I nearly fell into a puddle of water, but I managed to catch myself, getting only one-foot wet, although I did drop several large pieces of wood into the water and it splashed onto my shoes and stockings."

Several snickers were heard from the back of the courtroom, but Robert politely ignored them and continued. "I looked at Mr. Walley and he was grinning at me with a satisfied expression on his face."

"What do you mean by a 'satisfied expression'," Abraham asked Robert.

Robert looked directly at Mr. Walley and said, "I believe that he was trying to deliberately push me into the water for some unknown reason and when he failed to do that he became satisfied with the fact that he made me drop the wood and get my feet wet."

Mr. Walley tried to look stricken that anyone would think badly of him, but his expression did not fool Robert and he continued again.

"I started to apologize to Mr. Walley thinking that I had caused the wood to fall, but when I saw the smirk on his face I knew that this whole scene was a deliberate act on his part," Robert raised his chin and looked at Abraham again.

"What did you say or do then," Abraham asked knowing that Robert needed encouragement.

"I don't know what came over me," Robert said as he raised his chin a little higher, "I guess I was a little angry because I said, 'Why you big fat pompous walrus you did that deliberately'."

Several of the jurors smiled and then quickly covered their mouths with the back of their hands. The courtroom became a buzzing noise though several loud laughs were plainly heard.

The courtroom quieted after Judge John Crow banged his gavel several times.

Abraham said to Robert, "Did you apologize to Mr. Walley for your unkind words."

"Yes, I did immediately," Robert said, "but Mr. Walley only made a noise in his throat that sounded like 'harump' and turned around and walked away toward the road."

"What exactly did you say then Robert," Abraham asked.

"I said, 'excuse me Sir for my rudeness, I don't know what came over me,'" Robert answered, "and those were my exact words Mr. Blish."

The Judge asked if there were any other witnesses to the incident. No one stepped forward so he excused the jury to deliberate Robert's case.

In less than twenty minutes the jurors were back with their verdict and Robert was found guilty by his own confession of calling Mr. Walley a big fat pompous walrus.

The judge told him that as punishment he would receive five lashes the next morning.

Robert knew that it was a just punishment, as one did not call another man names, no matter how angry you were or how inconsiderate that person was.

The next morning in front of many townspeople Robert's punishment was carried out. It seemed only right that Mrs. Bursley took Robert into her home after his punishment and washed his wounds and applied the herbal salves that she had been given by Marie Dimmock.

As Mrs. Bursley treated Robert she apologized to him for not coming forward to help him in court and she confessed that she had witnessed the whole thing.

She also told Robert that Mr. Walley had been in her home trying to seduce her. She had been rude to him and would have nothing to do with him; after all he was much younger than she was and also a married man with a family, he became angry with her and left in a rage. He had taken his anger out on Robert.

Mary Bursley was crying softly as she finished confessing the guilt she felt for not helping Robert. "I did not want the whole town to know about this," she said. "I knew if some people found out about Mr. Walley's indiscretions, they might think that I was the one to start an affair and that is not the case at all." She sniffed and blew her nose and continued, "I do not like that man, preacher's son or not. He is a very vulgar person. I pity poor Little Hannah."

Robert patted her on the back and told her that he forgave her. A year later he proved it by marrying her. The talk died down and the situation was forgotten. Mr. Walley's evil ways and thoughts had still not caught up with him yet.

Shortly after Christmas Abraham got up in the morning to find" Daisy asleep in front of the fireplace as usual, or he thought she was. After he put a few small logs on the fire and she didn't move as she always did, he patted her head thinking that the old dog must be getting deaf, too.

She had been unable to see very well for the last year or so and she would often follow him wherever he went, stop and lay down when he stopped and then get up and trail along after him when he continued on. Lately she would only follow him to the end of the lane and then lay down and wait for him to come home.

This morning she didn't move when he stepped over her or even flinch her ear when he patted her head, he knew she was gone. He put his hand on her belly to see if he could feel her heart beating, she was cold to his touch. "You poor dear dog," he said out loud as he picked her up in his arms, I guess you've had a nice long life, but I'm sure going to miss you." He laid her back down in front of the hearth and then pulled his boots on, put his coat on and then picked Daisy up again and carried her out to the barn. He asked one of the hired men to see if they could dig a hole under the big Maple tree down the lane and bury her for him. He found a grain bag and put her in it and tied it closed. "Dig the hole as deep as you can, Jonas, I don't want anything digging her up again," he said.

"I will Mr. Blish," Jonas said with a tear in his eye, "I think the ground is still soft enough, I'll make her a casket, too if you don't mind."

"That will be kind of you, Jonas," Abraham said. "I guess I'd better go and write Johnny a letter." Abraham patted his hired man on his shoulder, "I'll tell him how you buried him, my friend."

Daisy had been a pet to everyone on the Blish farm for 15 years. She was 105 in a dog's age, they were all going to miss her.

Patricia Louise Blish Gould

CHAPTER THIRTY-SEVEN
1670

Overland traveling was getting easier. The settlers used well-worn Indian trails. The longest one from Plymouth to Barnstable was called the Cross Way to Sandwich. From this trail lanes led to scattered houses and to the Great Marsh and the Meetinghouse.

On May 29, 1670, at town meeting Abraham was again proclaimed to be a freeman along with Nathaniel Bacon, Sr. and Anthony Annable.

A month later on June 30, 1670, a horrible tragedy happened. Nathaniel Goodspeed died unexpectedly at the young age of 27; he left his wife Elizabeth Bursley Goodspeed with two small children to raise by herself. May age 3 and Nathaniel, Jr. age 1. Elizabeth was grief stricken for several weeks, though it was probably more guilt than grief that she felt.

Elizabeth Bursley had been a very spoiled child because, against her mothers wishes her father never made her do any of the chores that most children had to do. If she decided to disobey her mother's requests to help with the household duties, which was the way girls learned to become a good wife and mother, her father made excuses for her and would see that one of the maid servants children did her chores for her.

"Now you know that she's a little princess, Mary," John would say.

Mary Bursley had many discussions with her husband over this way of bringing up their daughter.

"She's no more a princess than Joanna is," Mary would reply.

Mary knew that Elizabeth would not make a good wife or mother if she did not learn to do any of the things that children had to learn at a young age.

Mary was right but John Bursley could never see any wrong in his beautiful daughter.

When she insisted on getting married at the young age of 17 her mother refused to even talk to her about it. But after several weeks of pouting and crying and pleading, Elizabeth convinced her father that she and Nathaniel Goodspeed were in love, her father relented and persuaded her mother to give in to her.

Mary Bursley knew that Nathaniel Goodspeed loved her daughter very much, but she wasn't sure if her selfish daughter loved Nathaniel or just the thought of getting her own way.

Nathaniel's father Roger and his mother Alice did not approve of the arrangement, but Nathaniel was in love with Elizabeth so they also gave their approval. Roger gave Nathaniel money enough to buy a nice lot across the meadow from their original home in Barnstable and helped him build a small house on it.

Elizabeth Bursley had dark blonde hair and pale blue eyes that seemed to sparkle every time she smiled at Nathaniel. However, after they were married for several weeks the real truth came out. Elizabeth so spoiled by her father expected Nathaniel to treat her the same way and give in to her every wish and whim. She found excuses each time he came home to a cold meal or dirty house.

Nathaniel put up with Elizabeth's laziness most of the time because she always convinced him that she was sick because of her pregnancy. Or she had a headache or it was too cold or too dark; she always had an excuse why she wasn't able to do her duty as a wife.

Most of the time she would get Henrietta Jackson, her neighbor, to help her or one of Henrietta's daughters, Milly 18 and Laura 17.

The Jackson's had eight children ranging from age 32 to 17 and their two oldest sons were married and they each had two young children and lived nearby. There always seemed to be someone Elizabeth could get to do her chores for her.

The smile she gave them always dazzled them into helping her, especially the younger boys, but not Henrietta's youngest daughter Laura.

Laura would not lift a finger to help Elizabeth after she found her asleep one day in the middle of the afternoon with a pint of beer spilled all over her clothes, the table and floor. May, only two years old at the time was asleep on the floor by her mother's feet and Laura could tell that she had been crying. The little girl's face was dirty and tear streaked and she was making little hiccups in her sleep.

Laura quietly went home leaving everything the way it was and told her mother that Elizabeth was drunk.

Henrietta went quickly to Elizabeth's rescue, cleaned her and baby May up, picked up her mess and made her promise never to do such a thing again or she would tell Nathaniel.

Joanna Bursley Dimmock helped her sister sometimes, but since her baby was born she had refused to call on her very often because every time she did, she would clean her house for her and get a good meal for Nathaniel.

Then Elizabeth would accept the credit for it not bothering to tell Nathaniel that her sister had been visiting her all day.

Elizabeth was good about concealing her drinking problem for more than a year after May was born.

During this time she became pregnant with Nathaniel Jr. she stayed sober during her pregnancy and for about six months after.

But lately Henrietta noticed that she had been relying on her and her daughters more and more.

She would have to tell Nathaniel, no matter how much it hurt him if Elizabeth didn't straighten herself out pretty soon.

Nathaniel and Elizabeth had had an argument the day that Nathaniel died. Nathaniel had asked Elizabeth every day for the past four days to wash his shirts for him. He had been planting for the last two weeks and had worn all three of his shirts several days each. They were dirty and stiff with perspiration and they made his underarms chafed and sore. The first day she complained of having a headache and told him she would see if Henrietta would do her wash for her the next day, after all she had no time for such hard work with two small children to care for. The second day she told him that Nathaniel, Jr. was fussy all day. The third day she had a very bad backache, he couldn't remember what her reason was for not washing his clothes yesterday. Maybe he hadn't bothered to ask her.

That morning when he got out of bed he asked, "Where did you put my clean shirts, Elizabeth?" He fumbled around in the darkness of the bedroom.

Elizabeth moaned slightly and rolled over pretending to be asleep. He poked her in the side with his finger and said a little louder, "Elizabeth, where did you put my clean shirts?"

She groaned and moved further toward the edge of the bed away from him and said, "Leave me alone."

Nathaniel really didn't want to wake the children but she was really beginning to irritate him, "Elizabeth," he said again louder, "I asked you where you put my clean shirts."

"Shush, Nathaniel, you'll wake the children," she told him sternly, "I couldn't find anyone to do the wash for me yesterday, I'll try again today."

Nathaniel became furious with her and this time he shouted, "You've been promising me that you would do the wash for the last four days," hoping he would wake the children, she never did anything during the day anyway. It wouldn't hurt her to get up early just once and take care of them. He put his dirty shirt back on and left the room.

Most mornings if the baby was awake before he left for the fields he would change his diaper and put him in bed with Elizabeth so she could feed him. He would kiss them both good-bye and then around 9 o'clock he would go home for breakfast that was usually prepared by one of Henrietta's girls. They would have their breakfast together and then he would put a couple of pieces of bread or some biscuits in a sack for his noon meal and be home just before dark for their evening meal. Lately however, Elizabeth would still be in her bedclothes when he came home for breakfast.

Once just a week ago when he came home for his morning meal little May was trying to change her baby brother's very soiled diaper and Elizabeth was still asleep in bed. He woke her up and asked, "Elizabeth, are you sick? Baby Nathaniel has made a mess and our little daughter is trying her best to clean him up."

Elizabeth moaned and put her hand to her head and sat up on the edge of the bed and said, "What is it? What time is it?"

Nathaniel thought that she reeked of stale beer, but lately she had not been keeping herself clean so he wasn't sure just what the odor was that he smelled.

"Get up," he said again, "the children need you. Now," he shouted as he but a half loaf of bread in a sack along with two apples and went out the door slamming it behind him. He could hear the baby crying and almost turned around and went back in, but he knew he had to do something to make Elizabeth a better wife and mother. Maybe letting her know how angry he was would help.

Elizabeth got out of bed slowly her head was spinning. She was so thirsty she thought as she made her way to the drinking pail on the shelf near the table. She drank a dipper of the cold water and sat down on the bench near the table.

Across the room May was still trying to clean her baby brother's behind with an old rag. The baby was wiggling and squirming against the coldness of the cloth and May was trying her best to hold her breath against the smell.

Elizabeth got another rag from the shelf beside the water pail and went over to them and kneeled down beside her children and cleaned up her baby and changed his diaper. She put the baby in his basket and asked May if she was hungry.

Little May shook her head yes. She went back to the water pail and took another clean rag and washed her little girl's face and hands. Tears ran down her cheeks as she covered a piece of bread with apple butter and put it in front of little May. She poured a mug of milk from the pitcher in the cupboard for her daughter and sat down beside her.

She was hungry too, but the smell of her daughter's breakfast, meager as it was, made her decide that she was more thirsty than hungry. She wanted a mug of beer but decided that she would have cider instead. Last years cider was bitter, but it always made her feel better faster than the beer. She went to the crock in the corner of the room near the door and lifted the cover, she moved a little of the scum that always formed on top and dipped her mug into the golden liquid. She shivered at the first swallow but then drank down the rest in several big gulps. She dipped her mug back in for a refill and then put the cover back on the crock. She sipped her cider while May finished her breakfast and then she helped her little girl get dressed.

Now, today, when Nathaniel left she got out of bed when she heard the door slam, she had to use the chamber pot, and when she pulled it out from under the bed it slopped over onto the floor. She had not emptied it the day before. She had no choice now, she carefully lifted it and carried it through the house out to the necessary in the woodshed and dumped it into the hole then she sat down and peed. She rinsed the pot out with the water that was in a bucket by the back door and took it into the house and slid it back under her bed.

Her feet were cold, she looked around for her shoes and found one under the chair and one under the pile of dirty clothes and slipped them on. Then went back outside to see if she could find her neighbor. Elizabeth saw her near the barn and called her name. Henrietta looked her way and called, "Good Morning Ma'am."

Elizabeth motioned for her to come to the house and as Henrietta came closer Elizabeth asked her if she would fetch enough water for clothes washing.

Henrietta said, a little reluctantly, "Yes, Ma'am, I'll get one of the children on it right away."

Elizabeth put her hand to her head and turned back toward the house. She had a headache again and her stomach gurgled. Baby Nathaniel was starting to wake up and was making little fussing noises. He had been sleeping a lot lately and it worried Elizabeth a little, but she thought it was best if he slept because the quiet helped her morning headaches.

Elizabeth gathered up Nathaniel's dirty shirts and her dresses and the rags that she had been using for her baby and found two of May's dresses and put them by the back steps.

"I have the wash water ready, Ma'am," Henrietta called through the open door.

Elizabeth handed her the dirty clothes and went back to the table, sat down and picked up her mug of cider and took a big gulp. The baby was crying hungrily now so Elizabeth got up and went to his cradle and picked him up. She sat down on the edge of the bed put him to her breast and tried to feed him, but he spit her nipple from his mouth and gagged.

She got up and went back to the doorway and asked, "Henrietta would you please find someone to feed my baby, he doesn't seem to want my milk anymore, he chokes and gags every time I put him to my breast."

The wash tub sat on a heavy table near the back door and Henrietta had the dirty clothes in it along with some lye soap and was stirring them with a big paddle. "Yes, Ma'am," she said a little disgruntled. She stepped into the house and trying not to gag from the smell, she took the baby from his mother. "I'll feed him at my house and take May with me," she said, trying to hold her breath. "We'll be back after the noon meal."

Henrietta took little Nathaniel out of his mother's arms and said, "Come with me little ones, Auntie Henrietta will get you something to eat." She sighed out loud as she put Baby Nathaniel over her shoulder and took May by the hand and headed toward her home across the yard.

"All right," Elizabeth said, "I have a lot to do," and looked around her messy house, the baby's dirty diapers were piled in a corner of the commonroom and there were dishes piled on the table and on the counter. The dishpan sat full of dirty dishwater with scum on the top of it. The scum made her think of the cider crock, maybe she would have just another little sip before she started cleaning she thought and picked up a mug from the table.

Henrietta's grandson was almost two and was eating table food as well as nursing. Her daughter-in-law, Bertha always seemed to have plenty of milk for both babies. Bertha didn't mind helping Elizabeth; many women fed their neighbor's babies for them. She had been nursing baby Nathaniel for almost four months now. Lately, however, she smelled the rank smell of stale beer or strong cider whenever she was near Elizabeth.

Henrietta agreed with her that Elizabeth was drinking too much beer and cider again but they were both in hopes that Elizabeth would stop soon.

Nathaniel was still angry as he walked back to the cornfield eating a slice of dry bread. It had started to cloud up just before he went home for breakfast and now it was starting to rain.

'Another reason for her not to do the wash,' he thought. Tears started to gather in the corner of his eyes as he thought about how happy they were just three short years ago.

'What is the matter with Elizabeth?' he wondered, 'could it be the children?'

Memories circled around in his head. 'She seemed so happy when we were first married and was really a good mother, of course I know that Henrietta is a big help to her, but all in all she cares very much for our children.'

He smiled to himself thinking, 'She still hasn't quite mastered her cooking yet, but Henrietta is helping her with that too.'

He signed out loud, 'Maybe there is something wrong with her head, she's always complaining of bad headaches.'

He rubbed the rain from his face with his wet sleeve, 'I'll have to talk with Marie Dimmock next Sunday at church, maybe she can give Elizabeth a tonic or something.'

The rain was coming down pretty steady by the time he reached the field and he could hear thunder off in the distance. 'If I hurry,' he thought to himself, 'I'll be able to finish this field before the storm gets here, it never hurts to plant in the rain,' he smiled to himself, 'I won't have to water the rows when I'm done.'

He was feeling a little better now that he had decided to confide in Mrs. Dimmock.

As the rain soaked into his shirt he said out loud, "well, she won't have to wash this one now," and he picked up his planting stick and his bag of seed.

Samuel Jackson and his two oldest sons had not yet returned to the field when he reached the row he had left off at earlier. He took his sack of seed corn and started down the next row with his sharp stick. He pushed his planting stick easily into the soft wet dirt and dropped a few seeds of corn into the hole then scuffed the soil around it and pushed down with the ball of his foot.

He didn't wear his shoes when he planted, he liked to feel the soft dirt under his feet and he could tell easier just how hard to push the seeds down into the soil when he was barefooted.

Nathaniel was half way down the row when he heard a loud clap of thunder; in fact he jumped a little pulling his head down into his shoulders. 'Wow,' he thought, 'that was close,' but he had about a cup full of seeds left and decided to finish planting them before he stopped to let the storm pass.

Nathaniel never heard the next thunderclap. His body flew off the ground about a foot and then it fell back to the ground making a few spasmodic movements on it own. The life had left Nathaniel Goodspeed's body as quickly as the flash was seen by Samuel Jackson who was walking down the road at the edge of the field.

Samuel saw the lightening bolt that hit Nathaniel and then smelled the burning flesh of the young man's feet. "Nathaniel," he yelled, "Oh, Nathaniel, Nathaniel," he kept repeating as he ran across the rows of newly planted corn.

His oldest son Jacob was right behind him staring with his mouth open in amazement.

"Go and get help Jacob," Samuel said as he bent over the lifeless body.

"Where?" Jacob asked bewildered.

"Run to Mr. Blish's," he said sadly, "Hurry." He knew that Nathaniel was dead and Abraham's house was the closest, he didn't know what else to do.

"What ever would happen to Elizabeth and the children now," he said quietly. Henrietta had told him during their breakfast what she suspected Elizabeth was doing. Mrs. Goodspeed, Nathaniel's mother, and Mrs. Bursley, Elizabeth's mother, would have to know, too, he thought, but Abraham will know what to do. Tears ran down his cheeks, "Oh, Nathaniel," he said again, his second son was standing beside him patting his shoulder, he was crying, too.

When Abraham reached the field Nathaniel's body was still smoking, the smell was horrible. The rain had slowed down and between him and Samuel they moved Nathaniel's body to the edge of the field onto the grass. Samuel sent Jacob to the barn to get the wagon.

Abraham banged on the door of Nathaniel's house and when Elizabeth Bursley Goodspeed answered it she was still in her nightgown.

"Elizabeth," Abraham said, "Please come out to the wagon, Nathaniel is dead he was struck by lightening."

Elizabeth said, "What? Nathaniel is in the field planting," and turned to go back into the house.

Abraham said, "Elizabeth, please get dressed and come with me to the Reverend's home, we're taking his body there."

By this time Jacob had told his mother what had happened and Henrietta came into the house through the back door and heard what Abraham was saying to Elizabeth.

"I'll help her Mr. Blish, I'll bring her to the Reverend's home as soon as I can," Henrietta said.

Abraham nodded and said, "Thank you," and closed the door.

He heard Henrietta raise her voice to Elizabeth saying, "Young lady you get yourself dressed this minute. Jacob is waiting to take you to the Reverend's house, now hurry." Henrietta took Elizabeth by the arm and marched her into her messy bedroom where Elizabeth lay down on the edge of the bed.

"Why are they taking Nathaniel to the Reverend's house?" she asked.

Henrietta found a dress that looked more or less clean and threw it in Elizabeth's direction, "Put this on Elizabeth, and hurry." She looked around a little more and found a clean apron on one of the shelves 'she must have forgotten that she had this,' she thought to herself.

Elizabeth slipped out of her nightgown and pulled the dress on over her head.

Henrietta put the apron around the waist of the inebriated young woman and turned her around so she could tie it. "Here, put your shawl on," she said as she pushed her toward the door.

Elizabeth hardly knew what was happening. Henrietta wanted to feel sorry for her, but she couldn't. It was all she could do to be as kind to her as she was.

Jacob called to his mother from the front door, "The buggy is ready, mother," he said.

"Elizabeth is ready too Jacob, she'll be right out," and she took Elizabeth's arm and led her out of the house toward the buggy. "The Reverend will know what to do with her I hope," she said to Jacob. "Tell him I think he should call Marie Dimmock, Elizabeth needs some medicine."

Marie Dimmock was already at the Reverend's home when Jacob arrived with Elizabeth. Abraham helped her down from the buggy and led her toward Nathaniel's body that was still laying in the wagon. The rain had washed most of the dirt off him and Marie had wiped his face and patted his hair back. When she looked at Elizabeth she knew immediately that she was drunk, not only from the smell of her but from the way her eyes were all blood shot and she stumbled as she walked toward her.

"I have some medicine that I will prepare for her Abraham," Marie said, "help her into the house," and she turned and went quickly into Reverend Walley's home. She mixed some Hops, Passion Flower, Golden Seal and Chaparral herbs together and put them into some hot water and by the time Elizabeth was in the house and seated at the table Marie had the strong tea ready.

She put her hand on Elizabeth's shoulder and said, "Elizabeth can you hear me?"

Elizabeth looked at Marie and said, "Marie, Nathaniel's dead."

"Yes, dear and you have to drink this medicine, all of it as quickly as you can," she said firmly and held the cup to Elizabeth's lips.

Elizabeth obeyed her and when she was finished Marie gave her another cup, she didn't make her drink it all at once this time, "Just sip this one my dear, you'll feel better in a few minutes."

Elizabeth said, "I have to see my mother, I want to go home to my mother's house."

Abraham said, "We have already sent for her Elizabeth, she'll be here soon."

Nathaniel Goodspeed was buried the next day and Elizabeth packed her belongs and moved back home with her mother. Roger and Alice Goodspeed took their son's children, May and Little Nathaniel, home with them to Marstons Mills. Elizabeth did not object, in fact some people thought she was relived.

• • •

Henry Cobb and John Chipman were made ruling elders at the annual town meeting held on June 4, 1670. They attended to the admission of members, ordination of officers; excommunication of offenders renounced by the Church and saw to it that they atoned for their wrong doings. Deacons attended to the 'temporal things of the church' leaving the Reverend to see to the religious needs of the congregation. Other members of the town council stayed in their respective offices for another year.

• • •

Abraham, Jr. was now 16 and wanted to go to College in Boston and study architecture. Sarah was willing to have him live with her and she promised to keep him safe. Abraham, Jr. had read all of the books that Abraham had in his collection as well as all of the books that were available to the children at school. He was a good student and a very bright young man.

Abraham reluctantly agreed to let him go after receiving confirmation for his enrollment from the Boston University on September 2, 1670. So at age 16, Abraham Blish, Jr. moved to Boston with Sarah and Richard to attend College. He threw himself into his studies majoring in architecture and theology and received excellent marks. He was a model student and was well known as an ambitious young man. He was thought to be a 'dandy' by many of his classmates because he was always meticulously dressed, and he was never seen with any of the young women that were forever seeking his attention.

Sarah sent several messages to Abraham that fall, assuring him that Abraham, Jr. was doing well in school and that she would see him soon. However, they were not able to go to Barnstable until just before Christmas.

They stayed for two weeks and had a wonderful holiday. The weather cooperated with them and traveling was easy. Abraham, Jr., Sarah and the children went back to Boston on December 31, 1670 soon after Sarah received a letter from Richard telling her he would be home on January 5th. She was delighted and could hardly wait to see him. She hated it when he had to be gone away on business during a holiday. He usually made it up to her though and lavished wonderful gifts upon her when he came home. She knew he would do the same this year. She missed him so much.

CHAPTER THIRTY-EIGHT
1671

Abraham received word from Richard More that his first mother-in-law, Sarah Pratt had passed away on February 12, 1671 and her funeral was to be held on February 15th.

Abraham immediately went to John Willis and made arrangements for him and Joseph to go to Duxbury. Richard also stated in the message that he had already notified Sarah and Richard Orchyard. They were all to meet at Richard and Mary's home and go to the funeral from there. It was a very sad day for Abraham and he was so glad to have his daughter and son with him.

Abraham and Joseph took the schooner to Boston with Sarah and Richard after the funeral and then they said their goodbyes with hugs and promises to see each other soon. Captain Willis brought them home to Barnstable.

Richard had been home only a few weeks before Sarah's grandmother passed away and she was so glad to have him home with her during her time of sorrow. After they were home from her grandmother's funeral for a week or so she rallied herself around knowing that her grandmother was in heaven and happy, and she had her children to care for. But Richard seemed to be grieving more than she was and she couldn't understand why he continued to be depressed and he seemed to be unhappy most of the time. She tried to coax him into a happy state of mind, but wasn't able to succeed. Finally in late February, Richard told her that several of his business partners in England had been robbing him blind. He had managed to find out in time before they stole everything from him, but their finances were not what they used to be and he was worried that she would leave him if he became penniless.

Sarah was appalled that his friends would do that to him, but convinced him that her love for him would never die and reminded him of their marriage vows, for richer or poorer. After several days of trying to console him and trying to help him decided who he could confide in, she convinced him that her father would probably be glad to help them. They still were not poor by any means; he still owned many properties. However, he would need help in deciding what properties he should keep and what he should sell. Somehow he had to make up for the losses he had taken in England.

Sarah sent a letter to her father by messenger explaining as well as she could the difficulty they were in and Abraham agreed to go over Richard's finances with him. So they all went to Barnstable on March 2nd.

After studying Richard's reports Abraham advised him about some of the options he had and suggested that they go to Duxbury and visit Richard More.

Sarah and the children stayed with Allice, it was too cold for the children to travel and she wasn't sure how long Richard and her father would be gone.

From Duxbury the three men went to Plymouth and Abraham introduced young Richard to some of the older more prominent businessmen there.

With Richard More's influence and Abraham's good word he did not have to sell any of his holdings.

Richard More was extremely happy to help and Abraham was as proud as a peacock when his son-in-law made a wonderful deal with the Plymouth Trade Commissioner.

On their way back to Barnstable Abraham and Richard had a chance to talk without any interruptions and he saw Richard in a different light. Abraham concluded that he and his son-in-law had finally become friends and he admitted to himself that Sarah had made the best choice after all.

Richard saw Abraham in a different light, too, not as a doting father that wanted to keep his daughter home forever to do his bidding, but as a very wise businessman.

Richard Orchyard actually made all of the decisions for the trade agreement; Abraham and Richard More only guided him to the right people.

Sarah and Richard stayed in Barnstable until the weather warmed up a bit, they left on April 10th they were anxious to get home. Abraham, Jr. had been left in the charge of Mr. Brattle and Sarah was anxious to see if everything had gone well with him while they were gone. It seemed to Sarah that she had been away from home a lot lately and she was pretty sure she was pregnant again.

• • •

Elder Henry Cobb was very proud of his third son Gershom when he was offered the job of Constable of Middleboro Colony. Gershom accepted and moved there in March of 1671. He was also in the militia and joined together with many other young men in the growing colonies to fight against any trouble that Metacomet's army might bestow upon them.

He was also proud of his oldest son for giving him another grandchild. James and Sarah Cobb had a daughter on March 28, 1671 they named her Hannah. Marie and Sarah helped her during her delivery.

"How many babies have we delivered?" Sarah Bourne asked her friend when they were on their way home.

"I don't know for sure but our first babies are now having babies," Marie said and they both laughed.

• • •

Samuel Crocker son of Deacon Job and Mary Crocker was born on May 15th, 1671. Samuel was their second son. Their first born child, two years before was stillborn and Mary was so afraid that Samuel would also be taken from her that she could hardly let him out of her arms.

Job would take the little one from her and lay him in his cradle whenever he thought that she had held him too long after feeding him. Sometimes she would cry and then he would hold her tight to his chest and try and soothe her telling her he was doing this only so his son could rest comfortably and he did not mean to hurt her. After a while she reluctantly gave in to his wishes and would put her baby in his cradle and just watch him sleep.

• • •

That September 3, 1671, Sarah Orchyard gave birth to her third son whom she named Richard. He was a small baby and was sickly and Sarah nursed him constantly for the first few months of his life until he grew strong enough so she could leave him for an hour or so with the nanny. By Christmas she was able to take him with her wherever she went, he had grown into a healthy bright-eyed baby. His hair was red like hers and just as curly and he had large blue eyes that seemed to laugh all the time.

Abraham wanted Sarah to bring little Richard to Barnstable for the Christmas holidays but she said she would rather not bring him out in the cold. She promised her father that if little Richard were healthy enough she would visit him in June.

Richard decided that messengers would do any business that he had to do in England during the winter months, he was going to stay home. He opened an office in Boston close to his home and was content to carry on his business from there. The messenger he hired had no authority to write his name on any papers so he did not worry about any bad deals that might be made.

The Blish farm was prospering and Joseph's cattle and horses were of a number where he could sell a few each spring and profit enough to set some money of his own aside.

Abraham was proud of his son and agreed most of the time with the decisions that he made in running the farm.

• • •

Elder Henry and Sarah Cobb had a daughter on September 11, 1671. Henry was 61 years old and Sarah was 43. They named her Experience, she was his 15th child and she was Sarah's 8th. Experience was not a very healthy baby her eyes were wide set and when she cried she made a gurgling sound.

Marie Dimmock did not hold much hope for the poor baby and told Sarah that she didn't think this baby would live very long. She was right, little Experience died on September 25, 1671. Marie Dimmock insisted that Sarah take her Blessed Tea and this time there was no argument about it. She made sure that Sarah didn't run out of the herb again like she did the previous winter.

• • •

Richard and Mary More visited with Abraham and Allice during the Thanksgiving holiday and spent a week with them. One evening when they were all together the children all wanted to hear one of Richard's stories. It was a little late so he told them that he had a short one for them this time. It was about the first wedding to take place in New England. The girls were all ears and the boys groaned but they all listened respectfully.

Mr. Edward Winslow and Susanna White were joined in marriage on May 22, 1621. This was the first marriage to be held in Plymouth, it was actually a marriage of convenience and not very romantic as I recall. You see Elizabeth Winslow wife of Edward, and William White, husband of Susanna died in the first sickness leaving both of them alone.

Widow White was left with two sons, Resolved, age two and a new baby Peregrine who was born November 30, 1620 on the Mayflower while it was still in the harbor. He was the first baby to be born in Plymouth. Mr. White was one of the first men to die in January; he developed scurvy and dysentery, as did many, and died on January 15, 1621. Mrs. White was in a horrible state of mind after that, not knowing how she would survive with two small children.

Edward Winslow's wife passed away shortly after that, I believe it was January 20 and he was left a widower with no one to care for his needs.

Mr. Isaac Allerton performed the wedding service; he was the Magistrate, or Judge, at the time, because our dear Governor Bradford was still not fully recovered from his near death sickness. He performed the service according to the custom of the Low Countries in England in which they lived. This marriage was more of a civil union because of a few questions that were brought up regarding any inheritance that the White children may receive from their late father. They considered the book of Ruth verse 4 in the bible as the kind of marriage that they would keep, a marriage of convenience.

Governor Bradford suggested that Mr. Winslow take the responsibility of caring for Mrs. White, after her husband died. She was in such a state of grief that Governor Bradford was afraid that both she and her baby would die. When he approached Mrs. White regarding this arrangement she agreed and seemed to regain her health soon after Mr. Winslow married her. Mr. Winslow also benefited from this arrangement and built them one of the first houses in the new colony.

The women tried to make this occasion joyful by picking wild flowers and strewing them over the ground where the bride and groom were to stand. They also prepared a little extra food for all those attending this special celebration. It turned out to be a lovely wedding taking place outside Mr. Brewster's home. None of the buildings were large enough to hold everyone, but the day was sunny and warm and for once the wind was almost at a standstill.

Susannah was a good wife and a good cook and Mr. Winslow enjoyed her company. After several weeks had passed, Mr. Winslow suggested to his new wife that they seek comfort in each other by sharing the same bed. He then asked Governor Bradford to bless their marriage with several bible verses during the next church service. Many of the verses that the Governor chose are still read to this day when two people are married.

Mr. Edward Winslow was well respected in our new colony and in 1649 he was chosen as one of the first selectmen in Plymouth. A selectman was appointed to act in behalf of the town in disposing of lands, to make inquiries into the state and condition of the poor and to provide for their comfort and find them employment. These men were also to direct the proper means of relief for the aged and decrepit and to attend other affairs of the town that might come up.

Mr. and Mrs. Winslow cared for each other deeply and they were married for over thirty years."

"Is that the end?" young Joseph asked.

"Yes, I'm afraid that it is," Richard said.

"You must remember more details next time you tell that story dear," Mary said smiling.

"I suppose I should," Richard agreed. "And I confess that there were a few more thoughts that I could have related if there were no little ears in the room, they may have made my story a little more interesting for the adults," Richard added.

"Maybe that's why it was just a short story," Abraham said chuckling as he got up from his chair.

"It is late and we should all be getting to bed," Allice said patting Richard on the shoulder, "I think it was a lovely tale."

"Thank you Allice," Richard said smiling.

"Come children," Mary said, "I'll tuck you in." The children followed her and the house was quite in no time.

Deborah and William bundled up their little ones and carried them across the yard to their nice warm beds.

Patricia Louise Blish Gould

CHAPTER THIRTY-NINE
1672

Marie Dimmock, age 56 and Sarah Bourne, age 55, were still helping babies into the world. Marie had been doing this for 32 years now and Sarah had been helping her for almost 28 years.

Sam and Mehitabel Annable had a baby girl on March 4, 1672 they named Hannah. Marie and Sarah helped Mehitabel through her delivery and both mother and child were in good health.

"Another granddaughter," Anthony Annable told Abraham that afternoon at their meeting, "so far I've been right, little Sam will be my only heir."

• • •

Richard and Mehitabel Child had a baby girl they named Abigail on June 16, 1672. Marie did not go to Watertown to help her daughter this time, but her delivery was easy and both her and the baby were healthy.

• • •

When Johnny Barker turned 21, on March 3, 1672 his Uncle, Captain John Williams, Sr. of Scituate, told him he had to leave giving him nothing for the hard work he had done for the past seven years. Johnny quietly left the Williams' farm and went directly to Boston. He found his stepbrother, Abraham, Jr. and told him what his Uncle had done to him. He hired a lawyer with the last few shillings to his name and a loan from Abraham, Jr. and sued his Uncle for breech of promise.

Although John Williams sent Johnny to school until he was 16, he treated his nephew as a "slave" for seven years and kept him employed in menial duties without wages. Captain Willims did not give him any of the profits derived from rents of land in Scituate that were owned by his father before his father had drowned twenty years before.

After several days of testifying as to how he was treated, Johnny Barker won his case.

The jury gave him 217 pounds and was appalled that Captain Williams had not allowed Johnny to learn a trade.

The jury also accused Captain Williams of being the wickedest man that ever was upon the face of the earth.

Johnny used the money wisely. He stayed with Richard and Sarah in Boston and went to college and studied law. He wanted to become an attorney and move back to Barnstable and engage himself in legal and business transactions.

Abraham thought that was a wonderful idea and told him if he needed anything he would be there to help him.

• • •

Joseph Blish joined the Barnstable Church on his 24th birthday, April 1, 1672.

• • •

On June 3 at the annual town meeting Joseph Blish was appointed Constable. Samuel Annable was elected Hayward and Abraham Blish, Joseph Hull, Nathaniel Bacon, Sr. and Job Crocker were appointed Selectmen.

• • •

On September 2, 1672 while visiting Richard and Mary More, Joseph Blish met Hannah Hull. Her father was Tristram Hull, a well-to-do landowner of Duxbury. Her Uncle was the late Joseph Hull, one of the founders of Barnstable. Abraham Blish and Joseph Hull had been town officials for many years both doing their part in keeping Barnstable growing.

Abraham had had a long talk with his son Joseph earlier in the summer. Their farm and Gristmill and other endeavors were prospering and their businesses were less demanding on their social lives.

"You need to start looking for a wife, Joseph," Abraham said one afternoon when they were on their way home from the Mill.

"I can't see myself married to any of the ladies here in town," Joseph replied, "they just don't appeal to me, Pa."

"I've noticed that several of them would consider you a suitable husband," Abraham said, smiling.

"Yes, Pa," Joseph answered, "I've seen their looks, I'm not blind, I'm just not ready."

Abraham was quiet for a minute and then he said thoughtfully. "Tristram Hull's daughter is an attractive young lady," Abraham looked at his son out of the corner of his eye and continued, "her name is Hannah." He knew he had his attention, so he finished his sentence, "Her father is a well-to-do landowner and businessman."

"I remember her from several years ago when we went to visit Richard and Mary More," Joseph said. "She's just a young girl, she can't be more than twelve years old."

"Tristram Hull and I have discussed this problem of yours and it seems that Hannah has the same problem that you do, she is not interested in getting married to anyone in Duxbury," Abraham chuckled. "See, you two already have something in common, neither of you can find anyone to marry."

Joseph smiled, "Two things, her name is Hannah, so was my step-mothers."

"Three things," Abraham laughed, "her uncle's name was Joseph and so is yours."

The two men walked a short distance amused with their own bantering.

"I guess I could meet her again and see for myself," Joseph said, "I suppose you have that all arranged, too?" Joseph questioned his father.

"No, I thought I would leave that up to you," Abraham answered smiling.

"Well, I guess I could send word to her father that I would like to meet her again, the next time we go to Richard's home," Joseph said. He wasn't sure if he wanted to commit to seeing her or not, "How old is she now?" he asked.

"She will be 15 in about six months and her father has confirmed in a document that she will collect her inheritance on her wedding day," Abraham said.

"Well, at least she won't be after my money," he laughed patting his father on the shoulder.

"I hear she's quite attractive now," Abraham said, "not the little freckled face girl you remember. She has blonde hair and blue eyes," he added when there was no response from his son.

"So what else do you know about her?" Joseph asked, his curiosity was beginning to get piqued a little.

"I am told that she also has a good child bearing figure," Abraham said, "but I'm not sure what that means exactly," he continued hastily.

"Hum, I guess I'll just have to see for myself," Joseph said. Blonde hair and blue eyes, he hoped all of their children would look exactly like her. His hair was red like his mothers and the boys had teased him when he was young. Girl's hair they taunted him especially on hot summer days when it curled about his face and ears. He made sure that it was long enough so that he could pull it tightly into a tail at the back of his head and tie it with a piece of ribbon, and he always wore his hat whenever possible.

"I'm planning to go to Duxbury day after tomorrow," Abraham said "would you care to go with me?"

"I think I could find the time," Joseph answered as nonchalantly as he could.

"How lucky I am to have a son that will do as I suggest," Abraham said smiling to himself.

"Always," Joseph said as he put his arm across his father's shoulder, he was almost three inches taller then his father now, and very proud to be Abraham Blish's son.

Needless to say Joseph was pleased to meet Hannah and they spent as much time together that week as possible talking about everything. He liked her very much.

CHAPTER FORTY
1673

At a special town meeting held January 16, 1673 Thomas Lumbart and James Cobb were chosen as Haywards and were asked to help Samuel Annable mend fences. About three feet of snow fell during the first two weeks of January and several hundred feet of fence was knocked down. Many men also needed help taking hay to their cattle and sheep.

• • •

Shubael and Joanna Dimmock had a son, their fourth baby, on February 16, 1673, they named him Shubael, Jr. Marie and Sarah helped Joanna with her delivery and everything went fine, both mother and son were healthy. Marie was a grandmother again.

• • •

At the annual town meeting held on June 6, 1673 Abraham was chosen as Grand Enquest again. Joseph Blish remained Constable for another year and Sam Annable was re-elected Hayward. James Cobb was elected Surveyor.

• • •

On July 8, 1673, James and Sarah Cobb had their fifth child, a son; they named James, Jr. James, Sr. was delighted to have a son at last, not that he didn't love his girls, but now he had a son to carry on his name.

Marie and Sarah helped Sarah Cobb deliver her baby and said they had not seen such a proud father for a long time.

• • •

On July 19, 1673 Samuel and Mehitabel Annable had their second son, they named him John. Samuel was happy to have another boy, now he had two to carry on his family name. Samuel was the only grown man left in New England named Annable. His four older sisters of course, had changed their names when they married.

When he picked up his new son for the first time he smiled and said, "Now its up to you and your brother Sammy to keep the Annable name going." He kissed his pretty wife Mehitabel and said, "but if they were all like Hannah I wouldn't care if the Annable name stopped with me."

He was delighted with his little girl Hannah. She was the image of her mother and smiled all the time. She never walked anywhere; she ran as fast as she could with her little short legs tagging along after her little brother. Mehitabel usually put a little apron around her because she often tripped over her dress, she looked like a little tiny housewife Samuel would say picking her up and snuggling her neck.

Samuel's happiness only lasted a little more than two weeks after his new son was born because his little daughter Hannah died accidentally on August 4, 1673. She was 17 months old.

Hannah was trying to follow her older brother Sammy down their front steps and fell, hitting her head on the corner stone at the bottom. Hannah lay there with out moving and it was a minute or so before her brother realized she was hurt and ran to get his mother.

When Mehitabel picked up her little girl she was bleeding from a large bump and gash on her forehead. She screamed to her husband, "Help, Samuel, Oh, Samuel, help," he had just left to go to the hay field; he was down the lane only a short distance.

Samuel turned around quickly when he heard Mehitabel scream his name and saw his frantic wife run into the house with his little girl in her arms.

Mehitabel grabbed a linen towel and wet it with cold water but the blood kept coming, she couldn't stop it. Hannah's eyes were large and round but Mehitabel knew she couldn't see anything and then the bleeding stopped.

"What happened," Samuel said breathlessly as he ran into the house. "Mehitabel, what happened," he said again taking the towel away from Hannah's little face.

"I think she fell off the steps," Mehitabel sobbed.

Sammy was crying too, "Baby fell down the steps," he said as he clung to his mother's skirts.

Mehitabel put her arm around her little boy and asked, "Did you see her fall Sammy?"

"Yes, she was going with me to the chicken house, she was going to help me get the eggs," he hiccuped between each sentence.

Samuel carried his baby girl into the bedroom and laid her on her bed. She didn't move. He closed her little eyes and covered her up with her quilt. Tears flowed down his face and he wiped them with the sleeve of his shirt as he went back into the parlor. "I'll go and get someone to help," he said to Mehitabel, "I'll be right back." He held her for a moment and whispered, "I think she gone."

Mehitabel collapsed into a chair and picked up her little Sammy, they cried together.

Samuel found his father about a half-mile away near the hayfield and collapsed in his arms. "What's the matter, Sam," Anthony asked hugging his son.

"Hannah fell off the steps, I think she's dead," Samuel sobbed and clung to his father.

"Oh, dear God," Anthony said and told one of the hired hands to go and find the Reverend.

When they got back to the house Mehitabel was in the bedroom holding her new baby and Sammy was holding his little sister's hand trying to get her to wake up.

"Papa, she won't wake up," the little boy said when his father and grandfather came into the room.

"Sammy, your little sister has gone to heaven," Samuel said as he picked up his son hugging him close.

Anthony examined his little granddaughter closely and put his ear to her chest. He heard nothing, he felt her neck to see if there was a pulse, he felt nothing. Tears rolled down his cheeks as he covered her head with the quilt. She was so beautiful he thought, as beautiful as any angel he had ever imagined. "She's gone to heaven," he whispered and said a prayer for her.

There was nothing for Reverend Walley to do when he arrived a little while later except to comfort the family. The funeral was held the next day and Mehitabel and Samuel grieved along with many of the other young parents that had lost a child.

As Grand Enquest, Abraham was obliged to record this terrible accident in the town records, so of course he had to question Mehitabel and Sam. He even had to ask little Sammy several questions. It broke his heart to see their grief.

"God needed another angel," he said giving Mehitabel a hug.

• • •

About two months later Nathaniel Bacon, Sr. died, it was October 2, 1673. He was only 59. His wife Hannah of 31 years was greatly saddened but she had known for several months that her husband was not going to live much longer.

Nathaniel had developed a severe pain in his stomach earlier that year causing excessive diarrhea and it had gotten progressively worse as the months went by. Lately he had been unable to eat anything except creamed soups or slightly flavored broth.

Marie Dimmock gave him some Culver's Root, Wild Lettuce, Willow Bark and Wintergreen leaves that she brewed into a strong tea; Hannah gave him just the right portion each day as Marie had directed. Marie also gave Hannah a strong tea made from the pain-killing herb, Wild Lettuce, and told her to increase the dose as often as Nathaniel needed it. She tried to make his last days as comfortable as she could.

Most days he was pain free when he took his medicine, but he was so frail and thin that he couldn't get out of bed. He told her he was ready to die and hoped that God would take him soon.

Hannah would say, "Nathaniel, you know you are much better today, we'll see if you can get out of bed for a while when I get my chores done."

He would always say, "As you wish my dear," and close his eyes and go to sleep.

On the afternoon of October 2ⁿᵈ they followed this same ritual, but when Hannah went in to check on him about an hour later he was gone. She sat beside his bed and cried for a while then got up and called to a hired hand to go and get the Reverend.

Nathaniel did not make a will but he left Hannah well to do. When his estate was settled at the end of the month it was appraised at 632 pounds sterling. He owned sixteen acres of land, a house lot containing twelve acres and another four acres west of Nicholas Davis' property. He also owned 32 acres of meadowland and several other tracts of land at Sandy Neck and at the commons. He was a tanner and a currier and had vats in the low grounds near his house, but he worked at tanning mostly in the winter planting and harvesting his fields during the remainder of the year.

Nathaniel was an active member of the town of Barnstable since its beginning. When he was young he was a poor man, without friends to assist him and did not have the advantage of a good education, but he had a good moral character, good business habits, and much energy and industry that more than compensated for those advantages that most men had.

Hannah was proud to be his wife and more proud that he was considered a prominent and influential man in the town of Barnstable serving as Constable for many years. He had also served the Colony Court faithfully all of his life as a member of the Council of War from 1658 to 1667 and a Deputy of the Colony Court for thirteen years from 1652 to 1665. He was also chosen as an assistant to the Court and elected annually from 1657 to 1673.

Hannah had always been there for him and they had raised a family together and were respected by everyone in town. What more could she ask for, except to have her husband back.

• • •

A few weeks later on November 5, 1673, Richard and Sarah Orchyard's baby Elizabeth was born their fourth child and first daughter. Sarah was delighted to have a girl at last. *"She looks like me too, Papa, she has red hair and blue eyes,"* Sarah wrote in the note that she sent her father.

Abraham had another grandchild, a total of eight now. He prayed everyday for her as he did for the rest of his family. During

Thanksgiving, Abraham and Allice went to Boston to see the new baby and they stayed for about a week.

When Abraham saw his new granddaughter for the first time it almost took his breath away, she looked just like Sarah did when she was born. "So beautiful," he whispered.

• • •

Abraham and Allice stopped in Duxbury to visit Richard and Mary on their way home from Boston. They arrived just as a terrible storm started and stayed for five days until it was over.

After a nice meal that Mary and Allice had prepared the men checked on the animals while the ladies cleaned the table.

"This storm is not unlike the great storm," Richard said, "except that it's the wrong time of year for a hurricane."

"I have seen many storms," Abraham replied, "this is most likely going to be from the Northeast and will probably last a day or two."

"Have I ever told you the story about the great storm?" Richard asked Abraham as they entered the warm house.

"Only in bits and pieces," Abraham answered.

The men took their coats off and stomped the snow from their feet and joined the women who were sewing by the fireplace.

"Then I shall tell you about it," Richard said as he lit his pipe.

"You may not believe me when I tell you about the great storm we had on, August the 14th, 1635. Although words can not describe its horror this is how I remember it. This great hurricane began very early in the morning, it was a Friday I remember, and lasted through late into the evening. There was a mighty blowing of wind and rain such as no one in this land, Indian or English, had ever seen. It blew down houses and uncovered others leaving them with no roofs. Blowing everything in them to the Four Corners of the earth, I do believe. It took off the roof of a house that belonged to the Plantation at Manomet and floated it to another place twenty miles away, leaving only the posts still standing in the ground.

The wind was so great that it blew down many hundreds of thousands of trees, turning up the stronger ones by the roots and breaking the taller ones off in the middle. Tall young oaks and walnut trees of good size were wound around each other into great piles looking like giant beaver

478

dams, it was all so very strange and fearful to behold. This great storm left horrible scars upon the good earth that are still very visible today.

Vessels were lost at sea with many men aboard. The sea swell to the south of here near Cape Ann rose above 20 feet high. Captain Isaac Allerton was sailing from Ipswich to Marblehead with the Reverends Peter Thacher and Joseph Avery and their families on board, and their boat was blown upon a rock just off the coast there. The Captain, the Reverends and their wives were saved by the good graces of God, but some of the servants, maids and three of the smaller children were washed overboard and drowned.

Much of our wheat crop was harvested, but many of our crops that were still in the fields were ruined. We did survive though, with the grace of our Lord Jesus, just as we did during those first months we were here in this new land many years ago.

On Monday, August 17th, 1635, just 3 days after the great hurricane, there was an eclipse of the moon and many people, especially the Indians, believed that God had sent a warning that there should be no more fighting and warring with one another. Englishmen and Indians alike were fearful of what might happen next.

I doubt that those who lived through this storm will ever forget it. Needless to say we spent most of the fall and winter of 1635 and much of the spring and summer of 1636, cleaning brush and cutting trees. The one good thing that has come of this is that there was plenty of firewood and we salvaged many of the trees and cut them into much needed lumber for homes that were being built here.

That was 38 years ago and we are still using wood and lumber that was felled by the great hurricane. I have no idea how many people were carried away in that storm. I dare say there were at least 150 people that were never accounted for in the weeks that followed.

Animals of all sorts, cattle, chickens and even wild animals were found scattered hither and yon. Men carried shovels with them wherever they went for weeks afterward, so they could bury any dead carcasses they might find. I found many animals lying dead and dug a hole beside their bodies and rolled them into it, then I covered them up. Luckily I never found any human remains."

"That must have been quite a fearful thing for you Richard," Abraham said. "How on earth did you survive without getting blown away?"

"You may not believe me when I tell you this but many people fled to their root cellars and caves that were near by," Richard said.

"Mr. Brewster and I along with Mr. Bradford and several others fled to the crypt that was in the hill near the burial ground."

"I must ask you if there were any bodies in there," Abraham said.

Richard smiled and said, "I will tell you that we were fortunate to have already buried everyone that had passed away earlier that year so we did not have anyone in there. However, the odor of the dead still lingered and you know yourself that the smell of a dead person is not the best odor to be near."

"That is true," Abraham said, "or that of a burned person," he added thinking of the way Nathaniel Goodspeed smelled when he was struck by lightening.

"Needless to say we were all very happy to leave when the storm was over," Richard said.

Later when they all went to bed they listened to the wind whistling around the house and through the trees and prayed that his storm would not become a hurricane.

CHAPTER FORTY-ONE
1674

It was cold and snowy outside on February 2, 1674, but in the Barnstable Church the atmosphere was warm and cozy as the Reverend Walley married Ruth Goodspeed, daughter of Roger and Alice Goodspeed to John Davis, Jr., nephew of Robert and Ann Davis. Most everyone went directly home after the ceremony because the snow was beginning to accumulate quite rapidly and they predicted that it would most certainly be over their boots by morning. Roger and Alice stayed with Abraham and Allice for several days until the weather cleared, and then they went back home to Marstons Mills about ten miles southeast of Barnstable.

• • •

On May 14, 1674 William and Deborah Burden had their fifth child, a son they named Abraham, after his step-grandfather, Abraham Blish. Marie and Sarah were with her and both mother and baby were in good health.

• • •

On May 15, 1674 Thomas Walley, Jr. was found dead by his wife Little Hannah when she went into his room to wake him up for breakfast. She did not cry. She smiled to herself and said, "It really works."

During the past year Thomas had gained over 100 pounds, by sheer gluttony. He would eat everything that Hannah cooked and then he would get up and go to his father's home and eat whatever was left of his evening meal. On top of that he would drink four or five mugs of beer or cider. Little Hannah was so disgusted with him that she told him he was not welcome in her bed. He smelled of terrible body odor and was unclean. Little Hannah could tell by his smell that when he went to the necessary to do his daily movement he did not bother to wipe himself. She would have nothing to do with him, she could not stand him any longer.

Little Hannah and her mother Hannah Bacon had a long talk the day before Thomas died. "He's killing himself slowly, he's eating himself to death," Little Hannah said, "and he is so smelly, mother, I can not get near him, his odor is so offensive," she added.

"Is he treating you badly?" Hannah asked her still pretty daughter.

"He often tries to get into my bed but I refuse him, and then he slaps me and punches me in the arm or leg where bruises don't show," Little Hannah said with tears in here eyes.

"I think I may have a solution to your problem Little Hannah," her mother said quietly, "Will you bring him to dinner at our house tomorrow evening?"

"Yes, of course mother," Little Hannah said wondering what kind of a solution her mother could possibly have that would solve her husband's unclean habits. "I'll try to get him to take a bath so he won't be so offensive, but I can't promise," she said a little embarrassed for her husband.

"We'll all try to hold our breath," Hannah smiled trying to ease her daughter's plight.

"What kind of a solution do you have in mind that will cure his dirty habits?" Little Hannah asked unable to hold back the question any longer.

"You'll see," Hannah said still smiling, "tell him we'll be having leg of lamb for our evening meal and a very special dessert."

"Thomas loves leg of lamb mother," Little Hannah said. She knew she would get no more questions answered today.

The next evening Thomas Walley, Jr. ate everything on his plate, in fact there was absolutely no food left on the table when they were all finished. "I have a nice raspberry tart for dessert if everyone is ready for it," Hannah said.

"Of course, I am," Thomas said, raspberry tarts are one of my favorite things to eat."

Hannah went to her cook shelf and sliced a large pie into regular portions and dished them out onto individual plates, Little Hannah helped her pass them around. Then she carried a large pie marked with the letter 'T' on top of the crust to the table and sat it down in front of Thomas, "I made this especially for you, Thomas," she said handing it to him. Within a few minutes it was gone.

Hannah walked Little Hannah and her children outside when they left to go home. Thomas had already left to go to his father's house, "To visit for a short while," he said. It was a beautiful spring evening and you could smell the flowers. "Oh, look Little Hannah the Lillie of the Valley are out and blossomed," she said, "I'll have to pick some tomorrow, they make the house smell so wonderful," she added.

"Yes they do," Little Hannah said as her children walked on ahead toward home. Then she looked at her mother and gasped as she remembered the way that Abigail Coggin Finney died. "Oh, mother," Little Hannah said, "What did you do?"

"I did absolutely nothing wrong my dear," she said firmly. "But, if you remember right, I told you ten years ago that he had two faces."

"I remember," Little Hannah said, "every time he hits me, I remember"

"Well, lets just say that I doubt very much if he'll ever hit you again, dear daughter," Hannah said.

"Oh, mother," was all that Little Hannah could say.

"You'd better catch up with them," Hannah said pointing to the children who were walking down the lane, "It'll be dark soon and I don't want anything to happen to you," she added smiling, "I love you."

"Yes, I love you too mother," Little Hannah said as she gave her mother a hug, "I'll see you tomorrow." She ran a little to catch up with her little ones and smiled all the way home.

• • •

In June of 1674 Abraham Blish, Jr. graduated from Boston University with a Masters Degree in Architecture. Abraham was proud of his youngest son and gave him 100 pounds sterling, part of his inheritance, as a graduation present.

Abraham and Allice went to Boston to a big celebration that Sarah held for her brother at her home. There were about a hundred relatives and friends there, among them were several young ladies that would have been pleased to marry Abe and they made their intentions known to him as well as Sarah as often as they could. But Abraham, Jr., or 'Abe' as he insisted on being called now, said he wanted nothing to do with women at this present time in his life. After all he was only 19 years old; his birthday wasn't until October 16th.

Whenever Sarah broached the subject with him he said his work kept him too busy to bother with a family and he was happy living the way he was. He built himself a nice home in Boston and had many male friends that he associated with, in fact they all belonged to a private club that many people whispered about. Abe had one particular young man about his own age that lived with him as his companion and his hired help included a cleaning person and a cook, they were both young men.

When the party was over and everyone was gone Abraham and Abe sat by the fireplace smoking their pipes. Abraham decided that he would question his son as to whether or not he would produce any grandchildren for him, Abe had always appeared to be a little effeminate, a dandy, as many would call him, and Abraham worried about him, not quite understanding his way of life.

"There were many beautiful young women here tonight, Abe," he said as matter-of-factly as he could, "is there any particular one that you're interested in?"

"I don't think that I will ever get married Papa," Abe said evenly but firmly, "and I wish you would please stop pestering me about my private life."

Abraham said just as firmly but with no irritation in his voice, "It is not my intention to tell you how to live your life, son, and I will not bring the subject up again."

Abe calmed down and lowered his voice and said, "I really want to pursue my career as an architect for as long as possible and I do not want a wife that would forever nag me to stay at home like Sarah nags Richard."

"I was not aware that she was like that," Abraham said keeping his voice low.

"I get very upset with my sister when she complains about Richard traveling so much, doesn't she know that he makes a lot of money staying on top of his business ventures?" Abe questioned, not expecting an answer.

"I guess many women are like that, maybe Sarah is insecure at times, especially when she's pregnant," Abraham said.

"I know that they are very happy together Papa, and Richard treats her well," he paused a moment, "he loves the children too."

"Yes, I know he does," Abraham said, "Sarah lost her mother when she was very young and I do believe that does more harm to little girls than it does when boys loose their mothers at a young age.

"I guess it might," Abe said quietly. He remembered his mother vaguely; he was four when she died.

Abraham stood up and tapped his pipe into the hearth and said, "I guess I'd better go to bed, I have a long day ahead of me tomorrow."

"Yes, I'm tired too Papa," Abe said as he stood up, he was taller than his father was now but much thinner, "I'll see you in the morning." He reached his arm out and put it around his father's shoulder, "Thank you for the money and everything you've done for me Papa, I know life has been hard for you at times, I will try to make you proud of me."

Abraham hugged his son tight for a minute then patted him on the back. "I am proud of you son," he said. He was quite happy to leave his youngest son alone in Boston after that, he really didn't want to know what he did in his leisure time.

Abe was a devout Christian and had become a good friend of Mr. Thomas Brattle of Boston, a very rich man and the owner of a large piece of land referred to as Brattle Close. Mr. Brattle was the architect of many churches in the Colonies and was forever hovering over the blueprints of a building he called his Cathedral.

After meeting Mr. Brattle earlier in the evening Abraham decided that his son was in good hands and would probably prosper in life if he associated himself with gentlemen like this rich man. Abraham knew that Abe was generous with his nieces and nephews and brothers and sisters and had always come home for the holidays. 'What more could I want from my children,' he thought.

• • •

On September 15, 1674 just a year after they met formally at Richard More's home, Joseph Blish age 26 and Hannah Hull age 16 daughter of Tristram Hull were married a the Duxbury Church. They spent their wedding night in the old house that Joseph's father and mother had lived in when they were first married. The next day they hired a schooner to move all of Hannah's things to their West Barnstable home.

Richard More once owned the little house and the land surrounding it and sold it to Abraham in 1637. Abraham in turn sold it to John Willis in 1638, who in turn sold it back to Richard More in 1640.

Abraham took Joseph aside just before they all retired for the night and told him several things that he should do for his new wife.

Joseph was a little embarrassed, but he listened respectfully and then thanked his father for his advice.

"I also hope that you and Hannah will be as happy as your mother and I were when we were married," Abraham said to his son. "Your mother was the most beautiful woman I ever met," he had tears in his eyes.

"I wish I could remember her better, Pa," Joseph said.

"I have never loved anyone as much as I loved Anne Pratt," Abraham said. Then smiling at his son he patted him on the back and chuckled, "I was so happy, I was in love."

Joseph laughed and said, "Yes, Pa, I know how you must have felt because I am so happy, I am in love, too."

• • •

Richard and Mehitabel Child had twins on November 10, 1674 and they named them Ebenezer and Hannah. It was a rare thing for two babies to be born at the same time and both live, they were quite small weighing only about four pounds each, but they were strong and Mehitabel had enough milk for both of them.

Both Marie and Sarah went to Watertown to be with Mehitabel when her time was close because she was so big with child that Marie was afraid that something might be wrong. She was so glad that Sarah was with her to help her when she realized what was happening as the babies were being born.

When Mehitabel had the first baby Marie laid him on the bed under he daughter's knees and cut his umbilical cord. Then when Mehitabel said she had to push again Marie could see the top of the head of another baby. "Oh my" she said smiling from ear to ear, "there's another one coming."

Sarah took the little baby out of the way and started cleaning him to make him cry.

"Go ahead and push again, dear," Marie said, "I see another little head, you're going to have twins."

Mehitabel pushed again and a little girl was born. Marie could not have been happier, she was the proud grandmother of twins. Sarah Bourne was delighted that she had witnessed this wonderful event and she doted over the two babies for a week after they were born before she went back to Barnstable.

They grew fast and by Christmas they both weighed about 7 pounds. Marie stayed with Mehitabel until after the holidays to help her. She now had eight children under the age of 11.

• • •

On December 3, 1674, Anthony Annable died in his sleep. He was 75 years old. He was one of the founders of Barnstable and had lived in the new colonies for 51 years. He had eight children and two grandchildren. He was laid to rest in his family's burial plot in Barnstable Cemetery beside his first wife Jane, who passed away in1643. His stillborn daughter who died in 1635, his infant son Ezekiel, who died in 1649 at age three months, and his granddaughter Hannah who died just five months before on August 4, 1672 at age seventeen months were also there.

The whole town mourned the death of Anthony Annable; he had been a distinguished gentleman of Barnstable since the beginning of the settlement. Anthony's title was not 'Mister' it was 'Goodman,' meaning that his property was worth less than two hundred pounds and that he was a man who was most useful in Church and State. Anthony had been a Deputy to the colony Court for thirteen years and was on a committee to revise colonial laws. He had been frequently employed in most important and difficult negotiations and was one of the 58 original purchasers of land in Barnstable.

Anthony also owned four acres of land that was given to him in the division of lands in 1623 to those who came to Plymouth in the ship called the *'Anne.'* He was a member of the first General Court held in 1639 and for the next 18 years held that membership twelve times. He was the chairman of many committees needed to run a successful town for the entire 35 years that he lived in Barnstable. He owned one of the best farms there and his moral character was impeccable and he was never a party to a lawsuit. He was a man of sound judgment, he was discreet, courteous, and a good neighbor and he exhibited his Christian character in his daily life.[1]

Anna Clark Annable was lost for many weeks in her memories. Her daughter-in-law Mehitabel helped her throughout this trying time as she had helped Mehitabel after her baby Hannah had died.

Abraham Blish missed Anthony more than anyone, except maybe his wife Anna. They had been neighbors for thirty-five years and helped each other build their homes and farm their lands. They had no secrets from each other and confided in one another in personal matters as well as the matters of the town government.

After Anthony's death Abraham went to Duxbury by himself to visit Richard for a while, he left shortly after Christmas. He went by horseback wanting the time alone to grieve for his friend. He knew that Richard More would understand him, he had always been there for him and knew he would help him through this sorrowful time, he dreaded the day when word would come of his best friend's death.

[1] In the Plymouth Colony, the Governor, Deputy Governor, Magistrates, Assistant Magistrates, Ministers of the Gospel and Elders of the church, School Masters, Commissioned Officers in the Militia, Men of great wealth, and Noblemen were the only ones entitled to be called Mister and their wives Mistress. This rule was rigidly enforced in those days and in all lists of names it was the custom to see that his rule was carried out. The title Goodman was the title that most men of everyday life were given.

'Where had the time gone,' he wondered, 'Richard is 62 now, I'm 58, Mary must be 60 and Allice is 57, Anne would be 54, only 54, I know she would still look the same he thought.' Tears filled his eyes. He shook his head as if to clear the sad thoughts away.

It took him two days to get there but the solitude of the ride was just what he needed. He left Allice home with her neighborly duties and her church friends knowing she would be doing the things she liked to do. She had not objected to his going and having been married for fifteen years she was used to his frequent visits to Duxbury. He was always in better spirits when he returned and she seemed happier to see him. 'Absence makes the heart grow fonder,' he mused.

When Abraham arrived at Richard's home he received his usual greeting and the men talked about their friend Anthony Annable and the other men that had been influential in their lives. And of course, Richard had a story to tell. This one was about the burning of a Pequot Indian village.

"This event happened just before you arrived in New England, Abraham," Richard said before he began his story.

"During January and the earlier part of February of the year, 1637, the Pequot Indians were quite restless and made an attack on the English in Connecticut along the lower part of the river killing men and women both while they were working in the fields. They also attacked Fort Saybrook but they did not succeed in killing anyone there. They tried to persuade the Narragansett Indians to join with them to rid their land of the English forever more. However, having suffered great losses at the hands of the Pequot, the Narragansett decided to join with the English.

After the attack on the Connecticut River Governor Vane of the Connecticut General Court requested help from Massachusetts Governor Winthrop asking him to send soldiers immediately. After careful consideration Governor Winthrop proceeded at once, sending 80 soldiers and about 50 Narragansett warriors to the fort. They surrounded them and made their attack with great courage and speedily forced their way in.

There was fierce resistance from the Pequot of course, and much shooting and fighting occurred. This followed with the English setting fire to the houses in the fort causing about four hundred Pequot Indians, men, women and even children to burn to their deaths.

The Narragansett Indians stood aloof from the danger during his encounter. Their only participation in the fighting was to stop any Pequot that might try to flee, leaving the whole execution of this attack to the English.

The three hundred Pequot that did remain alive were taken prisoner and divided into groups, some were sent to the English in the Connecticut River area, the male children were sent to the West Indies and the women and female children were distributed throughout the Massachusetts Colonies. The few that were left scattered themselves in all quarters of the country and surrendered themselves to the Narragansett or the Mohican to live under their leadership.

A year or so later the Narragansett turned against us and the Governor has had to deal with them every time a new chief is chosen. They are a very vengeful people.

Among the prisoners was a Pequot Medicine Chief named Monomotto his wife Nominito and their four children. Nominito was a modest looking woman of good behavior and was a tremendous help in saving three captured English girls that were taken prisoner by the Pequot the year before. She protected them and saved them from being abused and put to death and she treated the little girls most kindly. She requested that the English not kill her husband, abuse her body or take her children from her and being that she was a brave and kind soul, her wishes were granted. Chief Monomotto, his wife and children stayed in Plymouth under constant guard until a decision was made as to exactly what his involvement in the attack actually was.

The three English girls that were reunited with their families also pleaded with the Governor for mercy toward Chief Monomotto and to pardon him for any part he may have played in the attack.

After much thought Governor Vane and Governor Winthrop and other Colonial leaders granted a pardon to Chief Monomotto upon his promise to live in peace with the English. He was not to leave the Plymouth Colony for any reason. He died in 1657 and his wife still lives with one of their sons.

In all thirteen Pequot chiefs were killed and another Chief called Sassacus, having fled to the Mohawks for protection, was beheaded by them after they found him guilty of being a braggart and a vulgar human being.

There were some Pequot sub-chiefs that escaped and formed their own tribes, however, they had learned from this attack that they would never win a war with the English. They have lived with us as our friends since.

This horrible war between the English and the Indians ended after this burning. However, there were many skirmishes between the Indians themselves as many tribes, especially the Narragansett, were bitter en-

emies of each other. But, I think on the whole they have lived in peace with all Englishmen since.

I would like to say that there are many well-educated and reputable Indians in our colonies that are worthy of praise and have been God fearing men and women with well-behaved children for many years. They have much knowledge of the land and have always been willing to share it with us."

Richard ended his story saying, "It saddens me to think that the English would make such increasing demands on Wampanoag lands. The Governor of Rhode Island has allowed his people to encroach upon Metacomet's land for several years now. I wish this could all be settled peacefully. I'm afraid that Metacomet may form a confederation of all the tribes and that would lead to an uprising for all of the colonies and we would be forced to fight against the same Indians that we have all been friendly with for more than fifty years."

"I am certainly glad that we are at peace with most of them at the moment and hope that we can stay that way," Abraham said. "There is enough death and dying without war," he added sighing.

Richard was sorry that he told this story to Abraham, he should have told him something that would have cheered him up. "I should have saved this story for some other time, Abraham," Richard said.

"It's all right Richard, I don't think anything could cheer me up right now," Abraham said sadly.

"Let's talk about all of your grandchildren," Mary suggested.

Abraham laughed a little and said, "That would take the rest of the night my dear Mary, I think I'll go to bed if you don't mind. It's been a long day."

"Of course, Abraham you need sleep right now more than anything," Mary said kindly.

They all said good night.

CHAPTER FORTY-TWO
1675

Sarah sent word to her father at Richard's home that he had a new granddaughter and asked if he would like to stop for a visit on his way home. Little Hannah was born on February 2, 1675 to Sarah and Richard Orchyard. Sarah had an easy pregnancy and Hannah was born without much effort. It seemed that the little baby was just as anxious to see the world as Sarah was to have her in her arms. She was a good baby and easy to care for and her father doted on her. She now had three boys and two girls.

Every time she made a peep Richard would run to her to see if she was hungry or wet and he picked her up and carried her everywhere. Sarah was glad of his help but sometimes she felt a little left out, she wondered if this was the way Richard used to feel when their older children were young and she spent most of her time with them.

When Abraham arrived at Sarah's home he looked well and rested, she was so happy to see him. After a week of long talks and long walks, on days that were sunny enough to go out, both Abraham and Sarah felt better. They had always been able to talk to each other about everything and they understood one another, giving advice or taking advice from each other.

Abraham stayed in Boston until the 1st of March and then he decided it was time to go home. Joseph could very well run the farm while he was gone, but it would be spring soon and time for planting, and he missed his friends at church and yes he even missed his wife. He smiled as he thought about her gentleness.

When he arrived home Allice's greeting was one of the most affectionate he had received for quite some time. They were alone in the house and he returned her greeting the same way, he held her close and kissed her passionately, it was good to be home.

• • •

Anna Annable was born to Samuel and Mehitabel Annable on March 4, 1675. Their fourth child and they named her after her grandmother Anna. Mehitabel liked the spelling, the 'a' allowed the rhyming of her name, 'Anna Annable', she looked much like her grandmother, too. Anna Annable was pleased with her namesake and cared for her as much as Mehitabel would allow. Anthony had been gone for three months now and the new baby helped to fill her empty arms.

• • •

On February 16, 1675 Little Hannah Bacon Walley married Reverend George Shove of Taunton and she and her three children moved there with him. Reverend George Shove was a very thin man and very clean about his person. They were very much in love, everyone could tell, and all of her friends at her wedding wished her well.

• • •

In early July word came to Elder Henry Cobb that his son Gershom had been killed in Swanzey along with eight other young militiamen. They had held off the forces of Metacomet's men for several hours before they were killed. They were all buried on June 24, 1675.

On July 15th Elder Cobb held a memorial service for all of the families of the fallen men on a knoll near where they died; he also placed a stone marker as a monument in their honor for all to see and remember them.

• • •

On August 4, 1675 James and Sarah Cobb's sixth baby was born, they named him Gershom after his fallen Uncle. Marie and Sarah were with her and both her and the baby were healthy.

• • •

Joseph and Hannah Blish's first son Joseph, Jr. was born on September 13, 1675. He looked very much like his mother with blonde hair and blue eyes. A good baby with a great disposition and he was hardly ever fussy.

Abraham was delighted to have a grandson to carry on the Blish name, he was proud and held him as often as Hannah would let him.

She would try to take him away from Abraham if he went to sleep in his arms, but he would shush her away with a motion of his hand and say, "He's fine and I need the rest as much as Little Joseph does."

Hannah would smile and say, "you're going to spoil him and I won't be able to put him to sleep unless I hold him, Papa."

"I won't spoil him, Hannah, I promise," Abraham always answered.

William and Deborah Burden's son Joseph was born on September 20, 1675 only a week after Joseph and Hannah Blish's son Joseph, Jr. Abraham was a grandfather again. Although Deborah was not his real daughter, he had always thought of her as such.

Hannah was happy to have another baby to keep Abraham busy, now he could try to spoil both of them.

"Did you have to name him Joseph, too?" Abraham asked William.

"Well, I do believe that Joseph is a nice name," William replied, "but we shall call him 'Joey' so there will be no confusion as to who we are talking to."

Abraham smiled and said, "Joey it is then, and picked up the little baby and kissed him on his rosy cheek.

The little baby grimaced as if to say his grandfather's whiskers irritated him.

Abraham smiled and handed the new baby to his mother, "He's beautiful Deborah."

• • •

Two weeks later Elizabeth Bursley Goodspeed married her second husband, a man with the unusual name of Increase Clap, it was October 4, 1675 and she moved to Rochester with him. Though the weather was stormy the wedding was lovely and there was plenty of food at the reception.

Roger and Alice Goodspeed brought little May, now 7 years old and Nathaniel, Jr., 5, to the wedding. They hardly knew their mother, she had made no special effort to see them, except on Christmas and on their birthdays. "They would probably see her even less now," Alice said to some of her friends.

Some of the older children, remembering how Elizabeth's first husband Nathaniel had died, made up a rhyme that was repeated by even those that could not yet remember their alphabet.

"A man named Increase Clap
Came into Barnstable town,
A-riding on a good steed.
He passed a young lady walking fast
With her face all a-frown,
Her name was Elizabeth Goodspeed.
He smiled at her she smiled back,
He said, "Hello, I'm Thunder Clap,"
She said, "Hello, I'm Lightnin' Liz."
Now they were married in October
And said their vows with faces sober,
On the eleventh hour.
And from that day hence
They will be known as
Mr. & Mrs. Thunder Shower.

Of course not many of the parents heard them chanting this poem and those that did were obliged to scold their children and then try to quickly find a place to hide their faces so they could laugh out loud.

CHAPTER FORTY-THREE
1676

Johnny Barker, age 25, married Desire Annable age 23, youngest daughter of Anthony and Jane Annable on January 18, 1676 at the Barnstable Church.

When Johnny graduated from Boston College with a law degree in June of 1675, Abraham gave him 100 pounds sterling for a graduation gift. "You earned every cent of it," Abraham told him when he opened the pouch and counted it. "You've been a good son to me and your mother and father would be proud of you. I know I certainly am," Abraham said patting the young man on the back.

"Thank you Pa," Johnny said.

It pleased Abraham to hear Johnny call him 'Pa,' he very seldom called him anything except Sir. He smiled and shook Johnny's hand and said, "I'm very proud of you, son," and he hugged him. Johnny hugged him back.

Johnny soon became a prominent attorney in the colonies and while he resided in Barnstable he was one of the referees in many of the important cases that were brought to trial in the surrounding towns.

Now six months later he was a sergeant in the trainband, a group of local citizens that were trained militia to fight against Metacomet's army, and though they had had their differences in the past, he served under his Uncle, Captain John Williams of Scituate.

Except for the disturbances brought about by Metacomet's renegades, the militia was rarely needed against the Indians for the most part they all lived together in harmony. It was clear that the English in northern New England had not possessed one foot of land in the colony that wasn't fairly obtained by honest purchase from the Indians. A law had been made in the early days of settling Plymouth that no one could purchase, or receive as a gift, any lands from any of the Indians without the knowledge of the court.

The Indians were allowed to keep Mt. Hope, Pocasset and several other pieces of the best lands in the colony. Kenecompsit, Chief of the Mattakeese did sell a few acres of his land to some of the settlers with the courts permission.

Indian Micah owned Rafe's Pond and a large number of acres of woodland around the settlement that he allowed the townsmen to cut timber on for a small price. He had taught many of the early settlers to fish through the ice and showed them where the best fishing spots were. Life became easier for almost everyone in the new land as the years passed by. Barter and trading among the English and the Indians was a popular event that took place each fall as well as throughout the year.

• • •

No Militiamen had been seriously hurt or killed by Metacomet's men since the year before until Sergeant Johnny Barker, Esq. was wounded in the calf of his left leg in a battle near Watertown on August 7, 1676.

A large portion of the calf muscle was blown off and Captain Williams told him that his leg would probably get infected and it would have to be amputated.

Johnny refused to think such a thing and he demanded that he be taken back to Barnstable the following day. Captain Williams finally allowed two men to accompany him home on horseback.

It took them two days and three nights of constant travel to get there and by the time they arrived, Johnny was feverish and in great pain and could hardly stay on his horse.

The two soldiers helped Johnny into the Blish house and helped Abraham get him into his old bedroom. Abraham sent for Desire and for Marie Dimmock and Sarah Bourne immediately while Allice helped the young man take off his dirty clothes and get into a clean nightshirt. By the time he was in bed he had no more strength and he was asleep immediately. She washed his face and hands and the rest of his body as best she could while she waited for the ladies. She didn't touch his swollen leg, it smelled and there were little white maggots crawling around in it. It sickened her to look at it so she laid a clean linen cloth over it while she tended to the rest of him.

Desire ran into the Blish home crying and almost hysterical. Abraham allowed her to look into Johnny's room where he was sleeping making her promise not to wake him. When she saw that he was all right except for his leg she calmed down and agreed to sit quietly beside his bed until Marie and Sarah got there.

Marie and Sarah arrived to find Johnny Barker laying on his right side tucked snugly into his bed, he was sleeping or unconscious, they were not quite sure which. His left leg was propped up on a pillow with his wound covered with a linen cloth. Marie looked at the wound and immediately went to her medicine bag. Opening it she said, "Here Sarah please make some Echinacea and Blood Flower tea while I prepare a poultice for this leg," and handed her two little pouches. "Oh, here, put some Feverfew and Figwort in it, too," she added, handing her two more little pouches of herbs. "We'll relieve his pain and bring his fever down while we're cleaning his blood," she smiled at her very capable assistant. Sarah smiled back and took the little bags into the front room.

Marie gathered up several other pouches that were larger and followed Sarah into the front room. Abraham was sitting at the table with his head bowed in prayer. Marie put her hand on his shoulder and said, "I'm sorry to interrupt your prayers Abraham, but would you please get me a cup of cider vinegar."

Then she looked at Allice and said, "I also need a small dish, too Allice, please."

Marie took the small dish that Allice immediately handed her and poured a measured amount of each packet into it, Abraham handed her the mug of cider and she mixed a little of it with the herbs making a thick paste. She found some clean white linen strips of cloth in her bag and put a thick amount on one of them, then covered it over with another. She had a very potent poultice that was big enough to cover the entire wound.

"The tea is ready," Sarah said.

"Good, we're both ready," Marie said and they went into Johnny's room.

"Desire, dear, you may want to wait in the other room with Abraham and Allice," Sarah said gently, "you really should not see Johnny's wound, it may make you upset, dear."

Desire reluctantly went into the commonroom and sat down at the table and prayed with her father-in-law.

Abraham put his arm around her shoulders and hugged her, "He'll be just fine, dear," he said kindly.

"Johnny," Marie said loudly, "Johnny, wake up, you're home Johnny."

He turned his head toward the sound of Marie's voice and said, "My leg."

"Yes, Johnny, I'm going to fix it but I need you to wake up and drink some medicine for me," she said kindly, her voice lower now.

"Here Johnny, sip this for me," Sarah coaxed him as she held the mug to his lips.

Johnny took several small sips and then fainted, or went back to sleep, Sarah wasn't sure, "Well, at least he drank some of it Marie," she said.

"Good," Marie said, "it will keep him still for a few minutes while I work on his leg. Help me turn him over on to his stomach a little more," she said.

They turned Johnny so that Marie could see the complete wound when she removed the linen towel. Then she started picking the little white maggots out it.

"I'll need to wash the dried blood out Sarah, would you please get me a large towel and several small pieces of cloth. I'll also need a pitcher of hot water, too," she added.

Sarah went to the door and asked Allice where her linen towels were. She came back with several towels and six small white wash cloths and laid them on the bed.

Abraham came in carrying the pitcher of water, "Do you want me to pour some of this into the wash bowl, Marie," he asked. He needed to help.

"Yes, Abraham," Marie said looking at his worried face, "then if you'd like you can hold the bowl closer for me." He did as she asked and then watched her gently clean Johnny's wound.

When she was satisfied that she had removed all of the maggots Marie dipped the little pieces of linen into the hot water and then squeezed the water over the wound for four or five minutes.

The dirty blood soaked into the thick towel she had placed under his leg. Little pieces of blood and rotted flesh washed away as she trickled the hot water onto the wound and when she was done the dark red and blackened blood was completely gone. Only nice clean flesh remained.

She gently squeezed the wound and found that no puss oozed out of it. "Nice little maggots," she said and smiled, "they kept the wound from getting infected, I'm glad it wasn't covered too tightly."

Sarah said to Abraham who looked a little perplexed, "Maggots eat only the rotted flesh and infection."

"See Abraham," Marie said smiling, "even God's lowliest creatures have been put here on His great earth for a reason."

Abraham smiled and nodded. Then she took a clean needle out of her satchel and threaded it with a long piece of coarse horse hair and dipped it into the hot water. Next she pulled the pieces of skin together over the wound as much as possible and sewed them together with a crisscross stitch. Almost the entire wound was covered by the time she was through sewing. Then she applied the poultice and wrapped his leg snuggly with long strips of white linen.

Johnny slept the rest of the day and didn't wake up until the sun was shining the next morning. His leg was aching and it pained him when he tried to move it. "Oh," he groaned as Abraham came into his room.

"Well, my young son," Abraham said, "it looks like you're going to keep your leg for a while longer."

"It hurts real bad, Pa," Johnny said through clenched teeth.

"I have some medicine that Marie Dimmock left for you," Abraham said handing Johnny a mug of warm tea, "she said you had to drink it all and that she would be back this morning to make you some more."

"Oh, it taste awful," Johnny said after he obediently drank the bitter tea.

"I'm sure it does," Abraham replied, "but just think how good you'll feel in a few minutes."

"What did she say about my leg," Johnny asked as he looked down at the white bandage.

"She said you'll keep your leg but you may have to use a crutch for awhile," Abraham told him and then smiled and added, "you may have just a small limp but nothing more."

"You lost a large portion of the muscle," Marie said as she came into the room.

Johnny smiled at her and said, "Marie Dimmock, I think you are the greatest doctor alive."

"Now, now, Johnny flattery will only get you a permit to drink more of my bitter tea," she laughed, "and I just happen to have some right here."

"This isn't as bad as the other," Johnny said as he sipped the mug she handed him.

"You may also have to keep two stockings on that leg, too, Johnny," Marie said, "you may have trouble keeping it warm." She smiled at him again and said, "But it'll be better to have to wear three stockings instead of only one, right?" she laughed.

Johnny caught the little pun and said, "Right, they wanted to cut it off, I wouldn't let them, I made Uncle John give me an escort home."

"I think you got here just in time, too," Abraham said, "you were half dead from exhaustion."

"You'll be fine now Johnny," Marie said, "I'll be back every day to put a clean poultice on it starting tomorrow. I want to leave that one alone until then," she patted his foot and then pulled the quilt over his cold toes.

"Be sure to keep his toes warm, Abraham," Marie said, "he probably won't be able to feel them for a few days."

Abraham shook his head and said, "I'll take good care of him Marie, thank you for coming back this morning so early."

"You're welcome," she said as she left the room.

"Johnny, do know how fortunate this whole town is to have Marie Dimmock and Sarah Bourne living here?" Abraham asked his stepson.

"Yes, I do," Johnny said yawning.

Abraham left the room and Johnny went back to sleep.

• • •

Mehitabel Dimmock Child, wife of Richard Child and mother of nine children died on August 18, 1676 at the age of 34 the same day her ninth child was stillborn. Their seven living children ranged in age from 13 to not quite 2. Mehitabel's mother, Marie Dimmock, promised her that she would raise the motherless children while Richard ran his estate.

Marie was distraught that she could not help her daughter, she did everything she could for her but could not save her life. It was a sad time for their friends and family.

Richard and Marie laid Mehitabel to rest with her baby daughter on August 20,1676, the whole town of Watertown grieved with them.

After the funeral it seemed that Richard did not have time for anyone except his estate and his older children whom he often only tolerated for their usefulness as hired hands. He left the younger ones in the care of his mother-in-law and had very little to do with them. Some people thought that his grief made him insensitive to his children, but if the truth was known, he had never wanted to have as many children as he did. He resented them for the time they took Mehitabel away from him. They had argued about it on several occasions during their marriage. Now she was gone forever, 'why did she have to have so many children he wondered?'

Three weeks later Marie suggested she take her seven grandchildren to Barnstable with her so she could tend to some business that was waiting for her, Richard did not object. The children loved it in Barnstable, they felt free to be themselves and they wanted to go to school there.

Marie smiled and thought to herself that she would send word to Richard that she wanted to keep the children with her in Barnstable until next summer and suggested that he come there for the holidays to see them.

He sent word back that this arrangement was quite satisfactory for all of them.

At Christmas time he sent presents and his regrets that he would be unable to make the trip because of bad weather. Marie hadn't noticed any bad weather but she didn't say anything to anyone.

'Richard was Richard,' she thought, 'and he's the one that's losing out, not the children.'

She made sure that they all had a wonderful holiday.

• • •

On September 10, 1676 Job Crocker's wife Mary Crocker, age 32, died accidentally. She was the mother of Sam, age 5 and Thomas age 2. Mary was eight months pregnant and had gained a lot of weight with this baby and it made her loose her balance from time to time.

On September 8th she got up early so she could do her wash before little Thomas woke up. Her wash tub was set up in back of her house near the woodshed where rope was strung up so she could hang her clothes to dry.

Job had filled her tubs, one to wash and the other to rinse, the night before. This morning there were little crystals of ice floating on the top of the tubs and she knew if she put her hands in that cold water she would probably pee her pants.

It seemed like all she did was pee lately. So she went to the house and got the kettle of hot water that was hanging over the fireplace, she would pour some into each tub.

A little hot water in each would make it easier for her to hold her hands in long enough to scrub their clothes.

'My hands will probably be red as a rose anyway,' she thought, 'but at least they won't ache from being cold,' she smiled.

She stepped down onto the first step holding the hot kettle out in front of her in case it slopped over it wouldn't burn her, and as she went to step down onto the next step she lost her balance and fell forward. She instinctively put both arms down to catch herself and kettle of hot water splashed all over her face and arms and down the front of her. Her belly hit the edge of the kettle and she fainted.

Little Sam saw her fall and tried to help her get up but he couldn't wake her. He knew his father was at the church so he ran as fast as he could to get him. When he ran into the church, he screamed, "Papa, Mama fell down, I can't wake her up. Hurry, Papa."

Job had never seen his son so upset before and ran toward him. "What is it, Samuel?" he said picking the little boy up.

"Mama fell down the steps and I can't wake her up and she won't stand up for me," he said crying.

"Oh, my God in heaven," Job said praying, "please don't let her die."

William Crocker, Job's father heard what Samuel had said and ran to his son and taking his grandson out of Job's arms said, "I'll go get Sarah Bourne, you run home to Mary, hurry son."

"Mary, Yes, Mary, oh, God let her be safe," he prayed as he ran home.

When he found Mary she was lying on the ground near the back door where she had fallen, she was still unconscious. He touched her head carefully and then turned her over as gently as he could. Her face and arms were burned bright red and the front of her skirt was covered with blood, she was bleeding.

"The baby, oh Mary our baby," he sobbed. Her wet dress clung to her moving belly, their baby was moving, and it was still alive. Mary was still alive too, he could see the little pulse moving in the side of her neck and she was breathing little short breaths.

Job wasn't sure what he should do, he looked around and found a small towel that was on the washstand just outside the door, he wet the end of it in the cold water bucket. He wanted to wash the mud off her face, but it was burned, so red, he squeezed a little of the water onto the mud and it ran off down the side of her neck. She moaned a little. "Oh, Mary," Job sobbed and he wet the towel again.

After several trickles of water he had most of the mud washed off her pretty face. "Oh, Mary, Mary, can you hear me?" he kept asking her. She moaned again, but he couldn't wake her.

Sarah Bourne ran into Job's house through the front door with William right behind her and then she saw Job just outside the back door leaning over Mary. She ran down the steps quickly and asked, "Oh, Job, what happened?"

"I think she must have fallen," Job said. "She's bleeding and burned," he said tears rolling down his cheeks, "I can't get her to talk to me."

"We have to get her off the cold ground, Job," Sarah said calmly, "I think that the three of us can carry her without hurting her."

"We should put her on the bed in the small room," Job said, "then Thomas won't disturb her. Where is he?" Job said as he suddenly realized he had forgotten his little son.

"He must still be asleep," William said.

"Thank God," Sarah said, "at least he didn't see her fall or touch her burns."

"Let me fix the bed before we put her in it," Sarah said and went into the house. She found Mary's clean linen and then pulled the quilt from the bed and put a clean sheet over the one already there. Then she found a clean nightgown and placed it near the nightstand. She looked on a shelf near the bed and saw Mary's birthing pad and placed it on top of the clean linen sheet. Then hurried back out to where Mary was laying.

The three of them picked Mary up and took her inside and put her on the bed. "I'll take her clothes off, Job maybe you should go and see if you can find Thomas," she said. She looked at William and said, "Would you please go and get Marie Dimmock for me, I think I'm going to need her help." They didn't have to see poor Mary's naked body,' she thought, 'it would probably just upset them more than they were already.'

Mary's body from her face to her thighs was severely burned and the kettle left a horrible red line almost down the center of her belly. Sarah put both of her hands gently on Mary's belly and tried to feel the baby kick. It was still.

She knew that Mary's water had broken and the amount of blood on the ground and on her clothes was almost all that a person had in them. The wash basin by the bed was full of water and there was a clean little towel near it.

Tears ran down Sarah's cheeks as she gently washed the blood off Mary's legs and belly. Mary didn't move even when she washed the mud from her burned hands and arms. She found Mary's hairbrush and brushed the dirt out of her pretty dark hair.

Mary was still breathing when Marie got there, but it was very shallow, she might last a day or two, but not more than that. Blood was still slowly seeping out of her womb onto the birthing pad.

"I don't think she will live," Sarah said to Marie.

"Oh, Mary, you poor dear," Marie said and then put her hand on Mary's belly, she could not feel any movement from the baby. She looked at Sarah and shook her head 'No,' they both agreed, there was no hope for Mary or her baby.

When she was finished she went to the door and said, "I'm sorry Job, there is nothing we can do for Mary, or the baby," she put her hand into her apron pocket and pulled out her handkerchief and blew her nose.

"She'll probably be gone by morning. I'm so sorry," Sarah said.

Job came to the door of the room and looked in, "Oh, Mary," he said as he went in and knelt beside the bed in prayer, "Oh, God, no, please,"

William Crocker was holding Thomas and Samuel was standing beside them.

Samuel looked at Sarah and said, "Did Mama wake up?"

"No, Sammy, your Mama is on her way to heaven," Sarah said with tears still running down her cheeks, "we'll pray for her."

William Crocker sat Thomas on his feet and got down on his knees, "Let us all pray for your Mama, Samuel." Both little boys got on their knees and Sarah did the same.

Mary Crocker died two days later and was buried the following day. Job could not believe that his lovely wife and baby had been taken away in such a short time. Everyone grieved for him and his little children.

• • •

The rest of the year passed in Barnstable as usual and thankfully no one in town was saddened during the winter with any more deaths or injuries.

Marie and Sarah were glad that there were no more births that winter. They both said they were getting to old to go out in the middle of the night to deliver a baby.

Sarah said, "We should make all the pregnant women to come to us from now on."

Marie agreed saying, "The walk here would do them good too, and we wouldn't have so wait so long when they got here, their babies would just fall out," and then they both laughed.

• • •

News came in late August that Metacomet, better known by some as King Philip, was killed by the Rhode Island militia on August 10, 1676. During the last year or so the English had been encroaching on their land in Rhode Island and refused to pay for it or let them use it.

With the death of Metacomet, the war ended and resistance to further colonial settlements in southern New England ceased.

The people in the colonies were now confident that there would be no more conflicts with any of the Indian people. They knew of no other Indian chiefs that wanted war.

CHAPTER FORTY-FOUR
1677

Joseph and Hannah Blish had another son on February 17, 1677 they named him John. Abraham was delighted, he now had twenty grandchildren, though only two had the Blish surname but he loved every one of them.

• • •

On April 5, 1677 the Reverend Thomas Walley died. More dissension broke out in the church because no one could decide who would replace him. Abraham and several other men filled in as well as they could, but because ministers were still scarce in the colonies, they had to make do with Elders and other men of God.

• • •

Joseph told Abraham that Hannah was pregnant again the same morning that Little Johnny Blish died. It was June 30, 1677, a very sad day for Joseph and Hannah, but especially for Abraham, as Little Johnny looked just like his grandmother Anne, he had red curly hair and beautiful laughing blue eyes.

He was healthy and plump and had just started crawling around and jabbering away while pointing at everything that caught his eye. He was almost six months old.

He was playing near the fireplace with a cornhusk doll when Hannah heard him scream; she was in the kitchen area kneading bread.

A burning knot in a log burst, blowing fire and sparks out onto the stone hearth where little Johnny was sitting. A big ball of fire was all she could see as she turned, flames had engulfed her baby catching his clothes on fire.

She ran to the water bucket, grabbed it screaming to little Joseph to stay away, and threw the water onto her baby son.

He stopped screaming and was laying there breathing heavily as she dropped the bucket and hovered over him. She could only see black charred skin on her once beautiful white skinned baby.

He stared at her for a moment and then his little body shuddered and seemed to wither into a limp, soggy mess.

She wanted to touch him, and pick him up, but could not bring herself to do so. "Help," she screamed as she ran to the back door and flung it open.

The horrible smell of charred flesh was in her nostrils as she screamed Joseph's name, over and over for what seemed like hours until he finally appeared in front of her.

"What is it Hannah," he said as he ran into the house.

"The baby," she screamed, as she pointed toward the hearth. She could hear herself, but didn't seem to know it was she that was making that awful noise.

Joseph ran to his baby son and carefully touched him, "Oh my God, what has happened to him," he asked as he fell to his knees and picked up his lifeless child. The remains of the cornhusk doll were still clutched in his baby's hand. Joseph looked up at Hannah, "Oh Hannah," it was all that he could say, and then he repeated himself, "Oh my God, what has happened to our baby?"

"A log blew up, I think I heard it, and then I heard Johnny scream," she sobbed. "I only know that he was on fire when I saw him so I threw the bucket of water on him." She screamed again, a horrible sound. Little Joseph was crying big loud sobs in the corner of the room near the front door. Hannah looked in his direction and then called his name, "Oh Joseph, come to mother my dear son," she said. The little boy ran to her and she cradled him in her arms and they both sobbed holding each other tight.

Joseph got up still holding his baby and went to the door and shut it with his foot. Then he took a linen towel from the cupboard and laid it carefully on the table with one hand, holding his baby cradled in his other arm. Then he laid his son on the towel and carefully folded it around him. "I'm going to get father," he said tears were running down his face. He wiped them away with his sleeve leaving a black streak across his cheek and went out of the door closing it quietly.

When Joseph found Abraham at the Church, he ranted wildly about little Johnny and a fire. Abraham held Joseph around his shoulders tightly while his son sobbed and then gently held him at arm's length so he could question him. His face was smudged with black soot and he smelled like burned flesh. "What has happened Joseph?" Abraham asked sternly as he shook his son gently.

Joseph looked at his father and realized that he had found him, it seemed like he had been looking for him for hours. "Father, Little Johnny has been hurt bad," he sobbed, "please help him."

Abraham held on to Joseph's arm as he led him toward the house. "Oh, Joseph, tell me what has happened," he said.

"Hurry," Joseph said still sobbing, "my baby has been burned badly."

Abraham started running, pulling Joseph behind him by the hand. When they got to the house, Hannah was sitting on the front step holding little Joseph, both still sobbing. "Oh father," she said looking at Abraham, "please help him."

Abraham ran to the table where the little linen bundle was laying and looked at his grandson. He knew immediately that the baby was dead, he closed his grandson's beautiful blue eyes, 'so blue, like his grandmothers,' he thought as the tears flowed down his cheeks.

Joseph was standing next to him, "Please help him father," he repeated his wife's words.

"I'm so sorry, Joseph," Abraham said, "little Johnny's gone." He wrapped his arms around his son and they both cried for a few minutes. Then Abraham pulled himself together and said, "Come now, we have to make arrangements. Your son is in good hands now, with God and his Grandmother," he continued as he pulled the linen closer around his little body. "Go to Hannah and Joseph, they need you," he said as he picked up the little baby. "I'll take him to the Reverend's house and get someone to clean up here, you get yourself cleaned up and you and Hannah meet me there as soon as you can."

Abraham knew that Joseph had to have something to do now in order to keep his mind about him. His memory flashed back to

Anne, lying in a pool of blood in the middle of the garden. He shook his head as if to rid his mind of the horrible memory and left the house.

Little Johnny was buried the next day beside his grandmother in the Barnstable Cemetery. Everyone attending the service remembered the numerous tragedies that Abraham had endured during the last 25 years.

Abraham sat down at the table when he got home and wrote a letter to his brother John. It had been a while since he had written him.

July 3, 1677
Dear Brother John,
It has been a while since I last wrote to you and I do apologize to you for that. And it seems that the only time that I send you any news it is sad. I am sorry for that too.

I have just lost my little grandson Johnny. He was Joseph and Hannah's second son and he was only 6 months old. He was burned severely when a knot from the fireplace caught his clothes on fire. There was nothing anyone could do for him. It was just a horrible tragic accident. He was such a handsome little boy. He had red curly hair and nice blue eyes, much like his grandmother, my Anne.

I do have to tell you that Hannah is pregnant again and will have her new baby in February next year. That should help her cope with her loss, but I know it will never replace little Johnny.

Deborah and William will be having a baby sometime next month. This will be her seventh child. Mary and Sam have four children and Annie and John also have four now. Johnny and Desire do not have any children yet.

I now have twenty grandchildren living nearby. Though Sarah lives in Boston, I still see her and Richard and their five children quite often.

I hope you are all well and give my love to Molly.

Everyone has been asleep for a while now and I believe it is time for me to go to bed as well. I will close this letter now and hope to hear from you soon.

I leave you in God's hands and my prayers are with you always.
I will always be your loving brother,

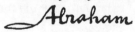

• • •

William and Deborah Barker Burden's daughter Anna was born August 26, 1677. She was a healthy baby and though this was Deborah's seventh child she was in good health soon after her baby's birth. Marie and Sarah marveled over Deborah, such a little thing to have such healthy babies. But enough was enough she didn't need any more children. They gave her Blessed Tea and she drank it every day for many years.

If Abraham counted all of his living grandchildren and step-grandchildren he now had twenty-two; they seem to be coming in twos he joked to William and Joseph.

• • •

Shubael and Joanna Dimmock had their sixth child on October 2, 1677, a baby girl they named Mehitabel after Shubael's sister. Marie and Sarah were with her and both mother and baby were healthy. They left several pouches of Blessed Tea with her.

• • •

On December 20, 1677, James and Sarah Lewis Cobb had their fifth child, a boy they named John. Marie and Sarah were with Sarah when her baby was born and everything went well. Blessed Tea was left with her and she was told it was a wonderful tea for her to take so that she could regain her strength before she had another baby. She took the tea for almost two years.

CHAPTER FORTY-FIVE
1678

Joseph and Hannah Blish's daughter Annah was born on February 20, 1678. Their third baby, Hannah was glad to have a girl. The loss of little Johnny would have been much too hard to bear if she had had another boy. "Thank you God," she said when she knew her baby was a girl.

Marie and Sarah were happy for her; they understood and thanked God, too.

• • •

Johnny and Desire Barker's son John, Jr. was born May 4, 1678, their first baby. Marie and Sarah were with Desire and she did wonderful and had a healthy baby.

Johnny Barker's sister Mary Pratt now had five children and his sister Anne Pratt had four.

Abraham had four more grandchildren in less than a year. "I think that makes twenty-six now," he said to Johnny patting him on the back. "I will have to count their names in my journal this afternoon when I add little John's," he said smiling.

• • •

Captain Matthew Fuller died on September 18, 1678. There were not very many people at his funeral because there had been a terrible icy rain on September 16th and the roads and paths were still covered with huge puddles of water. At the funeral Abraham sat beside John Mayo. The two men had walked together to the Captain's home to show their respect as neighbors. Abraham sat with his head bowed quietly thinking about the obnoxious man and smiled to himself as he remembered the time The Captain was sued by Governor Thomas Hinckley for calling the pompous Governor a liar. The accusation pleased more than one acquaintance of the stiff-necked Thomas, but the Captain acknowledged his fault and apologized publicly and the Governor dropped the lawsuit.

Abraham looked at the puckered scar on his hand and remembered the ax slicing through it and then the painful way Captain Fuller sewed it together. He rubbed the scar thinking about the Captain, he was the first regular physician to settle in Barnstable but Abraham couldn't remember very many people calling on him for his services more than once. He never went back, nor would he let his family call on him.

The Captain was never known for his gentle touch as a physician. Though he was Surgeon General in the colony forces during Metacomet's War, and ministered skilled medical attention to the wounded, he was considered a hotheaded soldier and very quarrelsome.

Abraham had to admit to himself that Captain Matthew Fuller had indeed performed many good services to his country and he admired him for that.

After the service Abraham and John both expressed their condolences to Frances, Matthew's wife, and told her she should call on them if she needed anything. She thanked them and they shook hands with the rest of the Fuller family.

Captain Fuller's servant Robert Marshall, a Scotsman, was particularly saddened by the Doctor's death. He had been with him for over fifty years. Abraham put his arm around the old man's shoulders and hugged him. "If you need to talk to someone come and see me," he said quietly to Robert.

Robert shook his head and wiped the tears from his eyes and whispered, "Thank you Mr. Blish."

Abraham and John Mayo went home after the service, they decided not to go to the cemetery with the pallbearers.

The weather was very cold and cloudy and most of the family members also decided to stay in the house instead of going to the cemetery. The servants carried Matthew Fuller's casket out into the cold, windy and gloomy afternoon. Several of them mumbled their displeasure about the job of carrying the heavy casket a mile through the deep puddles. They had not yet warmed up since digging the grave earlier and it was still cold and rainy and now the wind was blowing.

One of them said that the wind was as sharp as the Captain's tongue.

Another laughed at the remark.

Robert plodded along his feet as wet and numb from the cold as his heart was from loosing his master.

The old man became extremely distraught when the pallbearers carrying Captain Fuller stopped all of a sudden and sat the heavy box on the ground.

The smallest man, George Green stomped his feet on the path to warm them and said, "I'm not going a step further, I'm freezing."

He clapped his cold hands together and then put them under his arms to warm them.

Francis Fuller lifted her heavy skirt wet with water a little higher off the ground and said, "I'm sure you'll not freeze, George, your nasty disposition will keep you warm enough to go the rest of the way." The man groaned and bent down and together the six pallbearers picked up the heavy casket of Captain Fuller. He was buried as a soldier and with honor in the Barnstable Cemetery. No one else complained about anything the rest of the afternoon.

• • •

Samuel Annable, 32, died on June 9, 1678, leaving his wife Mehitabel Allyn Annable with three young children. Little Samuel was 9, Johnny was 5 and Anna was 3.

Samuel was in the militia with his brother-in-law Johnny Barker and had been sick with stomach cramps since he came home shortly after Metacomet was killed.

It seemed to Mehitabel when he first came home that he was hungry all the time and he ate everything she cooked, but he was still loosing weight. He weighed about 180 pounds when he joined the militia in1675 and now three years later he only weighed about 80 pounds. He had diarrhea almost every day now and nothing that Marie or Sarah gave him helped.

Samuel had no energy and he was so weak that he could not hold his little girl Anna.

Marie and Sarah concluded that he had eaten something bad while he was in the militia and gave him Culver's Root, Comfrey, Mullein and Slippery Elm.

Samuel went to bed early the night before he passed away and seemed to be sleeping peacefully when Mehitabel went to bed. She carefully put her arm around her husband and held him close. She whispered, "I love you, Samuel." And then she went to sleep, too.

He never woke up.

Mehitabel was heartbroken when she opened her eyes the next morning it was so quiet in the room. Samuel was not breathing. She carefully got out of bed and called to her mother-in-law Anna.

Anna came into her son's room and felt his neck and then listened to his chest. "He's gone my dear," she said and then fell to her knees beside the bed and cried and cried.

The children heard their grandmother's sobs and came into the room wondering what was happening.

Mehitabel told them that their father had gone to heaven. She let them each kiss his cheek and then she took them into the commonroom and they prayed for their dear loving father.

The grief over loosing her only living son caused Anna Clark Annable to take to her bed soon after his funeral. "He was so young," she kept saying over and over.

Mehitabel tried to console her but was also trying to cope with her own grief over the loss of her husband and take care of her children too.

A few weeks after Samuel's death Anna could hear her daughter-in-law sobbing one morning when she woke up, and when she called to her Mehitabel did not answer. She finally got out of bed by herself and found her clothes and dressed herself.

'What can be wrong,' she wondered as she made her way into the front room?

This was the day that Anna realized that she was not going to die because of her son's death and decided that she could probably make Mehitabel's life much easier if she offered to help her as much as her frail old body would allow. She was only 63, but she felt much older lately, Anthony had been gone four years now, it seemed much longer.

Mehitabel was strong but she had loved her husband very much and missed him terribly. Her mother-in-law had seemed like just another burden to her for several weeks until one day she just sat down at the long table where her husband used to sit and cried and cried.

When Anna found Mehitabel sitting at the long table all by herself her young body was shuddering with hiccups, her face was red and little Anna was leaning against her mother's side patting her back trying to console her.

Anna found a clean cloth and wet it in the water bucket on the shelf and took it to her and gently lifted her head and wiped her face and eyes. Then she pulled the young woman's head into her ample bosom and patted her hair brushing it back away from her face. "I'm so sorry Mehitabel for thinking only of myself," she said soothingly. "I will help you from now on as much as I can," she added as she bent her head and kissed Mehitabel on her hair.

Mehitabel looked up at her mother-in-law and was a little surprised that the older woman was out of bed and dressed. "I'm sorry too mother, I know I must be strong for the children, but today I just could not help myself," she sobbed. Then she said, "Everywhere I look I see Samuel, his chair I'm sitting in, his coat by the door, his boots, I'm just so sad," she sobbed again.

Anna held Mehitabel and let her cry. She remembered when she lost Anthony and both women cried for a while longer. Until baby Anna pulled on her mother's dress and held the wet cloth up to her sad mother's face trying to wipe the tears.

Both women gathered themselves together and as if nothing out of the ordinary had happened that day, they went about their daily chores. "Crying cleans the heart," Anna said and Mehitabel agreed.

His estate was settled on October 30, 1678 and it included the farm of his father Anthony Annable, though it was still in his mother's possession. Fifty-four acres on the south side of the highway, which Samuel held in his own right by a grant from the town of Barnstable; and also the estate of his wife, Mehitabel; which was hers alone, a gift from her father Thomas Allyn when he passed away.

The women would be fine, their husbands had left them well-to-do and the townspeople would see to their welfare if they ever needed help.

CHAPTER FORTY-SIX
1679

About a week after Captain Fuller's death Robert Marshall was suspected of stealing a box of Matthew's jewels. 'I still have not recovered from the horrible sadness I feel over my master's death and now this,' he thought. He had no will to live.

He had gone on about his duties, being very few now, and his body was weak from lack of food, he had hardly eaten a thing since his Captain had passed on.

Mrs. Fuller made sure that he was given a proper meal every day, but sometimes he just couldn't eat it.

Four months later on, January 18, 1679 Robert Marshall died, grief stricken over the death of his Captain and the accusation that he had stolen his master's jewels, he could bear no more.

Robert was to be buried in the Barnstable Cemetery on a knoll overlooking Captain Fuller's grave.

However, a horrible snowstorm covered the town with over two feet of snow the night that Robert died. His body was laid out at the Fuller's home and John Mayo conducted the service, with only a few of the Fuller servants in attendance.

Mrs. Fuller asked that they take Robert to the cemetery on the afternoon of the second day. It was too warm in the house to keep Robert's body any longer; he had to be buried.

The men waited until the sun was high in the sky before they went to the house to get Robert thinking that it would be warmer. But the sun did not show itself through the clouds and it was getting colder as the morning passed and now the wind was blowing icy pieces of snow everywhere.

It was just after noon when they entered the Fuller home to take Robert to the cemetery.

They walked about a half-mile when George Green, the same man that had been a pallbearer for Captain Fuller stopped suddenly.

The other men almost fell trying to hold up the extra weight of the casket.

"I'm not going a step further, I'm freezing," he said to the startled man next to him.

He clapped his hands together and then stomped his feet trying to warm them.

Another man said through chattering teeth, "George is right, I think we should bury the old man right here."

"I guess this is as good a place as any," said one of the older servants.

A big man who had been carrying the shovels handed one to the man beside him and said, "Here, start digging."

The man took the shovel and walked a couple of steps off the path and started shoveling big scoops of snow, "You don't have to ask me twice, I'm freezing, too," he said.

The other four men picked up a shovel and they all started digging Robert Marshall's grave right there beside the road. Taking a servant's body to the burying ground was no longer something that any of them thought they had to do. As long as he was buried what did it matter. They were near the northwest side of Scorton Hill.

One of the older servants was upset about burying a man so close to the road and suggested that they put the casket in the barn and wait until the weather cleared. But the others were against this suggestion because they'd have to carry it all the way back to the Fuller's so they all kept on digging.

"Let's just get the old man buried once and for all," George said his breath coming in big white puffs of steam.

When the hole was deep enough, the men roped the casket and lowered it into the grave and not any too gentle at that.

"We'll probably be punished for this misdeed," the older man said.

George laughed and said, "How?"

The older man looked at him with a scowl and said, "Who knows, maybe old Robert will come back and haunt us."

They all laughed a little and kept on covering up Robert's casket, they had all had enough of the great outdoors for one day and they wanted to go home to a warm fire and hot food.

It wasn't long after Robert's remains were buried when several reputable people traveling alone in the late evening claimed to have seen someone standing near the grave of Robert Marshall.

Two or three of the local servants swore that they had seen Robert's ghost standing over the Captain's grave. Some said that maybe they were both still watching over each other.

Abraham never believed that such a devoted servant would commit a crime against his master and did not approve of the way he was buried, but the town council would not agree with his proposal to have Robert's body moved to the cemetery. So the following spring when the ground had softened he and one of his hired hands secretly placed a stone on either end of Robert's grave.

Robert is still buried near the roadway and to this day no man has dared to disturb his grave. Over the years the elements have gullied away the roadside grave but the flowering locus still stand in full bloom all during the spring and summer where he was buried.

No one ever found any of Captain Fuller's jewels that Robert was suppose to have stolen. They may have been sold by the Captain before his death to support his business or taken by a family member that was in the house the day of the funeral. No one but the thief himself will ever know.

CHAPTER FORTY-SEVEN
1680

Joseph and Hannah Blish's son Abraham III was born on February 27, 1680. Little Abraham was their third baby born in February, first little Johnny who died in an accident, then Annah and now baby Abraham all just a year apart.

These children along with their little cousins, the Orchyards and the Burdens and the Pratts adored their grandfather Blish and they loved to hear his stories as much as he liked telling them.

• • •

Shubael Dimmock was given the rank of Ensign of the Plymouth militia and he was also a Deacon in the Barnstable Church. Shubael and Joanna Dimmock had a son they named Benjamin on March 4, 1680. He was their seventh child.

• • •

Job Crocker married Hannah Taylor of Yarmouth on July 19, 1680. She loved his little boys and they adored her. Samuel was 9 and Thomas was 6. They needed a mother as much as he needed a wife.

• • •

Summer and fall passed quickly with everyone going on about their business as usual. Abraham didn't write anything in his journal much anymore except to record the birth of a child or the death of a friend

Before everyone knew it a cold winter gale was blowing in from the ocean. Winter was upon them and it was Thanksgiving again and most of his family was gathered around the warm fireplace. He watched them all trying to remember their ages. He started with Deborah and William Burden's children, Mercy was 18, Deborah 15, Stephen 11, Abraham 6, Joey 5 and Anna 3.

Then there were Sarah and Richard Orchyard's children, Joseph 14, Edward 11, Richard, Jr. 9, Elizabeth 7, and Hannah 5.

Next there was Joseph and Hannah Blish's children, Joseph 5 and Annah 2. Then came Johnny and Desire Barker's children, Johnny was 2, and Desire was 10 months old.

Mary and Samuel Pratt's and Annie and John Pratt's children were not present so he was having trouble remembering their names and ages, he knew they each had five children now and Mary was pregnant again. 'What a great family I have,' he thought to himself.

"Grandpapa, please tell us a story," Hannah said as she crawled up into his lap.

"Yes," Joseph said, "tell us about the first Thanksgiving Grandpapa."

"Your Uncle Richard More told me that story, he tells it better," Abraham said smiling at them, "he was there you know."

"We like the way you tell it, too, Grandpapa," Hannah said touching his face with her little hand, "you make us laugh."

"Well, then," he said hugging his little granddaughter, "let me think. Ummm, where will I start?"

"Once upon a time," Hannah said matter-of-factly.

Abraham laughed and said, "Oh, yes," and began his story.

"Once upon a time at Plymouth Plantation a group of people called Pilgrims had just finished harvesting their crops of corn and beans and peas and pumpkins and squash and wheat and barley and cod and bass and lobsters."

"Grandpapa, you don't harvest fish," little Joey said as he climbed into his grandfather's lap to sit on his other leg.

526

"Oh, my mistake," he said and squeezed him a little. The other children laughed.

"So, the Pilgrims had just about everything harvested and put away into their storage house ready for winter. It was November 1621. The wood was all cut and stored away under cover and those that did the fishing had salted the cod and bass and other fish and stored it away.

They also had enough corn meal put away so that each Pilgrim could have a full peck every week, if he could eat that much."

Abraham pushed his belly out and puffed his cheeks up. The little children patted his belly and laughed together.

Joey said, "Grandpapa, you would be fat if you ate that much."

He laughed and said, "you would waddle like a duck if you ate that much."

"You would look like a pig if you ate that much," Hannah added.

Everyone laughed then Abraham cleared his throat and continued.

"Well, now the Pilgrims decided that God had been good to them and the Indians had helped them so much that first year that they would hold a celebration and invited them all to come and eat with them.

So four or five men went hunting for geese, ducks and turkeys and they came back with so many that it took them two days just to take the feathers off them.

Now don't you know they saved the biggest feathers to write with and to give to the Indians as gifts, they wore them in their hair you know.

The teeniest feathers they saved to stuff their pillows with, it takes a long time to save feathers, especially if the wind is blowing."

He paused for a minute chuckling, as the children laughed.

"Well, when the fowl were all plucked they cleaned them inside and out and then stuffed them with herbs and bread and oysters and wild onions and put them in their ovens.

The women did much of this kind of work, but they didn't mind it was warmer by the fireplace.

So, now the invitation went out to Chief Massasoit that he and all of his people were invited to a feast in their honor.

Governor Bradford declared that this feast would start on November 21, 1620 and last until all of the people had their fill and they could eat no more.

Now mind you, they did not touch any of the food that they had put away in storage, the food served at this celebration was extra.

The women spent four days making bread and pies and wonderful cobblers and hasty pudding. There were strawberry and rhubarb pies, pumpkin pies, blueberry pies and cranberries cooked with honey, there were blackberry cobblers and raspberry tarts."

"Grandpapa, you're making me hungry," Joseph said.

"Me, too," Joey said.

"We will have to see if there's any dessert left when we're through with the story," Abraham chuckled. They all laughed again.

"Well, now the women cooked some of the corn with the husks on it, roasting it on the coals after the birds were roasted.

They boiled the dried beans with pieces of salted venison and maple syrup, they cooked the squash and added spices and to the peas they added wild onions and they made the food fit for a king."

"Governor Bradford didn't invite the King did he Grandpapa," Hannah asked seriously.

"No, the King was unable to attend because he lived so far away," Abraham said just as seriously.

"What did the Indians bring, Grandpapa," Hannah asked.

"Well now Chief Massasoit came early in the morning and he brought ninety of his people with him.

The Pilgrims numbered about 90 now, with the 55 original that arrived in the Mayflower, that were still alive and about 35 of those that came on the Fortune, making a total of about 180 people at this wonderful feast called Thanksgiving."

"No, Grandpapa," Hannah said, "what did they bring to eat?"

"Oh," Abraham said chuckling.

"I believe they brought five deer, well, actually, they went out and hunted them and brought them back to the plantation and gave them to the Governor as a gift.

The women cooked them, too. But the Indian women also brought Bannock and flat sweet corn bread and large pots of honey and the sweet maple sugar.

They brought parched corn and they popped it over the coals at night and the men, both Indian and English told stories."

"I like the story Uncle Richard tells about parched corn, he says it funny," Joey said.

"That is a funny story isn't it, no one wanted to try it until Samoset and Uncle Richard did," Abraham said.

"Can we make some now Grandpapa?" Joseph asked.

All of the grownups were listening just as interested by his story as the children were.

Hannah said, "I think I can find some and maybe I'll even put some sweet butter on mine."

"Mine, too," Joey said.

"Mine, too," Hannah said.

"All right, I'll put it on everyones," Hannah said smiling as she went to get the corn and the popping pan.

"What happened next Grandpapa," Joey asked.

"Well let me think, where did I leave off," Abraham said smiling.

"They were all telling stories," Joseph said.

"Oh, yes," Abraham said, knowing exactly where he left off, but pretending not to, he was checking to see if they were paying attention. He smiled and continued again.

"The Indians told stories about the first white men that came to their land and gave them a bad sickness in 1614.

The Governor apologized and then told stories about why they had come to this new land, the Church would not let them believe in God the way they wanted to.

The Chief said it was not right for one to force his beliefs onto another.

These stories were all sad stories and they continued for a while until one of the Indians decided to perform a happy singing dance. He took out his flute and began to play happy little songs while some of the others sang, none of the Pilgrims knew what the words meant, but they sounded happy and made them smile.

Then five or six Indians got up and started dancing.

They all had their best buckskins on trimmed with fringes and dyed feathers of red and blue and yellow and green and they danced and swayed until they dropped from exhaustion.

The Pilgrims were fascinated by their gyrations and some of the younger men, your Uncle Richard included, tried to imitate them but they couldn't move about like the Indians did and they looked so funny that every one laughed at them, they even laughed at themselves.

During the day they played games. They played Rolling Hoops, one of the Indians made a hoop from a sapling and then he made a small straight stick to use as a guide; then they took turns rolling the hoop and running as fast as they could after it trying to keep it from falling over. The person that ran the furthest before his hoop fell over won the game."

"I can play that game," Hannah said proudly, "I can run a long, long way before my hoop falls down."

"Yes, you can I've seen you," Abraham said.

"They played Shuttlecock. One of the men made a Shuttlecock from a large cattail pod by sticking feathers into one end of it. Then he made two paddles from thin pieces of wood tapered on one end to fit his hand. The object of this game was to hit the Shuttlecock into the air and keep it there at all times. The first person that missed and let the Shuttlecock drop onto the ground lost the game and someone else took his turn.

Your Uncle Richard told me once that he played seven different men before he let the Shuttlecock fall to the ground."

"He must have been the champion," Joseph said.

"I do believe he was," Abraham said, "maybe when we see him again you can get him to play a game against you Joseph."

"I hope he hasn't forgotten," Hannah said seriously, "he's old now, Grandpapa."

"I don't think I'll tell him you said that, Hannah," Abraham laughed along with the other adults.

"I like that game Grandpapa," Joseph said.

"Yes, I've seen you play you are very good at it," Abraham added, "I think you have a much nicer shuttlecock and paddle than the Indian's had, don't you?"

"Yes, I do, and thank you for making it for me Grandpapa," Joseph said, "I take good care of it, I always keep it in my room when I'm not playing with it."

"You're a good boy, Joseph," Abraham said patting his grandson on his back.

The popcorn was done and Hannah and Deborah passed small clamshell dishes around to each child.

"Finish the story please, Grandpapa," Joey said.

"All right now," he said.

I believe they all ate more food and sang more songs and danced more dances and feasted for two more days.

The first Thanksgiving celebration lasted three days and two nights you know.

The Indians had never seen this kind of celebration, and the Pilgrims were delighted that their honored guests were pleased and promised to hold this event each year at the same time.

And to this very day we all celebrate Thanksgiving every year in November."

"We only have it one day though, Grandpapa," Johnny said.

"Yes, I know and that's because we don't have enough Indians here in Barnstable to keep us up for three days," Abraham chuckled.

The adults laughed out loud.

The children laughed too, not quite sure what was so funny.

"Well, now that's what happened at the very first Thanksgiving," Abraham said, "and if your popcorn is finished it is my bedtime, how about you?"

"I'm tired too," Joey said his popcorn was almost gone and his head was lying sleepily on Abraham's chest.

William got up and picked his little boy out of Abraham's lap and said, "Lets go to bed sleepy head," and took him up the stairs to the loft where they had all planned to stay the night.

Richard picked up Hannah and patted his father-in-law on his head and said, "Good story Pa."

"Thank you son," Abraham said getting out of the chair slowly, both his legs were asleep from the weight of the little children.

"Come along Joe, I'll tuck you in, too," Joseph said.

Little Joseph liked to have his father call him Joe it sounded all grown up, better than little Joseph like his mother called him.

Hannah and Deborah watched their husbands take the little ones up the stairs and then they hugged each other good night and went to their own rooms.

Alice stood by Abraham's side while he got his balance and then they too went to bed.

"That was a nice story to tell the children, Abraham," Allice said after they climbed into bed and then she kissed him good night on the lips.

Abraham pulled his wife close and held her for a long time thinking how fortunate he was now and how hard it must have been for the Pilgrims.

• • •

Samuel Cobb, son of the late Henry and Sarah Cobb, married Elizabeth Taylor on December 20, 1680. The meetinghouse was trimmed with holly and pine boughs and everyone in town attended the wedding.

This was a wonderful occasion to break up the monotony of the cold winter months. A wonderful meal was served at Sarah Cobb's home after the ceremony. The women of the church brought many delicious dishes to be served and when they were placed upon the large buffet table one could hardy see the table itself.

Everyone agreed that this celebration was a nice way to end the year.

CHAPTER FORTY-EIGHT
1681

Spring came and went with sheep shearing and planting as usual with nothing out of the ordinary happening.

On June 4, 1681 the town council elected to hire Reverend Johnathan Russell to serve as their full time minister. There had been no settled minister in the town of Barnstable for almost four years, since Reverend Walley died in 1677.

It was voted to allow the new Reverend the same pay that Reverend Walley received, 80 pounds per year, 40 pounds in money and the other 40 pounds in food.

Mr. Walley's house and land, which was built for the use of the minister residing in Barnstable, would also be used by the new Reverend.

He was allowed to keep any monies he received from anyone that hired him to perform a wedding or funeral or baptism at a price agreed upon between man and man.

• • •

Only one baby was born during the summer, on August 20, 1681, Samuel and Elizabeth Cobb had their first baby; they named her Sarah after her grandmother. Marie and Sarah were with her when her baby was born and both were healthy.

• • •

In the fall after the harvest Samuel Crocker, son of William Crocker was killed when Indian James kicked him in the bottom of his belly.

Indian James was indicted on November 20, 1681 for the murder of Samuel, whereof he died after three weeks of suffering from a great swelling in his groin. Samuel Crocker was just 39 years old when he died.

Johnny Barker, Esq. was Indian James lawyer and was determined that this trial would be fair and just. He allowed James to testify on his own behalf and called Job Crocker, Samuel's younger brother to the stand as a witness to the unfortunate event.

After the indictment was read by the Court Johnny immediately called Indian James to the stand. James was dressed in his finest buckskins and his hair was braided into two long braids that hung down the front of his fringe-decorated shirt.

The first question that Johnny asked him was, "Indian James, did you intentionally kick Samuel Crocker in the bottom of his belly causing him great pain?"

"No sir," James said clearly.

"Please tell the court and members of the jury how this most unfortunate incident happened," Johnny said to him.

"We were wrestling as we did once in a while to pass the time," James answered pausing, he thought he should wait for Johnny to ask him his next question.

"Yes, go on," Johnny said, "tell your story as you remember it."

"Well, Samuel and I have been friends since we were young," he looked down at his hands remembering the rivalry that had been between them for more than 25 years. They didn't dislike each other, but they had often challenged each other's strengths and weaknesses.

The Prosecutor, Nathaniel Bacon, Jr. interrupted saying, "I do not think you and Samuel were ever friends, Indian James."

Judge Crow pounded his gavel sharply and said, "No more out bursts Mr. Bacon, or I'll have you dismissed from the courtroom, you'll get your turn, if you keep quiet."

Attorney Bacon's face reddened from embarrassment. He had known Samuel Crocker all his life and though the man was a bit of a braggart and loud he had many friends, but he did not think that Indian James was one of them.

He sat up straighter in his chair and pretended to write some-thing on the paper in front of him.

Johnny Barker said, "James, please continue."

James looked at Nathaniel Bacon and then at the Judge and said, "Samuel and I and several other men were wrestling as we did often in the evening." He took a deep breath and continued, "We were in the barn at Mr. Crocker's place and we had all taken turns wrestling until one or the other of us lost. When we were down to the two of us, Samuel and I, we took our stance and then began. He put his hand behind my neck and pulled my head into a headlock and then I freed myself by bending down and twisting out of his hold. Before I could step away from him he grabbed me by my hair and pulled me down onto the floor. This is not how we wrestle; it is called a foul."

"What happened next," Johnny asked.

"That's when Job Crocker yelled, 'Unfair, Samuel, unfair.'" In-dian James said, "Samuel called back 'There are no rules for us tonight.' This frightened me for a second," James said, "because Samuel is bigger than I am and he could easily break my bones if we wrestled without rules. I backed away and said, 'Of course there are rules for us Samuel, we have all obeyed the rules tonight. Why do you say that,' I asked him." James looked at Johnny and said, "I have always obeyed the rules."

"Yes, I have heard that you are a fair man James," Johnny said as he walked over to James and patted his arm. "Please continue," he added.

The Indian straightened his shoulders and nodded his head in appreciation for the compliment, and continued. "Then Samuel rushed at me and I moved quickly out of the way and as I did I lost my balance and fell to the floor landing on my back. Samuel hit the side of the barn instead of me and then turned and jumped through the air toward me. I instinctively put my foot out to pro-tect myself. If he had landed on me with all of his weight it would have knocked the breath from me, I have seen this happen before to other men." James looked up at Johnny and sighed.

"I'm sure you would have been injured, James," Johnny said, then asked, "what happened next?"

James looked down at his hands and then back to Johnny and said, "Samuel's lower body landed on my left foot and my right knee. He gave a great gasp, collapsed and rolled away from me holding his manhood with both of his hands. His body had pushed my legs into my chest and I couldn't get up, all I could do was lay there for a minute, then I turned onto my side and got up on my knees. That's when I looked at Samuel's face, it was as white as snow. Job was leaning over him and asking him if he was all right. I crawled over to Samuel and tried to talk to him but all he did was moan, I don't think he could hear us. One of the other men left the barn to go and get Mr. Crocker and in a few minutes they came back and Mr. Crocker asked us what had happened. Job told his father that Samuel had hurt himself and Mr. Crocker and Job and two of the other men picked Samuel up and carried him into the house. No one said anything to me so I went home."

Judge Crow said, "Your witness, Mr. Bacon."

Nathaniel Bacon stood in front of Indian James for several minutes looking at the man trying to intimidate him, then he said, "I have just one question for you Indian James."

"Yes sir," James said.

"You said you always wrestle by the rules, when you put your foot out in front of you," he paused for a second, "were you playing by the rules then?"

"Don't answer that Indian James," Johnny said quickly, "badgering the witness your honor."

Nathaniel quickly said, "No more questions from this witness your honor." He didn't give the Judge time to say anything he had gotten his point across to the jury.

"Re-examine?" Judge Crow asked Johnny.

"No, your honor," he said. Then he looked at Indian James and said, "Thank you James, that will be all for now."

Johnny turned toward the courtroom and said, "I now call Job Crocker to the stand."

Johnny put his hand on Job's shoulder and said, "Job, I'm very sorry that your brother has been injured, I pray for his well being."

"Thank you, Johnny, ah Mr. Barker," Job said.

"Job, do you think that Indian James intentionally injured Samuel," Johnny asked him.

"No, sir," Job answered.

"Can you tell us what happened in the barn when Samuel and Indian James were wrestling?" Johnny asked.

"Everything that Indian James said was the truth and I can not add anything else to it, Mr. Barker," Job said.

"Thank you, Job," Johnny said. Then to the Judge he said, "No more questions for this witness your Honor."

"Your witness Mr. Bacon," the Judge said.

"I have no questions for this witness," Nathaniel said.

"The jury is excused to find a verdict in this matter," Judge Crow said looking at the jurors.

Abraham, Roger Goodspeed, Robert Davis, James Gorham, James Cobb, and Joseph Bearse were on the jury and had a hard time making their decision in this case. They deliberated for almost four hours before they passed judgment on Indian James. They jury found him *Not Guilty* of willful attempt to murder.

After the proceedings were over the Judge asked Indian James to leave town for his own good. Indian James obeyed and was never seen in Barnstable again.

Indian James told the Judge that he did not intentionally cause bodily harm to Samuel Crocker and the Judge believed him. In fact many people believed that Samuel Crocker caused his own death.

Marie Dimmock and Sarah Bourne did everything they could for Samuel. When they arrived at his home he was lying on his bed and was unconscious. His breeches were wet from the waist to the knees covered with urine and blood and his bowels had moved. Marie looked at Sarah and shook her head slightly, Sarah knew that her eyes were saying there was no hope.

"We will try to make him comfortable, William," Marie said, "but I think he has been injured inside and there is no way for us to heal him, he will have to do that himself."

"We have to get him undressed and out of those dirty wet clothes," she said looking at Sarah. "Alice will you get us some clean water and clean towels, please." Alice Crocker was still crying softly when Marie and Sarah entered their home, 'giving her something to do will calm her down,' Marie thought.

"William will you help Sarah while I make some medicine?" she asked him. She knew it would help him too if he thought he was doing something to help his son.

Marie made a strong tea from Marshmallow Root and Wild Lettuce and then made a poultice from oat straw.

Sarah noticed that blood was still oozing from Samuel's body when she was washing him and she asked Alice to find her a clean white linen sheet or a birthing pad to put under him.

Alice came back with both and handed them to Sarah then helped her slide the pad under her son.

Sarah covered him with the clean sheet and Alice held her son's hand while they waited for Marie to finish her poultice.

"Why did he always have to be such a rough character," William questioned not expecting an answer from anyone.

Marie and Sarah discussed Samuel's injuries between them and decided that his bladder or his large intestine may have been ruptured, maybe both, and they knew there was nothing they could do to heal him. They could only give him pain medicine and hope he didn't suffer too long.

"He is in God's hands now William and Alice," Marie said when she finished applying the poultice to his groin and giving Samuel some of the tea. She had taken several minutes to carefully put little droplets into his mouth hoping that his reflexes would let him swallow enough to relieve his pain.

Marie and Sarah took turns visiting him. They kept him as comfortable as possible, giving him the pain medicine and applying the warm poultices every few days. Nothing they tried helped him, his body fluids leaked steadily from him every day. He suffered greatly.

Samuel Crocker died on December 11, 1681.

William was thankful that his son was never married. He left no wife or children to suffer as he was suffering. William told Abraham that it left a hole in his heart when Samuel died, Abraham agreed with his friend knowing exactly how he felt.

CHAPTER FORTY-NINE
1682

Ensign Shubael Dimmock and his wife Joanna had their 8th child, a daughter, on March 12, 1682 they named her Joanna. Marie and Sarah were with her and both mother and baby were healthy.

• • •

Mehitabel Annable was considered a rich widow and was often sought after by many men of considerable less wealth than she was. She and Anna lived together at the Annable farm for five years after Samuel died, raising her children by themselves. Mehitabel did not want to replace her dear departed husband with anyone, she was content to be by herself.

Now five years later she met Cornelius Briggs of Scituate, married him and moved there with him taking young Samuel, age 14, John, age 10 now and Anna, age 8, with her. Cornelius was a widower and had a lovely home and much more money than she had.

Anna Annable wished her lovely daughter-in-law well and continued to run the farm by herself with the help of several hired hands.

When Samuel died the widow Mehitabel Annable was assigned all the moveable property and all of the livestock to dispose of as she needed; the money to go to the bringing up of the children hoping that she would give them the best education that the estate could afford her. She was to reap all of the profits from the land until the children were of age.

When Samuel, Jr., John and Little Anna become of age the Allyn farm will be given to Samuel and the Annable farm will be given to John. Samuel will have to pay Anna 25 pounds sterling for her share of the Allyn farm and John will have to give her 25 pound sterling for her share of the Annable farm. It was written this way in Anna Clark Annable's will.

• • •

There had been no skirmishes since the death of Metacomet and Captain Williams decided to excuse Johnny Barker from his duties as Sargeant in the militia with honor. Johnny Barker had completely recovered from the injury to his leg, it had healed well and he experienced no discomfort, except for the slight limp that he had that sometimes made his backache. There were plenty of other young men to take his place and he was released from the militia in April. About 20 other young men were also released with honor from the militia about this time.

Desire was happy to hear this because she was pregnant again and did not want to see her husband suffer anymore from any horrible injuries or fear that she would be a widow with several little children to raise by herself.

Johnny and Desire Barker's third child, a girl they named Anne was born on August 26, 1682. Desire was glad that Johnny was at home where he belonged. At least he was with her when her labor started, then she sent him to get Marie and Sarah.

Desire's labor went as usual and there were no complications for her, but the baby was very small and quiet.

"I don't hear my baby," Desire said when it was over.

"You have a tiny little girl," Marie told her and Sarah's trying to get her to accept her new surroundings.

"Is she alive," Desire asked worriedly.

"Yes, Desire," Marie said but she's having a hard time breathing. Sarah's doing everything she can for her.

"Oh, please God, don't let my baby die," Desire prayed as tears rolled down her cheeks.

Marie finished cleaning Desire and took the soiled birthing pad away. When she came back into the room she had a cup of new mothers tea for her.

"You must stay calm Desire so that your milk will be nourishing for your new baby," Marie said soothingly. "What are you going to name her?" she asked handing her the tea.

"Anne, spelled with an e," Desire said, "like her Aunt Annie."

"Like her Grandpapa's first wife, too," Marie said, "Anne Blish spelled her name that way."

"Yes, I know," Desire said sipping her tea.

"She was my very first helper you know," Marie said smoothing Desire's hair back, "in fact she and I helped you into this world."

"Yes, I know," Desire said and then smiled as she heard her baby start to cry.

Sarah cleaned the baby's little face and blew into her tiny mouth several times before the infant took a nice big breath then she made a very tiny noise. Sarah turned her over face down and rubbed her little back and patted it until mucus came out of her nose and mouth. Then she washed the little girl with a cool cloth hoping to stimulate her so she would cry and wiggle. Finally after about five minutes or so the tiny little baby decided she would make her presence into this world known to everyone and she started crying good and loud.

Desire was relieved and wanted to hold her daughter.

"In just a minute you can have her," Sarah said wrapping her in a blanket. "I want to make sure she knows how to eat so I want her to cry for a minute, it will loosen all the mucus from her lungs."

Sarah was a little worried because small babies didn't always keep their desire to live. She hoped little Anne would gain strength from her mother's milk and grow fast before cold weather set in. After a few minutes she handed little Anne to Desire and then helped the new mother sit up so the tiny infant could nurse. Sarah thought that the quicker she ate the better chance she had to live.

Little Anne did nurse, but only when her mother forced her to. If Desire did not wake her up in the middle of the night to feed her, the baby slept right through until morning. Desire was also worried which didn't help.

Marie and Sarah visited almost every day and Marie gave Desire strong doses of new mother's tea with Gentian hoping it would help to stimulate little Anne's appetite.

Sarah also held the baby and cooed to her rubbing her little legs and arms every time she was there. The tiny baby smiled very seldom and only gained about three pounds during the next three months.

Little Anne died on November 22, 1682. Desire and Johnny were heart broken.

Johnny remembered what Abraham had said when his mother, Hannah died and he held his wife and said, "God needed another angel," and they both cried together.

Johnny and Desire buried their tiny daughter the next day beside her grandmother, Hannah Williams Barker Blish.

Marie and Sarah cried all the way home that afternoon.

CHAPTER FIFTY
1683

On April 17,1683 Abraham's last will and testament was written and signed by him in the presence of Mary Hinckley and her husband Governor Thomas Hinckley.[1]

"I, Abraham Blish being weak in body but through the Mercy of God of sound and disposing mind and memory, calling to mind the uncertainty of this life on earth and being desirous to settle things in order, doe make this my last will and testament in manner and form following – That is to say:

I commend my soul to God in Jesus Christ my blessed Savior and my body to decent buriall as to my executor hereafter named shall seeme meet and convenient, and as touching such worldly estate as the Lord in Mercy hath sent mee, my will is that the same shall be imployed and bestowed as heerafter by this My will is expressed; and first I doe revoke, frusterate and make void all wills by mee heertofore made and doe declare and appoint this to be my last will and testament.

I give and bequeath unto Allice my loving wife the use of the east end of my now dwelling house which I have reserved for myself and doe now dwell in, during her naturall life, and the one moiety or half part of the yeerley rent of the lands belonging to the said dwelling house, which I have letten out to my son Joseph Blish during the said tearme, if she live so long; alsoe one cow to be att her owne dispose and the keeping thereof, together with the keeping of a mare or horse for her use to goe to mill and

---

[1] The spelling in this will is exactly as it is recorded in the town records in Barnstable, Massachusetts.

meeting during that tearm of the said lease, and one third of my household stuffe to bee at her dispose.

I will and bequeath to my son Joseph Blish the liberty to take in way of exchange that house and land belonging thereto which I now dwell on and hee hath the use of by virtue of a lease for years made therof unto him, if he shall see cause to chose it rather than that house and land which I heertofore gave unto him and his heirs forever by a deed of gift, together with the parcell of marsh lying at the northerly end of that marsh att the bridge, which parcell he hath reserved out of the said lands att the bridge, which hee leased out to John Barker and John Allin as by theer lease appeereth, provided always that he give legall sufficient deeds unto his brother my son Abraham Blish, of all the rest of the said lands att the bridge, with the houses and edifices therunto belonging now letten out to the said John Barker and John Allin, with the reversion therof to him my said son Abraham Blish, his heirs and assigns forever; but if otherwise my will is that my said son Abraham Blish shall have and enjoy my now dwelling house and all the lands therunto belonging, to him and his heirs or assigns forever and the other half of rent of said lands after my decease.

I will and bequeath unto my daughter Sara Orchyard five pounds to be paid her within one yeer after my decease, and five shillings apeece to her five children which she now hath to be payed by my executors when they have attained the age of twenty-one yeer.

I will and bequeath unto my grandson Joseph, the eldest son of my said son Joseph Blish, five pounds, and five shillings apeece to his other three children.

I will and bequeath to my son Joseph Blish all the rest of my goods and estate whatsoever to pay my debts and legacyes by me before given.

And I do hereby make and appoint him my son Joseph to bee my sole executor of this my last will and testament.

In Witness whereof I have heerunto set my hand and seale this 17ᵗʰ of Aprill, 1683.

Abraham Blish
In presence of Mary Hinckley
Thomas Hinckley, Governor

Abraham decided that Sarah didn't need his money so he left her only 5 pounds and gave each of his living grandchildren 5 shillings each payable upon their 21ˢᵗ birthdays.

Some people thought this strange, but Abraham had confided in Sarah about his wishes, and she had agreed.

She believed that Joseph and Abraham Jr. should inherit most of his wealth. She certainly didn't need it.

Richard and Sarah and their 5 children had visited Abraham and Allice just after the New Year began. They had a nice visit and though Abraham had been feeling poorly for several months he seemed much more energetic and enjoyed the company of his children and grandchildren.

Lately when he had to go out he was usually through with his chores and meetings and home by noon instead of his usual late afternoon.

Marie Dimmock told him earlier in the summer that he should slow down after he collapsed at church one Sunday afternoon in late March, shortly after His family had returned home to Boston.

His heart was not beating as it should and though Marie gave him some of her special tea that strengthened the heart Abraham did not regain his vigor.

Allice wished that he would take his medicine better.

Marie prepared a strong tea from Rosemary Leaves for him, but he complained that it was not to his liking and wouldn't take it unless Allice put it in his cider or beer.

Then as soon as he took a few sips he would refuse to drink the rest and would accuse her of trying to poison him.

Even Joseph's little five-year-old daughter Annah tried to persuade him to take his medicine. "Grandpapa," the little red-haired girl said, "I'll take some of your medicine if you do."

He laughed and said, "I'll be fine, I might take some later." He remembered that he had told her the same thing the year before when she had had a bad cold.

He would take a sip of the lemon and honey concoction and then she would.

"This medicine doesn't taste very good, you wouldn't like it," he told her as he made an awful funny face and patted her on the head.

Then she crawled up in his lap and said, "Grandpapa, tell me a story please."

As he put his arms around her he asked, "What one do you want to hear?"

"About my Grandmama, who looks like me," she said.

"Well then, where shall I begin," he teased.

"Once upon a time," Annah started the story for him.

Abraham smiled, he had told his children and grandchildren this story many times.

"Once upon a time, Annah," he repeated her, *"there was a beautiful girl named Anne. She lived in Duxbury near your Uncle Richard with her mother and father, Mr. John Pratt and Mrs. Sarah Pratt.*

The first time I saw her I knew I was going to marry her so she could be your Grandmama, Annah, he said. Then he added, *"I was so happy, I was in love!"*

Hannah giggled, patted his cheek and said, "Her hair was red like mine, right Grandpapa?"

"Yes it was Annah," and he hugged her tight and continued his story.

"Anne Pratt had little curls sticking out from under her bonnet and her eyes were blue as the sky. Her mother, your Great-Grandmama, had a wonderful meal ready for your Great-Grandpapa, your Uncle Richard and I as soon as we came through the door after doing the chores. The table was set in grand style with a lace cloth and lovely china."

"The same china that will be mine someday, Grandpapa?" Annah interrupted again.

"Yes, my dear, the very same china," Abraham answered. This was not entirely true but it made his story better and he smiled to himself.

"It's beautiful, I want to use it when I find my beautiful man," Annah said.

"Yes, you may use it when you find your 'handsome' man," Abraham corrected her chuckling and then he said, "Do you want to hear the rest of the story or do you want to tell it?"

"You tell it Grandpapa," Hannah said knowing that she should not interrupt. "I'm sorry, I won't talk anymore until your done."

Abraham kissed the top of her head and continued.

"I sat across the table from Anne and didn't take my eyes away from her unless someone spoke to me and then I was forced to be polite and look at them while I answered their questions.

I knew it was impolite to stare, but I couldn't help it.

I caught her looking at me several times, her eyes would crinkle into a smile and then she would look away quickly.

After we ate our wonderful meal your Great Grandpapa, your Uncle Richard and I sat in front of the fireplace and smoked our pipes and I watched Anne Pratt as she helped her mother clear the table, still trying not to be too obvious as I followed her every movement.

Later when it was time to go to bed, I couldn't sleep. I could hear her quiet breathing from the other room, or I thought I could, I wanted to be awake every minute she was near so I could see every move she made.

She was so graceful when she walked and her voice was as sweet as honey when she talked. But, I guess I must have fallen asleep after all because the next thing I knew your Uncle Richard was poking me and telling me that it was time to get up.

I was dreaming of Anne, I had never seen anyone so beautiful, I was so happy, I was in love!"

He squeezed Annah and she laughed up at him.

"We went to the barn and helped your Great Grandpapa with the chores and hitched up the oxen to the wagon then went back into the house and found another great meal ready for us. After we ate we thanked Mr. and Mrs. Pratt for their hospitality and went on our way to Uncle Richard's house. Uncle Richard was anxious to get home to see his wife, your Aunt Mary, and his new baby William. He missed them while he was gone and he was in love, too."

"Uncle William was a baby too?" Annah asked forgetting her promise.

"Yes, he was a baby 46 years ago, he's older than your papa," Abraham said. He really didn't mind her questions, he like her inquisitiveness.

"How old is papa?" she asked.

"He's only 35," he answered her remembering the day his oldest son was born.

"How old are you Grandpapa?" she asked

"I'm going to be 68 on my next birthday," Abraham answered her and then asked, "How old are you?"

She held up her little hand with her fingers spread apart and said, "Five."

"That's right and your Grandmama would be 62 now," he said quietly, wishing she were still here.

"Should I continue now," he asked Annah.

"Yes, Grandpapa, sorry," she whispered.

"I, however, did not want to leave, but of course, I had to. I shook Mr. Pratt's hand and hugged Mrs. Pratt. I wanted to kiss Anne but instead I stammered that it had been a pleasure to meet her. My face became red with embarrassment and my hand was wet when I held hers for a second in a polite handshake. She was smiling at me so brightly that I thought she might be laughing at me. Then to my amazement Anne put her other hand on top of mine and squeezed it. I was so happy, I was in love!"

Abraham paused for a minute remembering Anne's face until Hannah wiggled a little then he started his story again.

"I didn't see her again for two long months but I thought about her every day. Then one afternoon your Aunt Mary invited me to have my evening meal with her and Uncle Richard. When I arrived at their house Mr. and Mrs. Pratt and my beautiful Anne were there.
It was so wonderful to see her again I could hardly control myself. I shook Mr. Pratt's hand and hugged Mrs. Pratt and, oh how I wanted to kiss Anne, but of course I didn't. I just shook her hand and held it as long as I dared. She squeezed my fingers, I was so happy, I was in love!"

"You already said that Grandpapa," Annah said giggling.
"Yes, as a matter of fact I've said that many times," Abraham replied as he looked around the room.
Allice was off somewhere with her church ladies, 'It's probably a good thing,' he thought, 'speaking about Anne in front of her might have made her uncomfortable, she was a very sensitive lady.'

"After our meal the ladies of the house cleared the table while we smoked our pipes and chatted about the new settlement that was being planned. I was staying in a nice house that your Uncle Richard wanted to sell me, but I wanted to build my own home in the new settlement forty miles away."

"This house, Grandpapa?" little Annah asked.
"Yes, this very house, but it was much smaller then," Abraham answered. "Your papa and I have added many rooms on to it since then," he added.
"Oh," Annah said, "I like this house like it is."
Abraham paused, thinking of how hard it was to build a house with eight rooms and a large loft.

548

"Your papa and I worked very hard to make this house as nice as it is, all of the stones in the foundation were cut with a big hammer and chisel and it took many hours," Abraham said.

He looked at his hands, they were soft and smooth now but he could still remember the calluses and blisters that covered them once.

"Then when did you see Grandmama Anne after that Grandpapa," Annah asked patting his whiskered cheek.

"Oh, yes, we must get back to our story now," he said, a little embarrassed that he had let his mind wander.

"I didn't see Anne again after that evening until December, we had Christmas dinner with the Pratt's and it was shortly after that wonderful day that I decided to purchase Uncle Richard's house. I made many repairs to it while I lived there and I built a barn and stable, I paid him twenty-one pounds sterling for it.

It was cold that winter with a lot of snow and no one traveled very much until spring came and the snow melted. Then we had to walk through the mud if we went anywhere.

I missed her so much that winter that I made an excuse in February to go and talk to her father just so I could see her. She was just as beautiful as I remembered. I was so happy, I was in love!"

Annah giggled again, and Abraham chuckled. He loved to hear her laugh.

"It was in early fall, at a church meeting that I finally asked Mr. Pratt if I could court his daughter. I stuttered and stammered and talked about the weather and anything I could think of until finally I gained the courage and asked him if I could see his daughter and sit with her at church on Sunday. Do you know he laughed at me? And then he said, 'Yes.'

After that I saw her every Sunday at church or whenever I found an excuse to visit her father. I had never been so happy, I was in love!"

Annah said, "You was in love!" at the same time he did and they both laughed together.

"We were married a on a lovely day, September 7, 1640." He paused again remembering Anne's beautiful face, he could see her very clearly, and he said again, *"I had never been so happy, I was in love!"*

"And then you lived happily ever after, right Grandpapa?" Annah questioned looking at him with the same big blue eyes her grandmother had.

"Yes, we lived happily ever after, sweet Annah," he said and he closed his eyes tight to hold back the tears.

"I love you Grandpapa," his granddaughter said and patted his cheek again, then kissed his nose and ran off to play, chanting "I was in love, I was in love."

He smiled and said to Anne, "I'll see you soon my dear."

Joseph and Hannah Blish's son Reuben was born on August 14, 1683 their fifth baby and Abraham's ninth grandchild. He also had twenty-one step-grandchildren.

Abraham didn't feel like doing much any more, and he would sit for hours holding the new baby lost in his memories.

'When everyone comes to visit there are 44 people in this house counting me and Allice,' Abraham's thoughts were always of his family and friends now days. 'There was also Richard and Mary More and their five children, 7 more, 'Seven More's,' a little pun there,' he smiled and chuckled out loud. 'They should be counted as family they were so close to us and they were here at almost every important gathering we had,' he mused smiling to himself.

His thoughts continued, 'If I counted my blessings and my house full of love, though I was penniless, I would still be the richest man alive.'

Ruben looked very much like little Johnny and it still pained Abraham to think of how his little grandson had died, 'has it been five years already?' he thought to himself when he held Reuben for the first time.

He also remembered Johnny Barker's little baby, Anne that died last year in November when she was just a few weeks old.

He sighed, 'There would have been thirty-two little ones calling me Grandpapa if God had not taken them to be his angels,' he thought.

'I guess Anne needed some company,' he whispered, and then smiled at the face of his beautiful wife that was engraved in his memory.

"It's time to feed Ruben, Papa," Hannah would say whenever she knew it was time for him to nurse.

Abraham would say, "No, he's not fussing so he's not hungry."

Hannah was afraid that Abraham might drop off to sleep as he had often done in the past and drop her baby, but he didn't. However, when Ruben did start to fuss he would insist that Hannah come immediately and feed him. "You must care for your baby without haste," he would say firmly.

550

Hannah just smiled to herself and stopped whatever she was doing and took Ruben. Abraham would move about the house for a while or go to the barn and check on his animals, but he would be back as soon as he thought Hannah was finished with her baby.

On the afternoon of September 7, 1683 Abraham Blish went to his bedroom just after his noon meal to lay down where he would be comfortable. When Allice went in to check on him about an hour later he was gone. He was 67 years old. This day would have been Abraham and Anne Blish's 43rd wedding anniversary.

Abraham Blish left behind his third wife Allice two sons and a daughter, Sarah Blish Orchyard, Joseph Blish and Abraham Blish Jr. and nine living grandchildren, four with the Blish name, and twenty-one step-grandchildren.

He was buried in the Barnstable cemetery next to his first wife Anne Pratt, his second wife Hannah Barker and his little grandson Johnny Blish and granddaughter Anne Barker.

Allice and Joseph arranged for his funeral to be held on September 10, 1683 at the Barnstable Church giving his friend Richard More and his family time to get there.

Richard gave the eulogy.

"My friend Abraham Blish and I knew each other all of our lives, since we were small children living in the small town of Devon in Devonshire County England.

He went to Cambridge University in England and graduated from there in 1636 with a degree in Agriculture. He was a very well educated man but never looked down upon those who were not.

He came to Duxbury Colony by an invitation from me and with the good wishes of his parents and his brother John.

I remember that he wanted to come with me in 1620 when I came here on the 'Mayflower,' his parents would not allow him to do that. It is just a well, he was only about 4 years old at the time and he probably would have perished as so many of the small children did that year.

He told me once that he wanted to come to New England again in 1629 when he was 13, but again his father said no and insisted that he complete his education.

But as soon as he turned 21 and had finished his studies he collected his inheritance and was on his way."

Even through the hard times and the bad times he has never once told me that he was sorry that he came to this new country. Nor have I for that matter," Richard said interrupting himself. He wiped his face with his handkerchief and then continued.

"He came here in 1637 and stayed with me for a bout six months, then he bought a little house from me in Duxbury called 'Eagles Nest.'

He was one of the first settlers here in this wonderful little town of Barnstable. He built his house here in 1639 and 1640 and married Anne Pratt in September 1640. They have two children, Sarah born in 1644 and Joseph born in 1648. When Anne died Abraham married his second wife Hannah Williams Barker in January 1654 and their son Abraham, Jr. was born in October 1654. He raised Hannah's four children as his own, Deborah Barker Burden, Mary Barker Pratt, Annie Barker Pratt and Johnny Barker.

After Hannah passed away Abraham married his third wife Allice Derby in January 1659. They have been married for almost 24 years.

He was a Freeman five times during his lifetime the first was June 1, 1641, then in 1651, 1652, 1658 and then again in 1670.

He took the Oath of Fidelity in 1643 and again in 1657. He gained the right to bear arms in 1643 and held that distinction all his life.

He was a Grand Juror in 1642, 1643, 1658 and 1663.

He was a Surveyor of highways in 1645, 1650 and 1652.

He was elected Grand Enquest in 1658 and 1663.

He was Constable from 1656 to 1660 and again from 1667 until 1671.

He was Hayward in 1668 and 1673. He was known as a great farmer and landowner, owning 200 acres of land here in Barnstable at one time.

He led a Christian life and was highly regarded and respected as a friend to all those who knew him.

He was a very loving husband, father, stepfather, and father-in-law and was grandfather to 30 children, and he could remember every one of their names and ages.

Abraham did not have an easy life he worked very hard for all he had. He loved and cherished his family and friends giving them everything he could."

"I will surely miss my best friend," Richard said. He ended Abraham's eulogy with tears streaming down his face.

Mary held him close and cried with him.

Sarah sang a lovely hymn and then everyone went to Joseph's house.

Richard was getting older now and was the first one to admit it; he was 71 years old. His wife Mary was 68 and still beautiful with snow-white hair and blue eyes that still sparkled with life; the wrinkles around them made them seem even happier.

Mary held Sarah close while she cried for her father and then in turn she held each of her dear friend's children and grandchildren.

Little Annah patted her cheek and said, "Don't be sad Aunt Mary, Grandpapa has gone to see Grandmama Anne now, remember, he had never been so happy, he was in love."

Mary hugged the beautiful little girl tight, she looked so much like her grandmother Anne, and said, "Yes, I remember very well."

Everyone remarked that a finer man had never lived.

• • •

The last entry that Abraham wrote in his journal was a message to his children and grandchildren.

"Dear Children and Grandchildren,
When you live as a Christian you will always be happy and your sadness will turn into wonderful memories if you let it. The only things that I can leave behind in this world that may last forever are the following words of advice:
Your Generosity will keep you Wealthy
Your Wealth will keep you Generous.
Your Joyfulness will keep you Happy
Your Happiness will keep you Joyful.
Your Knowledge will keep you Influential
Your Influence will keep you Knowledgeable.
Your Kindness will keep you Friends
Your Friends will keep you Kind.
Your Humor will keep you Laughing
Your Laughter will keep you Humorous.
Your Loyalty will keep you Patriotic
Your Patriotism will keep you Loyal.
Your Love will keep your Children
Your Children will keep your Love.
Your Love for God will keep you Prayerful
Your Prayers will keep your Love for God."

THE END

Patricia Louise Blish Gould

Geneva Eldredge, of Sagamore, Massachusetts wrote a wonderful poem that happily expresses what happened around Old Cape Cod in the early years when the colonies were first settled.

CAPE COD LILACS

Long years ago on old Cape Cod
Strong men and women toiled with might,
From early dawn to candle light
To build plain homes and "lean to" sheds
A place to lay their wearying heads
On this wild, untried shore.
And when at last the task was done
They planted, "ere the set of sun
A lilac bush beside each door.
They plowed the fields and sowed the seed
To drive away the monster "Need,"
And watched as spring broke o'er the land,
Old Mother Nature's magic wand.
Bright purple bloom and fragrance sweet
Their winter-weary eyes to greet
Beside each kitchen door.
The pioneers are long since gone
Who labored in the dew drenched dawn,
Their homes are now but cellar walls,
Grown o'er by shrubs and weeds so tall,
Rough brier and brake and lichens gray
Seem all that's left of that far day
Until we glimpse trough tangled mass
A brave reminder of the past.
For here, where once was kitchen door
The lilacs bloom again once more.

Patricia Louise Blish Gould

Bibliography

William Franklin Atwood – "The *Pilgrim Story*" – 1940 – Seventeenth Edition – 1997

Matthew Rhodes Blish, *"Supplement to Genealogy of the Blish Family in America"* – 1957

J. R. Dolan, *"The Yankee Peddlers of Early America"* – 1964

Frederick Freeman, *"History of Cape Cod: The Annals of the Thirteen Towns of Barnstable County"* – 1862

Lucy Hall Greenlaw, *"Genealogical Advertiser, A quarterly Magazine of family History"* – 1974

Susan Meredith, *"The Osborne Book of World Religions"* – 1997

Amos Otis Papers, Revised by C. F. Swift *"Genealogical Notes of Barnstable Families"* – 1888

Louise Tenney, M.H., *"Today's Herbal Health"* – 1992

Donald D. Trayser, Barnstable – "Three *Centuries of a Cape Cod Town"* – 1971

"Pastimes of the Pilgrims " – Plimoth Plantation Publication – P 0 Box 1620, Plymouth, MA 02362–1620

"Curious Punishments of Colonial Days" – Historical Documents Co. – Plimoth Plantation Publication

"Mayflower Compact 1620" – Historical Documents Co. – Plimoth Plantation Publication

"List of Mayflower Passengers and Crew 1620" – Historical Documents Co. Plimoth Plantation Publication

Microsoft® Encarta 98 Encyclopedia © 1993-1997 Microsoft Corp.

(These 12 Articles were not read and considered and approved until August 1643 and were received in Boston on September 7, 1643. The Commissioners for the Massachusetts, Connecticut and New Haven governments signed them; John Winthrop, Gov. of Mass; Thomas Dudley, George Fenwick, Theophilus Eaton, Edward Hopkins and Thomas Gregson.)

ARTICLE I

The Style of this confederacy shall be "The United Colonies of New England.

ARTICLE II

The said United Colonies, for themselves and their posterities, do jointly and severally hereby enter into a firm and perpetual league of friendship and amity for offense and defense, mutual advice and succor upon all just occasions, both for preserving and propagating the truth and liberties of the Gospel and for their own mutual safety and welfare.

ARTICLE III

It is further agreed that the plantations which at present are, or hereafter shall be, settled within the limits of the Massachusetts shall be forever under the Massachusetts, and shall have particular jurisdiction among themselves in all cases as an entire body; and that Plymouth, Connecticut and New Haven shall each of them have like particular jurisdiction and government within their limits, and in reference to the plantations which already are settled, or shall hereafter be erected, or shall settle within their limits respectively; provided that no other jurisdiction shall hereafter be taken in as a distinct head or member of this confederation, nor shall any other plantation or jurisdiction in present being, and not already in combination or under the jurisdiction of any of these confederates, be received by any of them; nor shall nay two of the confederates join in one jurisdiction without consent of the rest, which consent to be interpreted as is expressed in the 6th article ensuing.

ARTICLE IV

It is by these confederates agreed that the charge of all just wars, whether offensive or defensive, upon what part or member of this confederation so ever they fall, shall both in men and provisions and all other disbursements be borne by all the parts of this confederation in different proportions according to their different ability in manner following, namely, that the commissioners for each jurisdiction, from time to time as there shall be occasion, bring a true account and number of all the males in every plantation or any way belonging to or under their federal jurisdictions of what quality or condition so ever they be from sixteen years old to threescore (60) being inhabitants there. And that according to the different numbers which from time to time shall be found in each jurisdiction, upon a true and just account, the service of men and all charges of the war be borne by the poll, each jurisdiction or plantation being left to their own just course and custom of rating themselves and people according to their different estates with due respects to their qualities and exemptions among themselves though the confederation take no notice of any such privilege; and that according to their different charge of each jurisdiction and plantation, the whole advantage of the war (if it please God to bless their endeavors), whether it be in lands, goods, or persons, shall be proportionately divided among the said confederates.

ARTICLE V

It is further agreed that, if any of these jurisdictions or any plantation under or in combination with them be invaded by any enemy whomsoever, upon notice and request of any three magistrates of that jurisdiction so invaded, the rest of the confederates, without any further meeting or expostulation, shall forthwith send aid to the confederate in danger but in different proportions; namely, the Massachusetts, 100 men sufficiently armed and provided for such a service and journey, and each of the west, 45 so armed and provided, or any less number, if less be required according to this proportion. But in any such case of sending men for present aid, whether before or after such order or alteration, it is agreed that at the meeting of the commissioners for this confederation the cause of such war or invasion be duly considered; and if it appear that the fault lay in the parties so invaded that then that jurisdiction or plantation make just satisfaction, both to the invaders who they have injured, and bear all the charges of the war themselves, without requiring any allowance from the rest of the confederates toward the same. And, further, that if any jurisdiction see any danger of any invasion approaching, and there be time for a meeting, that in such case three magistrates of that jurisdiction may summon a meeting at such convenient place as themselves hall think meet, to consider and provide against the threatened danger; provided when they are met they may remove to what place they please. Only

while any of these four confederates have but three magistrates in their jurisdiction, their request or summons
from any two of them shall be accounted of equal force
with the three mentioned in both the clauses of this article, till there be an increase of magistrates there.

ARTICLE VI

It is also agreed that for the managing and concluding
of all affairs proper and concerning the whole confederation, two commissioners shall be chosen by and out of
each of these four jurisdictions; namely two for the Massachusetts, two for Plymouth, two for Connecticut, and
two for New haven, being all in church fellowship with
us, which shall bring full power from several General
Courts respectively to hear, examine, weigh and deter-
mine all affairs of our war or peace leagues, aids, charges,
and numbers of men for war, division of spoils and whatsoever is gotten by conquest, receiving of more confederates for plantations into combination with any of the confederates, and all things of like nature, which are the
proper concomitants or consequence of such a confederation for amity , offense, and defense, not intermeddling
with the government of any of the jurisdictions, which by
the 3rd article is preserved entirely to themselves.

ARTICLE VII

It is further agreed that these eight commissions shall
meet once every year, besides extraordinary meetings (according to the 5th Article). To consider, treat, and conclude
of all affairs belong to this confederation.

ARTICLE VIII

It is also agreed that the commissioners for this confederation hereafter at their meetings, whether ordinary or extraordinary, as they may have commission or opportunity, do endeavor to frame and establish agreements and orders in general cases of a civil nature, wherein all the plantations are interested, for preserving peace among themselves and preventing as much as may be all occasion of war or difference with others, as about the free and speedy passage of justice in every jurisdiction, to all the confederates equally as to their own, receiving those that remove from one plantation to another without due certificates; how all the jurisdictions may carry it toward the Indians, that they neither grow insolent nor be injured with due satisfaction lest war break in upon the confederates through such miscarriage.

ARTICLE IX

It is also agreed that if any servant fun away from his master into any other of these confederated jurisdictions, that in such case, upon the certificate of one magistrate in the jurisdiction out of which the said servant fled, or upon other due proof, and said servant shall be delivered either to his master or any other that pursues and brings such certificate or proof. And that upon the escape of any prisoner whatsoever, or fugitive for any criminal cause, whether breaking prison, or getting from the officer, or otherwise escaping, upon the certificate of two magistrates of the jurisdiction out of which the escape is made, that he was a prisoner, or such an offender at the time of the escape, the magistrates, or some of them of that jurisdiction where for the present and said prisoner or fugitive abides, shall forthwith grant such a warrant as the case will bear for the apprehending of any such person, and the delivery of him into the hands of the officer or other person who pursues him. And if there be help required for the safe returning of any such offender then it shall be granted to him that craves the same, he paying the charges thereof.

ARTICLE X

It is also agreed that the justest wars may be of dangerous consequence, especially to the small plantations in these United Colonies, it is agreed that neither the Massachusetts, Plymouth, Connecticut, nor New Haven, nor any of the members of them, shall at any time hereafter begin, undertake, or engage themselves, or this confederation, or any part thereof in any war whatsoever (sudden exigents with the necessary consequence thereof excepted which are also to be moderated as much as the case will permit) without the consent and agreement of the forenamed eight commissioners, or at least six of them, as in the 6th article is provided; and that no charge be required of any of the confederates in case of a defensive war till the said commissioners have met and approved the justice of the war, and have agreed upon the sum of money to be levied, which sum is then to be paid by the several confederates in proportion according to the 4th Article.

ARTICLE XI

It is further agreed that if any of the confederates shall hereafter break any of these present articles, or be any other ways injurious to any one of the other jurisdictions, such breach of agreement or injury shall be duly considered and ordered by the commissioners for the other jurisdictions, that both peace and this present confederation may be entirely preserved without violation

ARTICLE XII

And Whereas it hath pleased the Governor of the United Colonies to incline the hearts of the commissioners that respectively represent the colonies to approve of, and to authorize us to ratify the said articles of confederation and perpetual union. KNOW YE that we the undersigned delegates, by virtue of the power and authority to us given for that purpose, do by these presents, in the name and in behalf of our respective members, fully and entirely ratify and confirm each and every of the said articles of confederation and perpetual union, and all the singular the matters and things therein contained: And we do further solemnly plight and engage the faith of our respective confederates, that they shall abide by the determinations of the United Colonies on all questions, which by the said confederation are submitted to them. And that the articles thereof shall be inviolably observed by the Colonies of Massachusetts, Plymouth, Connecticut and New Haven we respectively represent, and that the union shall be perpetual. In Witness whereof we have hereunto set our hands on this 6th day of June in the year of our Lord 1643 with full Commission and Authority in Name of the whole Court:

Edward Winslow, William Collyer, John Winthrop, Thomas Dudley, George Fenwick, Theophilus Eaton, Edward Hopkins and Thomas Gregson

The Oath of Freemen in Massachusetts

I _____ being by God's Providence an inhabitant and freeman within the jurisdiction of this commonwealth, do freely acknowledge myself to be subject to the government thereof; and therefor do swear by the great and dreadful name of the everliving God that I will be true and faithful to the same, and will accordingly yield assistance and support thereunto with my person and estate, as in equity I am bound; and will also truly endeavor to maintain and preserve all the liberties and privileges thereof, submitting myself to the wholesome laws and orders made and established by the name. And further, that I will not plot or practice any evil against it, or consent to any that shall so do; but will timely discover and reveal the same to lawful authority now here established for the speedy preventing thereof.

Moreover, I do solemnly bind myself in the sign of God that, when I shall be called to give my voice touching any such matter of this state, in which freemen are to deal, I will give my vote and suffrage as I shall judge in my own conscience may best conduce and tend to the public weal of the body, without respect of persons or favor of any man. So help me God in the Lord Jesus Christ.

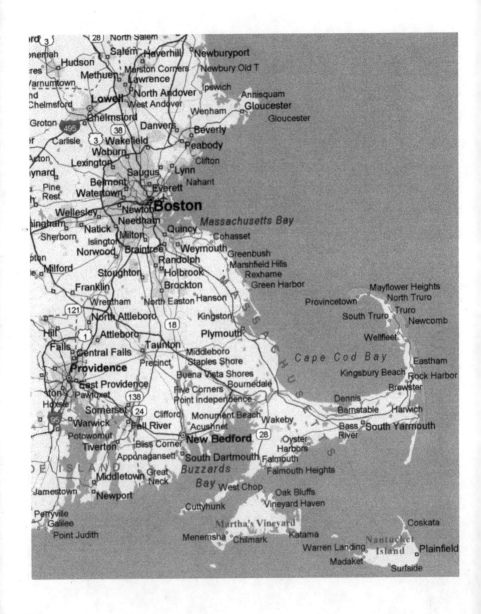